Teacher's Book
with Teacher's App

Fourth Edition

Ready for

ETHAN MANSUR

B2 FIRST

Macmillan Education Limited
4 Crinan Street
London N1 9XW

Companies and representatives throughout the world

Ready for B2 First 4th Edition Teacher's Book ISBN 9781380052360
Ready for B2 First 4th Edition Teacher's Book with Teacher's App
ISBN 9781380052308

Text, design and illustration © Macmillan Education Limited 2021
Written by Ethan Mansur

The author has asserted their right to be identified as the author of this work in accordance with the Copyright, Designs and Patents Act 1988.

This edition published 2021
First edition entitled "Ready for First Cert TB" published 2001 by Macmillan Education Limited.

All rights reserved. No part of this publication may be reproduced, stored in a retrieval system, or transmitted in any form or by any means, electronic, mechanical, photocopying, recording, or otherwise, without the prior written permission of the publishers.

Teacher's Edition credits:
Original design by EMC Design Ltd
Page make-up by SPi Global Content Holding Pte. Ltd.
Cover design by Restless

Authors' acknowledgements

I would like to express my deep gratitude to my wife, Antonia, and my two beautiful children, Lola and Dylan, for giving me the time I needed to write this teacher's book properly. And I would also like to thank Roy Norris for all his invaluable help and support during the writing process, as well as everyone at Macmillan who was involved in the project.

The publishers would like to thank Christina Anastasiadis (International House Madrid), Enric Prieto Puig (English Way Sabadell), Louise Brydges (City School), Fari Greenaway (IH Córdoba Sierra), Jo Johnson (CIC Escola D'Idiomes), Jeremy Knight (Hopscotch English Academy), Hannah Beardsworth (CLIC IH Seville), Violeta Chobotok (English Connection Barcelona Poblenou), Aidan Holland (British Council, Somosaguas Teaching Centre, Pozuelo de Alarcón), Sofija Berlot (Idiomes Tarradellas, Barcelona), Claudette Davis (City School of English), Patrick Doherty (City School), Rachel Kestell (Centro Idiomas Bilbao, Cámara de Comercio Bilbao), Howard Evans (Eli Sevilla), Matt Winship (M&M Language).

Student's Book credits:
Text © Roy Norris 2021
Design and illustration © Macmillan Education Limited 2021

The author has asserted their right to be identified as the author of this work in accordance with the Copyright, Designs and Patents Act 1988.

Designed by EMC Design Ltd
Illustrated by Martin Sanders (represented by Beehive Illustration) on pp22, 66, 131, 132, 165
Picture research by Emily Taylor

Full acknowledgements for illustrations and photographs in the facsimile pages can be found in the *Ready for B2 First Student's Book with Key* ISBN 9781380018069.

Printed and bound in Spain
2025 2024 2023 2022 2021
13 12 11 10 9 8 7 6 5

The author and publishers are grateful for permission to reprint the following copyright material:

Extract on p19 from Dan Glaister, "Inside the daredevil world of parkour, Britain's newest, gravity-defying sport" (14 Jan, 2017), The Guardian © Guardian News & Media Ltd 2019; Extract on p54 from Tim Lott, "Ditch the grammar and teach children storytelling instead" (19 May, 2017) The Guardian © Guardian News & Media Ltd 2019; Extract on p102 from Joe Sommerlad, "Black Friday 2018: How did the pre-Christmas shopping battle become an annual event?" (23 Nov, 2018), The Independent; Extract on p63 from Shaun Walker, "Yakutsk: Journey to the coldest city on earth" (21 Jan, 2008), The Independent; Extract on p135 from Marie Winckler, "On your marks, get set... get lucky" (20 July, 2011), Evening Standard. Data on p167: 'The Facts', Plastic Oceans © Plastic Oceans International 2020, https://plasticoceans.org/; Ian A. Kane, et al., 'Seafloor microplastic hotspots controlled by deep-sea circulation' (20 Apr, 2020), Science © 2020 American Association for the Advancement of Science, DOI: 10.1126/science.aba5899; 'Information About Sea Turtles: Threats from Marine Debris', Sea Turtle Conservancy © 1996-2020 Sea Turtle Conservancy, https://conserveturtles.org/; 'Factsheet: Marine Pollution', The Ocean Conference, USA, New York (5-9 June, 2017), Sustainable Development Goals © United Nations, https://sustainabledevelopment.un.org/; 'Ocean Waste', Cleaner Oceans Foundation © Cleaner Oceans Foundation Ltd, December 2017, https://www.blue-growth.org/.
Data on p235: Simone M. Ritter, Sam Ferguson 'Happy creativity: Listening to happy music facilitates divergent thinking' (6 Sept, 2017), PLOS ONE © PLOS, DOI: 10.1371/journal.pone.0182210; © Swedish Trade Federation.

These materials may contain links for third party websites. We have no control over, and are not responsible for, the contents of such third party websites. Please use care when accessing them.

The inclusion of any specific companies, commercial products, trade names or otherwise does not constitute or imply its endorsement or recommendation by Macmillan Education Limited.

Ready for conforms to the objectives set by the Common European Framework of Reference and its recommendations for the evaluation of language competence.

CONTENTS

Student's Book Contents	II
Introduction	IV
1 Lifestyle	TB1
2 High Energy	TB15
Ready for Use of English	TB29
3 A change for the better?	TB33
4 A good story	TB47
Ready for Reading	TB61
5 Doing what you have to	TB67
6 Relative relationships	TB81
Ready for Listening	TB95
7 Value for money	TB99
8 Up and away	TB113
9 Mystery and imagination	TB127
Ready for Speaking	TB141
10 Nothing but the truth	TB145
11 What on earth's going on?	TB159
12 Looking after yourself	TB173
Collocations Revision Units 1–12	187
Ready for Writing Sample answers and Key	TB188

STUDENT'S BOOK CONTENTS

	Language focus	Vocabulary	Word formation	Pronunciation
1 LIFESTYLE page 1	Habitual behaviour *Be used to*, *get used to* and *used to*	Lifestyle Clothes *Get*		Pronouncing questions
2 HIGH ENERGY page 15	Gerunds and infinitives	Music Sport	Affixes	Vowel sounds
READY FOR USE OF ENGLISH page 29				
3 A CHANGE FOR THE BETTER? page 33	Comparisons Articles	Technology Expressions with *as … as*	Nouns 1	Diphthongs
4 A GOOD STORY page 47	*So* and *such* Past tenses and time linkers	Films *Take*	Participle adjectives and adverbs	Silent consonants
READY FOR READING page 61				
5 DOING WHAT YOU HAVE TO page 67	Obligation, necessity and permission	The world of work	*en-* prefix and *-en* suffix	Connected speech: intrusive sounds
6 RELATIVE RELATIONSHIPS page 81	Defining relative clauses Non-defining relative clauses Causative passive with *have* and *get*	Relationships Describing people		Connected speech: consonant-vowel linking
READY FOR LISTENING page 95				
7 VALUE FOR MONEY page 99	Present perfect simple Present perfect continuous	Shopping Paraphrasing and recording Towns and villages		Contrastive stress
8 ON THE MOVE page 113	The future Contrast linkers	*Make* and *do* Travel and holidays Phrasal verbs	Adjectives	Chunking
9 MYSTERY AND IMAGINATION page 127	Modals for speculation and deduction Reported speech Reporting verbs	*Give*	Adverbs	Using intonation to show interest
READY FOR SPEAKING page 141				
10 NOTHING BUT THE TRUTH page 145	Passives Infinitives after passives	Crime and punishment Paraphrasing and recording Phrasal verbs with *out* and *up*	Participle adjectives and adverbs	Stress-shift words
11 WHAT ON EARTH'S GOING ON? page 159	*Too* and *enough* Conditionals	Weather *Put*		Consonant clusters
12 LOOKING AFTER YOURSELF page 173	Quantifiers Hypothetical situations Prepositions and gerunds	Food and drink Health	Nouns 2	Silent vowels
READY FOR WRITING page 188				

Collocations page 187   **Additional materials** page 198   **Ready for Grammar** page 204

Reading and Use of English	Writing	Listening	Speaking
Part 7 Multiple matching
Part 2 Open cloze
Part 1 Multiple-choice cloze
Part 4 Key word transformation	Part 2 Informal letter
Part 2 Article	Part 3 Multiple matching
Part 1 Multiple choice	Part 1 Interview
Part 2 Long turn
Part 6 Gapped text
Part 3 Word formation
Part 2 Open cloze
Part 4 Key word transformation	Part 2 Article
Part 2 Informal letter	Part 2 Sentence completion
Part 4 Multiple choice	Part 1 Interview
Part 2 Long turn
Part 3 Collaborative task
Part 4 Further discussion
Part 5 Multiple choice
Part 4 Key word transformation
Part 3 Word formation	Part 1 Essay
Part 2 Article	Part 2 Sentence completion
Part 3 Multiple matching	Part 1 Interview
Part 3 Collaborative task
Part 4 Further discussion
Part 6 Gapped text
Part 4 Key word transformation
Part 3 Word formation	Part 2 Report
Part 2 Review
Part 2 Informal letter	Part 1 Multiple choice	Part 1 Interview
Part 2 Long turn
Part 2 Open cloze
Part 7 Multiple matching
Part 3 Word formation
Part 1 Multiple-choice cloze
Part 4 Key word transformation	Part 2 Letter of application
Part 1 Essay
Part 2 Report	Part 2 Sentence completion
Part 4 Multiple choice	Part 1 Interview
Part 2 Long turn
Part 3 Collaborative task
Part 4 Further discussion
Part 1 Multiple-choice cloze
Part 5 Multiple choice
Part 3 Word formation
Part 4 Key word transformation	Part 2 Article
Part 2 Informal email	Part 3 Multiple matching
Part 1 Multiple choice	Part 1 Interview
Part 3 Collaborative task
Part 4 Further discussion
Part 6 Gapped text
Part 2 Open cloze
Part 4 Key word transformation	Part 2 Formal email
Part 2 Informal email
Part 1 Essay	Part 2 Sentence completion
Part 4 Multiple choice	Part 1 Interview
Part 2 Long turn
Part 5 Multiple choice
Part 3 Word formation
Part 4 Key word transformation
Part 1 Multiple-choice cloze	Part 1 Essay
Part 2 Article	Part 1 Multiple choice
Part 3 Multiple matching	Part 1 Interview
Part 2 Long turn
Part 3 Word formation
Part 7 Multiple matching
Part 2 Open cloze
Part 1 Multiple-choice cloze
Part 4 Key word transformation	Part 2 Review
Part 2 Report	Part 4 Multiple choice
Part 2 Sentence completion	Part 1 Interview
Part 3 Collaborative task
Part 4 Further discussion
Part 5 Multiple choice
Part 4 Key word transformation
Part 1 Multiple-choice cloze	Part 2 Article
Part 1 Essay	Part 4 Multiple choice
Part 3 Multiple matching	Part 1 Interview
Part 2 Long turn
Part 7 Multiple matching
Part 6 Gapped text
Part 3 Word formation
Part 4 Key word transformation
Part 2 Open cloze	Part 1 Essay
Part 2 Informal email	Part 2 Sentence completion
Part 1 Multiple choice	Part 1 Interview
Part 3 Collaborative task
Part 4 Further discussion
Part 7 Multiple matching
Part 2 Open cloze
Part 3 Word formation
Part 4 Key word transformation
Part 1 Multiple-cloze choice	Part 2 Report
Part 2 Article	Part 3 Multiple matching
Part 4 Multiple choice	Part 1 Interview
Part 2 Long turn

Audioscripts page 234 **Answer key** page 252

INTRODUCTION

Welcome to *Ready for B2 First*, a course consisting of both print and digital components designed to help students prepare for *Cambridge English Qualifications: B2 First*.

Student's Book/Digital Student's Book

Each of the 12 units in the Student's Book provides a balance and variety of activity types aimed at improving students' general English level. The exam sections include a variety of **tip boxes** which develop the language and skills students need to be successful in the exam.

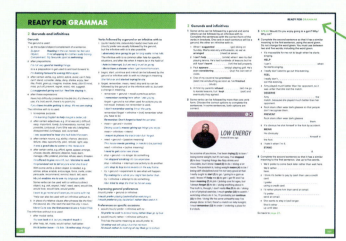

The Language focus sections contain a referral to the **Ready for Grammar** section with notes and extra activities at the back of the book.

At the end of every unit, there is a two-page **Review** containing revision activities and exam style tasks.

Every unit also has a **Pronunciation** lesson with listening and practice exercises, and games designed to help avoid common B2-level pronunciation errors.

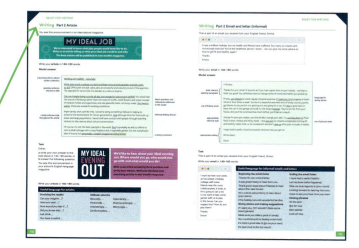

The book also contains five **Ready for** sections, which provide students with information, advice and practice on each of the four papers in the examination.

INTRODUCTION

Workbook/Digital Workbook

The Workbook has 12 units which provide consolidation of the language presented in the corresponding unit in the Student's Book. Each unit also contains further exam practice and skills work. There are useful **Phrasal verb** and **Word formation Lists** at the back of the book.

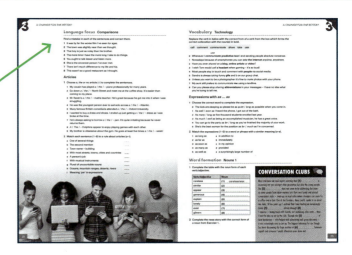

Teacher's Book

The Teacher's Book is **interleaved** with pages of the Student's Book. The answers to all of the Student's Book activities are **annotated** on the exercises, reading texts and audio scripts.

The procedural notes offer support to teachers on how to deliver the lesson. There are also **Teaching tips from Roy Norris** and ideas for **Extra activities**.

On-the-go practice

The Student's App allows learners to practice and perfect the language and exam skills in the Student's Book.

It also features 60 quick-fire **Are you ready?** questions to help students with practical tips to prepare for their exam day.

Classroom Presentation Kit

The Classroom Presentation Kit, accessible through the Teacher's App, is designed to be displayed on an interactive whiteboard (IWB) or projected onto a wall. It enables teachers to play **audio** or show **interactive Student's Book** and **Workbook activities** in class.
It is user-friendly and presents the lesson clearly to the whole class.
The Answer-by-answer reveal enables teachers to elicit student responses and check answers one by one.

VII

INTRODUCTION

Resource Centres

The Resource Centres contain **Wordlists** with definitions, IPA and example sentences for all of the lexis in the Student's Book Vocabulary sections. They also include all course **Audio**, **Answer keys** and **Audioscripts**.

Test Generator

Teachers can create tests or use the prebuilt tests to assign to students. There are **unit tests**, and **mid-** and **end-of-course tests** for each level, testing vocabulary, grammar, word formation and each part of the exam.

Overview of the Examination

Reading and Use of English 1 hour 15 minutes

Part	Task Type	Number of Questions	Task Format
1	Multiple-choice cloze	8	A text with 8 gaps; there is a choice of 4 answers for each gap.
2	Open cloze	8	A text with 8 gaps, each of which must be completed with one word.
3	Word formation	8	A text containing 8 gaps. The task is to complete each gap with the correct form of a given word.
4	Key word transformation	6	Gapped sentences which must be completed using a given word.
5	Multiple choice	6	A text followed by multiple-choice questions with four options.
6	Gapped text	6	A text from which sentences have been removed. Candidates replace each of these in the appropriate part of the text.
7	Multiple matching	10	A text preceded by multiple-matching questions which require candidates to find specific information in a text or texts.

Writing 1 hour 20 minutes

Part	Task Type	Number of Tasks	Task Format
1	Essay	1 (compulsory)	Candidates are given an essay title and notes to guide their writing.
2		3 (candidates choose one)	A writing task with a clear context, purpose for writing and target reader. Candidates write one of the following: article, email, letter, report, review.

Listening about 40 minutes

Part	Task Type	Number of Questions	Task Format
1	Multiple choice	8	Short, unrelated extracts of approximately 30 seconds each with one or more speakers. There are 3 options for each question.
2	Sentence completion	10	A monologue lasting approximately 3 minutes. Candidates write a word or short phrase to complete sentences.
3	Multiple matching	5	Five short monologues, each lasting approximately 30 seconds. The extracts are all related to a common theme. Candidates match extracts with prompts.
4	Multiple choice	7	An interview or conversation between two or more speakers lasting approximately 3 minutes. There are 3 options for each question.

Speaking 14 minutes

Part	Task Type	Time	Task Format
1	Interview	2 minutes	Candidates give personal information in response to questions from the interviewer.
2	Talking about photographs	4 minutes	Each candidate talks about two pictures for about 1 minute, and comments briefly on the other candidate's pictures.
3	Collaborative task	4 minutes	Candidates are given instructions with written prompts which they use for discussion. Candidates speak for about 3 minutes in total; the giving of instructions takes about 1 minute.
4	Further discussion	4 minutes	The interviewer leads a discussion which is related to the topic of Part 3.

1 LIFESTYLE

This first unit deals with the themes of lifestyles, routines and clothes. This, and every other unit of *Ready for B2 First*, gives the students the opportunity to improve their reading, writing, listening and speaking skills. All the activities are thematically connected. The grammar and vocabulary are taken from the reading and listening exercises, and students have the chance to consolidate this new language through controlled and freer practice.

Read the unit objectives to the class.

SPEAKING Part 1 Interview

This speaking activity gives students useful practice with the type of questions found in Part 1 of the *B2 First* speaking exam, where students are asked to give basic personal information about themselves. It's good to regularly practice Speaking Part 1 questions, as the more confidently and fluently students can answer the questions in Part 1, the more confident they will be going into the more challenging tasks to follow. These particular questions about the students' routines offer the teacher the opportunity to get to know the students at the beginning of the course. You may wish to use the **Speaking Part 1 cards** on the Teacher's Resource Centre to extend this into a 'Getting to know you' activity.

Put students into pairs to discuss the questions. Monitor and provide support as necessary. After five minutes, ask students to share something they learnt about their partner. Board any good vocabulary that surfaced during the activity. Note that too much error correction right away can be intimidating, so focus mostly on good language during your feedback in the first few lessons.

ONLINE MATERIALS

Speaking Part 1 cards (**Teacher's Resource Centre**)
Lifestyle questionnaire (**Teacher's Resource Centre**)
Unit 1 Test (**Test Generator**)
Unit 1 Wordlist (**Student's/Teacher's Resource Centre**)
Unit 1 On-the-go-practice (**App**)

1 LIFESTYLE

Vocabulary Lifestyle

1 Look at the verbs and adjectives that can all be used with the noun *lifestyle* to form collocations. Collocations are pairs or groups of words that are often used together.

| have / live / lead | a/an | active / alternative / busy / chaotic / comfortable / healthy / luxurious / outdoor / relaxed / sedentary / simple / stressful | lifestyle |

Underline those adjectives which could be used to describe *your* lifestyle.

2 **SPEAK** Work in pairs. Compare your adjectives with your partner, explaining your choices.

*I **have** quite **a healthy lifestyle** at the moment. I'm eating sensibly and doing a lot of exercise.*

3 **SPEAK** Discuss the following questions. As in other parts of this book, common collocations are shown in bold.
- Would you like to **change your lifestyle**? Why/Why not?
- Do you **lead an active social life**? What kinds of things do you do?
- What do you think is meant by the **American way of life**? How would you describe the **way of life** in your country to a foreigner?
- What are some of the positive and negative aspects of our **modern way of life**? In what ways, if any, was the **traditional way of life** in your country better?
- Why are people so interested in the **private lives** of celebrities? Do they interest you?

What might the people find difficult about their lifestyles?

LIFESTYLE 1

Lead-in

The Speaking Part 1 questions on page 1 act as a lead-in to the Vocabulary activities. A good transition to this section is to think of an adjective or two that describe the students' lifestyles based on their answers to the Speaking Part 1 questions, e.g. *Well, it sounds like some of you have a very busy lifestyle.* An alternative lead-in is to start with books closed and briefly describe your lifestyle (or that of a typical teacher). Put three choices for adjectives from Exercise 1 on the board. The students listen and choose the best adjective.

Vocabulary

1 Students read the instructions. Check they understand the meaning of 'collocation', as this term is used throughout *Ready for B2 First*. One good metaphor for collocations is relationships. Explain to the students that, just like people, words have strong relationships with certain other words and these combinations of words spend a lot of time together, just as you spend a lot of time with people that you have a strong relationship with, such as your friends and family. Focus the students' attention on the adjectives and check for understanding, e.g. *Which word describes the life of someone who is very rich?* Allow them time to do the task individually.

2 In pairs, the students discuss their lifestyles. Throughout the course, encourage students to use the **SPEAK** sections of *Ready for B2 First* as an opportunity to develop their fluency by speaking as much in English as they can. Remind them to provide reasons and examples for their ideas, as well as asking follow-up questions. Monitor the activity and make note of any of the adjectives that are being misused or mispronounced. Get feedback in open class when they have finished.

Note that one typical problem for students from all nationalities is 'spelling pronunciation', that is, pronunciation errors due to the complexity of the English spelling system. For example, in Exercise 1, students may be tempted to pronounce the last two syllables of *comfortable* as 'table', and the 'ch' in *chaotic* as /tʃ/ rather than /k/.

3 Organise the students into small groups and ask them to discuss the questions. Set a specific time limit, say five minutes, and politely end the activity by saying, *OK, I'm sure you have more to talk about, but I'm going to stop you there.* Nominate a member from each group to share ideas. Board any interesting vocabulary that came up during the discussion.

Teaching tip

Draw the students' attention to the fact the collocations appear in bold. Explain that this system is used throughout *Ready for B2 First*. Suggest that students use a separate notebook for new vocabulary items, which can be organised by theme. For homework, encourage students to record only the new vocabulary (not all the words) from today's lesson in their vocabulary notebooks under the theme of 'Lifestyles' with an example sentence for each one. Alternatively, ask student's to make use of the **Wordlists** on the **Student's Resource Centre**. You could set a spelling test for homework or ask students to revise the definitions of the words/phrases. Then test students on these as a warmer in the next lesson.

1 LIFESTYLE

Speaking

1 Students read the instructions. Explain that Speaking Part 2, or the Long Turn, is a speaking exam task in which they will have a minute to talk about a question and two photographs on their own. However, since this is the first time they are doing this task, you won't be timing them. Focus on the **How to go about it** box. Check understanding with a couple of yes/no questions, e.g. *Do you choose one of the photos to talk about?* (No). Now focus on the **Useful Language** box. Explain that throughout *Ready for B2 First* the phrases in these boxes have been carefully selected to help get students using the type of language that will help them do well on the exam. Put the students into new pairs. Allow them some time to plan what they are going to say about their photos, for example, one similarity, one difference, and then a few reasons why the people's lifestyles might be difficult (Student A) or enjoyable (Student B).

2 Student A does the speaking task and then the students switch roles. Monitor and make sure they are not simply describing the photos, but rather using the photos to help them discuss the question. In your feedback, concentrate more on how well the students carry out the task than on correcting errors, because the focus here is to introduce students to Speaking Part 2.

Teaching tip

When useful language is provided, encourage your students to produce it by having them choose one or two specific phrases to use during the speaking task. The partners who are listening can tick off the expressions they hear.

Extra activity

Ask the students to prepare role-plays based on the photographs from the Speaking Part 2 task. Put the students into pairs. One student is a journalist who is interviewing people from different professions about their lifestyles. The other student is one of the people in the photographs (assign or allow them to choose which one). Give the students some time to prepare questions or answers about the following:

- Daily routine
- What you like
- What you don't like
- Why you chose this profession.

Students perform the role-play asking for and giving details. Resist the urge to intervene unless communication is breaking down.

LIFESTYLE 1

Speaking Part 2 Long turn

1. Look at the four photographs. They show people who lead different lifestyles. Before you do the speaking task, read the information in the boxes below.

   Student A: Compare photographs 1 and 2 and say what you think the people might find difficult about their lifestyles.

   Student B: When your partner has finished, say whether you like working / would like to work in an office.

2. Now change roles.

   Student A: Compare photographs 3 and 4 and say what you think the people might enjoy about their lifestyles.

   Student B: When your partner has finished, say which lifestyle you would prefer to lead.

How to go about it

Student A

In part 2 of the speaking exam you are not asked to describe the photographs in detail, but to compare them. When doing this, comment on the similarities and differences:

Similarities: *In **both** pictures ...*

Differences: *In the first picture ... **whereas** in the second one ...*

Student B

In the exam you have time to develop your answer fully and give reasons for your opinions.

Useful language

Student A

I get the impression it's a stressful life.
She might/may have to travel a lot.
I doubt that they have much time for a social life.
They probably enjoy being outside.
I expect/imagine they prefer doing physical work.

Student B

(I don't think) I would like to be an office worker.
I wouldn't mind working in an office.
I'd prefer to have this lifestyle rather than that one.
I'd rather ride a horse all day than work at sea.

What might the people enjoy about their lifestyles?

1 LIFESTYLE

Reading and Use of English Part 7 Multiple matching

1 You are going to read an article in which four people talk about their lifestyles. For questions 1–10, choose from the people (A–D). The people may be chosen more than once.

> **How to go about it**
> - Read all the questions to see the kind of information you are looking for.
>   *To help you, one part of section A has been underlined. Match this part to one of the questions. Then look in the rest of section A for any more answers.*
> - Do the same for the other three sections. Underline the relevant parts of the text as you answer the questions.
> - If there are any questions you have not answered, scan the whole text again to look for the information you need.

Which person

admits to having an untidy house?	1	A
would not recommend their lifestyle to other people?	2	D
likes the unpredictable nature of their work?	3	C
is not particularly keen on taking exercise?	4	A
has a lot of free time?	5	B
has achieved an early ambition?	6	D
usually has no trouble getting to sleep at night?	7	A
does not normally have to go far to get to their place of work?	8	B
says that people have the wrong idea about their work?	9	C
is considering introducing more stability into their life?	10	B

2 Find the following phrasal verbs in the text and use context to help you work out their approximate meanings. The letters in brackets refer to the sections of the text in which the phrasal verbs appear.

turn up (A)   set off (B)   catch up on (B)   carry on (B)   make up my mind (B)
leave   *(sleep) a lot, because I didn't (sleep) enough before*   *continue*   *decide*

put off (C)   settle down (B, C)   grow up (D)   come across (D)   carry out (D)
discourage   *lead a more stable life*   *become an adult*   *find*   *do*

*I once **turned up** late for a play I was in.*

'Turn up' here means 'arrive'.

3 **SPEAK** If you had to choose, which of the four people would you prefer to change places with for a month? Why?

LIFESTYLE 1

Lead-In

This reading task continues with the theme of lifestyles. Ask the students to keep their books closed. Write or project on the board: *television and stage actor*, *ski and snowboard instructor*, *farm vet*, *mountaineer and wind turbine technician*. Check understanding of *vet* and *wind turbine*. Put the students in pairs and ask them to think about how having these jobs would affect people's lifestyles. Feedback the activity in open class. On the board, write any interesting vocabulary that comes up in the discussion.

Reading And Use Of English

1 The students read the instructions. Focus their attention on the **How to go about it** box. Elicit or check understanding of vocabulary items in the questions, such as *untidy* (1), *unpredictable* (3), *keen on* (4). Point out that the parts of the text that give you the correct answer do not usually include the same words as the questions, but rather uses examples or synonyms. As the students read, check to see they are underlining the parts of the texts which provide the answer. When finished, ask the students to check their answers in pairs, justifying their choices using the part of the text they underlined, before correcting the exercise in open class.

Teaching tip

For any challenging questions, take the time to explore why students choose the wrong answer. This develops valuable close reading skills that will help students identify, and not fall for, distractors.

Teaching tip

Although it would not be in keeping with the exam style, Exercise 1 could be made more communicative by setting up a jigsaw reading. Organise the students into groups of four. Give each member a short time to read one of the texts, i.e. Student A reads text A, Student B reads text B, and so on. The students then take turns giving oral summaries of their texts. This type of jigsaw activity is a nice way of integrating speaking into lessons that are a bit heavy on reading. It also helps students practice the valuable skill of summarising the content of a text in their own words, which is common in both academic and professional contexts.

LIFESTYLE

2 Students read the instructions. Put the students into pairs and allow them time to find the words together. This could also be done as a race in teams. The first team to find all the phrasal verbs in the text is the winner. Together, students discuss the meaning of the words in context. Nominate individual students to explain the words. Try to choose students randomly instead of going from one side of the room to another, to ensure that all the students are paying attention during this important feedback stage.

3 Students discuss the question in pairs or small groups. Note that these 'personalisation' speaking tasks give the students the chance to talk about their own ideas, feelings, preferences and opinions. Make sure to leave time for these tasks in your lesson plan, because this part of the lesson involves true communication – that is, students communicating real information about themselves.

READY FOR GRAMMAR

1 Habitual behaviour

Habitual behaviour in the present

A The present simple is used for habitual actions or permanent situations in the present.

*I **go** for a run twice a week. She **lives** near the park.*

B Frequency adverbs are used to indicate how often an action occurs. They are usually placed:

1 before the main verb.

*I **always** go to bed before midnight.*

2 after the verb *to be* or an auxiliary verb.

*She is **very often** late for work.*

*They have **rarely** been seen together.*

3 *Usually, normally, generally, frequently, sometimes, (very/quite) often* and *occasionally* can also be placed at the beginning of the sentence or clause.

***Occasionally** we go out for a meal, but **usually** we eat at home.*

NB *(almost) always/never, (very) rarely/seldom* and *hardly ever* cannot be used in the same way.

4 *Sometimes* and *quite/not very often* can be placed at the end of the sentence or clause.

*You say some very hurtful things **sometimes**.*

*I don't go to the cinema **very often**.*

5 Adverb phrases such as *now and again, from time to time, twice a week* and *every day* are placed at the beginning or end of a clause or sentence, but not between the subject and the verb.

*I see Paul at work **every day** and **from time to time** we have lunch together.*

Alternatives

1 The present continuous + *always* is used to talk about things which occur frequently and which the speaker finds annoying.

*He's **always complaining** about something!*

2 Adjectives can be used as an alternative to *rarely, normally* and *(not) usually*.

*It's **rare/normal/(un)usual/(un)common** for him to eat meat.*

3 *Tend to* + infinitive is used to make general statements about the habitual actions and situations of groups of people or individuals.

*British people **tend to drink** tea rather than coffee.*

*I **tend not to get up** very early on Sundays.*

4 *Will* + infinitive is used to talk about habitual behaviour. Frequency adverbs can also be added.

*She**'ll sometimes spend** the whole day reading.*

5 *It's not like someone to do something* is used to suggest that the way a person has behaved is not typical of their character.

*I'm surprised Graham didn't send me a card. **It's not like him to forget** my birthday.*

(He doesn't usually forget it.)

Habitual behaviour in the past

A The past simple is used for regular actions or habitual behaviour in the past, often with a frequency adverb.

*I **hardly ever went away** on holiday when I was young.*

B *Used to* + infinitive is used to refer to past habits and situations which no longer occur or exist now. Frequency adverbs can be used for emphasis and are placed before *used to*.

*We **used to have** a cat, but he died last year.*

*I **always used to walk** to work until I bought a car.*

Note the negative and question forms:

*I **didn't use to** like cheese. Where **did you use to** live?*

NB *use to* cannot express present habitual behaviour.

I usually (not use to) play tennis twice a week.

C *Would* + infinitive is used to refer to past habits, but not past situations. Frequency adverbs are placed after *would*.

Habit: *My father **would often** read to me when I was a young boy.*

Situation: *I **used to** (not would) have a bicycle.*

Stative verbs such as *have* (possession), *be, live, like, believe, think* (= have an opinion), *understand* and *know* are not used with *would* to refer to the past.

THIS IS YOUR LIFE

LIFESTYLE

Four more personal accounts in our series on lifestyles. This week we focus on people's work and how it shapes the way they live.

A Lucas Martín: *television and stage actor*

Normally I get out of bed around midday. I'll sometimes go for a run after I get up, though it's not really my idea of fun. I'm not a fitness fan, but I realise it's important.

When I'm not rehearsing or on tour, afternoons generally involve reading scripts or learning lines. My flatmates are also actors, so at home there are usually scripts lying all over the place. It's a bit of a mess, I'm ashamed to say. I'm passionate about history, and if I'm working away from home, I'll often spend the afternoon in a museum or historic building. I sometimes lose track of time, and I once turned up late for a play I was in. I felt terrible, so now I always get to the theatre early; I'm usually the first to arrive.

After a performance I eat and spend a few hours unwinding, so bedtime is often one or two in the morning. I'm normally out like a light as soon as my head hits the pillow.

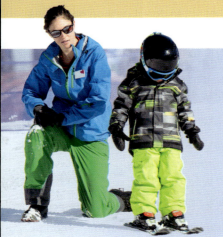

B Maja Andersson: *ski and snowboard instructor*

I generally spend six months in Europe and six in New Zealand, but I've also worked in Japan and Canada. Wherever I am, I love the fact that I usually live just a short walk from the slopes, so I can get up reasonably late and still have time for a decent breakfast before setting off for work.

When I started out eight years ago, I used to teach groups of young kids. Now I'm fully qualified, I tend to get the advanced classes, which I find more interesting. We get plenty of days off and when I'm not working, I go skiing by myself, or catch up on my sleep – I have no problem spending the morning in bed!

I love the lifestyle, but I'm not sure I can carry on doing this for much longer. It might be time to settle down and get a more normal job, something steady and secure. I haven't made up my mind yet, though.

C Reo Tanaka: *farm vet*

I used to have a dog and we'd go running together most mornings, but I gave him to my mum in the end. I tend to be out all day, visiting farms, and it wasn't fair to leave him alone. So now I don't get as much exercise as I'd like to.

I love my job, especially the variety and not knowing what you'll be doing from one day to the next. But being a vet – any type of vet – is not what most people think. It's not all cuddly lambs and cute little calves. We have to do some pretty unpleasant things sometimes, things which might put some people off working with animals for life.

My mum wants to know when I'm going to find someone to settle down with, but it's not as if I have loads of free time to go looking. There's not even room for a dog in my life, so I don't see how I'll be able to fit marriage in.

D Ben Adams: *mountaineer and wind turbine technician*

As a child, I would tell everyone that when I grew up, I wanted to climb Everest. I've actually climbed it three times now, and I've also scaled four more of the fourteen peaks over 8000 metres.

And when I'm not on a mountain, you might come across me hanging on a rope from a wind turbine, carrying out repairs to damaged blades at heights of up to 100 metres. That's how I make a living and pay for my climbing trips. I also sometimes get sponsorship from companies, which provide funding and maybe food and equipment. In return, I mention the sponsors in the talks I give and the articles I write when I get back from my climbs.

It's a fairly unconventional way of life, and not one I'd actively encourage others to adopt – there's a lot of danger involved – but it works for me. It's precisely that sense of danger that makes me feel alive.

5

1 LIFESTYLE

Language focus Habitual behaviour

1 Look at these two sentences from *This is your life*. Is the frequency adverb placed before or after:

  a the main verb? *immediately before the main verbs go and get, but after the main verb be.*
  b the auxiliary verb? *after the auxiliary verb will ('ll)*

  I'll **sometimes** go for a run after I get up.

  I **always** get to the theatre early; I'm **usually** the first to arrive.

2 Read the sentence and cross out the two adverbs that are used in the incorrect position.

  Normally / ~~Always~~ / Sometimes / ~~Never~~ I get out of bed around midday.

3 Read the sentence and cross out the incorrect option.

  Now I'm fully qualified, I **tend to get / ~~use to get~~ / usually get** the advanced classes.

4 Decide which of the following sentences 1–6 are grammatically incorrect. Change the position of the adverbs to correct them.

  1 I rarely go out on weekday evenings. *correct*
  2 I have usually my dinner in front of the television.
     I usually have my dinner in front of the television.
  3 Never I spend more than ten minutes doing my English homework.
     I never spend more than ten minutes doing my English homework.
  4 Someone is always telling me what to do and what not to do – it gets on my nerves. *correct*
  5 Hardly I ever play games on my phone – it hurts my eyes.
     I hardly ever play games on my phone – it hurts my eyes.
  6 It's rare for me to go to bed before midnight and quite often I'll stay up until two in the morning. *correct*

5 **SPEAK** Say whether or not the sentences in Exercise 4 are true for you.

6 Read these sentences from *This is your life* and answer the questions.

  As a child, **I would tell** everyone that when I grew up, I wanted to climb Everest.

  I used to have a dog and **we'd go running** together most mornings.

  1 Can *used to* replace *would/'d* before *tell* and *go*? Why/Why not?
     Yes, used to can be used to talk about both past states and past habits.
  2 Can *would* replace *used to* before *have*? Why/Why not?
     No, would + infinitive without to can refer to past habits, but not states. It is not used with stative verbs such as have to refer to the past.

7 Go to **Ready for Grammar** on **page 204** for rules, explanations and further practice.

8 In the following paragraph, decide whether the underlined verbs can be used with both *used to* and *would (a)*, only *used to (b)*, neither *used to* nor *would (c)*.

When my brother and I were little, my mum (1) <u>had</u>[b] an executive position in a pharmaceutical company. She often (2) <u>worked</u>[a] long hours and sometimes (3) <u>went</u>[a] away on business trips for two or three days at a time. Our dear old gran (4) <u>looked after</u>[a] us on those occasions, but it wasn't the same as having a mum around. We (5) <u>didn't like</u>[c] her being away from home, but we never once (6) <u>said</u>[b] anything, because we always (7) <u>thought</u>[b] she was happy in her work.

Then one day she (8) <u>announced</u>[c] she was giving up her job to spend more time with her family. My brother and I (9) <u>were</u>[c] delighted at the change in lifestyle, but I'm not sure about my mum: she often (10) <u>said</u>[a] afterwards that being a full-time mother was harder than being a business executive!

9 Write six sentences comparing your life now with your life five years ago.

  I used to be in a band, but I left a couple of years ago and now I hardly ever play my guitar.

10 **SPEAK** Work in pairs. Discuss your sentences from Exercise 8. Ask follow-up questions for more information.

  What type of music did you use to play?

  Why did you leave the band?

LIFESTYLE 1

Lead-in

On the board, write or project two groups of words 1) the adverbs of frequency *always, usually, sometimes, never,* and 2) the time expressions *at the weekend*, *on weekdays, in the morning, at night*. In pairs, students make sentences using language from both groups. This activity is meant to test the students' knowledge of the grammar before presenting it, so while monitoring make note of any strengths and weaknesses. You may wish to extend this or alternatively use the **Lifestyle questionnaire** on the Teacher's Resource Centre at this point.

Language focus

1-3 This grammar presentation gives students the chance to work out the grammar rules themselves. Give them a few minutes to do the exercises in pairs and then elicit the correct answers in open class. Ask the students to help you write rules on the board based on the examples. They should contain the following information: *Adverbs of frequency are usually placed before the main verb, but they go after the* be *verb. Some adverbs like* normally *and* sometimes *can go at the beginning of the sentence.*

4 Students read the instructions. Do the first sentence together. Ask students to do the activity individually. Then ask them to pair check before correcting in open class. Note that students may be less familiar with *hardly ever*. If you're working with a monolingual class and you share or feel confident enough with the students' L1, ask them to translate it to check understanding.

5 Students do the activity in small groups. Model by explaining why one sentence is true or not for you.

6 Give the students a couple minutes to read the instructions and think about the answers to 1 and 2. Then elicit the rules to the board.

7 Direct the students to the **Ready for Grammar** section on page 204 (see TB5 and below). However, if your students seem to have a good grasp of the grammar area, then you could set these exercises for homework and go straight to Exercise 8.

8 Students complete the exercise individually and then check in pairs. Ask them to justify their answers using the grammar rules discussed in class and from page 204. Correct in open class and try to resolve any lingering doubts.

9-10 While the students write their sentences for Exercise 9, monitor and check their work. Note that asking follow-up questions during pair work is a good habit for your students to get into. Before the students discuss their sentences, you may want to put one of your own sentences on the board and elicit possible follow-up questions.

READY FOR GRAMMAR

1 Habitual behaviour

1 Underline the correct alternatives.

1 *Always* / <u>Usually</u> I set my alarm for seven o'clock, but I <u>very often</u> / *from time to time* wake up before it goes off.

2 Chloe has <u>hardly</u> / *almost* ever had a day off school and she never *is* / <u>arrives</u> late.

3 My mum *every day* / <u>always</u> cooks lunch and my dad <u>normally</u> / *twice a week* gets dinner ready.

4 You're <u>always</u> / *sometimes* causing trouble these days! You <u>used</u> / *tend* to be so well-behaved.

5 It <u>doesn't</u> / *isn't* like Sadie to be late; *she use to be*/ <u>she's usually</u> so punctual.

6 We *would* / <u>used to</u> live in Shoreham-by-Sea, and it was <u>normal</u>/ *normally* for us to go to the beach after school in summer.

2 Complete the second sentence so that it has a similar meaning to the first sentence, using the word given. Do not change the word given. You must use between two and five words, including the word given.

0 She often went abroad on holiday before she got married.
   WOULD
   She __would often go__ abroad on holiday before she got married.

1 They don't usually arrive on time for anything.
   TEND
   They __tend to turn/show__ up late for everything.

2 Our local greengrocer would close his shop on Wednesday afternoons.
   USE
   Our local greengrocer __did not/didn't use to__ open his shop on Wednesday afternoons.

3 I almost always go out on Saturday night.
   EVER
   I __hardly ever stay__ or __am/'m hardly ever__ at home on Saturday night.

4 Anna rarely gets less than 70 per cent in her English exams.
   RARE
   It __is/'s rare for Anna to__ get less than 70 per cent in her English exams.

5 Richard is normally very talkative, so I'm surprised he was so quiet.
   LIKE
   I'm surprised Richard didn't say very much because it's __not like Richard/him to be__ so quiet.

6 From time to time you might find me sitting in the park reading a book.
   AGAIN
   Now __and again you might come__ across me sitting in the park reading a book.

Go back to **page 6**.

1 LIFESTYLE

Vocabulary

1 You could make this into a game by setting a time limit of two minutes. The pair with the most correctly identified items of clothing wins.

Answers

a belt; jacket; shirt; shoes; suit; tie; tie clip; trousers; waistcoat

b beanie/hat; gloves; jogging bottoms/ sweatpants; socks; sweatshirt/hoodie; trainers (Also: headphones)

c belt; clutch purse; dress; (dangly) earrings

d boots; fleece coat; gloves; headband; jeans; scarf

2 After the students read the instructions, do the first sentence together as a class. Students do the rest of the exercise individually. Check and model the pronunciation of *scruffy* /ˈskrʌfi/, *casual* /ˈkæʒuəl/ or any other words the students find challenging.

3 For stronger groups, an added challenge is to have the students cover Exercise 2 with their hand and use the words or collocations to describe the photos from memory.

4 Encourage the students to use vocabulary from Exercises 1 and 2, when appropriate. Remind them that we use the present continuous tense, not the past simple, to describe the clothes someone is wearing, e.g. *My partner is wearing jeans and a white shirt*.

Listening

1 ▶ 1.1 Since this is the first time they are doing this type of listening, ask students a few concept check questions after they have read the instructions. Ask: *How many different people will you listen to?* (Five) *How many possible answers are there?* (Eight). Now focus on the **What to expect in the exam** box. In pairs, give the students time to look at the options and discuss alternative ways of expressing the general idea contained in each sentence, e.g. *I always wear a business suit to work* (option A). Play the audio twice. Encourage students to justify their answers. (See answers highlighted in the **Audioscript** below.)

2 Students discuss the question in pairs.

Teaching tip

When teaching vocabulary, identify the words your students are having trouble pronouncing and then do a bit of choral repetition. First, say a word twice yourself. The students just listen the first time. Then they repeat all together after the second hearing. After, nominate individual students to listen to you again and repeat the word.

AUDIOSCRIPT

Listening Part 3 Multiple matching

▶ 1.1

Speaker 1 It's unusual for me to buy brand new clothes. I get most of what I wear from charity shops. Some people think that anyone who buys things that have already been worn by someone else can't really care much about clothes. But that's not true – you can find some pretty decent stuff in these places, even quite tasteful designer clothes that people, for whatever reason, have decided they don't want anymore. And they only sell clothes that are in good condition, often things that have only ever been worn once or twice. You get to support good causes, too, of course, because the money you spend goes to charity.
Ex 1 E

Speaker 2 Apparently, dressing smartly is supposed to increase your self-confidence, but I've never felt any different in a jacket and tie. And anyway, I'm not the kind of person who spends time worrying about what to put on in the morning. Some people take ages, umming and ahhing over what to wear, but I just throw on the first thing I find in my wardrobe and that's it. Job done. To be honest, I'd be happy just wearing the same two or three T-shirts all the time. The trouble is, I only have time to do my washing once a week, so that wouldn't work. I may not be fashionable, but I'm not dirty.
Ex 1 B

Speaker 3 I get suspicious when I go into a clothes shop and see that everything is incredibly cheap. If the prices are so low, then how much are the people who made them getting paid? And what are their working conditions like? I only buy from companies that sell ethical clothing, made by people who earn a decent salary and work in a safe environment. I usually get that kind of information online – it's easy enough to find. The clothes may not be as cheap and there's not necessarily any more guarantee of quality, but at least I can be confident that no one is being exploited.
Ex 1 D

Speaker 4 I spend a lot of money on clothes. I don't really care what they cost. They don't have to be designer clothes, but they do have to make me feel good about myself. I like to know that I can get something out of the wardrobe and any feelings of insecurity I have will just disappear as soon as I put it on. Then when I get to work and someone says, 'Hey, that shirt really suits you', it gives me a big lift. And I never wear the same thing more than once in the same month. My colleagues have got used to seeing me in something different every day.
Ex 1 H

Speaker 5 If I want to go out and get a new T-shirt, for example, then I always have to get rid of an old one first. And I only do that when I can't justify hanging on to it anymore – either because it's so scruffy I'm too embarrassed to wear it, or it's literally falling apart at the seams. That's why none of my clothes ever end up in a second-hand shop. I replace them, precisely because they're no use to anyone – not just me. I've been doing this for some time now, and I've noticed that clothes used to last a lot longer; the quality's got gradually worse and I have to replace things far more often than before.
Ex 1 F

TB7

LIFESTYLE 1

Vocabulary Clothes

1 **SPEAK** Work in pairs. How many of the items of clothing and accessories in the photographs (a–d) can you name?

2 Complete each gap with an adjective which is the opposite of the one in bold in the same sentence.

> baggy   brand new   casual
> colourful   scruffy   unfashionable

1 Charlie bought a great **second-hand** designer sweatshirt in *Vintage Gear* – it looks __brand new__.
2 Haven't you got a more **formal** jacket? That one's a little too __casual__ for the wedding.
3 My sister prefers **tight-fitting** tops and jeans, whereas I like everything to be really __baggy__.
4 Clothes that are considered **trendy** and worn by everyone one year, are often __unfashionable__ and too embarrassing to be seen in the next.
5 She wore a **plain** grey dress to the awards ceremony. We expected to see her in something far more __colourful__.
6 As a farmer, I don't have many **smart** clothes; I spend most of my time in __scruffy__ jeans and an old T-shirt.

3 **SPEAK** Which of the adjectives in Exercise 2 could you use to describe the clothes in the photographs? **a** formal; plain; smart **b** baggy; casual; colourful (trainers) **c** designer (dress); formal; smart **d** baggy (fleece); casual; colourful (scarf); tight-fitting (jeans)

4 **SPEAK** Work in pairs. Describe the clothes your partner is wearing.

Listening Part 3 Multiple matching

1 ▶ 1.1 You will hear five short extracts in which people are talking about the clothes they wear. For questions 1–5, choose from the list (A–H) what each speaker says. Use the letters only once. There are three extra letters which you do not need to use.

> **What to expect in the exam**
>
> - You will not hear exactly the same words as those in sentences (**A–H**). Before you listen, consider at least one alternative way of expressing the general idea contained in each sentence.
>
>   **A:** *I feel really comfortable in a white shirt and jeans, and that's what I wear nearly every day. Everything else seems to stay in the wardrobe.*
>
> - Each extract usually contains at least one distractor – a key word or expression which could cause you to make the wrong choice. Pay close attention both times you hear the recording.
>
>   *For example, although Speaker 1 mentions designer clothes, C may not be the correct answer.*

A I tend to wear the same clothes all the time.
B I don't really care what clothes I wear.
C I refuse to wear designer clothes.
D I'm careful to check the origin of the clothes I buy.
E I generally wear second-hand clothes.
F I only throw clothes away when absolutely necessary.
G I buy quality clothes that are guaranteed to last.
H I wear clothes that give me self-confidence.

Speaker 1 **E** 1
Speaker 2 **B** 2
Speaker 3 **D** 3
Speaker 4 **H** 4
Speaker 5 **F** 5

2 **SPEAK** Look again at the ideas expressed in sentences A–H above. How true is each one for you?

1 LIFESTYLE

Vocabulary Get

1 Read the extracts from the listening. Match each use of *get*, together with any associated words in bold, to one of the meanings in the box.

6	3	1	2	4	5
arrive at	become	buy	have the opportunity to	obtain	remove from

1 I **get** most of what I wear from charity shops.
2 You **get to** support good causes.
3 I **get** suspicious when … I see that everything on sale is incredibly cheap.
4 I usually **get** that kind of information online.
5 I can **get** something **out of** the wardrobe and any feelings of insecurity … will just disappear
6 When I **get to** work and someone says, 'Hey, that shirt really suits you', it gives me a real lift.

2 Underline the correct options to complete the phrasal verbs and expressions. There is an example at the beginning (0).

0 That jumper looks so scruffy. When are you going to **get** *away* / *along* / *lost* / <u>rid</u> **of** it?
1 Here's my phone number in case you need to **get in** *talk* / *speak* / <u>touch</u> / *tact* **with** me.
2 He was a lovely man – a pity you never **got the** *way* / *event* / *ability* / <u>chance</u> **to** meet him.
3 I asked Emma how much she **got** <u>paid</u> / *earned* / *money* / *salary* but she refused to tell me.
4 Come on, hurry up and **get** *moved* / <u>ready</u> / *ordered* / *fit*! Your bus leaves in five minutes.
5 Paul's parents are concerned about his behaviour. He's always **getting into** *problem* / <u>trouble</u> / *punishment* / *damage* at school.
6 Amy was upset when her sister moved out, but she **got** *out* / *off* / *by* / <u>over</u> it eventually.
7 I can't speak French, but I always manage to **get** *across* / *through* / <u>by</u> / *over* with a dictionary and a few gestures.
8 We **got** <u>stuck</u> / *held* / *kept* / *halted* in a traffic jam and missed the beginning of the concert.

3 SPEAK Discuss the following questions.
- How quickly do you **get ready for school/work** in the morning?
- How do you **get to school/work**? How long does it take you to get there?
- Did/Do you often **get into trouble** at school? What was the worst thing you ever did?
- Have you **got rid of** all your childhood toys and books? Why/Why not?
- What sort of things do you do when you **get angry**? How quickly do you **get over your anger**?

LIFESTYLE 1

Lead-in

Put the following sentences on the board and tell the students the missing word is the same for all three sentences.

I tend to _____ new clothes for my birthday.

I usually _____ home from work around 8 o'clock in the evening.

My best friend is going to _____ married next week.

Elicit the answer: *get*. Give them 10 seconds to study the sentences and then erase them. Elicit the three sentences back up to the board. Point out that, as seen in these examples, the word *get* can have many different meanings depending on which words it's combined with. These different meanings of *get* will be the focus of the lesson.

Vocabulary

1-2 Students read the instructions. Do the first sentence in each exercise together in open class. Get the students to pair check before eliciting the correct answers. To make this type of exercise more cognitively challenging for stronger groups, you could tell the students not to write anything down when they do the activity for the first time individually. They then have to pair check their answers from memory.

3 Students discuss the questions in small groups. During feedback, nominate a few students to tell you what other members of their group said. Note that students who watch films or TV series from North America might ask you about *gotten*. People in the United States and Canada use *gotten* for the past participle of *get* in most cases, but people from other English-speaking countries use *got* as both the past and past participle forms.

Teaching tip

Normally we place word stress on the main verb in a sentence, but with phrasal verbs the word stress falls on the particle instead. Select two sentences from the exercises, e.g. *I get that kind of information online. She got over it eventually.* Read them aloud and elicit the difference.

Extra activity

Put the students into groups of four or five. Assign each group five vocabulary items from page 8. Explain that the students are going to create a story that includes five expressions or phrasal verbs with *get*. Remind them that a good story has a beginning, middle and end. The beginning introduces the characters, setting and the problem or conflict. The middle consists of an event or series of events related to the problem or conflict. At the end of the story, the conflict or problem is resolved. Go around and monitor. Make sure each group's story has a clear beginning, middle and end. Regroup the students. They take turns telling each other their stories. The students listening have to listen for and write down the five vocabulary items used in the story.

1 LIFESTYLE

Writing

1 Students read the instructions and the letter. In pairs, they discuss the question.

2 Give the students time to read the letter quietly on their own. Encourage them to put a tick next to the advice they agree with.

3 Explain to the students that using these types of linking words and expressions help 'take the reader by the hand' and lead them through the ideas and messages you are trying to communicate.

4 Students do the exercise individually.

Suggested answers
Paragraph 2: To give the advantages and disadvantages of working as a ski instructor.
Paragraph 3: To outline the advantages of going to university.
Paragraph 4: To advise Paula on what she should do.
Paragraph 5: To make some closing comments.

5 Have students look at the task and then focus their attention on the **How to go about it** box. Put students in small groups to come up with advantages, disadvantages, and possible advice. Elicit ideas from the class and show them how they could be organised logically into paragraphs.

Teaching tip

B2 First examiners are really only hard on errors that are seen as being below the level expected or those that impede communication. So these are the types of errors you should focus on while giving students feedback on their writing. Particularly with the first piece of writing students turn in, focus more on what they do well.

Sample answer

Dear Tom,

It was great to hear from you! That's a very important choice to make, and I think you should think carefully about it before choosing.

I'm certain you would enjoy working in a hotel and that you would do it very well and, obviously, that would be a great experience and you would earn a great deal of money. However, it's true you would be far from your family and friends and, if you are not used to work many hours, you will find it exhausting.

On the other hand, as your parents need help, if you stay, you will be giving them a rest from work and also you will be in your city and in your free time you will be able to hang out with your friends.

Because of that, in my opinion the best thing for you to do is to stay at home and help your parents in the shop. You will have more opportunities to travel abroad when you are older.

In any case, regardless what you decide, I'm sure you will have a great summer.

A hug

Lucía

187 words

Examiner comments

Content: All the content is relevant and informative. The writer considers both options before advising Tom which to choose.

Communicative achievement: The conventions of letters are used appropriately. The opening and closing comments are generally appropriate, although 'A hug' is not usual. The register is consistently informal and the tone friendly and helpful.

Organisation: The letter is well organised into logical paragraphs. A range of linking words is used, particular at the beginning of sentences (*However; On the other hand; Because of that; In any case*). However, there is an over-reliance on *and* to link ideas within sentences.

Language: A reasonable range of everyday language is used (e.g. *think carefully; earn a great deal of money; exhausting; have more opportunities to travel abroad; hang out with your friends*). Both simple and complex forms are used with good control (e.g. *if you stay, you will be giving them a rest from work; the best thing for you to do is to stay at home*) and errors do not prevent understanding (*you are not used to* ~~work~~ *working; regardless [of] what you decide*).

Mark: Good pass

AUDIOSCRIPT

Listening Part 1 Multiple choice

▶ 1.2

M = Man W = Woman

1 You hear two people talking about a friend of theirs.
M: How many houses has Mike got now?
W: Well, there's this one here, the flat in Brighton, the cottage in Devon, and that villa of his in Spain. So, four altogether.
M: Hmm. Easy for some, isn't it?
W: I don't know. I get the impression he's fed up with it all – always moving around. I wouldn't be surprised if he got rid of everything over here and lived in Spain permanently.
M: Is that what he's said he'll do?

Writing Part 2 Informal letter

1 SPEAK Read the following Writing Part 2 instructions. What advice would you give Paula and why?

You have received a letter from your English-speaking friend, Paula.

> As you know, this is my last year at school, and I can't make up my mind what to do when I leave. My parents want me to go to university, but I'd really like to work as a ski instructor. What do you think I should do?
>
> Thanks, Paula

Write your letter in 140–190 words.

2 SPEAK Read Hugo's reply below to Paula's letter, ignoring the gaps. Do you agree with Hugo's advice? Why/Why not?

LIFESTYLE

Dear Paula

It was great to hear from you. You've certainly got a difficult choice to make. I know how much you love skiing and I'm sure you'd be a brilliant teacher, **(1)** ___but___ maybe you should think more carefully about your future.

The good thing about being a ski instructor is that you could have an exciting lifestyle, working in different countries, meeting lots of interesting people and doing something you really enjoy. The trouble is, though, it's not very well-paid work, and the career prospects are not fantastic **(2)** ___either___ – you might still be in the same job in twenty years' time. **(3)** ___On the other hand___, if you go to university, you'll have more chance of getting a decent job later. It'll be great fun **(4)** ___as well___, especially if you choose a university in a different town and live away from home.

(5) ___So___, if I were you, I'd do what your parents suggest and study for a degree. You could always work in a ski resort in the holidays – students get really long breaks!

(6) ___Anyway___, good luck and let me know what you decide. Looking forward to hearing from you.

All the best,

Hugo

3 Complete gaps 1–6 in the letter with the linking words or expressions in the box.

> anyway   as well   but   either   on the other hand   so

4 What is the purpose of each of the paragraphs in Hugo's reply?

Paragraph 1: To express an initial opinion on the choice that Paula has to make.

5 Do the following Writing Part 2 task.

You have received a letter from your English-speaking friend, Tom.

> Hi
>
> I'm not sure what to do during the summer holidays next year. My parents want me to help out in the shop they own, but I'd quite like to work in a hotel in your country – there are plenty of jobs available. What do you think I should do?
>
> Write soon, Tom

For more information on writing informal letters, see **page 193**.

How to go about it

› Plan your answer carefully. For this type of question, list the advantages and disadvantages of each option.

Advantages of working in parents' shop: easy work; live and eat at home …

› Decide which of these points you will include in your answer and what advice you will give.

› Write your answer using logical paragraphs, a variety of linking devices, and a range of language.

Underline any expressions in Hugo's reply that you could use in your own letter, e.g. It was great to hear from you.

1 LIFESTYLE

Listening Part 1 Multiple choice

▶ 1.2 You will hear people talking in eight different situations. For questions 1–8, choose the best answer (A, B or C).

What to expect in the exam

› The eight recorded extracts are either monologues or conversations. You hear each one twice.
› The introductory sentence is read out before each recording.
› For question 1, for example: you will hear the sentence *You hear two people talking about a friend of theirs.* You will not hear the question *What does the woman say about the friend?* or the three options A–C.
› As in all parts of the Listening paper, you will hear distractors.

1 You hear two people talking about a friend of theirs.
　What does the woman say about the friend?
　A He talks a lot about his lifestyle.
　B He leads a comfortable lifestyle.
　(C) He may change his lifestyle.

2 You overhear a man talking to a friend on his phone.
　Why is he phoning?
　A to persuade his friend to do something
　(B) to ask for some information
　C to change an arrangement

3 You hear a woman talking about her family's financial situation.
　What is she going to do?
　A ask someone to help her
　(B) try to sell something
　C look for a new job

4 You hear a man talking about his job.
　Who is the man?
　A a hotel manager
　B a hotel receptionist
　(C) a hotel doorman

5 You hear two people talking about the value of their time spent living abroad.
　What do they agree about?
　(A) It has helped them develop their personality.
　B It has made them appreciate their own country.
　C It has given them better job prospects.

6 You hear a man talking on the radio.
　What is he doing?
　(A) reviewing a book
　B advertising a product
　C reading a news report

7 You hear two people talking about the village they both live in.
　What does the woman think of the village?
　A People are not always very friendly.
　(B) Some of the roads are dangerous.
　C There are not enough children.

8 You hear a man talking about a country in which he once lived.
　What surprised him about the people?
　(A) the importance they give to clothes
　B the type of food they eat
　C their attitude to work

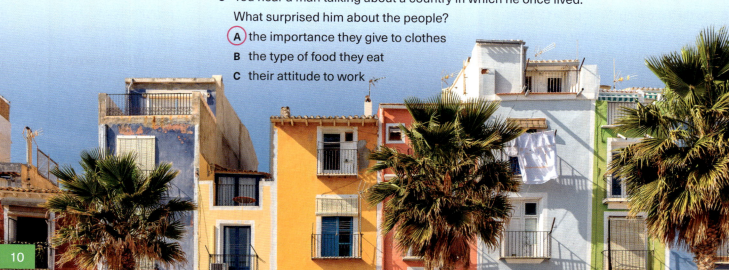

LIFESTYLE 1

Listening

▶ **1.2** Give students time to read the **How to go about it** box and the questions. Then play the recording twice.

AUDIOSCRIPT continued

W: Well, you know Mike. It's not like him to talk much
Q1 about his plans. But he did say he might settle down one day – stay in one place. And you know how much he likes Spain.

2 You overhear a man talking to a friend on his phone.

M: I'm stressed out, to be honest, what with work and all the problems with the house. I need something to help me relax. … Well, yeah, I did think about yoga, but the class is on Friday and I play squash then. And then I saw they do pilates on Tuesdays and Thursdays, which would be ideal
Q2 for me. … Yeah, I know you did. And actually, I was wondering if you could tell me what it was like, what sort of things you did. I had a quick look online, but it's always better to talk to someone with firsthand experience.

3 You hear a woman talking about her family's financial situation.

W: We just about get by, but it's a bit of a struggle. I can only get part-time work and Frank lost his job at the furniture factory last August. He's sent off loads of applications, but no luck so far. My mum and dad could probably help out, but somehow it doesn't seem right borrowing from them. They've been saving all their lives and I want them to *enjoy*
Q3 their money, now they're retired. There's nothing for it but to put my car on the market and see if I can get a decent price for it. The kids'll just have to get the bus in the morning.

4 You hear a man talking about his job.

M: I don't get to wear a uniform – you know, with a cap and all, like they do at some of the other hotels, but I do wear a suit. A decent one – tailor-made – not just any old suit. Inside, at the front desk they reckon I look smarter than the boss. I'm not so sure about that, but I do like to look good for the
Q4 guests – I'm the first person they see before they go into the hotel. And I've got this long black overcoat, as well – it can get pretty cold standing outside on the steps in winter, I can tell you.

5 You hear two people talking about the value of their time spent living abroad.

W: I've gained so much from these two years living abroad.

M: Yeah, me, too. I reckon we'll have no trouble finding work when we get back home.

W: I'm not sure that's true. But anyway, I was thinking more about the benefits to me as a person.

Q5 I've become much more tolerant since I've been here, more willing to accept difference.

M: That's what I mean. We've grown as individuals, we're more open-minded and independent, so that makes us more employable.

W: Well, I admire your optimism. I just know that I'll miss being here.

M: It's alright, but the whole thing has made me value life at home more.

6 You hear a man talking on the radio.

M: The world today is faster and more dynamic than when our great-grandparents were alive, but as a result, life is often more stressful and unhealthy. Self-help gurus offer people the hope of finding a solution to their problems, improving their health and wellbeing, and generally making their lives
Q6 better. The author of *Back to Basics* says his guide will help you achieve all these things in a matter of weeks. He's lying – the only thing it's good for is sending you to sleep, and you'd be wasting your money if you bought it and your time if you read it.

7 You hear two people talking about the village they both live in.

M: Are you enjoying it here in the village?

W: Yes, I am. I think I know nearly everyone now. When I came here last year everyone went out of their way to introduce themselves and make me feel welcome.

M: That's good. So you feel comfortable here, then?

W: Yes, I do. And the children have settled in well, too.
Q7 I just get a bit nervous about the traffic sometimes.

M: What, on the main road?

W: Yes, and a couple of other spots as well. There are certain places I won't let the children go without me. Some drivers just don't slow down for them.

8 You hear a man talking about a country in which he once lived.

M: On my travels I've had to get used to eating all kinds of strange dishes, so I was prepared for their rather unusual cuisine. If I was offered something I knew I wouldn't like, I used to cover it in lemon and salt to hide the taste. And it's a hot country, so the slow pace of life and relaxed approach to work
Q8 were only to be expected. What I hadn't anticipated was their way of dressing. I'm not used to being with people who take so much care over what they wear and I felt quite scruffy by comparison. Colour, style, fashion – it all mattered to them. I had no idea before I went.

1 LIFESTYLE

Lead-in

Put students into groups A, B and C. Group A has to talk about how life was different 100 years ago; group B, 1,000 years ago; and group C, 10,000 years ago. Board a few ideas to get them started, e.g. *100 years ago people used to cross the ocean by ship, but now they usually fly.* Regroup students to report their original group's ideas.

Language focus

1 Give students a minute to look at the examples on their own before comparing their ideas with a partner.

2 Discuss this in open class. In monolingual groups, if you share or are familiar with the students' L1, you could ask them to translate *be used to* and *get used to* check their understanding.

3 Elicit to the board: *be/get used to* + gerund/noun phrase. Contrast this with *used to* for past habits, which is followed by the infinitive without *to*.

4 Direct students to the **Ready for Grammar** section (see below). Alternatively, if your students are confident with the grammar by this point, you could set this section for homework and go directly to Exercise 5.

5 Students discuss the situations in groups. Monitor and check their use of the target language. Make a note of any errors to address later. Elicit their ideas for a couple of the situations as a class. Finish with some corrective feedback.

Reading and Use of English

1 Students answer the question in pairs. Elicit a few ideas from the class.

2 Give the students time to read the text. Ask if any of their ideas were mentioned.

3 Before doing the exercise, direct the students to the **How to go about it** box. Remind them to only use one word per gap. Individually, students fill the gaps. They then compare in pairs before checking in open class.

4 In small groups, students discuss the question. Get brief feedback from the class.

READY FOR GRAMMAR

1 Be used to/get used to + noun or gerund

Be used to + noun/gerund means 'to be accustomed to'.
She's a nurse so she**'s used to seeing** sick people.

Get used to + noun/gerund means 'become accustomed to'.
I want to leave Athens; I can't **get used to the heat**.

---

1 Be used to/get used to + noun or gerund

1 Write the words in the correct order. Begin each sentence with the word in bold.

0 trouble school? **Did** use into you at to get
   Did you use to get into trouble at school?

1 bike school to to to a **Lucy** use used get
   Lucy used to use a bike to get to school.

2 got used morning to in up the **She's** getting early
   She's got used to getting up early in the morning.

3 every dad to to me **My** his clean Sunday used get car
   My dad used to get me to clean his car every Sunday.

4 paid worked didn't much waiter he as to a when use **Paul** get
   Paul didn't use to get paid much when he worked as a waiter.

5 not doing are people **Many** work used hard young to
   Many young people are not used to doing hard work.

2 In the first gap write either the correct form of *be* or *get*, or leave it blank. In the second gap write the correct form of the verb in brackets. There is an example at the beginning (0).

Life after retirement

To The Daily Times

I enjoyed your article about the pros and cons of retirement in yesterday's edition. I (0) _____ **used to** _own_ (own) a small grocery shop, where I worked for over forty years. Six months ago, I sold the business and started to draw my pension. I was looking forward to retiring; I (1) _____ **used to** _dream_ (dream) about it and think how wonderful it would be not to have to work anymore. It's not that simple, though. I suppose I should (2) _be or have got_ **used to** _having_ (have) so much free time by now, but I (3) _am_ just not **used to** _being_ (be) able to do what I want, when I want. I can't seem to (4) _get_ **used to** not _having_ (have) to get up early every morning and I still wake up at six. When I had the shop, I (5) _____ **used to** _spend_ (spend) ten hours a day there, and to be honest, I miss the routine. However, I'll have a new routine soon; my wife and I have just become grandparents (to twins!) so no doubt we'll have to start (6) _getting/to get_ **used to** _looking_ (look) after children again. I'm certainly looking forward to that!

David Rumsey
Worthing

Go back to **page 11**.

1 LIFESTYLE

Language focus Be used to, get used to and used to

1 Look at the following sentences from the last extract in the listening. In which of them does *used to*:

a mean 'accustomed to'   b refer to past habitual behaviour?

1 On my travels I've had **to get used to eating** all kinds of strange dishes. a
2 If I was offered something I knew I wouldn't like, **I used to cover** it in lemon and salt to hide the taste. b
3 **I'm not used to being** with people who take so much care over what they wear. a

2 What is the difference in meaning between *get used to* and *be used to*?
If you *get used to doing something*, you gradually become familiar with doing something which is new to you.
If you *are used to doing something*, you are now familiar with it because you have done it before.

3 What form of the verb is used after *be used to* and *get used to*?
the gerund

4 Go to Ready for Grammar on page 204 for rules, explanations and further practice.

5 **SPEAK** Talk about all the things you have to *get used to* in the following situations.

- you start your first job
- you become famous
- you go on a diet
- you get married
- you have children
- you move to another country

In a new job, you might have to get used to working together with other people.

Reading and Use of English Part 2 Open cloze

1 **SPEAK** What do you think are the key ingredients for a long life?

2 Read the text below quite quickly, ignoring the gaps. Are any of your ideas from Exercise 1 mentioned?

3 For questions 1–8, read the text again and think of the word which best fits each gap. Use only one word in each gap. There is an example at the beginning (0).

How to go about it

Before you decide what the missing word is, consider the meaning of the whole sentence, and the words both before and after the gap.

For gaps 1–3, key words have been underlined to help you make your decisions. No words are underlined in the exam.

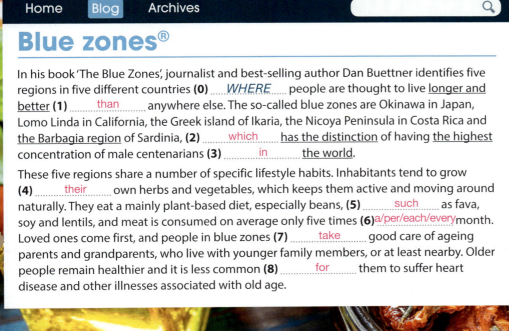

Blue zones®

In his book 'The Blue Zones', journalist and best-selling author Dan Buettner identifies five regions in five different countries (0) __WHERE__ people are thought to live longer and better (1) __than__ anywhere else. The so-called blue zones are Okinawa in Japan, Lomo Linda in California, the Greek island of Ikaria, the Nicoya Peninsula in Costa Rica and the Barbagia region of Sardinia, (2) __which__ has the distinction of having the highest concentration of male centenarians (3) __in__ the world.

These five regions share a number of specific lifestyle habits. Inhabitants tend to grow (4) __their__ own herbs and vegetables, which keeps them active and moving around naturally. They eat a mainly plant-based diet, especially beans, (5) __such__ as fava, soy and lentils, and meat is consumed on average only five times (6) __a/per/each/every__ month. Loved ones come first, and people in blue zones (7) __take__ good care of ageing parents and grandparents, who live with younger family members, or at least nearby. Older people remain healthier and it is less common (8) __for__ them to suffer heart disease and other illnesses associated with old age.

4 **SPEAK** Which of the lifestyle habits mentioned in the last paragraph are common to your region? Are they part of your own lifestyle?

1 REVIEW

Language focus Habitual behaviour

Complete each gap with a word from the box. You do not need to use all the words.

always almost hardly like never not tend
use used usual usually very will would

1 My grandad's got a car, but he __hardly__ ever uses it. He'll only drive in good weather.
2 __Usually__ we play football on Sunday morning, but this week's game is in the afternoon.
3 This nocturnal bird is __not__ often seen in daylight, so these early-morning images are a rare treat.
4 It's not __usual__ for students to bring sandwiches; most eat in the school canteen.
5 We __very__ rarely go into the town centre to shop these days; it's far too crowded.
6 We __tend__ not to go abroad on holiday; there are so many places to visit here in this country.
7 When I was at school, I __would__ often get into trouble for talking during lessons.
8 Where did your mum __use__ to work before she retired?

Reading and Use of English Part 1 Multiple-choice cloze

For questions 1–8, read the text below and decide which answer (A, B, C or D) best fits each gap. There is an example at the beginning (0).

YOUNG ENTREPRENEURS

A growing number of school-going teenagers are using the internet to (0) __D__ their pocket money by selling clothes and accessories online. One shopping app has over seven million users worldwide, (1) __C__ many enterprising under-18s who have decided they would (2) __D__ work for themselves than look for a part-time job in a shop or restaurant.

Sixteen-year-old Eva Laidlaw, who has (3) __B__ up in a family of successful business people, buys second-hand garments then sells them via the app, more (4) __A__ than not, at a decent profit. 'I get most of my clothes from charity shops and car boot sales,' she says. 'You can (5) __C__ across good quality items if you're (6) __A__ to spend the time looking.'

Katie Simmons is another young entrepreneur. (7) __C__ on holiday in Tuscany three years ago, she discovered that clothes sold in the markets there were extremely cheap. So, every two months, Katie, now eighteen, (8) __B__ for Italy and hunts for items she thinks will sell easily at home. 'I had intended to go to uni,' says Katie, 'but now I have a business to run.'

0	A advance	B lift	C rise	D <u>boost</u>
1	A containing	B consisting	C <u>including</u>	D introducing
2	A better	B prefer	C like	D <u>rather</u>
3	A turned	B <u>grown</u>	C brought	D raised
4	A <u>often</u>	B ever	C always	D sometimes
5	A get	B find	C <u>come</u>	D take
6	A <u>prepared</u>	B disposed	C organised	D equipped
7	A Whereas	B Whenever	C <u>While</u>	D Whether
8	A goes away	B <u>sets off</u>	C carries on	D catches up

12

LIFESTYLE 1

Reading and Use of English Part 4 Key word transformation

For questions 1–6, complete the second sentence so that it has a similar meaning to the first sentence, using the word given. Do not change the word given. You must use between two and five words, including the word given. Here is an example (0).

0 How long was your journey from London to Manchester?
TAKE
How long ..*DID IT TAKE YOU TO*.. get from London to Manchester?

1 Why don't you throw away that old coat?
RID
How about ..*getting rid of*.. that old coat?

2 I still find it strange to wear glasses.
USED
I still haven't ..*got used to wearing*.. glasses.

3 He never asks when he borrows my things!
ALWAYS
He is ..*always borrowing my things without*.. asking!

4 Simon doesn't usually drink coffee.
UNUSUAL
It ..*is/'s unusual for Simon to*.. drink coffee.

5 Helen is not usually so pessimistic.
LIKE
It is ..*not/n't like Helen to be*.. so pessimistic.

6 I can't wait to see you again.
FORWARD
I'm really ..*looking forward to seeing*.. you again.

What to expect in the exam

› The second sentence of a transformation is a paraphrase of the first sentence; it expresses the same idea but with different words.
› Transformations test your knowledge of grammar, vocabulary and collocation. *In these transformations, all the language which is tested appears in Unit 1, including the Grammar reference on page 208.*
› More than one feature of grammar and/or vocabulary may be tested in a single transformation.
  In number **1**, for example, consider:
  – the verb and preposition used with the word *rid*.
  – the form of the verb used after the words *How about*.
› You must write at least two words and no more than five, and you cannot change the key word in any way.
  In number 2, for example, you must include the word used, *and not* use, uses *or* using.
› In the exam, when you transfer your answers to the separate answer sheet, you write only the missing words in CAPITAL LETTERS.

Vocabulary Get

Match each beginning 1–7 with an appropriate ending a–g.

1 Please do not hesitate to **get**
2 Come in. I have to finish **getting**
3 I want to change jobs. I don't **get**
4 I'm sorry I'm so late. My bus **got**
5 I don't own a car; I can easily **get**
6 When we lived in Australia, I **got**
7 I enjoyed the party once I had **got**

a **ready**. I won't keep you waiting long.
b **the chance to** go diving on a coral reef there.
c **in touch with** our sales team if you have any questions.
d **over** my shyness and talked to a few people.
e **paid** enough for the work I do here.
f **stuck** in the snow and I had to walk.
g **by** without one. I just use public transport.

Writing Part 2 Article

Write a short article of 140–190 words about your lifestyle and how you feel about it.

You could include information about some of the following:

your daily routine   your work or studies   your free time activities
your social life   your family life   your eating habits

Use texts A–D in *This is your life* on page 5 for ideas on how to structure your article. Include some of the vocabulary and grammatical structures you have studied in this unit

Please go to the Teacher's Resource Centre for a Sample answer with Examiner comments for this Writing task.
For more information on writing articles, see **page 192**.

1 LIFESTYLE

LIFESTYLE

Pronunciation Pronouncing questions

1 ▶ 1.3 Listen to two speakers asking the questions below. What differences do you notice in the way they speak? Who is easier to understand?
   1 Why do you like that film?
   2 What do you want to talk about?
   3 How did you do that?
   4 Where did you live?

2 Read the information in the box to check your answers to Exercise 1.

> **Pronouncing questions**
>
> Many English speakers join words together when they speak quickly. In questions with *do/did + you*, it can be difficult to hear whether the speaker is saying *do* or *did*.
> - What do you want to do? /wɒdʒə wɒnə duː/
> - How did you travel? /haʊdʒə trævəl/

3 ▶ 1.4 Write down the four questions you hear.
   1 Who do you want to speak to now?
   2 Where did you go this morning?
   3 When do you have to be there tomorrow?
   4 Why did you say that earlier?

4 **SPEAK** Work in pairs. Practise saying the questions in Exercise 3 as clearly as possible.

5 **SPEAK** Now say the questions in Exercise 3 joining the words together.

> **What to expect in the exam**
>
> One of the criteria for marking in the Speaking paper is Pronunciation. The examiner will consider the following:
> - Are the answers clear? Can the speaker be generally understood?
> - Is the speaker's intonation appropriate?
> - Does the speaker use sentence stress correctly? Is word stress correct?
> - Are individual sounds clear? Are they correctly produced?

14

Pronunciation

Understanding connected speech, in particular how words are joined together in fast speech, is an important listening skill.

1-2 ▶ 1.3 In open class, discuss the differences and who the students thought was easier and why. Note that the surrounding context usually makes it clear whether the speaker is saying *did* or *do*, even if the difference is difficult to hear in a single utterance.

3 ▶ 1.4 Play the recording at least twice.

4-5 Students read the instructions and practise saying the questions. Note that in both fast speech and slow careful speech, information words, such as nouns and verbs, are usually stressed in English, while grammatical words like prepositions, articles and auxiliaries are usually unstressed, e.g. Where did you go this morning? The last noun in a sentence usually receives more stress than the other information words. You could practise this by eliciting the stressed words in the sentences from Exercise 3 on the board and doing some choral drilling.

2 HIGH ENERGY

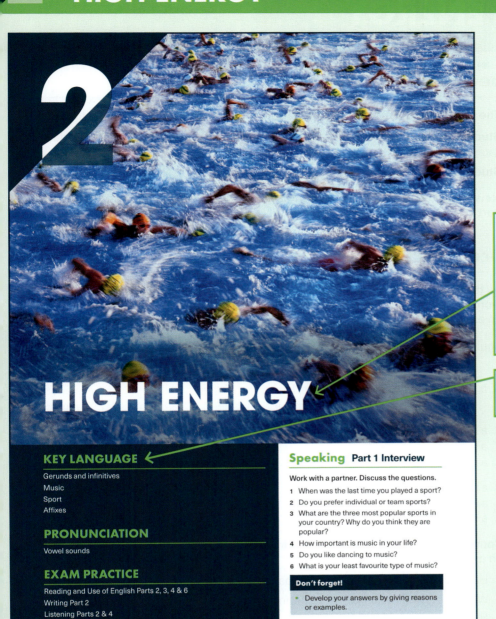

Sport and music are the themes of this unit. Vocabulary related to these two topics is contextualised through the reading and listening tasks, as well as the important grammar point of gerunds and infinitives.

Read the unit objectives to the class.

KEY LANGUAGE
Gerunds and infinitives
Music
Sport
Affixes

PRONUNCIATION
Vowel sounds

EXAM PRACTICE
Reading and Use of English Parts 2, 3, 4 & 6
Writing Part 2
Listening Parts 2 & 4
Speaking Parts 1, 2, 3 & 4

Speaking Part 1 Interview
Work with a partner. Discuss the questions.
1 When was the last time you played a sport?
2 Do you prefer individual or team sports?
3 What are the three most popular sports in your country? Why do you think they are popular?
4 How important is music in your life?
5 Do you like dancing to music?
6 What is your least favourite type of music?

Don't forget!
- Develop your answers by giving reasons or examples.

SPEAKING Part 1 Interview

Focus students' attention on the picture. Board the following question words: *who, what, when, where, why,* and *how*. In pairs, students brainstorm some ideas for each one, e.g. *For who, they could be amateur athletes.* Bring the class back together to share their ideas.

Both sport and music are topics that often come up in Speaking Part 1. These questions will give the students useful practice discussing these topics. You could illustrate the importance of giving full answers to questions with a demonstration. A student asks you the first question twice. The first time give a short, abrupt answer, e.g. *Last weekend*. The second time give a fully developed answer that includes an example or reason, e.g. *Last weekend I played football with my mates at a local pitch. We just get together sometimes and play for fun. It's not an official team or anything.*

Give students five minutes to discuss the questions in pairs before getting whole class feedback. Write any interesting vocabulary that comes up during the conversation on the board.

ONLINE MATERIALS

Gerunds and infinitives dominoes (**Teacher's Resource Centre**)
Vowel sounds board game (**Teacher's Resource Centre**)
Unit 2 Test (**Test Generator**)
Unit 2 Wordlist (**Teacher's Resource Centre**)
Unit 2 On-the-go-practice (**App**)

2 HIGH ENERGY

Speaking Part 2 Long turn

Don't forget!

Student A
› Do not describe the photographs in detail; talk about the similarities and differences.
› The second part of the task is written as a question above the photographs.

Student B
› Develop your answer fully, giving reasons for your feelings or opinions.

1 The photographs below show people listening to music in different situations.

Student A: Compare the photographs and say why you think the people have decided to listen to music in these situations.

Student B: When your partner has finished, say where you like listening to music.

2 Now change roles. Go to the Additional materials on page 198 and do the Speaking Part 2 task.

Vocabulary Music

1 All the words in each of the groups below can be used in combination with one of the words in the box. Write an appropriate word from the box in each of the gaps. There is an example at the beginning (0).

guitarist   in   instrument   live (adj)   on   play (v)   playlist   ~~rock~~   song

0	a _rock_	band musician star	3	download a perform a mime a	_song_	6	a _live*_ *pronunciation /laɪv/	album performance music venue
1	a lead a session a bass	_guitarist_	4	_on_	tour stage the radio	7	_in_	the charts concert tune
2	a percussion a wind a stringed	_instrument_	5	_play_	a track a tune a chord	8	create a shuffle a delete a	_playlist_

2 Complete each gap with an appropriate word combination from Exercise 1. There is an example at the beginning (0).

0 Have you been to see a singer or a band perform in _a live music venue_ ?
1 Who would you most like to see perform live _in concert/ on stage_ ?
2 Have you ever performed or spoken _on stage_ in front of an audience?
3 Can you _play a tune_ on any instrument?
4 Can you sing _in tune_ or do people cover their ears when they hear you?
5 Do you listen to songs that are _in the charts_ or do you prefer less commercial music?
6 When you _create a playlist_, how do you decide which songs to include on it?

3 **SPEAK** Work in pairs. Discuss the questions in Exercise 2, giving as much detail as possible.

Why have the people decided to listen to music in these situations?

HIGH ENERGY 2

Lead-in

Ask everyone to choose one photo on their phone (or that they've brought from home) which they don't mind showing to their classmates. The students then get up and walk around the room and do a 'mingle' activity, where they have to show each other their photos and try to find a connection between them. Encourage them to ask each other questions and briefly discuss each other's photos before switching partners.

Speaking

1-2 This speaking task is about music, a topic which is further explored in the vocabulary and listening activities on pages 16 and 17. Get the students to read the instructions and then focus on the **Don't forget!** box. Ask a few *yes* or *no* concept check questions: *Do you describe both photos in detail?* (No) *Do you compare the photos?* (Yes) *Is this speaking task a dialogue between you and a partner?* (No). While the students do the task, make notes on what they do well and what could be done better. Look out for common problems, such as not answering the question, only talking about one of the photos, describing the photos in too much detail, quickly running out of things to say, talking about the photos with their partner etc. Give the students some feedback on their performance in open class.

Vocabulary

1 Students read the instructions. Focus on the example (0). Remind the students what a *collocation* is. *Rock band*, *rock musician* and *rock star* are all very common noun + noun collocations of the word *rock*. Students could do this task individually and then pair check. They could also do it in pairs and then check their answers with another pair. Correct as a class.

Clarify the meaning of any vocabulary students are unfamiliar with, such as *chord* (three or more notes played together) or *shuffle* (to move things into a different order). Elicit and drill the pronunciation of *chord* /kɔːd/, *percussion* /pəˈkʌʃn/, *stringed* /strɪŋd/, or any other words you think your students will have trouble with.

2 Students do Exercise 2 as suggested. Correct as a class. Give the students one minute to study the vocabulary items in Exercise 1. Then ask them to close their books and write down as many as they can remember.

3 Put the students into new pairs and ask them to discuss the questions. Monitor and make a note of any emergent language you would like to exploit during the feedback stage.

Teaching tip

Get students to do speaking tasks twice. It will give them the opportunity to do them better the second time. Task repetition is particularly useful after students have received feedback on their first attempt, which they can then incorporate into their second one. Ask the students to reflect on their performance. What went better (or worse) the second time? Why?

UNIT 2

Speaking Part 2 Long turn

The photographs below show people listening to music in different situations.

Student A: Compare the photographs and say why you think the people have decided to listen to music in these situations.

Student B: When your partner has finished, say where you like listening to music.

Why do you think the people have decided to listen to music in theses situations?

Go back to **page 16**.

HIGH ENERGY

Listening

1 Give students some time to discuss the questions and then conduct brief feedback.

2 After the students have read the instructions and the information in the **What to expect in the exam** box, set up a role-play to check their understanding of the task. Put the class in pairs and assign roles A and B. A is a student in this class; B is a student from another class who knows nothing about the *B2 First* listening paper. Student A explains in their own words what to do in this part of the test, while Student B asks questions. Bonus points for students in role B who purposely misunderstand, e.g. *So let me see if I understand, I have to listen and write down one word for each answer, right?*

3 This exercise practises a useful exam strategy for Listening Part 2. On the day of the exam, they will only have 45 seconds to read the text and make predictions, but since this is the first time encountering this task, give them as much time as they need. When you elicit their ideas in open class, make sure they justify them.

4 ▶ 2.1 Allow the students to compare their answers in pairs after the first and second time they listen (see answers highlighted in the **Audioscript** below). Ask how many of their predictions made in Exercise 3 were accurate.

5 Organise the groups so the students are with people they have not yet talked to. During their conversation, encourage students to share a snippet of their favourite soundtrack (quietly!) using their phone.

6 Direct the students to the **Additional materials** section on page 199 (TB18).

AUDIOSCRIPT

Listening Part 2 Sentence completion

▶ 2.1

Hi, I'm Jack Suggs and on today's programme we're going to take a look at what's <u>going on</u> in the world of music. Apparently, the average person in Britain listens to around three thousand five hundred songs a year. And in the case of young adults aged between 18 and 24, that figure is more than <u>six thousand</u>, an average of about three and a half hours of music a day. *(Ex 4 Q1)*

Music's all around us – in shops, restaurants, gyms and even in the workplace. Not so long ago, the idea of employees listening to music in offices was almost unheard of; now it's becoming increasingly common. In fact, almost as common as it used to be in <u>factories</u>, where many employers have got rid of it because it can be distracting, and an obvious safety risk. *(Ex 4 Q2)*

In an office, though, it can be very beneficial, depending on what you're trying to achieve. According to some recent research, if the work involves creative thinking, then positive, stimulating music can help you <u>come up with</u> original ideas. But if it's anything that requires <u>problem-solving</u>, then it's better to work without any noise at all – including music, of course. *(Ex 4 Q3)*

Background music can also help increase business in restaurants. There are music-streaming services that design playlists to suit different types of restaurants and their brand or image. In a study <u>carried out</u> recently, one such service led to an increase of roughly 11 per cent in the sales of <u>side dishes</u> in one establishment, and orders of smoothies and shakes rose by 15 per cent! Restaurants have to be careful, though, because if they get the music wrong or play it too loud, they can <u>put</u> people <u>off</u> eating, and sales will fall. *(Ex 4 Q4)*

And there's some really interesting research that's been done by scientists at the University of Oxford. They <u>found out</u> that traditional music played in Indian restaurants can make the food taste up to 10 per cent <u>hotter</u>. They haven't <u>worked out</u> exactly why this is, yet, but it seems we associate the fast beat and high-pitched, distorted sounds of Indian music with high energy, and that reflects the sensation of eating spicy food. *(Ex 4 Q5)*

Now, if you like watching TV series, you may have noticed that many directors nowadays tend not to use <u>famous</u> musicians and composers to create the soundtracks for their work, but <u>turn</u> instead <u>to</u> relatively unknown artists – the band *Survive* in *Stranger Things*, for example, or *Mogwai* for *Les Revenants*. And they're such an important part of the process that they often compose the music before filming even begins, and so help to shape the series that's being made. *(Ex 4 Q6)*

They also use <u>technology</u> to create their sound, so there's less need to hire large orchestras and big studios these days. In fact, there's a move away from the dramatic sounds of the orchestra towards music that doesn't <u>stand out</u> so much, music that's more in the background so that it won't distract the viewer. *(Ex 4 Q7)*

Which is very different to what's happening with video games. Orchestras are an important element of these, and composers like Eimear Noone, are in constant demand. Eimear comes from Ireland, but has <u>set up home</u> in <u>California</u>. She's worked on games like *World of Warcraft* and *Legend of Zelda*, which are played by hundreds of millions of people, and she travels the world performing sell-out concerts of her soundtracks. *(Ex 4 Q8)*

Video game music is also played on the radio. On the commercial station Classic FM, there's a very popular, one-hour programme which plays music exclusively from games. Its name, appropriately, is *High Score* and it's presented by Jessica Curry, who co-founded a game development company called *The Chinese Room* and composed the music for the game *Dear Esther*. Many classical music lovers were sceptical at first, but the first series <u>turned out</u> to be a huge success, so they made more programmes. *(Ex 4 Q9)*

Now, on *this* programme, before we <u>go on</u>, you're going to hear a piece of <u>jazz</u> from somebody we all normally associate with rock music, and I want you to decide who it is we're listening to. *(Ex 4 Q10)*

HIGH ENERGY 2

Listening Part 2 Sentence completion

1 **SPEAK** Work in pairs or small groups. Discuss the questions.

  1 What type of music do you like listening to?
  2 How many hours do you think you spend listening to music each day?

2 Read these Listening Part 2 instructions and the What to expect in the exam box.

  ▶ 2.1 You will hear a man called Jack Suggs talking on the radio about music. For questions 1–10, complete the sentences with a word or short phrase.

  > **What to expect in the exam**
  >
  > - The words you *read* in the question may not be the same as the words you *hear* in the recording. For example, in question 6 **you read** ... *directors of TV series avoid using* _____ *artists to write soundtracks*, but **you hear** ... *directors nowadays tend not to use* _____ *musicians and composers to create the soundtracks for their work.*
  > - However, the word(s) you need to write are actually heard in the recording.
  > - For many of the questions, you will hear distractors, information which could fit the gap but does not answer the question.
  >   *For question 1 below you will hear more than one number. Listen carefully to ensure you choose the right one.*
  > - You do not need to write more than three words for each answer.
  > - Minor spelling errors can be made (e.g. *musicall*) but the words must be recognisable.

3 **SPEAK** Work in pairs. Read sentences 1–10 and discuss the type of information you might need to write for each one.

  1 will be a number, possibly quite a high one.

4 ▶ 2.1 Listen to the recording twice and complete the sentences.

  Jack says that people in Britain aged between 18 and 24 listen to an average of over (1) *six thousand/6,000/6 thousand* songs a year.
  Jack says that music is no longer played in many (2) *factories* for safety reasons.
  The findings of one recent study recommend silence when doing work which involves (3) *problem-solving/solving problems*.
  Jack says that sales of (4) *side dishes* increased by about 11 per cent in one restaurant, when the right type of music was played.
  Scientists at Oxford University discovered that a certain type of music could make some food taste even (5) *hotter*.
  Jack says that many directors of TV series avoid using (6) *famous* artists to write soundtracks.
  Jack says that many musicians make use of (7) *technology* when recording soundtracks for TV series.
  Eimear Noone, a composer of video game soundtracks, lives in (8) *California*.
  Jack mentions a radio programme called (9) *High Score*, which is dedicated to video game music.
  Jack says he is going to play some (10) *jazz* music on his radio programme.

3 Possible answers

  2 A plural noun, possibly referring to types of places, buildings or events.
  3 A noun or gerund, perhaps an activity, or possibly certain types of people or objects.
  4 Probably a type of food or drink.
  5 The comparative of an adjective (after *even*) describing food.
  6 Probably an adjective describing *artists*, though perhaps a noun to form a compound noun.
  7 A noun, possibly plural, perhaps with an adjective; something that musicians can use.
  8 Probably the name of a place, such as a town or a country.
  9 The name of a programme; there are numerous possibilities.
  10 A style of music.

5 **SPEAK** Work in groups. What is your favourite soundtrack from the following? Why?

  - a film
  - a TV series
  - a video game

6 Go to the **Additional materials** on **page 199**.

17

2 HIGH ENERGY

Reading and Use of English   Part 6 Gapped text

1 **SPEAK** Work in pairs. Look at the photographs of people doing parkour, and discuss the questions.

1. What does parkour involve doing?
2. What type of people do it and what skills do you think are required?
3. What benefits does it have for participants?

2 You are going to read an article about parkour. Read through the base text (the main text with the gaps). Are any of your ideas from Exercise 1 mentioned?

3 Six sentences have been removed from the article. Choose from the sentences A–G the one which fits each gap (1–6). There is one extra sentence which you do not need to use.

To help you, some words and phrases are written in **bold**. These show connections between the language in the text and the language in the missing sentences. A number of grammatical words such as *he*, *its*, *their*, *this* and *those*, are written in *italics* to show further connections.

Note that these connections are not shown in the *First* examination.

> **How to go about it**
>
> - Check that the whole sentence fits in with the meaning of the text before *and* after the gap.
> - When you think you have found the correct missing sentence for a gap, read the whole paragraph again to check that it fits.
> - When you have finished the task, check that the sentence which you have not used does not fit into any of the gaps.

4 **SPEAK** Work in groups. Discuss the questions.

1. Do you think parkour should be taught in schools? Why/Why not?
2. Are there any high-risk or extreme sports you would like to try?

HIGH ENERGY 2

Lead-in

Books closed. Divide the class into two teams, A and B. Explain that each team has three minutes to write down as many sports as they can think of, but they only get points for sports not also mentioned by the other team. The team with the most points is the winner.

Reading and Use of English

1 Ask if anybody in the class has heard of parkour — or perhaps even tried it. Put the students into pairs and focus their attention on the photos. Give them a few minutes to answer the questions. Instead of the pictures, or in addition to them, you could find a short video on the internet.

2 Allow the students no more than three or four minutes to read the article. The idea is to read quickly to get the general idea. In open class, ask if any of their ideas are mentioned.

3 This is the first time students are encountering this type of reading task, so do take the time to familiarise them with it. Before they read the instructions and the **How to go about it** box, give the students a couple of minutes to look at page 19 and together with a partner discuss *what* they have to do in this task and *how* to do it. Nominate a few students in open class to share their ideas. Then get the students to read the information on page 18 and report back on how many of their ideas are included there.

As a class, find the missing sentence for the first gap together, using the words in bold and italics. At this point, if you think your students are going to find this reading challenging, tell them which sentence is not used (B) before they do the rest of the gaps.

4 While the students discuss the questions in small groups, circulate and offer further ideas where necessary.

Teaching tip

Ready for B2 First often provides students with useful language to help them improve their performance on the Speaking paper. This same logic can be applied to any activity in class which involves speaking, for example, checking answers in pairs. Useful language for pair checking could include:

- *What do you have / What did you put for number 1?*
- *I have/put A.*
- *What made you choose A?*
- *I was doubting between A and B.*

- *I put A because here in the text it says …*
- *It can't be B because …*
- *I ended up with A by process of elimination.*

To come up with useful language, take a moment and role-play the speaking task your students will be doing and ask yourself, what would I say? Put this useful language up on the board so students can easily refer to it.

UNIT 2

Listening Part 2 Sentence completion

1 Look at the **listening script** on **page 235** and use the context to help you work out the meanings of the phrasal verbs in **red**.

… we're going to take a look at what's **going on** in the world of music.

'Go on', here, means happen.

2 **SPEAK** Talk about at least five of the following with your partner.

1 a <u>person</u> you usually **turn to** for help if you have a problem
2 a <u>place</u> in the world where you would happily **set up** home if you could
3 a <u>problem</u> for which politicians need to **come up with** a solution soon
4 a <u>moment</u> that **stands out** as being particularly important in your life
5 a <u>holiday</u> that **turned out** to be a complete disaster
6 an <u>activity</u> you have been **put off** doing again because of a bad experience
7 an interesting <u>fact</u> or piece of <u>information</u> that you have **found out** recently
8 an <u>experiment</u> you **carried out** in a school science lesson which made an impression on you

Go back to **page 17**.

1 Possible answers

go on = happen
come up with = think of
carry out = do/conduct (a study)
put off = discourage
find out = discover
work out = manage to understand
turn to someone = go to someone for help
stand out = be easy to notice
set up home = begin living in a place
turn out (to be) = become
go on = continue

2 HIGH ENERGY

READY FOR GRAMMAR

2 Gerunds and infinitives

Gerunds

The gerund is used:

1 as the subject/object/complement of a sentence.
   Subject: **Reading** in the car makes me feel sick.
   Object: I find **shopping** for clothes really boring.
   Complement: My favourite sport is **swimming**.

2 after prepositions.
   I'm not very **good at making** things.
   to is a preposition in *get used to* and *look forward to*.
   I'm **looking forward to seeing** Millie again.

3 after certain verbs, e.g. admit, adore, avoid, can't help, can't stand, consider, delay, deny, dislike, enjoy, feel like, finish, give up, imagine, involve, keep, (don't) mind, miss, put off, prevent, regret, resist, risk, suggest.
   Liz **suggested going out** but I **feel like staying** in.

4 after these expressions:
   have (no) difficulty/problems/trouble (in), it's/there's no use, it's (not) worth, there's no point (in).
   If you **have trouble getting** to sleep, **it's no use crying**.

The infinitive with *to* is used:

1 to express purpose.
   I'm learning English **to help** me get a better job.

2 after certain adjectives, e.g. (It is/was etc.) difficult, easy, important, lovely, (un)necessary, normal, (im)possible, (un)usual, (I am/She was etc.) delighted, disappointed, (un)happy, sad, surprised.
   I was **surprised to hear** she had failed the exam.

3 after certain nouns, e.g. ability, chance, decision, failure, idea, opportunity, plan, refusal, right, way.
   It was **a good idea to come** to this restaurant.

4 after certain verbs, e.g. afford, agree, appear, arrange, choose, decide, demand, deserve, hope, learn, manage, offer, pretend, promise, refuse, seem, threaten.
   He **offered to give** me a lift, but I **decided to walk**.
   He **promised not to tell** anyone what she'd said.
   With some verbs a direct object is needed, e.g. advise, allow, enable, encourage, force, invite, order, persuade, recommend, remind, teach, tell, warn.
   My job **enables me to use** my language skills.
   Some verbs can be used with or without a direct object, e.g. ask, expect, help*, need, want, would like, would love, would hate, would prefer.
   I **want to go** home and I **want you to come** with me.
   *help can also be used with an infinitive without *to*.

5 in place of a relative clause after phrases like *the first/the second, etc./the next/the last/the only* + noun.
   Marie Curie was **the first woman to win** a Nobel Prize.

The infinitive without *to* is used:

1 after modal verbs.
   You **can look** at it, but you **mustn't touch** it.

2 after help, let, make, would rather, had better.
   We**'d better leave** – it's late. I**'d rather stay**, though.

Verbs followed by a gerund or an infinitive with *to*

1 (quite/really) like, (absolutely/really) love/hate and (much) prefer are usually followed by the gerund, but the infinitive with *to* is also possible.
   I **absolutely love going/to go** for long walks in the hills.
   The infinitive with *to* is common after *hate* for specific situations, and after *like* when it means *be in the habit of*.
   I **hate to interrupt**, but we really must be going.
   I **like to have a shower** when I get home from work.

2 begin, start, continue and intend can be followed by the gerund or infinitive with *to* with no change in meaning.
   She fell over and **started crying/to cry**.

3 forget, remember, mean, need, stop and try can be followed by the gerund or the infinitive with *to*, but with a change in meaning.
   • remember + gerund = recall a previous action
      I **remember coming** here when I was young.
      forget + gerund is not often used for actions you do not recall. Instead, *not remember* is used.
      I **don't remember seeing** Jim at the party.
      remember/forget + infinitive = (not) remember what you have to do
      Remember/Don't forget to feed the cat later.
   • mean + gerund = involve
      Dieting usually **means giving up** things you enjoy.
      mean + infinitive = intend
      I **meant to phone** the electrician but I forgot.
   • need + gerund = (passive meaning)
      This house **needs painting**. (= needs to be painted)
      need + infinitive = (active meaning)
      I **need to get** some new shoes.
   • stop + gerund = no longer do something
      I've **stopped smoking**: it's too expensive.
      stop + infinitive = interrupt one activity to do another
      Let's **stop to buy** some sweets on the way home.
   • try + gerund = experiment to see what will happen
      Try resting for a while: you might feel better then.
      try + infinitive = attempt to do something
      Alan **tried to stop** the thief as he ran away.

Expressing general preferences

(much) prefer + gerund *or* infinitive
I **much prefer** playing basketball **to** watching it.
I **much prefer to** play basketball **rather than** watch it.

Preferences on specific occasions

1 would (much) prefer + infinitive with *to*
   I**'d prefer to** walk to school today **rather than** go by bus.

2 would (much) rather + infinitive without *to*
   This has the same meaning as *would prefer to*.
   I**'d rather not** talk about it at the moment.
   I**'d much rather** do nothing all day **than** go to school.

Inside the daredevil world of PARKOUR

HIGH ENERGY 2

An expression of attitude, exploring boundaries and calculated risk, free running has official status in the UK.

Frazer Meek jumps down from a wooden platform and jogs across the floor of the Fluidity Freerun Academy, a huge warehouse in an industrial estate on the outskirts of Cardiff. It is a wintry Thursday evening and there are only a few people practising their leaps and swings on the purpose-built equipment, designed to imitate the bollards, railings and concrete building blocks of the great urban outdoors.

In early 2017, the UK became the first country in the world to recognise parkour as a sport. **1 D** *Its* **participants are capable of leaping to improbable heights** while almost always seeming to land, cat-like, on their feet.

Also known as free running and *art du déplacement*, the sport attracts thousands of mainly young, mainly male **participants** across the country. **2 A** *This* **includes the opening sequence of the James Bond film** *Casino Royale*, as well as **advertising and music videos**.

'A lot of people from the pedestrian world don't understand parkour,' says **Meek**. 'It's not just about technique, it's about the attitude. It's about exploring boundaries sensibly, seeing danger and calculating risk.' **3 G** 'I really hated conventional sports,' he remembers. '**I was a nervous kid** who liked playing video games. Then I started to come across it on internet forums, and it seemed to be a lot of people who didn't fit in with more conventional stuff, shy people. That's what appealed to me about it.'

Some years ago, **Meek** got together with some like-minded spirits and rented a gym to practise parkour. Within weeks, hundreds of kids were turning up. **4 C** *It is one of a* **handful of purpose-built parkour centres** in the UK, offering a daily timetable ranging from 'Little Ninjas' for ages two to four, to adult drop-in sessions.

Their business reflects the coming of age of a sport that started in the late 1980s as little more than **some friends playing around after school** in a Paris suburb. **5 F** An early ambassador for parkour in the country, *he* appeared in *Jump London*, the television documentary that introduced the activity to a wider public in 2003 as he and two friends leapt across the capital's rooftops. He also played Mollaka, the bomb-maker chased by Daniel Craig's Bond in the memorable sequence at the start of *Casino Royale*.

Participants point to the **minimal equipment requirements** as one of parkour's advantages, arguing that now that it is recognised as a sport, parkour can extend its work in schools. This is a view echoed by Parkour UK chief executive Eugene Minogue. ' **6 E** It goes back to the core of what PE is about.'

Charlotte Blake is the chair of Free Your Instinct, a charity that brings parkour to the field of mental health. It has, she says, been an effective tool in helping people with anxiety, depression and bipolar disorder to build resilience and overcome the obstacles in their lives. 'Parkour helps you to move naturally within your environment and to develop a new dialogue with your environment, to play with it and to open up a world of opportunity,' says Blake.

A *Their* interest has been propelled by parkour's high profile on YouTube and **in popular culture**.

B Some highlight **the apparent risks** associated with parkour, but the organisation insists that the injury rate is lower than in other sports.

C *Later*, in 2016, *he* **set up Fluidity Freerun** with fellow parkour enthusiast Craig Robinson and a £50,000 loan.

D Parkour is defined as the discipline of **moving 'freely** over and through any terrain using only **the abilities of the body'**.

E Given the lack of outdoor space and the funding challenges, the great thing about parkour is that **all you need is a pair of trainers**.

F **One of** *those* **children, Sebastien Foucan,** became president of Parkour UK, the sport's governing body.

G *He* started when he was just **twelve years old**.

2 HIGH ENERGY

Language focus Gerunds and infinitives

1 Look at the underlined words in the following extracts from the reading text. For each one, explain why a gerund, an infinitive without *to*, or an infinitive with *to* is used.

   1 … the UK became the first country in the world <u>to recognise</u> parkour as a sport.

   1 to recognise: the infinitive with to is used in place of a relative clause after 'the first' + noun. Here it means 'the first country … which recognised parkour'.

   2 Its participants are capable of <u>leaping</u> to improbable heights …
   leaping: a gerund is used after a preposition, in this case, of.
   3 I was a nervous kid who liked <u>playing</u> video games.
   playing: a gerund is used after certain verbs, in this case, like.
   4 … it seemed <u>to be</u> a lot of people who didn't fit in with more conventional stuff…
   to be: an infinitive with to is used after certain verbs, in this case, seem.
   5 … Meek … rented a gym <u>to practise</u> parkour.
   to practise: an infinitive with to is used to express purpose, the reason why something is done.
   6 Parkour can <u>extend</u> its work in schools.
   extend: the infinitive without to is used after modal verbs, in this case, can.

2 Go to **Ready for Grammar** on **page 206** for rules, explanations and further practice.

3 One way of talking about your likes and dislikes is to use verbs such as *love* or *hate*, followed by a gerund. Certain adjectives can also be used, together with a preposition and a gerund.

   In 1–6 below, complete the first gap with a word from box a, and the second gap with a preposition from box b. The first one has been done for you.

   a absolutely   can't   don't   much   quite   ~~really~~

   b ~~about~~   at   in   of   on   with

   1 I __really__ **don't enjoy** going for walks in the countryside; I just can't get **excited** __about__ being in the open air, like some people.
   2 I __don't__ **mind** listening to jazz now and again, but I wouldn't be **interested** __in__ going to a concert.
   3 I __absolutely__ **love** cooking, and I'm especially **fond** __of__ baking cakes.
   4 I __quite__ **like** watching basketball, but I'm not very **good** __at__ playing it.
   5 I __much__ **prefer** watching films at home; I've never been very **keen** __on__ going to the cinema.
   6 I __can't__ **stand** playing board games with my family, but I never get **bored** __with__ playing games on my phone.

4 **SPEAK** How true are the statements in Exercise 3 for you?

5 Write eight sentences about your likes and dislikes using the verbs and prepositions in Exercises 3. For each sentence, add an extra piece of information.

   *I'm very **interested in watching birds**. I can identify over a hundred different species.*

   *I really **hate going to shopping centres**. There are too many people and I always seem to get a headache.*

6 **SPEAK** Work in pairs. Compare your sentences from Exercise 5. Ask follow-up questions for more information.

   A: *I'm very interested in watching birds. I can identify over a hundred different species.*
   B: *How did you learn to identify so many?*
   A: *I've got several books about birds and I watch a lot of videos on the internet.*
   B: *When did your interest in birds begin?*
   A: *When I was about eight, I was on holiday in Scotland with my family and we saw an eagle. It was so close I thought it was going to attack us!*

HIGH ENERGY 2

Language focus

1. Ask the students to look at the sentences from the reading in pairs and, based on their own knowledge of the grammar point, explain why one of the three patterns is used. Explain that it's OK at this stage if they don't know the reason. Go around the room and prompt the students with questions, such as *In 6, what kind of word is can?* (modal verb). Elicit a few explanations from the students as a class, but don't tell them if they are right or wrong at this stage.

2. Direct the students to the **Ready for Grammar** section on pages 206 and 207 (see below, TB19 and TB21). Give them time to read only the rules in the column on the left and check their explanations for the sentences in Exercise 1. Note that you only need to do as many of the exercises in this section as there is time for or that you think is necessary. It is even possible to come back to exercises 3–6 later and teach them as a separate lesson, as this section can work independently. Since there are quite a few rules to go through, the students may need some help finding them. Check the explanations for the sentences in Exercise 1 as a class.

3. After they read the instructions, give the students a few minutes to complete the task individually. Correct in open class. If there is time, students could quickly quiz each other.

4. Students discuss the sentences in pairs. Get brief open class feedback.

5-6. Monitor as the students write their sentences individually and check their use of the target language. Students could role-play the dialogue before doing the speaking activity in order to provide a model for how to ask follow-up questions. Circulate and make note of any interesting emergent language to address after the speaking task.

You may wish to use the **Gerunds and infinitive dominoes** on the **Teacher's Resource Centre** at this point.

READY FOR GRAMMAR

2 Gerunds and infinitives

1. Some verbs can be followed by a gerund and some others can be followed by an infinitive with *to*. Complete the sentences with the correct form of the verbs in brackets. One verb in each sentence will be a gerund, the other an infinitive with *to*.

   1. When I **suggested** ___going___ (*go*) skiing on Sunday, Marta was very enthusiastic, so we've **arranged** ___to meet___ (*meet*) at seven.
   2. I **can't help** ___smiling___ (*smile*) when I see my dad playing tennis. He's had hundreds of lessons but he still hasn't **learnt** ___to hit___ (*hit*) the ball properly.
   3. Paul **appears** ___to enjoy___ (*enjoy*) playing golf. He's even **considering** ___buying___ (*buy*) his own set of clubs.
   4. One of my cousins has **promised** ___to take___ (*take*) me windsurfing as soon as I've **finished** ___studying___ (*study*).
   5. At first my parents **refused** ___to let___ (*let*) me go to karate lessons, but I **kept** ___asking___ (*ask*) and eventually they agreed.

2. Some verbs can be followed by more than one verb form. Choose the correct options to complete the sentences. In some sentences, both options are correct.

3. **SPEAK** Would/Do you enjoy going to a gym? Why/Why not?

4. Complete the second sentence so that it has a similar meaning to the first sentence, using the word given. Do not change the word given. You must use between two and five words, including the word given.

   1. It's impossible for me not to laugh when he starts singing.
      HELP
      I can't ___help laughing___ when he starts singing.
   2. I really don't want to go out this evening.
      FEEL
      I really don't ___feel like going___ out this evening.
   3. Amy played much better than her opponent, so it was unfair that she lost the match.
      DESERVE
      Amy ___didn't/did not deserve to lose___ the match, because she played much better than her opponent.
   4. Rock stars often wear dark glasses so that people don't recognise them.

TB20

2 HIGH ENERGY

Lead-in

Books closed. Write or project on the board: *What makes you happy? Why?* Give the students a few minutes to discuss in pairs. Elicit a few ideas in open class.

Speaking

1-2 Students read the instructions and the **How to go about it** box. Since this is the first time students are doing a Speaking Part 3 task, ask them whether the following statements are true or false to check their understanding.

- *It's okay to disagree with your partner.* (True)
- *In the exam, you will have four minutes in total for this task.* (False)
- *You should wait until task two to reach a decision.* (True)
- *In the exam, the speaking examiner gives you a piece of paper with the diagram for task 1 and the question for task 2.* (False)

Monitor and try to write down one example of students 1) agreeing, 2) disagreeing politely, 3) giving opinions, 4) asking partners for their opinions, 5) giving reasons or examples for opinions. Share these examples in open class.

Speaking

Give the students time to read through the instructions and the **What to expect in the exam** box. Ask the class whether the following statements are true or false to see how well they've understood the task.

- *Sometimes the examiner asks a question that both students can answer.* (True)
- *Candidates can only talk to the examiner in this task.* (False)
- *It's a good idea to fully answer the questions, instead of just saying yes or no.* (True)

Organise the students into groups of three. Nominate one student from each group to be the examiner, who reads the questions.

READY FOR GRAMMAR

LOW ENERGY
Posted 30 mins ago

So as some of you know, I've been **trying (1)** *to lose* / *losing* some weight, but it's not easy. I've **stopped (2)** *to buy* / *buying* things like fizzy drinks and chocolate, but I know I **need (3)** *to do* / *doing* a lot more. The problem is, losing weight **means (4)** *to be* / *being* self-disciplined and I'm not very good at that. I really ought to **start (5)** *to go* / *going* to a gym as well. I know it'll **help** me **(6)** *to get* / *get* fit and I've been **meaning (7)** *to join* / *joining* one for ages, but I always **forget (8)** *to do* / *doing* anything about it. The truth is, though, I don't really **like (9)** *to do* / *doing* a lot of physical exercise; I much **prefer (10)** *to watch* / *watching* others do it. So, I'll probably just **continue (11)** *to live* / *living* life the same unhealthy way I've always done. In fact, there's a match on telly tonight; I must **remember (12)** *to order* / *ordering* a pizza for 8 o'clock.

PREVENT
Rock stars often wear dark glasses ____to prevent people (from) recognising____ them.

5 It's obvious he shot himself in the foot by accident.
MEAN
He obviously ____didn't/did not mean to shoot____ himself in the foot.

6 I hate it when I'm ill.
STAND
I ____can't/cannot stand being____ ill.

5 Complete the second sentence so that it has a similar meaning to the first sentence. Use up to five words.

1 We'd prefer to come back later rather than wait here.
We'd rather ____come back later than wait____ here.

2 I think it's better to pay by cash than use a credit card.
I prefer ____paying by cash to____ using a credit card.

3 I'd rather phone him than send an email.
I'd prefer ____to phone him rather than____ send an email.

4 She wants to stay in bed longer.
She'd rather ____not get____ up until later.

Go back to **page 20**.

HIGH ENERGY 2

Speaking Part 3 Collaborative task

1 **SPEAK** Work in pairs. Here are some things that many people believe are important if we want to feel happy. Talk to each other about how important these things are for our personal happiness.

2 Now decide which two things are most important for our personal happiness.

How to go about it

- Part 3 is an interactive task. As well as giving your own opinions, ask your partner what they think, and respond to their comments by agreeing, disagreeing or adding a further comment. Give reasons for your opinions.
- Do not start to make your decisions for task **2** while you are doing task **1**. In the exam you will not know what task **2** is until you have finished task **1**.
- In task **2** you do not have to agree with your partner when making your final decision.
- In the exam you will have two minutes for task **1** and then one minute for task **2**. However, while practising for the exam, in the early units of *Ready for First*, you can allow yourself more time.

Speaking Part 4 Further discussion

SPEAK In Part 4 of the Speaking test the examiner will ask you questions which are related to the topic in Part 3. Discuss the following questions.

What to expect in the exam

- A particular question may be directed specifically at you or your partner. Alternatively, you may both be asked the same question and encouraged to discuss your ideas together.
- In either case, you are expected to give full answers to the questions asked, with reasons for your opinions.

- What other things make you feel happy?
- Do you think having longer holidays would make people feel happier?
- Some people say that the best way to be happy is to make other people happy. What do you think?
- If something is making you feel unhappy, is it better to talk about it with your friends or your family?
- Some people like listening to happy music when they feel happy, and sad music when they feel sad. Why do you think this is?
- Do you think it is possible to be happy all of the time?

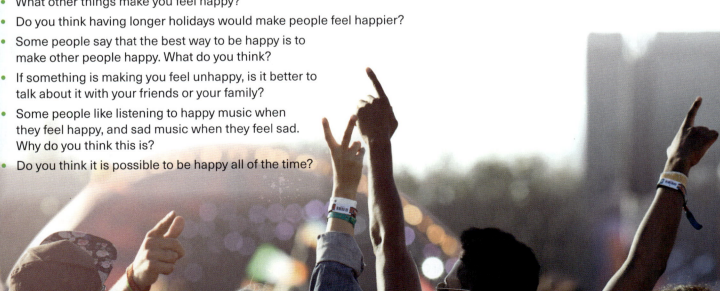

2 HIGH ENERGY

Vocabulary Sport

1 Can you name all the sports in the illustrations in the quiz below? Write the name of each sport next to the verb with which it is used. The first one has been done for you.

do _athletics_ gymnastics

go skiing, cycling, swimming

play volleyball, tennis, basketball/handball, football, golf

2 Write the name of the sport which each group of nouns is associated with. The first one has been done for you.

1	_tennis_	court	net	racket	backhand
2	football/hockey	pitch	referee	corner	foul
3	golf	course	green	clubs	hole
4	skiing	slope	sticks	run	goggles
5	athletics	track	field event	lane	meeting
6	cycling	saddle	helmet	pedals	peloton

3 Add each of these nouns to the appropriate group in Exercise 2.

fairway   gears   lift   red card   service   triple jump
golf   cycling skiing football/hockey tennis athletics

4 Complete the questions with the verbs in the box.

beat draw hit kick pass take take win

1 Which sports ___take___ **place** on an ice rink?

2 Which country's football team ___beat___ Croatia to win the 2018 World Cup Final?

3 Which **medal** does a runner-up ___win___?

4 In which sports do you ___hit___ **the ball** with a racket?

5 How many players from each team can ___take___ **part** at one time in a game of basketball?

6 If two hockey teams ___draw___ **nil-nil**, how many goals are scored?

7 In football, if you ___pass___ **the ball back** to your own goalkeeper using your chest, can they pick it up?

8 In which international team sport can you score points if you either ___kick___ **the ball** with your feet over one post and between two others, or touch it down over the opponents' line using your hands?

5 **SPEAK** Work in groups. Do the quiz in Exercise 4.

6 **SPEAK** Work in pairs.

Student A: Choose a sport and explain the rules to your partner.

Student B: Imagine that you are not familiar with your partner's sport. Ask your partner any questions that are necessary to help you fully understand the rules.

When you have finished, change roles.

HIGH ENERGY 2

Lead-in

Dictate the following typical Speaking Part 1 questions to your students. Read each one twice at a regular speed. Allow the students to compare in pairs before displaying the questions with a projector or eliciting them to the board.

- *What are the most popular sports in your country?*
- *Are there any sports you are really keen on?*
- *What sports do you dislike?*
- *What is your experience taking part in sports?*

Get the students to discuss the questions briefly in pairs. Feedback in open class.

Vocabulary

1 After the students read the instructions, focus their attention on the quiz at the bottom of the page. Ask them to point to the picture of athletics with their finger. (Note that in North America *athletics* is known as *track and field*.) Students can do this exercise in pairs or small groups. Elicit that in general sports with a ball collocate with *go*; sports ending in *-ing*, with *play*; martial arts and recreational activities, with *do*. Note that *practise* does not usually collocate with sports; we practise an aspect of a sport in order to improve, e.g. *practise my backhand*.

2-3 Put the students into small groups for this exercise. Provide monolingual dictionaries, if available. In the case that mobile phones are allowed, direct them to the Macmillan online dictionary. Correct in open class. If students ask you for the meaning of any words, try to elicit them from other students in the class. Check the pronunciation and drill *goggles* /ˈgɒg(ə)lz/, *peloton* /ˈpelətɒn/ and *slope* /sləʊp/. Exercise 3 could be done in open class or in pairs. Note that many of the words in Exercises 3 and 4 have a clear visual representation and could be revised later using pictures.

4-5 Students do the exercises in pairs as suggested.

Quiz answers

1 ice hockey, figure skating, curling
2 France
3 silver
4 tennis, badminton, squash
5 five
6 none
7 Yes. If the player uses their head, chest or knee (but not their foot), the goalkeeper can pick it up.
8 rugby

6 Put students into new pairs. Give students time to prepare. Help them with any unknown sports related lexis. While they do the role-play, monitor and make note of any common errors to address after the activity.

Teaching tip

Particularly with vocabulary, revision is very important. The more times students encounter a word and engage with it meaningfully, the more likely they are to remember it. Train your students to revise regularly at home using their vocabulary notebooks, flash cards or apps like Quizlet. One good study habit to encourage is revising vocabulary within 24 hours, because research shows that most forgetting happens immediately after we learn something, and that the rate of forgetting slows downs afterward. As a teacher, you can prioritise revision by including a bit of it in every lesson, for example, in a five-minute slot at the beginning or end.

Extra activity

Pictionary is a fun game to play with students of all ages. It of course works better with words that are easy to draw, such as the sports vocabulary in this lesson. Put students into two teams. One member of each team comes to the board to draw and the other members of the team have to guess the word based on the drawing. No talking or gestures allowed. The first team to guess the word provided by the teacher gets a point. A variation is to give each student who is drawing a list of words and set a time limit. The team that guesses the most words from the list is the winner.

2 HIGH ENERGY

Listening

1. Ask the class a few more questions about the photographs: *What do you think are the names of these sports? What would make people interested in participating in these sports?*

2. This exercise aims to raise students' awareness of distractors. The words in the options will almost never appear in the part of the listening which provides the correct answer.

3. ▶ 2.2 Play the recording twice. Students can check their answers in pairs before you check the answers as a class. (See answers highlighted in the Audioscript below.)

4. After students have discussed the questions in groups, bring the class back together to share their ideas. Add any interesting emergent language to the board.

AUDIOSCRIPT

Listening Part 4 Multiple choice

▶ 2.2

I = Interviewer M = Mike Taylor

I: Octopushing, elephant polo, or cheese rolling. Our sports correspondent, Mike Taylor, has been finding out about some of the world's strangest sports. Which is the most unusual one for you, Mike?

M: Well, it has to be chess boxing, because it's such a bizarre combination. A match starts off with a four-minute round of speed chess, followed by a three-minute round of boxing. There can be up to six rounds of chess and five of boxing before a **winner** is decided. Sounds like just a bit of fun, but when I watched two men competing on German television recently, **I was amazed by their level of skill in each of these two very different disciplines.** [Ex 2 Q1] After all, boxing is such an aggressive, physical sport, whereas chess is all about using the brain. You don't expect a **boxer** to be good at chess, or a chess **player** to be good in the ring.

I: Have you found any other unusual combinations like that?

M: No, but you mentioned octopushing, which is underwater hockey – so it's an unusual setting for a familiar game. I haven't seen it played, but I've read that it's a very exciting **spectator** sport – major tournaments have TV screens that show the images captured by underwater cameras. **Apparently, you don't have to be very fit to play. But I'm not convinced – it seems physically very demanding to me.** [Ex 3 Q2] The good thing, though, is that no individual player has to stay underwater for long periods at a time. People like me who can't hold their breath for very long can keep coming up for air.

I: OK. What else have you got?

M: Well, one of my favourites is sport stacking, which involves individuals or teams building pyramids with plastic cups. It doesn't sound very impressive, nor do **competitors** need to be in particularly good physical condition. But if you watch a video of some of the best stackers, **you'll appreciate just how fast they are. It's quite staggering.** [Ex 3 Q3] There are adult competitions, and I'm thinking of having a go at it myself, but most **participants** are teenagers and children, some as young as four. Mind you, in sport we're used to seeing very young competitors outdo older ones, so that's nothing new.

I: Indeed. And are there any of these sports that you definitely wouldn't want to do?

M: Yes, there are, and not because they're in any way tough or there's too much danger involved. Far from it. It's just that I find them a bit ridiculous. There's toe wrestling, retro running – that's running backwards – or even pillow fighting, which is now a sport in Japan. **They all seem rather silly to me, and they're not sports I'd particularly want to do or even watch.** [Ex 3 Q4]

I: You mentioned toe wrestling. What does that involve?

M: Well, basically, competitors lock big toes and try to force their opponent's foot onto the side board of a wooden frame. I mean it's fine for kids, and a toe wrestling competition is the kind of thing you might expect them to organise in the school playground. But for grown men and women to hold a World Championship every year, and then for **organisers to apply for toe wrestling to become an Olympic sport** [Ex 3 Q5] – well, it's too daft for words. I'm just pleased the application wasn't accepted.

I: Alright. And which of the sports you've seen is the most impressive, would you say?

M: Well, probably the Man Versus Horse Marathon, which takes place every July in Wales. Human **runners** race cross-country against **riders** on horseback for 22 miles – that's around 35 kilometres – and on two occasions in the last forty years, a human **contestant** has won. Now that's not as astonishing as it might seem – horses are fast in short races but not so good over long distances. But **it does seem a little unfair that the human victories are not mentioned in the same breath as some of the world's more famous sporting achievements. These people are heroes, but they're virtually unknown outside Wales.** [Ex 3 Q6]

I: Yes, it's the first time I've heard of the race. You're a runner, aren't you, Mike?

M: I was, **but I damaged my knee when I was skiing and had to stop.** [Ex 3 Q7] I was a real enthusiast – used to run for a couple of hours after work every evening – but even then, I wouldn't have beaten a horse, that's for sure.

I: There's no shame in that! Right, thanks Mike. Time now for …

TB23

HIGH ENERGY **2**

Listening Part 4 Multiple choice

1 **SPEAK** Work in pairs. Look at the photographs of unusual sports. What do you think contestants have to do in each one?

2 You will hear a man talking on the radio about unusual sports. Read question 1 and the extract from the Audioscript, The underlined sections in the extract contain words which are the same or similar to words in all three of the possible answers A, B and C. Only one of these sections matches an answer; the others are distractors. Choose the best answer (A, B or C) and say why the others are incorrect.

1 When Mike saw a chess boxing match, he was surprised by
   - **A** how skilled the competitors were at both parts of the sport.
   - B how much fun the competitors were having.
   - C how aggressive the competitors were.

> Sounds like just a bit of fun, but when I watched two men competing on German television recently, I was amazed by their level of skill in each of these two very different disciplines. After all, boxing is such an aggressive, physical sport, whereas chess is all about using the brain.

3 ▶ 2.2 Read questions 2–7. Then listen and choose the best answer (A, B or C).

What to expect in the exam

- As with all parts of the **Listening** paper, you will hear distractors. Listen carefully both times you hear the recording.
- Although a particular option may be true, it may not be the correct answer to the question you are asked.

In question 2, all three statements are true but only one is something that Mike finds it difficult to believe.

2 Having read about octopushing, Mike finds it difficult to believe that
   - A players do not have to hold their breath for long intervals.
   - **B** a high level of fitness is not required to play it.
   - C it is an exciting sport to watch.

3 What impresses Mike most about the competitors in sport stacking?
   - A their fitness
   - **B** their speed
   - C their age

4 What is Mike's criticism of some of the unusual sports?
   - A They are far too dangerous.
   - B They should not be called sports.
   - **C** They are difficult to take seriously.

5 What do we learn about the organisers of toe wrestling?
   - A They apply what they learn from international competitions.
   - B They have arranged a number of events in schools.
   - **C** They made a request which was rejected.

6 How does Mike feel about the human triumphs in the Man Versus Horse Marathon?
   - A They are very surprising.
   - **B** They deserve more recognition.
   - C They are unlikely to be repeated.

7 Why did Mike give up running?
   - **A** He was injured.
   - B He lost interest.
   - C He had no time.

4 **SPEAK** Work in groups. Discuss the questions.
   1 Would you be interested in taking part in or watching any of the sports Mike mentions? Why/Why not?
   2 Do you have any strange sports in your country? What do the competitors do?

23

2 HIGH ENERGY

Word formation Affixes

1 Add an appropriate suffix, *-or, -er* or *-ant*, to each of the verbs in the box to form nouns for the people who perform these actions. You may need to make further spelling changes to the verbs.

win – winner

~~win~~ box play spectate compete participate organise run ride contest
boxer player spectator competitor participant organiser runner rider contestant

Check your answers in the **Audioscript** on **pages 235–236**.

2 Add either *-ist, -eer, -ee* or *-ian* to the pairs of words below to form the nouns for the corresponding people. Use the same suffix for both words in each pair. You may need to make further spelling changes.

employ/train electric/politics mountain/engine novel/science
employee/trainee electrician/politician mountaineer/engineer novelist/scientist

3 In 1–7, use the same prefix from the box with all three adjectives to make them negative. The first one has been done for you.

dis- il- im- in- ir- un-

	Adjectives	Negative
1	ambitious/likely/reliable	unambitious/unlikely/unreliable
2	experienced/decisive/tolerant	inexperienced/indecisive/intolerant
3	legal/logical/legible	illegal/illogical/illegible
4	moral/mature/mortal	immoral/immature/immortal
5	practical/patient/perfect	impractical/impatient/imperfect
6	regular/responsible/relevant	irregular/irresponsible/irrelevant
7	honest/obedient/satisfied	dishonest/disobedient/dissatisfied

4 What is the meaning of the prefixes in bold?

former	outside or beyond	very big	very small	wrongly
ex-wife	**extra**terrestrial	**hyper**market	**micro**electronics	**mis**spell
oversleep	**pre**historic	**post**graduate	**re**write	**under**cook
too much/ excessive(ly)	before	after	again	too little/ not enough

Writing Part 2 Article

1 **SPEAK** Work in pairs. Read the following Writing Part 2 task. Talk to your partner about what ideas you would include in your answer.

You see this notice in an English-language magazine.

ARTICLES WANTED!
MY FAVOURITE SPORT

Write us an article telling us about your favourite sport. Why do you like it and what advice would you give to someone who wants to take it up?

The best articles will be published in this magazine.

Write your article in 140–190 words.

HIGH ENERGY 2

Word formation

One strength of *Ready for B2 First* is its comprehensive approach to word formation. In this unit, students get valuable practice with *affixes*, which refer to morphemes which are added to the beginning (prefixes) or the end (suffixes) of words to change their meaning.

1 Students read the instructions and do the task individually. Direct students to the **Audioscript** on page 235 (TB23), where the words appear in bold. Invite the students to discuss in pairs the meaning of these words in context.

2 In pairs, have the students take turns quizzing each other on the words in Exercises 1 and 2, e.g *What do you call a person who …?*

3-4 Ask the class to work through the exercises with a partner. Check in open class.

Writing

1 Students do the task as suggested. Check the meaning of *take up*. Get some brief class feedback.

Extra activity

Elicit and drill the pronunciation of the following pairs of words: *compete* /kəmˈpiːt/ and *competitor* /kəmˈpetɪtə(r)/, *contest* /ˈkɒntest/ and *contestant* /kənˈtestənt/, *organise* /ˈɔː(r)gənaɪz/ and *organiser* /ˈɔː(r)gəˌnaɪzə(r)/, *politics* /ˈpɒlətɪks/ and *politician* /ˌpɒləˈtɪʃ(ə)n/.

Teaching tip

Encourage students to start a new page in their vocabulary notebooks dedicated to word formation, where they can collect and revise new forms of words.

Suggest making columns labelled NOUN, VERB, ADJECTIVE, and ADVERB.

Teaching tip

In class, get students into the habit of spending a few minutes brainstorming ideas before starting to write. In the writing paper, students often lose points for poor structure when they don't dedicate enough time to developing and organising their ideas. One popular and useful way of brainstorming a topic is a mind map, also known as a spider diagram. Encourage students to think of more ideas than they need and then narrow them down to a few of the best ones.

HIGH ENERGY

2 Students should be able to do this fairly quickly by skimming the article. Check the meaning of *give up*, *feel on top of the world*, *warm up*. Check the answers in open class. To add an element of cognitive challenge, put the students in pairs and ask them to cover the article with their notebooks. Together, they try to remember what the article said about a–d. They then uncover the article and check their ideas. Ask the students, *Why did the writer decide to put the information in this order?* Note that organising your ideas into paragraphs is an important skill to develop for all the types of writing on the *B2 First*.

3-5 These exercises encourage students to notice important elements of the genre. Explain that in the exam you can be marked down for using a register that is either too informal or too formal, or for inappropriately mixing informal and formal language. Having a clear idea of who you are writing for helps you decide on the most appropriate register. Tell your students that their goal should be to write an article that looks and sounds like an article. To achieve this effect, it helps to use language typical of articles, such as contractions and informal linkers, as well as rhetorical devices like direct questions.

6 Focus on the **How to go about it** box. Elicit in what ways the example article in Exercise 2 follows the advice in the box, for example, by starting with a direct question. Direct the students to the **Ready for Writing** section on page 192 to make students aware of this useful resource. The final writing could be done in class or set for homework. However, it would be a good idea to give the students some time during the lesson time to organise their ideas from their initial brainstorm into paragraphs. In pairs, they could share ideas and help each other think of interesting titles or where to include a direct question.

Extra activity

Articles are in their nature descriptive, so it's important to include a range of adjectives. To encourage this, write or project the list of adjectives related to sports on the board:

exciting, competitive, challenging, popular, dangerous, enjoyable, silly, violent, outdoor, indoor, simple, complicated

In small groups, students think of different sports that could be described with these adjectives, justifying their answers with reasons and examples. Challenge the groups to think of a single sport that could be described using as many of the adjectives as possible.

Teaching tip

It can be useful to create writing checklists for each writing assignment. This helps students to avoid missing something out, but more importantly it helps them develop the habit of checking and evaluating their own work. Instruct the students to tick off the items on the checklist and hand it in with their writing. A word of warning: effective checklists should ideally have between three and six points. That way they don't give the student too much or too little to think about. A possible checklist for the article task on page 24 could be:

- *Does the article say why I like the sport and give advice to someone taking it up?*
- *Has an appropriately informal style been used?*
- *Have the ideas been organised into paragraphs?*
- *Does the article use a variety of informal linkers?*
- *Does it have an interesting title?*

HIGH ENERGY 2

2 Read the model answer below and match the paragraphs 1–4 to the summaries a–d.

a Benefits of the sport and reasons for liking it.   2
b Closing comment.   4
c What the sport is and what is special about it.   1
d Advice to people who want to do this sport.   3

A STRANGE WAY TO ENJOY YOURSELF

1 Have you ever seen a smile on the face of a long-distance Ex 4 c
runner? Running ten kilometres or more certainly doesn't
sound much fun, but this sport is a powerful addiction and
Ex 4 a
once you've started, you'll find it difficult to give it up. Ex 4 d
Ex 4 c
2 So what is the attraction of running? For me, whether I'm Ex 4 a
working or studying, there is no better way of getting rid of
stress. I can think through my problems and at the end of the Ex 4 d
race I have the answers. And simply completing a half or full Ex 4 b
marathon increases my confidence and makes me feel on top
of the world.
Ex 4 a
3 If you're thinking of taking it up yourself, don't try to do too Ex 4 d
much at the beginning. You should set yourself realistic
targets and always do warm-up exercises before you run. Also, Ex 4 b
make sure you buy a good pair of running shoes to protect
your knees and back from injury.
Ex 4 b Ex 4 a
4 And don't be put off by the expressions on the faces of the Ex 4 d
runners – they're enjoying every minute, and so will you! Ex 4 a

3 Who is the article written for (the target reader)?
Is it written in a formal or informal style? It is written for readers of a magazine. The style is informal.

4 Find examples of the following in the model answer:

a Contractions: e.g. *doesn't, you've*
b Informal linkers: e.g. *So*
c Direct questions
d Phrasal verbs

5 Match each of the features 1–3 with its purpose a–c.

1 The title — a to involve the reader
2 Direct questions — b to encourage the reader to take up the sport
3 The final sentence — c to attract the reader's attention

6 Now write your own answer to the task in Exercise 1.

> **How to go about it**
>
> - Decide which sport you are going to write about, then plan your answer.
>   *You could use the same paragraph plan as the model answer in Exercise 2.*
> - Begin your article with an interesting opening paragraph. You could start with an interesting fact, a surprising statement or a direct question, as in the model answer.
> - Aim to hold the target reader's attention. Use a lively, engaging style throughout the article. You could involve the reader by talking to them directly, as in the model answer.
> - End with a statement or question which summarises your thoughts and/or leaves the reader something to think about.
> - Give your article a title to attract the reader's attention. You could write this when you have finished your article.

For more information on writing articles, see **page 192**.

2 REVIEW

Reading and Use of English Part 3 Word formation

For questions 1–8, read the text below. Use the word given in capitals at the end of some of the lines to form a word that fits in the space in the same line. There is an example at the beginning (0).

The Celebrated Pedestrian

Pedestrianism, an early form of racewalking, was an **(0)** _EXTREMELY_ popular sport in 18th- and 19th-century Britain, attracting huge crowds of **(1)** _spectators_. Individuals would either aim to walk a certain **(2)** _distance_ within a specified period of time or else compete against other pedestrians. Cash prizes were offered but **(3)** _participants_ could also earn substantial amounts from the money gambled on events.

Perhaps the most famous **(4)** _walker_ was Captain Robert Barclay Allardice, whose **(5)** _extraordinary_ achievements earned him the title of 'The Celebrated Pedestrian'. The Scotsman's most memorable **(6)** _performance_ took place in 1809, when he walked 1000 miles (1609 kilometres) in 1000 hours for a bet of 1000 guineas. Many considered it **(7)** _unlikely_ that he would complete the challenge, which required him to walk a mile an hour, every hour, for forty-two days and nights. He proved them wrong, though the task was so **(8)** _physically_ demanding that by the end of the walk he had lost nearly fifteen kilos in weight.

EXTREME
SPECTATE
DISTANT
PARTICIPATE
WALK
ORDINARY
PERFORM
LIKELY
PHYSICAL

Reading and Use of English Part 2 Open cloze

For questions 1–8, read the text below and think of the word which best fits each gap. Use only one word in each gap. There is an example at the beginning (0).

How to go about it

- Look at the title and read the whole text through once before writing your answers.
- Look carefully at the words before and after each gap. You may need to write the plural form of a noun, or the negative form of an adjective.

SUMMER HOLIDAY MUSIC CAMP

If you're aged **(0)** _BETWEEN_ 12 and 18 and you're interested **(1)** _in_ music, come along to the One Music school in August and **(2)** _take_ part in our school holiday music camp. There's a wide range of activities on offer and you'll have the chance **(3)** _to_ learn from professionals, improve your musical skills and discover your true potential. You're guaranteed to make lots of new friends **(4)** _as_ well!

You'll get to try out a variety of instruments and then play them **(5)** _on_ stage in front of your family and friends at the end-of-camp concert. And if you feel **(6)** _like_ having a go at singing, there are classes to suit all types of voices and singing styles. Or maybe you **(7)** _would_ rather learn how to write songs, in which case our songwriting workshops will be perfect for you. Whatever your musical interests, join us this summer – it's impossible **(8)** _not_ to have fun on a One Music holiday camp!

REVIEW 2

Reading and Use of English — Part 4 Key word transformation

For questions 1–6, complete the second sentence so that it has a similar meaning to the first sentence, using the word given. Do not change the word given. You must use between two and five words, including the word given.

1 Elisa said it wasn't a problem if she had to work an extra hour on Saturday.
   MIND
   Elisa said she ___didn't/did not/wouldn't/would not mind having to___ work an extra hour on Saturday.

2 Rob thinks he's always right, so it's pointless to argue with him.
   POINT
   There's ___no point (in) arguing___ with Rob, because he thinks he's always right.

3 I would prefer it if nobody gave me money for my birthday.
   WANT
   I don't ___want anybody/anyone/people to give___ me money for my birthday.

4 It wasn't difficult for Alison to find work when she left school.
   DIFFICULTY
   Alison had ___no difficulty (in) finding/getting a___ job when she left school.

5 Try not to get into trouble on your first day back at school.
   AVOID
   Try ___to avoid getting___ into trouble on your first day back at school.

6 The lead singer was not in favour of recording a live album.
   IDEA
   The lead singer didn't think it was a ___(very) good idea to record___ a live album.

Vocabulary — Sport

Complete each gap with a suitable word.

1 We stayed in a hotel next to the golf ___course___, and our room overlooked the fairway of the eighteenth ___hole___.
2 When the ___referee___ blew the final whistle, several fans ran onto the football ___pitch___.
3 I'm useless at tennis: I can't even ___hit/get___ the ball over the net with the ___racket/racquet___.
4 The ___lift___ taking us to the top of the steepest ski ___slope(s)/run(s)___ broke down halfway up and we were left hanging in the air for over an hour.
5 Last night, Liverpool ___beat/defeated___ Chelsea 2–0, and Everton ___drew___ 1–1 with Arsenal.

Writing — Part 2 Informal letter

You have received a letter from your English-speaking friend, Suzy:

> Hi!
>
> My brother's 21 next month and I want to do something special for him. He's a big rock music fan so I was thinking of either buying him a decent speaker so he can play his music really loud, or getting him a three-day ticket for next summer's rock festival here. What do you think I should do?

Write your letter in 140–190 words.

For more information on writing informal letters, see **page 193**.

Please go to the Teacher's Resource Centre for a Sample answer with Examiner comments for this Writing task.

2 HIGH ENERGY

  HIGH ENERGY

Pronunciation Vowel sounds

1 Underline the word with the different vowel sound in each group.

1	caught	cart	court	4	live	leaf	leave
2	fool	pool	wool	5	third	heard	where
3	cough	front	some				

2 ▶ 2.3 Listen to check your answers to Exercise 1.

3 For each pair of words, underline the one whose vowel sound is the same as the word in bold on the left. The first one has been done for you.

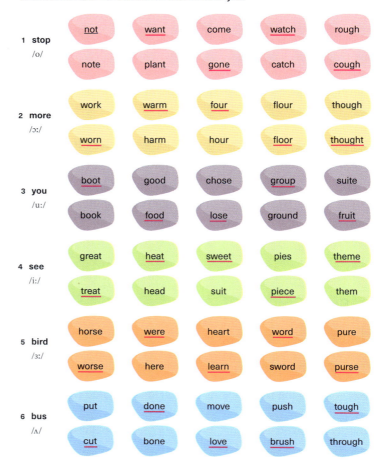

1 stop /ɒ/
2 more /ɔː/
3 you /uː/
4 see /iː/
5 bird /ɜː/
6 bus /ʌ/

4 Write down a sequence of numbers that is important to you, e.g. a phone number or date of birth.

5 **SPEAK** Work in pairs. Use the code below to communicate your number sequence from Exercise 4 to your partner. Make sure you pronounce the words as clearly as possible.

| 0 seat | 1 sit | 2 saw | 3 ship | 4 salt |
| 5 surf | 6 sheep | 7 sat | 8 sort | 9 sheet |

Student A: My number is ...seat, sheet, sit, saw, sort, salt.
Student B: Is your number 091284?

28

Pronunciation

1–2 ▶ 2.3 Elicit the answers as a group by letting students listen to each set of words twice. Students just listen the first time and then raise their hand for the odd one out on the second listen. Raise awareness of long and short vowel sounds by encouraging students to 'feel' the difference. For long vowels like /uː/, the muscles of the lips and the tongue tighten; for short vowels like /ʊ/, the mouth is more relaxed.

3 If students are unfamiliar with the idea of phonetic symbols, say that each symbol represents an individual speech sound. They are useful to learn while studying English due to its complex spelling system.

4–5 While students do the activity, monitor their pronunciation of the target vowel sounds and model when necessary. Make note of any particularly problematic sounds for future reference. You may wish to use **Vowel sounds board game** on the Teacher's Resource Centre.

READY FOR USE OF ENGLISH

Introduction

The first four parts of the Reading and Use of English paper are Use of English tasks. In this unit we will look specifically at three of the tasks: **Part 1 Multiple-choice cloze**, **Part 2 Open cloze** and **Part 3 Word formation**.

Information on the content of **Part 4 Key word transformation** appears at frequent intervals throughout this book.

What do you know about the Use of English tasks?

Look at the following statements and decide which are true (T) and which are false (F). If you think a statement is false, give reasons for your answer.

1. All four Use of English tasks are in the form of a text. **T / (F)**
   All except Part 4 (Transformations) for which the six questions are unrelated.
2. You should read texts through at least once before you attempt the task. **(T) / F**
3. One mark is given for each correct answer in the Use of English tasks. **T / (F)** *There is one mark for each correct answer except in Part 4 (Transformations): in this part, two marks are given for a completely correct answer, one mark if it is partly correct.*
4. Parts 1, 2 and 3 each contain eight gaps. **(T) / F**
5. All four parts of the paper contain an example. **(T) / F**
6. You should not write the answer for the examples on your answer sheet in the exam. **(T) / F**
7. In **Part 1** (Multiple-choice cloze) if you are not sure of the answer it is better to leave a blank. **T / (F)** *Marks are not deducted for incorrect answers. If students are unsure, they should eliminate any alternatives they consider to be clearly wrong and then, if they still cannot decide on the correct answer, make a sensible guess.*
8. In **Part 2** (Open cloze) you sometimes have to write two words. **T / (F)** *Only one word. Note that contractions (e.g. can't, won't, I've) and hyphenated words (e.g. one-way) count as two words.*
9. In **Part 3** (Word formation) an answer is given no marks at all if the word is misspelt. **(T) / F**
10. In **Part 4** (Key word transformation) the key word must not be changed in any way. **(T) / F**

Reading and Use of English — Part 1 Multiple-choice cloze

What to expect in the exam

Reading and Use of English Part 1 focuses mainly on vocabulary. The following examples show some of the different features of the language which are tested in the Multiple-choice cloze.

Look carefully at the words in italics and underline the answer (A, B, C or D) which best fits each gap.

1. **Knowing the meaning of a word.**
   It was a fast-flowing *game of football*, despite the poor condition of the __C__.
   A green   B lawn   C pitch   D floor

2. **Knowing the grammar of a word.**
   His doctor __C__ *him to eat* less and do more exercise.
   A said   B suggested   C advised   D insisted

3. **Knowing which words form collocations.**
   a The carnival parade had to be postponed because of the __D__ *rain*.
   A strong   B hard   C forceful   D heavy
   b Lily laughed at Tom's jokes, but I __C__ *the impression* that she didn't really like him.
   A made   B thought   C got   D reached

4. **Phrasal verbs**
   He was offered the job, but he *turned* it __B__ because of the low salary.
   A up   B down   C off   D on

5. **Linking words**
   We'll let you buy a motorbike __D__ you ride it carefully.
   A as if   B whenever   C although   D as long as

29

READY FOR USE OF ENGLISH

Introduction

Before doing the quiz, you may want to quickly show the students an exercise for each of the four parts, to help them remember which one is which. Pre-teach *gap* and *leave something blank*. The quiz could be done in pairs or individually. Check the answers together as a group. Make sure the students have no other questions about this part of the exam before moving on.

Reading and Use of English

Students complete the task following the instructions in the **What to expect in the exam** box. Correct in open class. Explain that students can greatly improve their knowledge of vocabulary, and therefore their Use of English Part 1 score, by collecting and revising new collocations, phrasal verbs, linking words and other new language in an organised way in their notebooks. Teachers should encourage this practice throughout the course.

READY FOR USE OF ENGLISH

READY FOR USE OF ENGLISH

1 **SPEAK** Look at the photograph and the title of the text below. What do you think you will read about?

2 Now read the text through quickly, ignoring the gaps, and check your predictions.

3 Read the text again and for questions 1–8, decide which answer (A, B, C or D) best fits each gap. There is an example at the beginning (0).

Don't forget!
› Read the whole sentence before and after the gap.
› Consider meaning, grammar and collocation when making your decisions.

BIRD BRAINS

The word 'bird-brain' is sometimes used to **(0)** _B_ to someone who is considered stupid. But the behaviour of New Caledonian crows **(1)** _B_ that birds can be extremely intelligent creatures. It is **(2)** _D_ known that they use sticks to extract food from holes in trees, **(3)** _C_ creating hooks at one end to make the task easier. Experiments conducted at the University of Auckland and recorded on film also show that they have a good **(4)** _A_ of the principles of water displacement. The crows work **(5)** _D_ that the best way to reach a piece of food floating in a half-filled tube of water is to drop objects into the tube to **(6)** _C_ the water level. What's more, they are capable of distinguishing between objects that will **(7)** _B_ and those that will float; faced with a choice, the birds select the heavier ones, ignoring those that will be too light, and they reject hollow objects in **(8)** _A_ of solid ones.

0	A describe	B _refer_	C apply	D signify
1	A assures	B _proves_	C concludes	D results
2	A strongly	B hugely	C deeply	D _widely_
3	A until	B yet	C _even_	D still
4	A _understanding_	B learning	C knowing	D informing
5	A up	B towards	C on	D _out_
6	A expand	B grow	C _raise_	D enlarge
7	A drown	B _sink_	C plunge	D dive
8	A _favour_	B advantage	C request	D wish

4 **SPEAK** What other examples of animal intelligence have you seen or read about?

1-2 In open class, elicit some ideas and then give students a few minutes to read the text and check their predictions. Explain to students that a tried and true exam strategy for Use of English Parts 1–3 is to read the text quickly to get a general idea before focusing on the gaps.

3 Before the students do the task, focus on the **Don't forget!** box. Check the answers as a class. Take the time to explore why any incorrect answers given by students are wrong.

4 Students discuss in small groups. Get brief feedback in open class.

READY FOR USE OF ENGLISH

READY FOR USE OF ENGLISH

Reading and Use of English Part 2 Open cloze

1 **SPEAK** What do you know about the habitat, food and behaviour of wolves?

2 Read the following text. Are any of the points you discussed in Exercise 1 mentioned?

GREY WOLVES

(0) **At** one time grey wolves, whose Latin name is *Canis lupus*, could be found over large areas of Europe. Over the last century, however, (1) **their** numbers and range have been considerably reduced, mainly as a result of hunting and the widespread destruction of habitat. Consequently, it is (2) **not** as easy to see them in the wild as it used to be.

There are (3) **a** number of subspecies of grey wolf, including the Italian wolf and the Iberian wolf, (4) **which** inhabit the forests of northern Portugal and north-western Spain. All wolves hunt for food in small packs, often preying on animals that are much larger (5) **than** themselves. And (6) **although** they will eat almost anything, including deer, sheep, rabbits and even fish and fruit, wolves rarely attack people.

Grey wolves usually (7) **give** birth to between four and seven cubs. The cubs leave the den when they are eight to ten weeks old, after which they (8) **are** cared for by all members of the pack until they reach maturity.

What to expect in the exam

In **Reading and Use of English Part 2** there is a text with eight gaps to be filled. This task focuses mainly on grammar, though some aspects of vocabulary may also be tested. The following are some of the types of words which are omitted. Look at the words in **bold** in the text above and write its number next to the corresponding type below. The first one **(0)** has been done for you.

- _3_ Articles
- _2_ Negative words
- _4_ Relative pronouns
- _8_ Auxiliary verbs
- _1_ Possessive adjectives (*my, your, his*, etc)
- _5_ Words in comparisons
- _6_ Linking words
- _0_ Prepositions
- _7_ Verbs in collocations

3 Read the text below and think of the word which best fits each gap. Use only one word in each gap. There is an example at the beginning (0).

WOLVES AND HUMANS

Wolves have something in common with dogs that may come (0) _AS_ a surprise to you. A recent study carried (1) _out_ by Dr Dorottya Ujfalussy and her colleagues at the Eötvös Loránd University in Budapest has shown that wolves, like dogs, can become fond (2) _of_ humans. For three months, ten researchers each raised one wolf cub at home as (3) _if/though_ it were a normal puppy; they cuddled the cubs, fed them from bottles and (4) _took_ them for walks.

The first discovery they made (5) _was/is_ that young wolves are difficult to control and make terrible pets. It seems there is (6) _no_ safe place for your cup of coffee with a wolf cub in the home. It also became clear, though, that they are able to form lasting relationships with humans. Aged two to four months, the cubs were relocated to the animal park where they (7) _had_ been born. Here, they were visited regularly by their caregivers, who found that even after two years, the wolves greeted them (8) _more_ warmly than they did a human stranger.

Reading and Use of English

1-2 Ask students to look at the picture and identify the animal. Note that *wolf* has an irregular plural. What do the students associate with wolves? Get the students to discuss the question in Exercise 1 in pairs. After they read, elicit any of their ideas mentioned in the text. Focus on the **What to expect in the exam** box. The aim of this activity is to raise students' awareness of the kind of words that are usually gapped in Use of English Part 2. Students could do this in pairs or individually.

3 Before they do the exercise, quickly elicit the following useful exam strategies:
- use the title and/photo to predict the topic/content
- read quickly for general idea before focusing on the gaps
- consider the type of words that could be missing

Go through the answers as a class. Ask the students if they put into practice the exam strategies.

READY FOR USE OF ENGLISH

READY FOR USE OF ENGLISH

Reading and Use of English Part 3 Word formation

What to expect in the exam

- **Part 3** contains a text with eight gaps, each of which has to be filled with the correct form of a word given in capital letters.
- The missing words are usually nouns, adjectives, adverbs and occasionally verbs. Sometimes the word you write will need to be in the plural, and sometimes a negative form is required. The meaning of the text surrounding the gaps will help you decide
- No marks will be given for answers which are misspelt.

1 For questions 1–8 use the word given in capitals at the end of each line to form a word that fits in the space in the same line. Use the words in bold to help you decide on the correct form of your answer. There is an example at the beginning (0).

0	The _LENGTH_ of the Channel tunnel is roughly fifty kilometres.	LONG
1	His third book is a **lively and** _humorous_ account of family life.	HUMOUR
2	The company took on **two thousand new** _employees_ last year.	EMPLOY
3	Rising prices have forced consumers **to** _tighten_ their belts.	TIGHT
4	It is **becoming** _increasingly_ **difficult** for young people to find work.	INCREASE
5	Unfortunately, the train was **both noisy and very** _uncomfortable_	COMFORT
6	Desert animals cope with **the** _heat_ in a number of ways.	HOT
7	**Cook** the mixture on a low heat **in a medium-sized** _saucepan_.	SAUCE
8	This _extraordinary_ **achievement** won her a place in the **record books**.	ORDINARY

2 Describe each answer in Exercise 1 using the words in the box below.

adjective   adverb   compound noun   negative   plural   spelling change   verb

(0): 'Length' is a noun. A spelling change is required to form it: the 'o' in 'long' becomes an 'e' in 'length'.

1 adjective; spelling change required (the 'u' in 'humour' is dropped)
2 noun; in the plural
3 verb
4 adverb
5 negative adjective
6 noun; spelling change required
7 compound noun
8 adjective

3 Look at the title of the paragraph below. What do you think the text will say?

4 Read through the text quite quickly, ignoring the gaps, and check your predictions.

5 Now read the text again and for questions 1–8, use the word given in capitals at the end of some of the lines to form a word that fits in the space in the same line. There is an example at the beginning (0).

Don't forget!
For Parts 2, 3, and 4 of the Reading and Use of English paper, write your answers in CAPITAL LETTERS when you transfer them to the answer sheet in the exam.

CAREERS INFORMATION: CIRCUS PERFORMERS

Here is some brief (0) _INFORMATION_ for anyone thinking of following a career in the circus. There is, of course, a wide range of jobs available: trapeze artists, acrobats, clowns, (1) _magicians_, fire-eaters and tight-rope walkers are all to be found in the big top.   **INFORM / MAGIC**

A few circuses train their own performers, but usually they are more (2) _interested_ in someone who can already demonstrate a circus-related (3) _ability_ or skill. Circus schools are the best way for aspiring artists to develop their talents, and can be either connected to a large circus or else totally (4) _independent_. Circus performers need to be physically fit and possess the necessary mental (5) _strength_ to cope with the intense training and obvious demands of the job. They are also flexible and able to adapt (6) _easily_ to new situations, particularly as circuses are frequently on the move.   **INTEREST / ABLE / DEPEND / STRONG / EASY**

Additionally, for many jobs within the circus, good concentration is essential. Fire-eaters and acrobats cannot afford to be (7) _careless_ as mistakes can have (8) _disastrous_ consequences.   **CARE / DISASTER**

Reading and Use of English

1 Put the following on the board: *the correct form, plural, negative, the meaning of the text, misspelt*. Give students a minute to read the **What to expect in the exam** box and then, with their books closed, they have to tell you what the text says in relation to the words or phrases on the board.

2–3 Students could do this in pairs and then compare their answers with another pair, or individually and then pair check. Circulate and provide help if needed. Check as a class and then do Exercise 2 in pairs or all together. You may want to check their understanding of *compound noun*.

4 Remind the students to take a moment to predict the content of the article and read it quickly for gist before attempting the answers. Note that while this task focuses mostly on forming individual words, at times students will need to show understanding of the text beyond the sentence level to get the correct answer. Finish by asking if anyone in the group would be interested in working in the circus. Why or why not?

3 A CHANGE FOR THE BETTER?

Technology and the associated changes in society are the themes of this unit. As with previous units the grammar and vocabulary are clearly contextualised and linked to the reading, listening, speaking and writing tasks.

Read the unit objectives to the class.

KEY LANGUAGE
Comparisons
Articles
Technology
Expressions with *as ... as*
Nouns 1

PRONUNCIATION
Diphthongs

EXAM PRACTICE
Reading and Use of English Parts 3, 4 & 5
Writing Parts 1 & 2
Listening Parts 2 & 3
Speaking Parts 1, 3 & 4

Speaking Part 1 Interview

Work with a partner. Discuss the questions.
1 How often do you change your phone?
2 What apps do you use the most?
3 How do you think your life will change in the next twelve months?
4 Talk about someone you know who has changed in some way in recent years.
5 What changes do you think should be made to your school, college or workplace?

SPEAKING Part 1 Interview

Focus students on the photograph. Ask students what the photograph represents. Ask the class for ideas on how they think the photo relates to the unit title. You could also ask students what their favourite season is and why.

Remind students that in Speaking Part 1 they should avoid giving one-word answers. They should develop their answers by giving reasons and examples. They should not pre-prepare answers and instead aim to sound as natural as possible. Model this behaviour by answering the first question.

Put students into pairs to discuss the questions. Monitor and help with vocabulary and grammar as necessary. After five minutes, bring the class back together. Nominate two or three students to share the main points from their discussions.

ONLINE MATERIALS

Sentence auction (**Teacher's Resource Centre**)
Your own idea (**Teacher's Resource Centre**)
Unit 3 Test (**Test Generator**)
Unit 3 Wordlist (**Teacher's Resource Centre**)
Unit 3 On-the-go-practice (**App**)

3 A CHANGE FOR THE BETTER?

Listening Part 2 Sentence completion

1 SPEAK You will hear an Australian student called Paul giving a talk about RoboCup, an international robotics competition. Look at the photographs. What do you think happens at this event?

2 ▶ 3.1 Listen to the recording and for questions 1–10, complete the sentences with a word or short phrase.

RoboCup was held for the first time in **(1)** ....Japan.... in 1997.

The categories in the children's competition are Soccer, OnStage and **(2)** ....Rescue/rescue.....

Paul says he didn't watch any videos of teams performing a **(3)** ....magic show.... in the OnStage event.

Paul's favourite video of an OnStage performance featured a robot dressed as a **(4)** ....penguin.....

Team members in the OnStage event are interviewed about their involvement in the design and **(5)** ....programming.... of their robots.

The maximum total time each team can spend on the stage is **(6)** ....six/6.... minutes.

Paul was impressed by the fact that the robots in RoboCupSoccer are all **(7)** ....autonomous.....

Paul says that all of the robot soccer teams he watched lacked a good **(8)** ....(solid) defence.....

In RoboCup@Home, designers have to communicate with their robots by using their **(9)** ....voice(s).....

Paul watched robots fetch objects from the **(10)** ....kitchen.... and give them to their designer in another room of the apartment.

3 SPEAK Would you be interested in attending and/or taking part in RoboCup? Why/Why not?

Do you agree with Paul that robots 'might become a reality in the home in the future'? Why/Why not?

> **Don't forget!**
>
> › Before you listen, read the questions and think about the kind of information which might fit each gap: is it, for example, a place or a number, a noun or an adjective?
>
> › You may hear information which could fit the gap but does not answer the question.

A CHANGE FOR THE BETTER? 3

Listening

1 Ask students to look at the photographs and discuss the question. You can ask the students to do this in pairs before feeding back or do this as a whole class discussion. Ask a few questions if necessary to generate discussion, e.g. *Have you ever seen robots like this before? What do you think the two men are doing?*

2 ▶ 3.1 Focus the students' attention on the **Don't forget!** box. Ask them *What type of information is likely to go in the first gap?* Elicit that it will be a place (*country*, *city*, etc). Explain that this is useful practice for the exam, where they will be given 45 seconds to read the task. They should use this time to predict the type of answers they will hear. Put students in pairs to discuss the type of information that you might need to write in the rest of the gaps.

Play the recording twice and let students compare their answers together between listenings. (See **Audioscript** below).

3 Students discuss the questions in pairs or small groups. Feedback in open class and make sure students give reasons for their answers.

AUDIOSCRIPT

Listening Part 2 Sentence completion

▶ 3.1

P = Paul

P: Hi, my name's Paul and I'm going to talk to you about the world robotics championship, RoboCup, which I've been looking into on the internet for a project I'm doing. The competition is usually organised in a different country every year, though **[Ex 2 Q1]** it's been held no fewer than four times in Japan, which is where the first event took place in 1997. The first time it was hosted here in Australia was in 2000 in Melbourne.

Now, RoboCup is short for 'Robot Soccer World Cup', and actually, the ultimate aim of the event is to encourage the development of robots which can beat the Football World Cup champions by 2050. Well, good luck with that, guys! But there are other challenges, too – including RoboCup@Home and RoboCup@Work in the adult competition, and the **[Ex 2 Q2]** OnStage and Rescue categories in RoboCupJunior, which is for kids up to the age of nineteen.

Let me just explain a little bit about the OnStage event. That's where teams get the chance to show what their robots can do through a stage show. And that can be anything from storytelling to a dance or a **[Ex 2 Q3]** theatre performance … or apparently, even a magic show, though I didn't find any videos of that one on the internet. The robots generally wear costumes and their designers can be part of the show, too. Many of the performers I saw were dressed up as characters from films, but the star of the video **[Ex 2 Q4]** I enjoyed most was a robot in a penguin costume. It was great fun and the audience loved it.

But there's also a serious side to the whole thing. For example, all the teams have a technical interview with the judges, and each member has to answer questions about the part they played in the **[Ex 2 Q5]** design and programming of their robots. And the competition rules are really strict. Points are taken off if a robot moves outside the area that's marked out on the stage, or if a team goes over the time limit. They have a total of five minutes for their performance, which includes setting it up and introducing it, and then an extra minute to clear **[Ex 2 Q6]** up – so no more than six minutes altogether on the stage. It's all very quick, so there's no chance for the audience to get bored.

I saw some videos of some of the other events, as well, like RoboCupSoccer, which is pretty impressive. What amazed me most about it is the fact that there are no radio signals, or remote controls or any other kind of communication from **[Ex 2 Q7]** the designers – all the robots are autonomous. They all communicate with each other and make their own decisions about what to do … almost like human players – except the ones I saw kept falling over for no apparent reason, which was quite funny to watch.

I have to say, though, there was some pretty good passing of the ball, but none of the teams had **[Ex 2 Q8]** what you could call a solid defence. Sometimes a robot would kick the ball from one end of the pitch to the other, and the other team just stood by and watched as it went into the goal! But hey, it's good entertainment and a great way for the public to learn about the latest developments in robot technology.

For me, though, RoboCup@Home seemed the most educational event. For this one, designers have to interact with their robots, and the only way **[Ex 2 Q9]** they can do that is by voice. A kind of apartment is set up in the venue and the robots have to follow their designers' spoken instructions to perform a number of different tasks. I saw them do things like open the curtains in the bedroom, or go into **[Ex 2 Q10]** the kitchen and get something like a bottle or a cup and take it back to the designer who was in the lounge.

This kind of thing might become a reality in the home in the future, so it's really interesting to see robots doing things in this context.

A CHANGE FOR THE BETTER?

Word formation

1. Students read the instructions. Do the first word together as a class. Students can either check their answers in the **Audioscript** on page 236 (TB34), or you could correct them as a class.

2. Check that students understand that the last word in each group requires a spelling change. Correct the exercise together. Ask students to spell the words out loud where there is a spelling change.

3. Students should read the whole of each paragraph before filling in any words. Explain that this will help them decide if the missing words are singular, plural, positive or negative. Mention that in this text, all the words are nouns, but that in the exam there will be a variety of word forms. Students do the exercise in pairs. Circulate and help them with spelling if necessary. Correct together.

Vocabulary

Ask students to work in pairs and note down the technological devices they use in a typical day and find three that they have in common. Get feedback from the class. Ask various pairs what their common devices were and which of these they would find it hardest to live without.

Put students in small groups to discuss the choices. Encourage them to give as much information as possible when discussing the different alternatives. As well as giving reasons for their preferences, they might, for example, talk about when they do each thing and/or for what purpose. For the first bullet point, they could also discuss which method they prefer using when calling people online e.g. Skype, Zoom, Houseparty, Facetime, Whatsapp, etc. And when discussing social media they could say whether they prefer using Twitter, Instagram, Snapchat and so on. Note that in everyday speech people usually refer to their smartphone as their 'phone' or 'mobile'.

Extra activity

You may want to practise word stress so that students see some common patterns. Draw this table on the board.

• • ● •	• ● • •	● • •	• ● •	● •
information				

Ask students to look at the answers from Exercise 2 (excluding *originality* and *popularity*) and match them to the stress patterns in the table. Elicit the word stress of the first few nouns from the class and write them on the board in the correct column. Then students work in pairs and add the remaining nouns. Circulate and model words students have problems with. Check the answers and then choral drill each column.

• • ● •	• ● • •	● • •	• ● •	● •
information	ability	carelessness	appearance	difference
explanation	majority	government	assistance	sadness
resignation	obedience	argument	enjoyment	treatment
presentation		loneliness	annoyance	weakness
		tolerance	existence	
			dependence	

Extra activity

Write the following on the board as a filler or a warmer. You could do this as pair or group work, or as a competition. You could also ask students what messaging abbreviations they use in their language and what they mean. The answers are underlined below. Do not underline on the board.

Choose the correct alternative to complete the meanings of the items of messaging abbreviations.

1. **TL; DR** <u>too long; didn't read</u> / talk later; do ring / too late; don't respect
2. **BRB** bring/<u>be</u>/bounce right back
3. **LOL** laugh off/over/<u>out</u> loud
4. **BTW** <u>by</u>/back/beyond the way
5. **IDK** I don't kiss/<u>know</u>/kick
6. **IMHO** <u>in my honest opinion</u> / it's my home office / I'm moving her out
7. **HBD** home before dark / <u>happy birthday</u> / had a big dinner
8. **FYI** find your identity / free young individuals / <u>for your information</u>
9. **ROFL** rolling <u>on</u>/off/out (the) floor laughing
10. **OTT** over the total/<u>top</u>/table

3 A CHANGE FOR THE BETTER?

Word formation Nouns 1

1 Write the correct noun form of the words in brackets to complete these extracts from the listening. You may need to use a plural form.

1 The __competition__ (*compete*) is usually organised in a different country every year.
2 And that can be anything from storytelling to a dance or a theatre __performance__ (*perform*).
3 It's good __entertainment__ (*entertain*) and a great way for the public to learn about the latest __developments__ (*develop*) in robot technology.
4 ... the robots have to follow their designers' spoken __instructions__ (*instruct*) ...

2 Use the suffixes in the box to create nouns from the words in 1–6. The same suffix is required for all four words in each group. The final word in each group also requires a spelling change. There is an example at the beginning (0).

| -ance | -ation | ence | -ion | -ity | -ness | -ment |

0	object	react	predict	convert
	objection	*reaction*	*prediction*	*conversion*
1	enjoy	treat	govern	argue
	enjoyment	treatment	government	argument
2	original	popular	major	able
	originality	popularity	majority	ability
3	appear	assist	annoy	tolerate
	appearance	assistance	annoyance	tolerance
4	sad	weak	careless	lonely
	sadness	weakness	carelessness	loneliness
5	inform	resign	present	explain
	information	resignation	presentation	explanation
6	differ	exist	depend	obey
	difference	existence	dependence	obedience

3 Use the word given in capitals at the end of some of the lines to form a noun that fits in the gap in the same line. You may need to use a plural form. The first one has been done for you.

1 Carla could not hide her _amusement_ at the sight of her father's first-ever laptop. He had quite a __collection__ of what he called 'technological antiques' and this was his favourite. It had plenty of __similarities__ to her own model, but it was the weight and __thickness__ of it that caused her to smile. — AMUSE / COLLECT / SIMILAR / THICK

2 One of the many __activities__ during our Science Week this year is a trip to the Technology Museum. A single __payment__ of £15 should be made by Friday, 7 October. Please also sign the attached form giving __permission__ for your child to attend. — ACTIVE / PAY / PERMIT

3 Aunt Gwen's __generosity__ on birthdays was unquestionable but it had to be said that most of her present-buying __decisions__ were not the best – a pink jumper and a romantic novel, for example. Prepared for __disappointment__, Paul unwrapped her gift and was amazed to find a top-of-the-range smartphone. — GENEROUS / DECIDE / DISAPPOINT

Vocabulary Technology

SPEAK Look at the choices below. Which, if any, of the alternatives do you do? Which do you prefer doing? Give reasons for your answers.

- call people using a landline, smartphone, tablet, laptop or desktop computer
- communicate with people via email, text or social media
- use predictive text, abbreviations or whole words when messaging people
- access the internet via smartphone, tablet, laptop, desktop or other device
- comment on posts, threads, blogs or photos
- share memes, GIFs or links on social media
- use a headset or chat to communicate with other players when gaming
- take photos with a camera, phone, tablet or other device

3 A CHANGE FOR THE BETTER?

Reading and Use of English Part 5 Multiple choice

1 **SPEAK** Do you think you spend too much time on your phone?

2 **SPEAK** Look at the following tips for reducing the amount of time you spend on your phone. How difficult do/would you find it to follow each one? Give reasons for your answers.

   1 Leave your phone outside your bedroom overnight.
   2 Keep it away from the table at mealtimes.
   3 Leave it at home when you go out for a meal or to an event, such as a concert.
   4 Keep notifications for social media apps turned off.
   5 Leave your phone in the kitchen and always go there to check for messages.
   6 Keep it switched off for a whole day.

3 Read through the article below quite quickly. Which of the tips in Exercise 2 does the writer say he follows? Tips 1, 3, 4, 5. He also says he keeps the phone switched off for a whole morning or afternoon, but not the whole day (6).

MY DIGITAL DETOX

According to a recent survey by Ofcom, people in the UK spend an average of two and a half hours each day on their smartphones, which they check every twelve minutes. Journalist Steven Rice reveals the steps he took to combat his own obsession.

Some weeks ago, I downloaded a screen time tracking app onto my phone, just one of a series of measures I adopted to tackle my growing, and potentially unhealthy addiction to the device. Looking back, I had been in obvious denial about how it was affecting my ability to concentrate, and the impact this was having on my work. But I could not ignore my wife's increasingly loud tutting at my frequent scrolling, nor the fact that even my digitally native, generation-Z daughters were rolling their eyes whenever they caught me chuckling at memes or watching cat videos on YouTube. It was clearly time for a change; time for a detox. [Ex 4 Q1]

My newly installed app told me that I was picking up my phone over forty times each day and spending more than four hours online; not as much as some people, perhaps, but this was no consolation. It was still above the national average and no less cause for concern. We shouldn't, of course, go all out to demonise phones; they have become indispensable items, and our online life is often closely intertwined with our offline one. My phone enables me to deal with work-related issues, arrange to meet up with friends, book concert tickets and holidays, and yes, even buy books to read. [Ex 4 Q2]

But as we all know, there is another, darker side to it all. Our phone addiction, we are told, is making us more anxious and depressed. Social media can cause young people, in particular, to feel less confident, as they continually compare themselves to their peers; so-and-so looks better, wears trendier clothes, has more expensive holidays, leads a more interesting life. And we are constantly bombarded with information, challenging our ability to focus, causing us to skim briefly rather than pause to reflect on what we read. Our minds have become like butterflies flitting from one subject to another, hindering our ability to apply ourselves for any length of time to one task. [Ex 4 Q3]

In planning my detox, I took what I considered to be the most useful ideas from a number of books and websites I consulted, with names like *How to break up with your phone* and *Time to Log Off*. Despite the titles, none advocated anything as final as a permanent break-up or logging-off. The phone itself is not the problem, but how you use it, so the route to a healthier relationship with technology is to learn moderation and good habits. And since this can be quite daunting, it's better to ease yourself into it with a step-by-step rather than an all-at-once approach. My first step was to switch off notifications for all social media apps on my phone. [Ex 4 Q4]

The result was disappointing. Having my phone on my desk when I worked at home was still a distraction; I kept looking at it, wondering if I was missing out on anything, and sometimes, I'm afraid to say, secretly giving in to temptation. 'Out of sight, out of mind,' I thought, and promptly moved it to the kitchen. If I wanted to check for messages, I'd have to get up and go to the other end of my flat. As predicted, I soon stopped thinking about the phone and was able to give all my attention to my work. Likewise, I banned the device from my bedroom; no more late-night screen time before I turn the light out, or early-morning scrolling as soon as I wake up. I sometimes take a book to bed instead – though I often nod off after just a page or two. [Ex 4 Q5]

By the end of the first week, I began switching off my phone completely for a whole morning or afternoon, and now I occasionally leave it at home if I go out in the evening. And what are the benefits? For one thing, I can concentrate on living my own life rather than worrying about what others are doing with theirs. The less time I spend on my phone, the more time I have to myself. My imagination wanders more freely, ideas for articles come more easily and assignments are completed more quickly. Oh, and yesterday, only nine pick-ups and forty-three minutes online. Can't be bad. [Ex 4 Q6]

A CHANGE FOR THE BETTER? 3

Lead-in

Tell students about something you have given up in your lifetime and why you did it. Focus the students' attention on the heading of the article. Elicit the meaning of *digital detox* (a period during which someone deliberately avoids using electronic devices such as computers, mobile phones, or tablets). Put them into pairs to discuss something they gave up and how they did it. Monitor and help with new vocabulary as necessary. Bring the class back together to share their ideas. Add any useful emergent language to the board.

Reading and Use of English

1 Ask this question as part of a general class discussion. If your class are comfortable with each other, you could ask the students to look on their phone analytics and share how much time they've spent on their phone in the past week – though you should probably be willing to do this yourself too!

2 This exercise could be done as a whole class discussion, but you may decide to put students in pairs or small groups to discuss each scenario. An alternative approach could be to conduct a survey with students saying how easy or difficult they would find each scenario on a scale of 1 (very easy) to 5 (extremely difficult).

3 Allow just three or four minutes for students to skim the article. Get feedback from the class.

4 Read the **What to expect in the exam** box as a class. These boxes draw attention to key features of the exam so that students become comfortable with the style and format.

Students read the instructions and the **How to go about it** box. Then ask them the following questions:
- *Why should you read the whole text before looking at the questions?* (to get an overall understanding)
- *Do the questions appear in the same order as the information in the text?* (Yes)
- *Do you lose marks for incorrect answers?* (No)

Ask students to read the questions, and check that they understand the vocabulary, e.g. *gestures*, *fragile*, *frustrated*, etc. They then answer the questions. Check the answers together. If students have chosen the wrong option, ask them which part of the text they thought the answer came from. Warn them to be careful of distractors.

5 Elicit a few useful expressions for giving opinions and write them on the board. You could also add the following language which came up in the reading task: *(no less) cause for concern*, *affecting/ challenging/hindering one's ability to*, *concentrate on*. Then students discuss the questions in pairs.

Teaching tip

While students are mainly working on reading or listening skills, you are less likely to spend time on lexis, as this might clash with the reading, listening or other aims. During such stages, you are likely only to:
- deal with an item when a student specifically asks about it
- give brief, to-the-point explanations or translations, rather than detailed presentations
- offer help quietly to the one or two students who ask, rather than to the whole class
- sometimes refuse help and tell students to do their best without knowing some items.

After the first phase of listening or reading work, once the learners have become comfortable with the text (and if there is time in the lesson), you can focus on lexical items in the text and how they are used. Here are some things that you could ask:
- *Can you guess the meaning of this word from the meaning of the text around it?*
- *Find some words in the text that mean …*
- *Find some words in the text connected with the subject of …*
- *In line X, what does … mean?*
- *Find specific words and sort them into three separate groups under these headings: …*
- *Why does the writer use the word … here?*
- *Find words in the text that match this list of synonyms.*
- *What words come before/after the word … What other words collocate with this word?*
- *Can you remember any other phrases you know with this word in them?*
- *Can you find any multi-word items (i.e. groups of words that go together / lexical chunks)?*
- *What's the opposite of this word?*
- *How many different words does the writer use to describe the …?*

3 A CHANGE FOR THE BETTER?

READY FOR GRAMMAR

3 Comparisons

Form

- Add *-er* and *-est* to form the comparative and superlative of regular one-syllable adjectives, or *-r* and *-st* for adjectives ending in *-e*. Double the consonant if the adjective ends in a short vowel and a consonant.

Adjective	Comparative	Superlative
cheap	cheap**er**	the cheap**est**
late	late**r**	the late**st**
thin	thin**ner**	the thin**nest**

- Use *more* and *the most* before adjectives with more than one syllable. Change *-y* to *-i* and add *-er* and *-est* to adjectives ending in *-y* after a consonant.

sincere	**more** sincere	the **most** sincere
happy	happ**ier**	the happ**iest**

- Two forms are possible with some two-syllable adjectives, e.g. *clever, common, friendly, gentle, likely, narrow, pleasant, polite, quiet, simple, stupid, tired*.

clever	clever**er**/**more** clever	the clever**est**/the **most** clever

- Use *more* and *the most* before most adverbs. Add *-er/-r* and *-est/-st* to the following adverbs: *fast, hard, late, long, soon*.

quietly	**more** quietly	the **most** quietly
fast	fast**er**	the fast**est**

- Some adjectives and adverbs have irregular forms.

good/well	**better**	the **best**
bad/badly	**worse**	the **worst**
far	**further/farther**	the **furthest/farthest**

Use

- To talk about people or things that are different in some way, use comparative forms of adjectives/adverbs + *than*

  *I think listening is **more difficult than** reading.*

  For small differences use *a bit, a little, slightly* before comparatives.

  *Your lounge is **slightly bigger than** ours.*

  For big differences use *much, (quite) a lot, far, significantly*.

  *My new car's **much faster than** my old one.*

- To emphasise the difference between one person or thing from all the others, use *by far* or *easily* before superlatives.

  *This is **by far the best** book I've ever read.*

  Use *in* before a noun when specifying the group.

  *Steven's **the naughtiest** boy **in the class**.*

- *Less* and *least* are the opposites of *more* and *most*.

  *Rugby is **less popular** than football here.*
  *This is easily the **least friendly** bar in town.*

  Like *more* and *(the) most,* they can be used without a noun.

  *You should **eat less** and **exercise more**.*

  Use *less/least* with uncountable nouns, and *fewer/fewest* with plural countable nouns.

  *I'm eating **less chocolate** and **fewer sweets**.*

- Use *(just) as* + adjective/adverb + *as* to show similarities.

  *She's **just as intelligent as** her sister.*

  So can replace the first *as* after *not*, when describing differences.

  *It's **not so difficult as** I thought it would be.*

  Not so becomes *not such* if a noun is used.

  *Maybe this isn't **such a good idea as** I thought.*

  To describe small differences, use *not quite, nearly, almost.*

  *He's **not quite so impatient as** his brother.*

  To describe big differences use *not nearly.*

  *Her new film isn't **nearly as bad as** her last one.*

  Use *as much* with uncountable nouns, and *as many* with countable nouns, or on their own.

  *I haven't got **as many chips as** Sally.*
  *I don't weigh nearly **as much** as I used to.*

- Use *be (just, (not) nearly, almost, not quite) the same* + noun + *as* to show similarities and differences. Possible nouns include *age, colour, height, length, size, weight, width.*

  *My mum **is almost the same age as** my dad.*

- Use *the* + comparative, *the* + comparative for changes which occur together; the second is often the result of the first.

  ***The more** money I have, **the faster** I spend it.*

- Use the following structure to describe similarities and differences: *little/no/(not) a lot of/(not) a great deal of/not much difference between.*

  *There isn't **much difference between** my job and yours.*

- Use verb + *more of a/an* + noun in some collocations, e.g. *make more of an effort/a difference, be/become/pose more of a problem/challenge/threat/danger.*

  *In a fire, smoke can **pose more of a danger** than the actual flames.*

A CHANGE FOR THE BETTER? 3

4 Read the article again. For questions 1–6, choose the answer (A, B, C or D) which you think fits best according to the text.

1 What encouraged the writer to begin a digital detox?
   A the negative effect his phone use was having on his work
   B the disapproving gestures of his family at his phone use
   C the realisation that his phone use was harming his health
   D the results of an app he installed to help limit his phone use

2 What feeling does the writer express in the second paragraph?
   A He is annoyed at the influence internet has on our daily lives.
   B He is pleased that others have worse phone habits than him.
   C He is convinced of the fact that the phone is a useful tool.
   D He is worried about how other people might judge him.

3 The writer compares our minds to butterflies in line 33 in order to highlight
   A the speed with which we are able to process information.
   B the attractiveness of our ability to multitask.
   C the delicate and fragile nature of our brains.
   D the difficulty we have in concentrating.

4 What advice does the writer give for reducing phone use in the fourth paragraph?
   A Obtain help from a variety of sources.
   B Switch off the phone regularly.
   C Introduce changes gradually.
   D Stop using social media.

5 The writer uses the expression 'Out of sight, out of mind' in lines 49–50 to indicate that
   A he could not see enough progress, so he considered giving up the detox.
   B he could check his messages because he knew nobody could see him.
   C he felt frustrated at not being able to see the messages on his phone.
   D he believed he would forget about his phone if he could not see it.

6 What improvement to his life does the writer mention?
   A He has become more creative.
   B He socialises more than before.
   C He sleeps more deeply at night.
   D He reads much more than he used to.

5 **SPEAK** Do you think people have become too dependent on information technology? Why/Why not?

How to go about it

> Read the article first for an overall understanding. (You did this in Exercise 3.)
> Find the part of the article which relates to the question you are answering. The questions appear in the same order as the information in the text.
> Eliminate the options which are clearly wrong, then check the option or options you have not eliminated.
> If you still cannot decide, choose one of the options. Marks are not deducted for incorrect answers.

What to expect in the exam

In the exam, the six multiple-choice questions may focus on some of the following features:
- a detail in the text, e.g. question 1.
- the attitude or opinion of the writer, e.g. question 2.
- the writer's use of comparison, e.g. question 3.
- the meaning of a word or phrase in context, e.g. question 5.

Questions might also focus on features such as the main idea expressed in a paragraph, or the writer's purpose. Sometimes the last question tests global understanding of an aspect of the whole text, including the writer's reason for writing it or the overall tone of the text.

37

3 A CHANGE FOR THE BETTER?

Language focus Comparisons

1 Complete the following sentences from *My digital detox*. If a word is given in brackets, write the correct form of that word. You may need to write more than one word.

1 But as we all know, there is another, _____darker_____ (*dark*) side to it all. (line 25)
2 I was ... spending more _____than_____ four hours online; not as much _____as_____ some people, perhaps ... (lines 15–17)
3 Our phone addiction, we are told, is making us _____more anxious_____ (*anxious*) and depressed. (lines 26–27)
4 Social media can cause young people in particular to feel _____less confident_____ (*confident*), as they continually compare themselves to their peers; so-and-so looks _____better_____ (*good*), wears _____trendier_____ (*trendy*) clothes, has _____more expensive_____ (*expensive*) holidays, leads a _____more interesting_____ (*interesting*) life. (lines 27–31)
5 I took what I considered to be the _____most useful_____ (*useful*) ideas from a number of books and websites I consulted. (lines 37–38)
6 The _____less_____ time I spend on my phone, the _____more_____ time I have to myself. My imagination wanders _____more freely_____ (*freely*), ideas for articles come _____more easily_____ (*easily*) and assignments are completed _____more quickly_____ (*quickly*). (lines 65–68)

Now check your answers in the article on page 36.

2 Why are the following forms of the bracketed words in Exercise 1 incorrect?

more dark   anxiouser   expensiver   usefullest   freelier

2 Suggested answers

The comparative and superlative of adjectives with one syllable, like *dark*, are formed by adding the suffixes *-er* and *-est* respectively (*darker/darkest*, not *more/most* dark).

The comparative and superlative of most adjectives with two or more syllables are formed by preceding the adjective with the words *more* and *most* respectively (*more/most anxious*, not *anxiouser/anxiousest*; *more/most expensive*, not *expensiver/expensivest*; *more/most useful*, not *usefuller/usefullest*).

The comparative and superlative of adverbs like *freely* are all formed by placing the words *more* and *most* respectively before the adverb (*more/most freely*, not *freelier/freeliest*).

3 What are the comparative and superlative forms of these adjectives and adverbs.

~~strange~~   fast   hot   happy   slowly   difficult   common   bad   far

strange, stranger, the strangest

4 Go to **Ready for Grammar** on **page 208** to check your answers to Exercises 2 and 3, and for further rules and practice.

5 Write down one example for each of the following:
- the best type of pet
- the best smartphone
- your favourite singer or band
- a film you really enjoyed
- a sportsman or woman you admire
- a favourite holiday destination

3
fast: faster, the fastest
hot: hotter, the hottest
happy: happier, the happiest
slowly: more slowly, the most slowly
difficult: more difficult, the most difficult
common: more common/commoner, the most common/the commonest
bad: worse, the worst
far: farther/further, the farthest/furthest

6 **SPEAK** Work in small groups. Try to persuade the other members of your group that your choices are better than theirs.

Cats are the best pets to have. They're far more independent than most other animals.

A CHANGE FOR THE BETTER? 3

Language focus

1 This task is designed to see how much students already know. Students read the instructions. Check they understand them by asking: *What do you have to do with the words in brackets? Do you only have to write one word?* They then complete the sentences. Either ask them to look back at the text to check their answers or check the answers together as class. you may wish to extend this section by using the **Sentence auction** on the Teacher's Resource Centre.

2-3 Give students time to do the exercises on their own. Then, ask them to check their answers in pairs before doing open-class feedback.

4 Direct students to the Ready for Grammar section on page 208 (see TB37 and below).

5 If necessary, model your own examples first.

6 Students read the instructions. Elicit the expressions they might need for giving an opinion or agreeing and disagreeing. Write appropriate suggestions on the board. You might include the following: *I'm afraid I don't really agree; Do you really think so?; Yes, but don't you think …; Well yes, but it depends on …; I suppose you're right ….*

Roleplay the example dialogue with two students, then ask them to discuss their choices in their groups. Encourage students to use the expressions from the board and a variety of comparative forms during their conversations.

READY FOR GRAMMAR

3 Comparisons

1 Complete the sentences with adjectives from the box. You may have to use the comparative or superlative form or you may not need to make any changes.

| boring | careful | cold | early | fast |
| good | hard | hot | quiet | tired |

1 I knew the exam would be difficult, but I didn't expect it to be as __hard__ as that.

2 Last summer was the __hottest__ since records began, with temperatures reaching 40º in some parts of Britain.

3 There are too many mistakes in this essay. You need to be a lot __more careful__.

4 He was very ill last week, but I'm pleased to say he seems to be getting __better__ now.

5 They put the heating on today so the school wasn't quite so __cold__ as it was yesterday.

6 That was the __most boring__ film I've ever seen. I almost fell asleep near the end.

7 The later you go to bed, the __tireder/more tired__ you'll feel tomorrow.

8 We were the first guests to arrive at the party. We got there half an hour __earlier__ than anybody else.

9 Life in the countryside is so much __quieter/more quiet__ than in the city; no traffic, no crowds and no neighbours!

10 The cheetah, which can run at a speed of 110 kilometres an hour, is the __fastest__ animal in the world.

2 In 1–7, complete each gap with a word from the box, so that sentence b has a similar meaning to sentence a. You will need to use some words more than once.

| as | between | great | many | more |
| much | not | same | such | the |

1 a Our television is almost as big as a double bed!
  b Our television is almost the __same__ size __as__ a double bed!

2 a I used to be far more interested in playing video games than I am now.
  b I'm __not__ nearly as interested in playing video games now __as__ I used to be.

3 a My taste in music is very similar to that of my best friend.
  b There's not a __great__ deal of difference __between__ my taste in music and that of my best friend.

4 a The most stylish phone I've ever owned is the one I have now.
  b I've never owned __such__ a stylish phone __as__ the one I have now.

5 a If I have a lot of screen time in the evening, it takes me a long time to get to sleep.
  b The __more__ screen time I have in the evening, __the__ longer it takes me to get to sleep.

6 a I study far less than I should; I'll need to work harder if I want to pass the *First* exam.
  b I don't study nearly as __much__ as I should; I'll need to make __more__ of an effort if I want to pass the *First* exam.

7 a I had fewer problems with this exercise than I thought I would.
  b I didn't have as __many__ problems with this exercise __as__ I thought I would.

3 SPEAK Work in pairs. Discuss how true the sentences in Exercise 2 are for you.

Go back to **page 38**.

TB38

A CHANGE FOR THE BETTER?

Listening

1 Discuss the first bullet point as a class. Give students five minutes to discuss the changes.

2 ▶ 3.2 Ask students to read and do the task in the **How to go about it** box. Play the recording twice.

3 Feedback as a class (see answers highlighted in the **Audioscript** below).

4 The post-listening question provides an opportunity for personalisation.

Vocabulary

1 Ask students to complete the gaps from memory before checking their answers in the **Audioscript**.

2 Students complete by themselves. Check answers as a class.

AUDIOSCRIPT

Listening Part 3 Multiple matching

▶ 3.2

Speaker 1 Next year we're starting lessons at 10, rather than 9 every day. The head says teenagers need more sleep than adults, and they'll be more receptive during class if they come in an hour later. It's a fairly radical idea and it's attracting a lot of attention from the press. I just think it's another one of the head's schemes to get publicity for
Ex 2 herself. *She clearly has her own interests at heart*
E *rather than those of the kids.* Perhaps I should have spoken out at the consultation meeting, but she's got the support of the whole teaching staff, and they don't seem to care that her motives are all wrong.

Speaker 2 I'm really fed up with our head of department. We all are. As *well* as having absolutely no interpersonal skills, he has a habit of making changes without bothering to find out what anyone else thinks first. He told us in a meeting last week that we're going to be using a different coursebook for Year 8 next term, and he's ordered three class sets already. I'm not saying that a change wasn't necessary – I think we're all a bit tired of the book
Ex 2 we're using at the moment – but *I do think he could*
D *have let us have some say in the matter before going ahead.* It's no way to run a department.

Speaker 3 Until now, a student's end-of-term report consisted of a mark for each subject, followed by a summarising comment from the tutor. With the new system, each subject teacher has to write a comment as well – and since I teach maths to as *many* as two hundred students every year, it'll take me absolutely ages. The head says the tutor's comment isn't enough to give parents a full picture of how their child's getting on, but I think it's fine as *long* as it's carefully written. Most parents won't read the comments anyway – they're just
Ex 2 interested in the marks. *It's a waste of time* as *far*
H as I'm concerned, and I know the majority of my colleagues feel the same.

Speaker 4 The situation in Year 10 is not much better than it was before. Mixing up the classes like that – splitting up the troublemakers – is a
Ex 2 step in the right direction, but *it doesn't go far*
C *enough.* They're still there, and they're still causing disruption to lessons. The head should have asked the parents to come in and got the kids to make certain guarantees in front of them, made them promise to improve their behaviour and so on. Then if the promises aren't kept, expel them from the school. We told her that, but she said expelling them would just create problems for other schools. She needs to be much tougher.

Speaker 5 There's some building work going on outside the music room. The windows are double glazed, but they're not thick enough to keep out the noise, so I've been moved to a room on the other side of the school. I've changed rooms many times
Ex 2 before, but never to one as bad as this. *The ceiling's*
A *high and the acoustics are terrible for the piano. Plus I have to shout to make myself heard, so my throat is suffering. And then the sun streams in during the afternoon and sends the kids to sleep.* I'm telling you, as *soon* as the work's finished, I'm moving straight back to my old room.

Extra activity

Tell students that someone in another class wrote the following incorrect answers. This will help students to identify the distractors.

1 D 2 H 3 C 4 A 5 B

Turn to the **Audioscript** (see above). Identify the language in each extract which may have caused the student to choose the wrong answer.

Example: *1 Perhaps I should have spoken out at the consultation meeting.*

Possible answers

2 *I'm not saying that a change wasn't necessary …*

3 *The head says the tutor's comment isn't enough to give parents a full picture of how their child's getting on …*

4 *… she said expelling them would just create problems for other schools.*

5 *I've changed rooms many times before …*

In order to prepare students sufficiently for this kind of task, it is essential that they are given practice in predicting the content of listening exercises.

Also note the following phrasal verbs in the listening script. Get students to underline and work out their meaning from context: Speaker 1 *speak out*; Speaker 2 *find out, go ahead*; Speaker 3 *get on*; Speaker 4 *split up*; Speaker 5 *go on*.

A CHANGE FOR THE BETTER? **3**

Listening Part 3 Multiple matching

1 **SPEAK** You will hear five short extracts in which secondary school teachers are talking about changes that have been made in their schools. With your partner, discuss why each of the following changes might have been made.

- starting the school day later
- using a different coursebook
- writing longer school reports
- mixing up students to form new classes
- moving to a different room

2 ▶ 3.2 For questions 1–5, choose from the list (A–H) what each speaker says about the changes. Use the letters only once. There are three extra letters which you do not need to use.

A The change has resulted in <u>a number of new problems</u>.
B <u>Too many changes</u> have been introduced.
C The change is <u>insufficient</u> to solve a problem.
D <u>We should have been consulted</u> about the change.
E The change is being made <u>for selfish reasons</u>.
F <u>Most parents support</u> the change.
G The change has brought <u>unexpected benefits</u>.
H <u>Most</u> of the <u>teachers</u> feel the change is <u>unnecessary</u>.

Speaker 1 E 1
Speaker 2 D 2
Speaker 3 H 3
Speaker 4 C 4
Speaker 5 A 5

> **How to go about it**
>
> › Underline the key words and phrases in the eight options. The first one (A) has been done for you. However, if you hear one of these words or phrases, do not assume that the question which contains them is the answer.
>
> › Listen carefully both times before making your final decision.

3 Check your answers using the **Audioscript** on **pages 236–237**. Underline those parts of each extract which guide you to the correct answers.

4 **SPEAK** Work in pairs. Tell your partner about at least two changes which have occurred recently in your life. Describe the reasons for the changes and your attitude towards them.

Vocabulary Expressions with *as … as*

1 Complete these sentences from the listening using a word from the box.

far   long   many   soon   well

1 **As** ___well___ **as** having absolutely no interpersonal skills, he has a habit of making changes without bothering to find out what anyone else thinks first. (Speaker 2)
2 I teach maths to **as** ___many___ **as** two hundred students every year. (Speaker 3)
3 I think it's fine, **as** ___long___ **as** it's carefully written. (Speaker 3)
4 It's a waste of time **as** ___far___ **as I'm concerned**. (Speaker 3)
5 **As** ___soon___ **as** the work's finished, I'm moving straight back to my old room. (Speaker 5)

2 Match each of the completed expressions in bold in Exercise 1 to a word or expression below with a similar meaning.

in addition to¹   in my opinion⁴   immediately⁵
provided³   a surprisingly large number of²

39

3 A CHANGE FOR THE BETTER?

Speaking Part 3 Collaborative task

1 SPEAK Your class has decided to do a project on changes and developments over the last century. Talk with your partner about some of the changes that have taken place in the different areas of our lives below.

2 SPEAK Now decide in which two areas the most positive changes have taken place.

Useful language

Relevant grammar areas

Present perfect: e.g. Technology **has changed** the way we communicate.
Past habitual behaviour: e.g. We **used to play** outside more.
Present habitual behaviour: e.g. **It's quite normal for** schools **to** provide tablets now.
Comparisons: e.g. We're **a lot healthier** now, thanks to medical advances.

Asking questions

Can you think of any more changes?
Do you have any other ideas?
Do you agree with me on that?

Agreeing and disagreeing

| That's right/true. | I think so, too. | I agree (up to a point). |
| That's not right/true. | I really don't think so. | I completely disagree. |

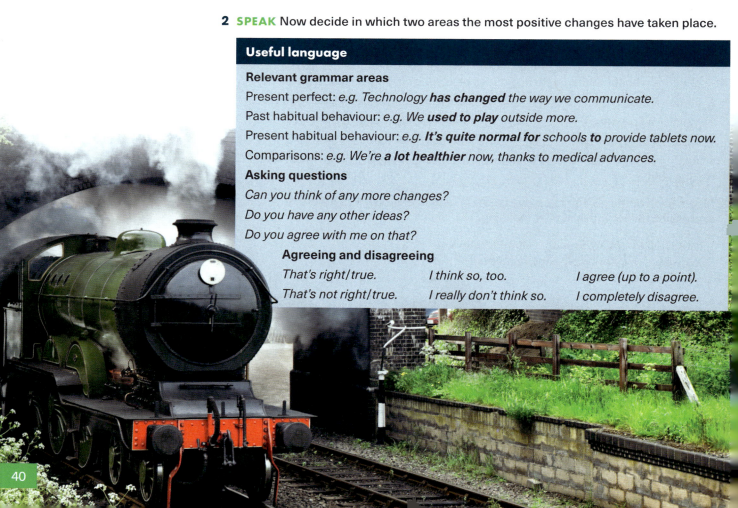

A CHANGE FOR THE BETTER? 3

Speaking

1–2 Students read the instructions. Ask the class whether the following statements are true or false about the Speaking Part 3 task to check their understanding:

- *You have to discuss changes that have taken place over the last ten years.* (False)
- *You have to choose one area which has experienced the most positive changes.* (False)
- *You should interact with your partner.* (True)
- *There will be pictures to help you in the Speaking exam.* (False)
- *You must not make your decisions for task 2 while you are doing task 1.* (True)
- *You don't have to agree with your partner when making your final decision.* (True)
- *The timing for the different tasks is flexible.* (False)

Focus students' attention on the **Useful language** box. Mention that most of the structures are from Units 1–3. (The present perfect isn't covered until Unit 7, but students should already be able to use it at this stage). Explain that they will be awarded points for the range of grammar they use, so they should use a variety of structures. Points are also awarded for interaction, so they should listen and respond appropriately to their partner.

Mention that the pictures are designed to help them, but they can talk about other aspects of each topic, e.g. in the Travel and transport section they could mention low-cost airlines.

Circulate and write down some good examples of student language. Get feedback from the class. Ask one pair which two changes they chose as being the most positive and see if the other students chose the same two. Write examples of good language on the board as positive feedback.

Speaking

If necessary, give students some guidance on what to talk about for each of the questions. For example:

1. Think about work conditions, leisure, health, education, etc.
2. Consumerism, availability of non-seasonal food all year round, etc. What are some of the negative and positive effects.
3. More/less technology, more subject choices, more government investment, more/less homework, different teaching styles, etc.
4. Where you live, your job, your car, free-time activities, etc.
5. Whether they like routines, they are afraid the change will have negative consequences, etc.
6. Think in terms of climate, inventions, medical breakthroughs, space exploration, fashion, food, etc.

Get feedback from the class. Ask a few pairs to share some interesting points from their discussion.

Extra activity

Before students do the Speaking Part 3 task, you could use the photos to help think of three different aspects for each of the changes. This will help to get students to generate lots of ideas to discuss when doing the Part 3 task. Do one as a whole class then ask students to do this in pairs.

Possible ideas

1. **Education**
   Classroom resources: technology, availability of books, science equipment.
   Discipline: corporal punishment, strictness of teachers.
   Availability of education: possibility of university (or any) education, school leaving age.
   Content and methodology: types of subjects, level of students' participation.

2. **Communication**
   Technology: email vs letter, immediacy, free calls via internet worldwide, smartphones vs landline phones, face-to-face vs screen languages.
   English as a world language: number of people learning foreign languages.
   International relations: technology and international travel facilitating closer ties between countries, businesses, individuals.

3. **Travel and transport**
   Within towns: buses, cars, bicycles, levels of density, pollution, danger.
   Inter-city: types of road, types of train, air travel.
   International: in particular, air travel (frequency, cost, distance …).
   Tourism: increase in international travel, positive and negative effects on tourist regions.

4. **Free time**
   Amount of free time: shorter working hours, longer holidays.
   Games: social (family, friends) vs individual (screens); time spent outside vs time spent in the house.
   Other free-time activities: organised sport, television vs radio, music and concerts, following vloggers, hanging out with friends.
   Holidays: amount of holiday, destinations, activities.

5. **Medicine**
   Availability: national health systems.
   Resources: number of hospitals, technological advances.
   Cures: cures found and diseases eradicated, use of antibiotics, life expectancy.

3 A CHANGE FOR THE BETTER?

Language focus

1 Ask students to read the text and answer the questions in Exercise 1. Explain that reading the text before filling in the gaps will help them understand the overall gist. Elicit answers from the class.

2 Alternatively this could be done as a jigsaw reading. Do number 1 as a whole class and then split the remaining 14 into two groups of 7. Allow students to check their answers with a partner.

3 Direct students to the **Ready for Grammar** section on page 210 (see below and TB42).

READY FOR GRAMMAR

3 Articles

- **The definite article** (*the*) is most commonly used:
  1 when there is only one of something.
     *I'd like to speak to **the manager**, please.*
  2 when something is mentioned again.
     *I bought a shirt and a tie. I'll wear **the shirt** tonight.*
  3 when both listener and speaker know what is being referred to.
     *Hurry up! **The film** starts in 10 minutes.*
  4 when talking about a specific aspect or part of something.
     *We're studying **the history of** architecture.*
     *I missed **the beginning of** the film.*
  5 to speak generally about certain groups of singular countable nouns, such as inventions and animal species.
     ***The mop** was invented in Spain by Manuel Jalón.*
     ***The whale** is still hunted by countries such as Japan.*
  6 with adjectives referring to general classes of people, e.g. *the homeless, the blind, the deaf, the rich, the poor, the old, the young, the French.*
     *Not enough is being done to help **the homeless**.*
  7 with superlatives.
     *Who is **the greatest footballer** in the world?*
  8 with musical instruments.
     *I'd love to learn to play **the piano**.*
  9 with types of transport which have a fixed timetable.
     *Shall we get **the bus** or take **a taxi**?*
  10 with some countries, e.g. *the USA, the UK.*
  11 with oceans, mountain ranges, deserts, rivers etc, e.g. *the Atlantic, the Pyrenees, the Sahara, the Thames.*
  12 with some geographical areas.
     *We're going to **the mountains** rather than **the coast**.*

- **The indefinite article** (*a/an*) is most commonly used:
  1 when first mentioning a singular countable noun.
     ***A man** went into **a bar** with **a fish**.*
  2 when referring to any one of several things.
     *Could you pass me **a biscuit**, please?*
  3 when talking about a person's job.
     *My father is **a nuclear scientist**.*
  4 with some numbers, e.g. ***a hundred** metres, **a thousand** people, **a million** pounds*
  5 meaning *per* in expressions like *twice **a day** or 50 miles **an hour**.*

- **No article** is used:
  1 when referring in a general sense to plural or uncountable nouns, including abstract nouns.
     *Do you think **computers** will replace **teachers**?*
     *Alan won't eat **cheese** or **meat**.*
     *We sang songs of **love** and **peace**.*
  2 with most streets, towns, cities and countries.
     *I went to **Bond Street** when I was in **London**.*
  3 when a town's name is used with a building, e.g. **Luton Airport, Oxford University**.
  4 in many common expressions, e.g. *to go home, to be at home, to go to or be at work/school/university, to be in hospital/church/bed/prison, to go by car/bus/coach/train/plane, to go on holiday, to have breakfast/lunch/dinner, at night.*

A CHANGE FOR THE BETTER?

3

Speaking Part 4 Discussion

SPEAK Discuss the following questions on the topic of change.

1. Do you think the quality of life in general is better now than it used to be?
2. Some people say we have too much choice nowadays. What do you think?
3. How could the education system in your country be improved?
4. If you could change one thing in your life, what would it be?
5. Some people don't like change. Why do you think that is?
6. What do you think will be the biggest changes in the next 100 years?

Language focus Articles

1. Read the extract from *A century of change* below, ignoring the spaces for the moment, and answer the following questions.

   - Which two areas from the speaking activity on page 40 are mentioned in the extract?
     Travel and transport and Communication
   - Which of the changes mentioned in the extract did you discuss in the speaking activity?

2. Now read the extract again and complete each of the gaps with *a*, *an* or *the* or leave it blank. There is an example at the beginning (0).

3. Go to **Ready for Grammar** on **page 210** for rules, explanations and further practice.

A CENTURY OF CHANGE

Since **(0)** *the* beginning of the last century there have been enormous changes in the way **(1)** *–* people live. **(2)** *The* world has become a much smaller place and **(3)** *–* life is much faster. In the first half of the twentieth century, **(4)** *the* horse was gradually replaced by **(5)** *the* motor car as **(6)** *the* most popular form of transport. One hundred years ago, air travel was still in its infancy; now there are around 100,000 commercial flights **(7)** *a* day worldwide. In the 1940s, **(8)** *–* steam trains were still a common sight on the world's railways. They have now all but disappeared from mainline routes and in several countries electric-powered high-speed trains can be seen racing across **(9)** *the* countryside at around 300 kilometres **(10)** *an* hour.

And **(11)** *–* information travels faster, too, thanks to developments in information technology, telecommunications and mass media. Having your own computer at **(12)** *–* home was almost unheard of in 1970, but just forty years later in 2010 there were over **(13)** *a* billion personal computers in use worldwide. Now, however, smartphones have taken over as the world's favourite computing device. **(14)** *The* telephone was already fairly widely in use by 1920, with some twenty million installed in the United States alone. But who could have predicted that a century later over half the world's population would own **(15)** *a* mobile device that could do everything a telephone can and much more besides?

3 A CHANGE FOR THE BETTER?

Writing Part 1 Essay

1 **SPEAK** Read the following Writing Part 1 instructions and the model answer. Do you agree with the writer's conclusion? Why/Why not?

Your English class has been discussing the effect of technology on sport. Now your English teacher has asked you to write an essay.

Write an essay using **all** the notes and giving reasons for your point of view.

> **Has technology made a positive contribution to sport today?**
> **Notes**
> Write about:
> 1 the use of technology to improve performance
> 2 the use of technology in refereeing decisions
> 3 ………………………………… (your own idea)

HAS TECHNOLOGY MADE A POSITIVE CONTRIBUTION TO SPORT TODAY?

Some people feel that technology has helped to improve our enjoyment of sport and they approve of its use. Others, however, believe it has a negative effect and would prefer to see its influence limited.

On the positive side, the use of technology in football to decide if a goal has been scored or not, or in tennis to judge whether the ball is in or out, clearly helps to make the games fairer. Communication between sports officials via microphones also improves the quality of their decisions. Another positive influence of technology is its role in increasing safety for competitors. Modern helmet design in cycling is an example of this.

On the negative side, the use of technology to improve performance can give some sportspeople an unfair advantage over others. For this reason, full-length swimsuits and so-called 'superbikes' have now both been banned from some swimming and cycling competitions.

In conclusion, I think that as long as sporting achievements remain the result of human effort, rather than scientific advances, then the contribution of technology will always be positive.

2 The third note in the question asks for 'your own idea'. What is the writer's own idea in the model answer?   *The safety aspects.*

3 The model answer in Exercise 1 is sometimes called a 'balanced' essay. In what way is the essay 'balanced'? *The essay is 'balanced' because the writer considers both sides of the argument, the positive and negative aspects of technology in sport, before giving their opinion.*

4 What is the purpose of each paragraph?
Paragraph 1: a general introduction
Paragraph 2: Advantages/Positive aspects of technology
Paragraph 3: Disadvantages/Negative aspects of technology
Paragraph 4: Conclusion

5 Add the underlined linking expressions from the model answer to the table below.

Introducing one side of the argument	*Some people feel; On the positive side; On the one hand*
Introducing the other side of the argument	*Others, however, believe; On the negative side; On the other hand*
Making additional points	*Another positive influence; In addition (to this); Furthermore; Moreover; Firstly/Secondly/Finally*
Introducing a result	*For this reason; Consequently; As a result*
Concluding	*In conclusion; On balance; To sum up*

3 A CHANGE FOR THE BETTER?

READY FOR GRAMMAR

3 Articles

1 In 1–5, decide which gaps require an article. Write *a*, *an*, or *the*, or leave the gap blank.

1 I read that __the__ electric toaster was invented at __the__ end of __the__ nineteenth century, but __–__ consumers didn't show __-/an__ interest in it until much later.

2 When we were on __–__ holiday in __the__ mountains last week we saw __a__ bear.

3 She works as __a__ teacher in __a__ school for __the__ blind in __–__ Northern Ireland. __The__ school has over __a__ thousand pupils.

4 I have to say that __–__ life has been good to me. I've been happily married for over __–__ fifty years and I have __a__ wonderful family. My wife and I were lucky enough to be able to give up __–__ work in our fifties and we've spent __the__ last thirty years travelling to __–__ different countries – we've been all over __the__ world.

5 **Moira:** I'm looking forward to __the__ concert. You've got __the__ tickets, haven't you?
   Jack: Oh no! I've left them at __–__ home on __the__ kitchen table. Don't worry, though. I'll get __a__ taxi – I can be there and back in half __an__ hour.

2 Match each paragraph to one of the inventions from the box.

compass(2) microwave(6) oven radar(5) space blanket(3) video(4) Walkman(1)

1 This invention completely changed the lives of ~~the~~ music lovers around the world. At first, Sony® executives thought the idea of people walking round with headphones on their heads would not be ˄a success. But ˄the device's creator, Akio Morita, always knew that the portable device, smaller than a paperback book, would be popular.

2 This device was probably ~~a~~ the most important navigation instrument to be invented in the last millennium. Originally, sailors used ˄the position of the sun and the North Star to guide them, but clouds often caused them to lose their way. This invention made possible the exploration of distant lands, including America, one of the most significant events in ~~the~~ history.

3 This is made from a material called Mylar, a type of ~~the~~ plastic covered with a microscopically thin film of metal. It is used, for example, for exhausted marathon runners or for keeping ~~the~~ mountaineers warm. The material existed in the 1950s but its production became much more sophisticated as a result of ~~the~~ man's efforts to land on the Moon in the following decade.

4 The first machines were built in the 1950s but for many years its cost limited its use to ~~a~~ the television and film industry. By ˄the early 1980s much cheaper versions were introduced and became nearly as common as television sets. It was ˄the first device to enable viewers to watch their favourite programmes whenever they chose and as often as they liked.

5 The name of this invention comes from the phrase 'radio detection and ranging' and is used to detect the presence of objects and calculate their distance, as well as their size, shape and speed. Although originally developed as an instrument of ~~the~~ war, it is now used for controlling ~~the~~ air traffic and predicting the weather. In addition, it has important applications in ~~an~~ astronomical research.

6 No well-equipped kitchen would be complete without this appliance. The first domestic version made its appearance in 1955. It was big, bulky and at over ˄a thousand dollars it was not ~~an~~ immediately successful. It was only in 1967, when the countertop model became widely available, that it began to grow in ~~the~~ popularity.

3 Each paragraph in Exercise 2 contains three errors in the use of articles. Correct the errors by adding, changing or deleting a word.

Go back to **page 41**.

3 A CHANGE FOR THE BETTER?

Writing

1 Ask students to read the instructions and example answer, and then discuss the questions with a partner. Get some feedback from the class.

2 Ask students to identify the writer's own idea. You could use **Your own idea** on the Teacher's Resource Centre to extend this exercise.

3 Discuss this in open class. Ask students to find examples in the sample (e.g. discourse markers: *On the positive side; On the other hand*).

4 Students should work individually first before comparing their answers with their partners. This will give them time to think and concentrate.

5–6 Students work in pairs to complete the table.

7–8 Ask them to read the instructions and the **How to go about it** box. If you prefer, you could offer students a choice of essay titles, e.g. *The mobile phone has greatly improved our lives today* or *Technology has improved life for the consumer* or *Technology has improved the quality of education*.

As some students may not be used to planning an essay, ask them to think of ideas for each section with their partner. Circulate and offer further ideas if necessary.

9 You can either do this as a timed task in class (40 minutes) or set this as homework.

Sample answer

The internet is everywhere and there are many advantages for have it. However, it is not sure that we must have it for to enjoy the life completely.

On the one hand it is much better to speak with your friends personally and don't get in touch with them online all the time. The only way to keep your friends and have a good relationship with them is see them regularly, rather than to chat on the social media. Also, about the entertainment, it is better to play the games or watch the films with other people, not by your own.

On the other hand, shopping online is better that go to the shops. There are more products for to choose and it is not so tired as walk round shops all the day try the clothes.

To conclude, we don't really need the internet to enjoy the life to the full. A computer or a phone cannot give you the good relations you have when you are with another people. However, it is useful for some things, like the shopping.
181 words

Examiner's comments

Content: All content is relevant and the target reader is on the whole informed, though not fully. The student refers to both friendships and entertainment, but the latter point is not fully developed. Shopping is the student's own idea. A clear conclusion is reached in the final paragraph that computers and phones are no substitute for contact with real people, although they can be useful.

Communicative Achievement: The conventions of writing an essay are used appropriately to hold the reader's attention. There is a clear essay structure with an opening statement, two paragraphs outlining the pros and cons of the internet in our lives and a concluding paragraph expressing the writer's opinion. The essay is written in a consistently neutral register with, in most cases, some more formal language to introduce ideas (*On the one hand; On the other hand; To conclude; However*)

Organisation: The text is organised into clear paragraphs, and there is a reasonable selection of linking words, particularly across paragraphs (*On the one hand; On the other hand; To conclude*). The student probably means *as for entertainment* when writing *about the entertainment*.

Language: In general, the frequent errors do not impede communication; however, the sheer number of them does distract the reader. The writer has particular problems with verb forms (*there are many advantages for have it; for to enjoy; it is much better ...; don't get; rather than to chat; There are more products for to choose; it is not so tired as walk round shops all the day try the clothes*) and articles (*enjoy the life; chat on the social media; play the games or watch the films; try the clothes*). Other errors include *by your own; better that; not so tired; another people*.

Some complex grammatical forms and less common lexis are used successfully (*it is much better to speak with your friends personally; get in touch with them online; the only way to keep your friends; social media*).

Mark: Pass

A CHANGE FOR THE BETTER?

6 Add the following linking devices to the table in Exercise 5.

> In addition (to this)   Consequently   On balance   On the one hand
> Furthermore   To sum up   Moreover   As a result
> Firstly/Secondly/Finally   On the other hand

7 You are going to write an answer to the following Part 1 question. Read the question, but before you write your essay, do Exercise 8 and read the advice in the How to go about it box.

Your English class has been discussing the role of information and communications technology in today's world.
Now your English teacher has asked you to write an essay.
Write an essay using **all** the notes and giving reasons for your point of view.

> **Do we really need the internet to enjoy life to the full?**
> **Notes**
> **Write about:**
> 1 friendships
> 2 entertainment
> 3 .... (your own idea)

8 Decide what the third point (your own idea) will be. Look at these possible options and consider how information and communications technology does and/or does not help us to enjoy life to the full.

Reference material: the internet enables quick, easy access to information for study or work, so gives us more time for leisure. Apps with maps and GPS also help save time.

- Reference material
- Shopping *simple to shop online, wider range of products than in shops; but perhaps less enjoyable than going to shops (especially with friends)*
- Working at home *the internet enables homeworking, so more time with family; but working alone can be lonely and boring*
- Health *some people are so dependent on technology that their health would suffer if they had to live without it; the internet encourages a sedentary lifestyle, with consequences for health (e.g. back problems, eyesight)*

9 Now write your essay in 140–190 words.

> **How to go about it**
>
> - Plan your essay. For each of the three points in the Notes section, make a list of relevant ideas which you could include in your essay. *For this question, consider both the positive and negative effect of the internet, e.g. friendships.*
>
>   Positive: it enables us to be in constant contact with friends.
>
>   Negative: we might not develop good social skills; it is not a good substitute for face-to-face conversations.
>
> - From your lists, select the points you want to include in your essay. Make notes, developing your ideas.
> - Decide how you will introduce and conclude your essay.
> - Write your essay. Make sure you:
>   a organise your ideas and opinions using paragraphs and linking devices.
>   b include a range of vocabulary and grammatical structures and avoid repetition wherever possible.
>   c write in a consistently formal or neutral style.
> - Check your work for grammar, vocabulary, spelling and punctuation errors.

For more information on writing essays, see **pages 189–191**.

3 REVIEW

Language focus Comparisons

Complete each gap in the paragraph with a word from the box. You do not need to use all the words.

by   in   less   little   lot   many   more   most
much   nearly   of   so   such   the   to

Max has changed since our days at school together. The older he gets, **(1)** __the__ more sociable he seems to be. He was never the **(2)** __most__ confident boy **(3)** __in__ the class and he didn't have as **(4)** __many__ friends as he probably would like to have had. But he's **(5)** __much__ less reserved now, and not **(6)** __nearly__ as nervous. Physically, he's different as well. He's quite a **(7)** __lot__ larger than he used to be and not **(8)** __so__ pale and sickly looking. In those days he was **(9)** __by__ far the thinnest of my friends, but he's put on a bit of weight and he looks **(10)** __less__ delicate now.

Articles

Each numbered line in the text below has one mistake in the use of articles. You may have to add, change or delete an article. The first two have been done for you.

1 Is it always ^a good idea to introduce changes into our lives?
2 Some people feel that change is positive and enjoy doing things in ~~the~~ different
3 ways. Others, however, prefer ~~a~~ stability and avoid change as much as possible.
4 One advantage of altering ^the way you do things is that it gives you the chance to
5 make improvements and become ^a better student, employee or person. It enables
6 you to consider different approaches and decide which is ^the best one. Another
7 positive aspect of change is that it adds variety to ~~the~~ life and prevents you from
8 becoming bored. This also helps to make you ~~the~~ more dynamic and interesting.
9 On ~~a~~ ^the negative side, change can be stressful if you constantly have to get used to
10 new situations, like moving house or switching jobs. For this reason, ~~the~~ many
11 people like to stay in ^the same place all the time, preferring familiarity to uncertainty.
12 In ~~the~~ conclusion, I think it is easier and more beneficial to introduce changes
13 into your life when you are young and more flexible. ^The Older you are, the more
14 ^an effort it takes to do things differently, and the more you want predictability.

44

REVIEW 3

Reading and Use of English — Part 4 Key word transformation

For questions 1–6, complete the second sentence so that it has a similar meaning to the first sentence, using the word given. Do not change the word given. You must use between two and five words, including the word given.

1 The new version of this phone isn't nearly as big as I thought it would be.
   MUCH
   The new version of this phone ……… **is much** smaller than ……… I thought it would be.

2 This is easily the most boring game I've downloaded recently.
   ENJOYABLE
   This is by ……… far the least **enjoyable** ……… game I've downloaded recently.

3 There are fewer teachers in my school than there were last year.
   NOT
   There ……… are **not** as/so many ……… teachers in my school as there were last year.

4 If you work harder now, you won't have to do so much later.
   THE
   The harder ……… you work now, **the** less ……… you'll have to do later.

5 Lucy is as tall as her mother.
   HEIGHT
   Lucy ……… is/'s the same **height** as ……… her mother.

6 Technology has had a bigger effect on our lives than we could ever have imagined.
   MORE
   Technology has ……… made **more** of ……… a difference to our lives than we could ever have imagined.

Reading and Use of English — Part 3 Word formation

For questions 1–8, read the text below. Use the word given in capitals at the end of some of the lines to form a word that fits in the space in the same line. There is an example at the beginning (0). Write your answers IN CAPITAL LETTERS.

Michael Hart

Michael Hart (1947–2011) was the (0) *FOUNDER* of Project Gutenberg, one of the (1) *earliest* and longest-lasting online literary projects. His life's aim was to digitise the world's literature and make it freely available online. As a result of his work, he is widely considered to be the (2) *inventor* of the eBook. In 1971, Hart typed a copy of the United States Declaration of Independence into the computer at the University of Illinois, where he was a student. The internet was used only by academic and military (3) *researchers* : the World Wide Web would not come into (4) *existence* for another two decades. Yet Hart spent the next fifteen or so years typing up historic texts such as the works of Shakespeare and the American Constitution, using (5) *equipment* he had begged, borrowed or made himself. In 1987, with over 300 books in the online (6) *collection* , he took on an (7) *assistant* , and together they recruited volunteers worldwide to help with typing and proofreading (8) *responsibilities*. Project Gutenberg now offers more than 60,000 free eBooks to download in over 60 different languages.

FOUND
EARLY

INVENT

RESEARCH
EXIST

EQUIP
COLLECT
ASSIST
RESPONSIBLE

Writing — Part 2 Article

You have seen this announcement in an international magazine.

Write your article in 140–190 words.

For more information on writing articles, see **page 192**.

Please go to the Teacher's Resource Centre for a Sample answer with Examiner comments for this Writing task.

LIFE CHANGES

Write us an article about a time in your life when something changed. Mention the reasons for the change and describe your feelings before and after it.

We will publish the most interesting articles next month.

45

3 A CHANGE FOR THE BETTER?

Pronunciation   Diphthongs

1 The words in the box below are from *My digital detox* on page 36. Match the words with their correct pronunciation.

change   clearly   compare   continually   disappointing   home   loud   time

1 /tʃeɪndʒ/ — change
2 /taɪm/ — time
3 /laʊd/ — loud
4 /həʊm/ — home
5 /kənˈtɪnjʊəli/ — continually
6 /kəmˈpeə(r)/ — compare
7 /ˈklɪə(r)li/ — clearly
8 /ˌdɪsəˈpɔɪntɪŋ/ — disappointing

2 ▶ 3.3 Listen and check your answers to Exercise 1.

3 The words in Exercise 1 all contain diphthongs. Choose the best word or phrase to complete the rules.

> **Diphthongs**
> 1 British English has **eight** / ten diphthongs: /eɪ/, /ɪə/, /ɔɪ/, /aɪ/, /əʊ/, /aʊ/, /eə/ and /ʊə/.
> 2 Diphthongs are long consonant / **vowel** sounds made from two / **three** short sounds.
> 3 We pronounce diphthongs by saying the two sounds separately / **moving quickly from one sound to the next**.

4 Add the words from Exercise 1 to the correct column in the table.

/ɪə/	/eɪ/	/ʊə/	/ɔɪ/
year	break	sure	boy
clearly	change	continually	disappointing
fear	space	during	annoyed

/əʊ/	/eə/	/aɪ/	/aʊ/
phone	hair	life	down
home	compare	time	loud
robot	aware	decide	without

5 ▶ 3.4 Listen and add the words you hear to the correct column in the table in Exercise 4.

6 Write a sentence using at least four words from the table in Exercise 4.

7 **SPEAK** Work in pairs. Practise saying your sentences from Exercise 6.

Pronunciation

1–2 ▶ 3.3 This first exercise is meant to introduce the students to the phonemic symbols for diphthongs, so if they don't know them for the first matching, that's all right. They will hear them when they check their answers with the recording.

3 Depending on where you are from, or where you learnt your English, you may not use all eight of these diphthongs in your accent. For example, /ɪə/, /eə/, and /ʊə/ do not occur in General American.

4–5 ▶ 3.4 Do some choral drilling to give the students practice with the diphthongs.

6–7 Circulate while the students practise saying their sentences, checking their pronunciation of the target sounds. Nominate a few stronger students to read their sentences to the class.

4 A GOOD STORY

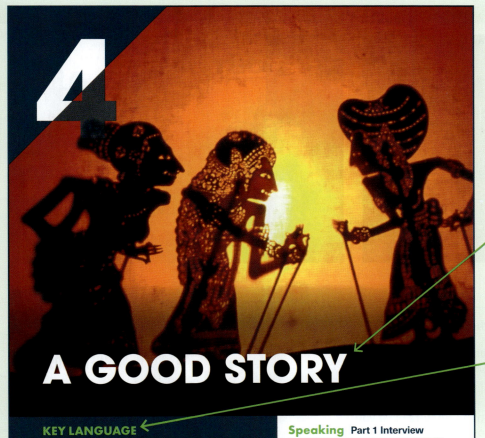

The unit deals with the theme of stories in the context of books and films, with reading and listening tasks related to these topics. The vocabulary and grammar input in this unit aims to help students express themselves better while writing or talking about books and films. Students will also get valuable practice writing reviews and reports.

Read the unit objectives to the class.

KEY LANGUAGE
So and *such*
Past tenses and time linkers
Films
Take
Participle adjectives and adverbs

PRONUNCIATION
Silent consonants

EXAM PRACTICE
Reading and Use of English Parts 3, 4 & 6
Writing Part 2
Listening Part 1
Speaking Parts 1 & 2

Speaking Part 1 Interview

Work with a partner. Discuss the questions.
1 Do you prefer watching films at home or in the cinema?
2 What TV series have you enjoyed watching recently?
3 When was the last time you wrote a story?
4 Talk about a day you've enjoyed recently.
5 Describe a time when something went wrong.

SPEAKING Part 1 Interview

You could start your lesson in a light-hearted way by getting the students to create a meme or joke involving a comical exchange between the characters in the photo. Model this by drawing speech bubbles on a piece of paper to hold above the photo or projecting the image on the board and drawing them there.
For example:
A: I love skiing.
B: Me too.
The students create their own and then vote on which one they find the funniest.
Now turn to the Speaking Part 1 questions. Remind them to extend their answers a bit by providing examples or reasons. Elicit a few useful phrases to the board, such as: *because, because of* + noun phrase, *since, for example, one good example is*, etc. Make note of any good examples of students extending their answers and share them with the group in open class.

ONLINE MATERIALS

Film crossword (**Teacher's Resource Centre**)
Presenting a report (**Teacher's Resource Centre**)
B2 First for Schools writing lessons (**Teacher's Resource Centre**)
Unit 4 Test (**Test Generator**)
Unit 4 Wordlist (**Teacher's Resource Centre**)
Unit 4 On-the-go-practice (**App**)

4 A GOOD STORY

thriller

musical

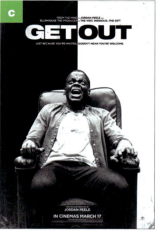
horror film

historical drama

Vocabulary Films

1 Match the film posters (a–j) with the genres in the box.

action film   comedy   fantasy   historical drama
horror film   musical   romance
science fiction film   thriller   western

romance

2 SPEAK Which, if any, of the films in the posters have you seen? Do you think you would enjoy those you haven't seen? Why/Why not?

3 For Exercises A and B, decide which word best fits each space.

A   terrible   terrific   terrifying

1 I'm not surprised it won an Oscar – it was a __terrific__ film.
2 Absolutely __terrifying__! I've never been so frightened in all my life.
3 This was probably the worst film I've seen all year. The plot was non-existent and the acting was __terrible__.

B   critic   criticism   review

It seems that every **(1)** __review__ I read of this film gives a different opinion. The **(2)** __critic__ who writes for *The Times*, for example, is very enthusiastic about it and has nothing but praise for Tim Burton. The same director, however, comes under strong **(3)** __criticism__ in the magazine *Premiere*.

4 SPEAK Work in pairs. Read the following review of *Blade Runner 2049*, which appeared in a student magazine. Does this type of film appeal to you? Why/Why not?

action film

BLADE RUNNER 2049

Blade Runner 2049 is a rare example of a <u>sequel</u> which is just as entertaining as the original. The film is <u>set</u> in the future, thirty years after the events of the first *Blade Runner*, and <u>stars</u> Ryan Gosling as K, with Harrison Ford returning in the <u>role</u> of Deckard.

K works as a blade runner, an agent whose job is to find and 'retire' older models of the androids known as replicants. At the beginning of the film, he discovers a secret from the past that leads him to try to solve a mystery about his own origins.

The <u>scenes</u> with Ryan Gosling and Harrison Ford are enjoyable to watch, and even quite amusing at times, so I was surprised and disappointed that they only appeared together towards the end. As for the rest of the <u>cast</u>, Silvia Hoeks gives an impressive performance as the terrifying Luv, and Ana de Armas is very convincing as K's virtual girlfriend, Joi.

This is a visually stunning film, with an amazingly atmospheric <u>soundtrack</u> and a slow, but gripping <u>plot</u>. I would recommend it to anyone who likes science fiction films which require concentration and make you think.

A GOOD STORY 4

Lead-in

Start off the lesson with an A–Z brainstorm about the topic of films. In this activity, students have to think of a word related to the topic for each letter of the alphabet, e.g. *action* for letter A. Film titles are ok as long as they are in English. This could be done all together up on the board with small classes. For bigger classes, put the students into groups of three or four and give them a handout with the alphabet written vertically in columns. Make sure to set a short time limit. In open class, ask a few questions based on some of the words from the students' A–Zs.

Vocabulary

1-2 Students do the exercise in pairs. Quickly check as a class. Discuss the questions in Exercise 2 all together. Then give students a few minutes to think of another couple of examples for each genre. It's fine if the film titles are in the students' first language(s). Switch pairs. Students tell each other about a few of the films mentioned they would or wouldn't recommend and why.

3 This exercise aims to clarify words related to films that are often misused at a B2 level. Students do Exercises A and B individually. Model and check the pronunciation of *terrifying* /ˈterɪfaɪɪŋ/. Ask the students if they would describe any of the films from their earlier discussion as *terrible*, *terrific* or *terrifying*.

4 Tell students they are going to read an example of a review. They ignore the underlined words the first time they read.

5-6 Students read the instructions and do the exercise. Encourage them to use the context to guess the meaning of any unknown words. While you correct in open class, you could elicit the film described along the way or wait until after.

Answers

1 *Blade Runner*
2 *Harry Potter and the Philosopher's Stone*™; *Harry Potter and the Chamber of Secrets*™; *Harry Potter and the Prisoner of Azkaban*™
3 *It*
4 *The Dark Knight Rises*
5 *Titanic*
6 *A Star is Born*

7 Put the students into new pairs. While they discuss the points, note down examples of usage – both effective and less effective – and of any words or phrases that you find yourself helping the students with. Then feed back these examples of emergent language in open class. To finish off this section or for revision at the start of the the next lesson, you may wish to use the **Film crossword** on the **Teacher's Resource Centre**.

Teaching tip

One way of helping students improve their accuracy and range is to engage with language that comes up during the lesson, often unpredictably, while students are talking to each other or the teacher. This is often referred to as *emergent language*. The idea is to pick up on this language and focus on it, usually by taking notes during the lesson and writing the examples of student language up on the board. If you put up words, collocations or even full sentences that students produce successfully, this gives the other members of the group the chance to learn from each other. If you put up examples of less successful usage, the students can correct themselves and, together with the teacher, explore more natural-sounding ways of expressing those ideas or messages.

Extra activity

Ask the students to prepare a short presentation about a favourite film. Their presentations should include the same information, and be structured similarly, to a film review. This will help students internalise the structure of the genre. The introduction in a film review gives basic information, such as the title, theme, setting, etc. Then comes a brief plot summary, followed by some criticism, where you express your opinions on what was good or bad about the film. A review always finishes with a recommendation. To spice up their presentations, students could show a short clip from the film or its trailer. For small classes, the presentations could be done in open class; for bigger ones, in groups of four or five.

A GOOD STORY

Language focus

1 Students read the instructions and discuss the questions with a partner. Elicit rules to the board. Ask students to write two sentences, one using *so* and the other *such*, about a film they really like or dislike. Nominate a few students to share their sentences with the class.

2 Direct students to the **Ready for Grammar** section on pages 212–213 (see below). Use your judgement on how much to do here before moving on to the key word transformations.

3 Students will have had some practice with key word transformations in the review sections of units 1–3, but you may want to do the first one together, preferably up on the board, to remind them how to do this task. Allow students to do 2–4 individually and then check their answers in pairs. Ask students to explain the use of *so* or *such* in the exercises with reference to the rules in the **Ready for Grammar** section.

4 Circulate and check the students' use of *so* and *such*. Make note of at least one or two successful uses of the target language to share with the class afterwards. If students are using *so* and *such* unsuccessfully during this activity, don't be afraid to interrupt and provide on-the-spot correction. The main aim of this activity is the correct use of this particular grammar point.

READY FOR GRAMMAR

4 So and such

These intensifiers are used to give emphasis.

1 *So* is used before:
   a adjectives and adverbs without nouns.
   *I'm **so tired**. I'll have to go to bed.*
   b *much, many, little, few*.
   *You shouldn't eat **so much**, Ian.*
   *Rachel can speak **so many languages**! She's amazing.*

2 *Such* is used with or without an adjective before:
   a singular countable nouns (the indefinite article *a/an* is also needed).
   *I can't stand him. He's **such an idiot**.*
   *I'd never heard **such a wonderful voice** before.*
   b uncountable nouns and plural countable nouns (the article is not needed).
   *I haven't eaten **such good food** for a long time.*
   *Our neighbours are **such friendly people**.*

3 *So* and *such* can both be used with a *that* clause to talk about the results or consequences. The word *that* can be omitted.
*It was **such a bad film that we** left before the end.*
*It was raining **so hard we** had to stop the car.*

---

4 So and such

1 Complete the sentences with *so* or *such*.
   1 We had ___such___ a lot of homework to do at the weekend!
   2 Marco didn't expect there to be ___so___ many questions in the exam.
   3 It was ___such___ delicious food that I couldn't stop eating.
   4 It really is ___such___ an interesting book – I was up reading it all night.
   5 Lara enjoyed herself ___so___ much she didn't want to go home.

2 Correct the mistake in each sentence by changing, adding or deleting one word.
   1 Anthony and Sasha are ~~so~~ *such* good friends.
   2 It snowed so heavily during the night ~~which~~ *(that)* we couldn't get to school the next day.
   3 Seville is such ^*a* beautiful city and there's so much to see and do.
   4 Why did so few people vote in such an important election? Perhaps it's because they have so ~~a~~ little confidence in our politicians.
   5 I need a break – this is such ~~a~~ hard work!
      such a hard job

Go back to **page 49**.

A GOOD STORY 4

5 Complete the gaps in 1–8 using the underlined words from the review of *Blade Runner 2049*. You may need to change the form of a word. There is an example at the beginning (0).

0 The most memorable ___scene___ comes at the very end of the film, when Humphrey Bogart and Ingrid Bergman say goodbye.
1 The original film is ___set___ in Los Angeles in a futuristic 2019.
2 John Williams composed the ___soundtracks___ for the first three of the eight films about the boy wizard.
3 Finn Wolfhard, one of the younger members of the ___cast___, also appears in the hit TV series *Stranger Things*.
4 The ___sequel___ to *The Dark Knight,* and the third instalment in the trilogy, was released in 2012.
5 Leonardo DiCaprio ___stars___ as a poor artist who falls in love on board the ill-fated ship with Kate Winslet, in the ___role___ of a seventeen-year-old aristocrat.
6 The basic ___plot___ involves a country music star who helps a young singer, played by Lady Gaga, to find fame.

6 SPEAK Can you name the films in Exercise 5?

0 *Casablanca*

7 SPEAK Work in pairs. Talk about the following using some of the vocabulary in Exercises 1–5.
- a film you didn't enjoy
- your favourite film
- the most frightening film you have seen
- the most gripping film you have seen

Language focus *So* and *such*

1 SPEAK Work in pairs. Why are *so* and *such* used in the following sentences? What types of words follow *so* and *such*?

Both words intensify the adjective or adjective + noun that follow.

I was **so** impressed with the soundtrack of the film that I downloaded it as soon as I got home.   *so* + adjective (or adverb)

such + (indefinite article +) adjective + noun

She has **such** a wonderful voice that it seems a shame to dub her films into English.

2 Go to **Ready for Grammar** on **page 212** for rules, explanations and further practice.

3 For questions 1–4, complete the second sentence so that it has a similar meaning to the first sentence, using the word given. Do not change the word given. You must use between two and five words, including the word given.

1 We decided to see the film as it had such good reviews.
   THAT
   The reviews for the film ___were so good that___ we decided to see it.
2 The weather was so bad that we decided to come home.
   SUCH
   It ___was such bad weather___ that we decided to come home.
3 I got so absorbed in the film I forgot to phone Amy.
   SUCH
   It ___was such an absorbing___ film I forgot to phone Amy.
4 The party was so crowded we could hardly move.
   PEOPLE
   There ___were so many people___ at the party we could hardly move.

4 SPEAK Work in pairs. Each of you should choose one of the following topics and talk about it for one minute. Use *so* and *such* as many times as possible.
- a singer or band whose music you like
- an activity you enjoy doing
- a memorable holiday
- a celebration or party you attended

fantasy

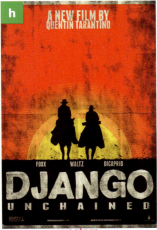
western

science fiction film

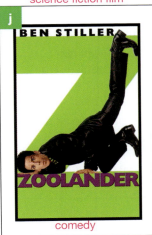
comedy

4 A GOOD STORY

Word formation Participle adjectives and adverbs

To describe how we feel about something or someone we can use past participles as adjectives. *My younger brother got quite **frightened** during the final scene.*

To describe the thing or person that produces the feeling we can use present participles as adjectives. *It was quite a **frightening** scene.*

Adverbs can be formed from present participle adjectives.

*It's expensive to go and see a film these days. Not **surprisingly**, cinemas are often half empty.*

1 Look back at the review of *Blade Runner 2049* on page 49 and find examples of adjectives and adverbs formed with *-ing* and *-ed*.

2 Write the past participle of each of the regular verbs from the box in the appropriate column in the table below, according to how the *-ed* ending is pronounced.

annoy   bore   disappoint   disgust   embarrass   fascinate
frustrate   impress   relax   shock   surprise   tire   worry

/d/	/t/	/id/
amused *bored surprised*	astonished	excited
annoyed *tired*	*embarrassed relaxed*	*disappointed fascinated*
worried /wʌrid/	*impressed shocked*	*disgusted frustrated*

3 The present participle (*-ing*) form of the verbs in Exercise 2 can all be used as adjectives, except in the case of one of the verbs. Which one is it and how is the adjective formed?   *impress impressive (adj)*

4 Complete each gap with the present or past participle form of an appropriate verb from Exercise 2. You may need to use an adverb. More than one answer may be possible.

1 Ninety minutes is the ideal length for a film – after that I start to get __*bored/tired*__.
2 I find it so __*annoying/frustrating*__ when people talk during a film. Why can't they keep quiet?
3 I tend not to watch sequels; you expect them to be as good as the first film, but they're often __*frustratingly/disappointingly/surprisingly*__ poor.
4 I fell asleep in the cinema once. I felt so __*embarrassed*__; people were laughing at me.
5 Documentary films about wildlife are __*fascinating*__; I learn so much from them.
6 There's a __*shocking/disgusting/worrying/surprising*__ amount of violence on television and in films – I think they should impose stricter limits.

5 **SPEAK** Work in pairs. Discuss how true the sentences in Exercise 4 are for you.

Writing Part 2 Review

1 Read the following Writing Part 2 question then follow the instructions below.

> Your teacher has asked you to write about a film you have seen recently for the school's English magazine. Write a review for the magazine, including a brief description of the plot, giving your opinions on the film and saying who you would recommend it to.

Put the stages (a–d) in the correct order to show a possible paragraph plan for a review. Then use the *Blade Runner 2049* review on page 49 to check your answer.

a   A brief description of the plot.   2
b   Comments on other aspects of the film and a recommendation.   4
c   Introduction to the film, including an overall opinion and one or two facts, *e.g. the main actors, type of film, etc.*   1
d   Opinions on specific scenes and the acting.   3

2 Write your answer to the question in Exercise 1 in 140–190 words. Follow the paragraph plan in Exercise 1 or use your own.

Useful language

In your review, include elements of the following language from this unit:

> relevant film vocabulary, e.g. *stars ... as, is set in, plot, cast*
> participle adjectives to express your opinion, e.g. *stunning, disappointed.*

A Good Story 4

Word formation

On the board, write: *My English teacher is boring. My English teacher is bored.* Elicit the difference.

1 Remind students they have now looked at word formation twice, focusing on affixes (Unit 2) and nouns (Unit 3). In this lesson they are going to focus on forming adjectives and adverbs. Ask the students to read the rules. Elicit examples from the *Blade Runner 2049* review to the board. Note that students might be more familiar with the term *past participle* than *present participle*. The *-ing* form of a word is called a *present participle* when it is used to form continuous tenses, e.g. *She's running away*, or adjectives, e.g. *an embarrassing moment*. The *-ing* form of a word is called a *gerund* when it functions like a noun, e.g. *Running is fun*, or *I love running*.

Answers

To describe how we feel about something or someone:

… *I was surprised and disappointed that they only appeared together towards the end.*

To describe the person or thing that produces the feeling:

… *a sequel which is just as entertaining as the original. The scenes … are … even quite amusing at times ..*

.. Silvia Hoeks gives an impressive performance as the terrifying Luv and Ana de Armas is convincing as K's virtual girlfriend, Joi.

This is a visually stunning film with … a slow but gripping plot.

Adverbs formed from present participle adjectives:

… *an amazingly atmospheric soundtrack …*

2 Say the three example words aloud so that students can hear the difference. Say a couple more from the list and students listen and put them in the correct column. Students could do the exercise on their own and then check their answers with a classmate, or in pairs and check their answers with another pair. Note the *ied* in *worried* is pronounced /ɪd/.

3-4 Students complete the activities as suggested. Check in open class.

5 As always, encourage the students to take advantage of this **SPEAK** activity to work on their conversational fluency by giving reasons for their views and asking follow-up questions.

Writing

A good way to introduce this activity would be a quick review of the film vocabulary from pages 48–49. Students could, for example, write a couple questions using the vocabulary and then discuss them in pairs or small groups.

1 Ask students to read the task and underline the points in the task rubric that need to be included in their reviews: *a brief description of the plot*, *opinions on the film* and say *who you would recommend it to*. Elicit in open class. In pairs, students put the stages in order and then check their answers with the *Blade Runner 2049* review on page 48.

2 The final writing assignment could be done in class (timed, 40 minutes) or set for homework. Remind students to refer to page 197 in the **Ready for Writing** section, which is dedicated to reviews and provides useful language and a good model.

Teaching tip

Pronunciation is something we hear, but it's also something we can *feel*. For the *-ed* endings, we can help students feel the difference by asking them to put their hands on their vocal cords, located in the neck. Have them pronounce /t/, then /d/. Elicit the difference: the vocal cords vibrate for /d/. This is called a voiced consonant. /t/ is unvoiced. This will help them understand the general rule: We pronounce *-ed* /d/ when a word ends in a voiced consonant, e.g. *surprise*. When we add *-ed* to a word ending in an unvoiced consonant, e.g. *relax*, we pronounce it /t/. We only pronounce *-ed* /ɪd/ when added to words ending in the letters 'd' or 't'. This last rule is the easiest one for students to learn and remember, and perhaps also the most important.

Extra activity

Give students time in class to decide on the film they are going to review and write notes for each of the paragraphs in their plan. Then ask them to work in pairs and tell each other about their films, following the notes they have made. Their partner should listen carefully to check that they have included a balance of information and opinions in their plan, as well as a recommendation with reasons.

4 A GOOD STORY

Speaking

Ask students what they remember about the Long turn before they open their books and read the instructions. Focus on the **Useful Language** box. Check students' understanding of *tightrope* and *engrossed*. Students could match the words and expressions in pairs or individually.

When you feedback the exercise as a class, ask the students to justify their answers. Explain that if they produce this kind of 'good' language on the exam they will receive higher marks.

Point out that on the day of the test the examiner will be listening to their English for the first time, so if they play it safe and only use simple language that is below the level of the test, their speaking mark may be low even if they are fairly accurate. Tell students to 'show what you know'. This is a good motto to return to again and again throughout the course every time do you do practise speaking exam tasks.

Focus on the **Don't forget!** box. Stress that when in the role of Student B, students should remember this is still an important part of the speaking exam — in other words, a chance to impress the examiner with how good their English is. A very short answer here is a missed opportunity.

Teaching tip

Once students are better acquainted with this speaking task, it's a good idea to start timing them, so they get feel for what it will be like in the exam. Let students time themselves with a clock or watch — or, if allowed, mobile phone. You could also keep the time yourself, starting and stopping all the pairs together. Students describing the pictures have one minute; their partners have 30 seconds to respond to a question related to the topic. Note that on the official exam students can't bring timers or phones to the speaking exam and will not know how much time they have left, but the above procedure is useful because it helps student know what a minute 'feels' like. Later in the course, you can have students time each other with the timer hidden, to better approximate exam conditions.

Listening

1 Students should be familiar with Listening Part 1 from Unit 1, but it may be worth taking a minute to go back and quickly read the What to expect in the exam box on page 10. In this lesson, students will get useful practice with a key exam strategy: identifying distractors. Make sure the students understand that they must go down the page and look at the first multiple choice question in Exercise 3 and then look for the answer in the shaded part of the Audioscript on (see below). Students compare in pairs. Get open class feedback.

2 Focus on the **What to expect in the exam** box. Students then discuss the questions in Exercise 2 with a partner. Feedback in open class. Ask the students how the advice in the **What to expect in the exam** box would be helpful for this question. Note that the better the students understand how exam questions are constructed, the better they will be at answering them correctly.

3 ▶ 4.1 Pre-teach *overhear* (question 5). Remind them about the advice regarding question 3 in the **What to expect in the exam** box. Then play the recording for each question twice. You could check the answers to each question one at a time or check all of them at the end.

Extra activity

Direct students to the Audioscript on page 237 (see below and TB52) for questions 2 and 3 and find examples of the use of *but* in the creation of distractors.

Answers

2 B a historical novel

At times it reads like a novel set against a background of huge political change across the continent. But this is the story of a life in which fact is stranger – and far more absorbing - than fiction.

3 A It wasn't as enjoyable as the first film in the series.

You never expect a sequel to compare well with the original, but in some ways this one was better, more entertaining.

3 C The comedy scenes were not very funny.

Yeah, I didn't laugh out loud like you – I never do – but I know what you mean.

A GOOD STORY 4

What are the people enjoying about watching these different performances?

1

2

one-man show; street performer; walking on a tightrope; in the open air; being outdoors; audience; pass the time

on stage; audience; cultural event

Speaking Part 2 Long turn

Before you do the speaking task, read the information in the boxes below.

Look at photographs 1 and 2. They show people watching different types of performance.

Student A: Compare photographs 1 and 2 and say what you think the people are enjoying about watching these different performances.

Student B: When Student A has finished, say which of these performances you would prefer to watch.

Useful language			Don't forget!

The following words and expressions could be used when talking about the photographs 1–4 on this page. Match each word or expression to one or more of the photographs.

on stage	audience	in the open air
one-man show	pass the time	consult reference books
read for pleasure	street performer	walking on a tightrope
being outdoors	cultural event	be engrossed in a book

Don't forget!

Student A
Talk about the similarities and differences, then answer the question in the box.

Student B
Develop your answer fully, giving reasons and/or examples.

Now change roles. Look at photographs 3 and 4. They show people reading in different places.

Student A: Compare photographs 3 and 4 and say why you think the people have chosen to read in these places.

Student B: When Student A has finished, say where you like reading.

consult reference books; read for pleasure; pass the time; be engrossed in a book

consult reference books; read for pleasure; pass the time; be engrossed in a book; in the open air; being outdoors

Why have the people chosen to read in these different places?

3

4

51

4 A GOOD STORY

Listening Part 1 Multiple choice

1 You will hear people talking in eight different situations. Read question 1 below then look at the shaded **Audioscript** on **page 237** and choose the best answer (A, B or C).
   C

2 Look at the shaded **Audioscript** on **page 237** again and answer the following questions.

   a In which part of the script does the answer to question **1** appear; near the beginning, the middle or the end?   *near the beginning*

   b Which nouns are used in the script to avoid using these words from options **A** and **C** in the question?
   soundtrack: music, songs;
   - soundtrack
   - plot   *plot: storyline*

   c The man makes positive comments about the acting (*the actors do their best with their lines*) and the soundtrack (*people are saying good things about the music*). Which linking word does he use in both cases to introduce a more negative comment immediately afterwards?   *but*

3 ▶ **4.1** For questions 1–8, choose the best answer (A, B or C).

   1 You hear a man talking to a friend about a TV series he is watching.
   The man is impressed with
   A the soundtrack.   B the acting.   **(C)** the plot.

   2 You hear a woman reviewing a book on the radio.
   What type of book is it?
   (A) an autobiography
   B a historical novel
   C a travel guide

   3 You hear two friends talking about a film they have just seen.
   What did they both find disappointing about it?
   A It wasn't as enjoyable as the first film in the series.
   (B) The pace of the film was too slow at one point.
   C The comedy scenes were not very funny.

   4 You hear a man telling a woman about a storytelling course he attended.
   What does he say about the course?
   A It was better than he had expected.
   B It will be useful for his work.
   (C) It helped to build his confidence.

   5 You overhear a woman calling a bookshop.
   Why is she calling?
   A to make a complaint
   (B) to make a suggestion
   C to apologise

   6 You hear a man talking to a friend about a story writing competition he won.
   What did he feel nervous about?
   (A) being interviewed about his success
   B reading out his story on live radio
   C receiving his prize from a famous person

   7 You hear two friends talking about an actor in a play they have just seen.
   What do they agree about him?
   A He looked too young for the part.
   (B) He did not always speak clearly.
   C He moved around unnaturally.

   8 You hear part of a talk by a writer.
   What is she doing?
   A encouraging the audience to read to their children
   (B) explaining the importance of a past event
   C promoting a new book she has written

What to expect in the exam

› You may hear the key language which guides you to the answer near the beginning, the middle and/or the end of the extract.

In question 3 the key language appears in two different parts of the extract.

› You will not necessarily hear the same words as those in options **A**, **B** and **C**.

› Sometimes, contrast linkers, such as *but*, *although* or *however*, are used to create distractors (*as in Exercise 2c above*).

A GOOD STORY

AUDIOSCRIPT

Listening Part 1 Multiple choice

 4.1

W = Woman   M = Man

1 You hear a man talking to a friend about a TV series he is watching.

W: Enjoying the new series?

M: *(Ex 3 Q1)* Well, yeah, it's OK. The writers have done a great job with the storyline. It draws you in, makes you want to keep watching – like a book you can't put down. It's a shame about the actual script, though – I mean, the actors do their best with their lines, but they all sound very unnatural. And people are saying good things about the music, but I really don't understand why they've used modern songs in a series set in the 1920s.

W: So you're not a fan then?

M: I wouldn't say that. I watched three episodes in a row last night.

2 You hear a woman reviewing a book on the radio.

W: *(Ex 3 Q2)* All too often we are told that the author 'takes us on a journey', but the phrase is entirely appropriate for this, the first volume of Gray's memoirs, since each chapter is named after a different European location where she lived out a particular stage of her colourful life. At times it reads like a novel set against a background of huge political change across the continent. But this is the story of a life in which fact is stranger – and far more absorbing – than fiction. The map at the beginning of the book is a useful addition, by the way, as many of the place names may be unfamiliar to you.

3 You hear two friends talking about a film they have just seen.

M: *(Ex 3 Q3)* I thought the pace dropped a bit half way through the film, but apart from that it was really good.

W: Yeah, it was great. You never expect a sequel to compare well with the original, but in many ways this one was better, more entertaining.

M: Especially the bits with those twins. I haven't laughed so much in ages.

W: Yeah, I didn't laugh out loud like you – I never do – but I know what you mean.

M: Definitely a candidate for an award or two.

W: Right. But it's true, the director could have speeded up the action a bit in the middle.

4 You hear a man telling a woman about a storytelling course he attended.

W: So what made you decide to do a storytelling course?

M: Well, a friend of mine who did it last year recommended it to me. She thought I might enjoy it – and she was right. It was great fun, really laid back and everyone was very supportive. *(Ex 3 Q4)* It gave me the courage I needed – and the self-belief – to be able to stand up and speak in front of a group of people.

W: So are you going to be leaving us to take up a career as a storyteller, then?

M: No, I like working here too much.

W: Ha-ha! That's a good story.

5 You overhear a woman calling a bookshop.

W: Hello, yes, it's about a book I bought in your shop last week. A Katharine Adams novel. I just wanted to point out that there were one or two pages missing … No, no, there's really no need to apologise. I mean it's not as if it was the last page or anything. And I got the gist of what was happening without the pages. *(Ex 3 Q5)* I just thought you ought to know so you can check the rest of your stock, or talk to the publishers or something … That's OK … Yes, pages 60 to 63…

6 You hear a man talking to a friend about a story writing competition he won.

W: Hey, I saw you on the telly last night, talking about your competition win. You kept that quiet.

M: Well, yeah, it was a bit of an ordeal, to be honest.

W: Why's that?

M: *(Ex 3 Q6)* Well, it's a live chat show, so I was worried I might make a mess of it.

W: But you'd already been on national radio.

M: Yeah, but I didn't have to say much then – just read the story out. That's much easier than talking about yourself in front of millions. And anyway, I wasn't surrounded by all those celebrities when I was on the radio. It was just me and the other three finalists in the studio with the presenter.

7 You hear two friends talking about an actor in a play they have just seen.

W: The actor who played the grandfather looked familiar. Did you recognise him?

M: Yeah, I did. I've seen him in one or two of those period dramas on telly. He usually plays much younger characters, though – he can't be much older than forty.

W: Well, make-up did a good job, then – he looked very convincing.

M: Yeah, he did, and his movements and gestures were really authentic. He's a natural.

W: Right, but I did think he tried a bit too hard with the voice. *(Ex 3 Q7)* He mumbled a lot, so it wasn't easy to make out what he was saying sometimes.

M: Yeah, I had trouble understanding him, too.

8 You hear part of a talk by a writer.

W: Now, you're all avid readers, so you know all about the wonders of books. Your bookshelves are probably full of novels – some of them mine, hopefully! – and it's likely you started reading from an early age. So it may surprise you to know that until I was fifteen I had never actually read a book from beginning to end. *(Ex 3 Q8)* My parents didn't read, and nor did I. Then one day, a local writer came to my school and read extracts from her latest novel – and I was hooked. I bought the book and when I'd finished it, I knew exactly what I wanted to do in life.

TB52

A GOOD STORY

Vocabulary

1. Elicit the meaning of *take up* as a class. Explain to the students that, similar to the vocabulary section dedicated to *get* in Unit 1, in this lesson they will look at another very common verb, *take*. This word also has a wide variety of different meanings depending on which words it is combined with. *Taking the bus* is very different to *taking out the rubbish*, for example.

2. Students read the text on their own, and then decide on the best title in pairs. Tell them to ignore the underlined words for now. Check the answers as a class.

3. Check the students' understanding of *resemble*, *employ* and *gain* control. It would be better to do this exercise in pairs or small groups, as some students may find it challenging.

4. Explain that now that they have examined some phrasal verbs with *take*, they will look at some common expressions with this same verb. Tell the students to ignore the letters for now. Pre-teach *blame* and *stray cat*. Instead of pair-checking out loud, students could exchange books (or notebooks, if the answers are written there) and check each other's work. They then explain to their classmate why they think any answers are wrong. Check the exercise in open class.

5-7. You could make Exercise 6 more dynamic by inviting four students up to the board, one for A, B, C and D, to write the answers. Different students could come up after and write the expressions in Exercise 7 in the right place. If you think your class needs more support with these lexical items, give them a few minutes to translate them into their L1. Make sure the students use a proper translation site, such as *Linguee.com*, which provides example sentences in both languages. If you have a monolingual class, they could finish by quizzing each other, e.g. *How do you say ... in English?*

Note that there are **translated wordlists** available on the **Teacher's Resource Centre** in several different languages.

8. If your students find this task too open-ended, you could suggest a specific topic — sports, for instance. Alternatively, do this activity as pair work and then ask students to share their stories with the class. Vote on the best or most interesting, funniest, etc.

Teaching tip

Get the students to create a separate page for common delexicalised verbs like *get*, *take*, *give*, *go*, *have*, *put*, *make* and *do* in their vocabulary notebooks.

Throughout the course, encourage students to record any new expressions or phrasal verbs containing these verbs.

Extra activity

To give your students extra support with the phrasal verbs with *take*, you could exploit the short story in Exercise 2 by asking the students to answer some comprehension questions about it which include the phrasal verbs. Write or project the following questions on the board.

- *Who does Roisin take after?*
- *How does she take after him?*
- *When she was eight, what activity did she take up?*
- *Did she take to this new activity quickly or slowly?*
- *A part of her body takes over when she dances – what is it?*
- *Why did her teacher take her aside?*
- *What did she find hard to take in?*
- *When and how did her career take off?*

When the students have answered the questions, erase everything but the phrasal verbs in the order above (the order they appear in the text). With their books closed, students have to retell the story in pairs using all the phrasal verbs.

4 A GOOD STORY

Vocabulary Take

Phrasal verbs with *take*

1 Read this extract from the listening text. What is the meaning of the phrasal verb in bold?

*So are you going to be leaving us to **take up** a career as a storyteller, then?*   start (a new job or activity)

2 Read the following short story and choose the best title (a–c).

a The dangers of Irish dancing   b The end of a promising career   (c) Winning isn't everything

> **Roisin** always <u>took after</u> her dad. Her mother was a calm, laid-back person, but Roisin, like her father, was ambitious. She had to be the best at everything, and that included Irish dancing, which she <u>took up</u> at the age of eight. She <u>took to</u> it immediately, and knew after just a few lessons, that she wanted to be a world champion. Her teachers were impressed: once she'd learnt a new dance routine, her feet seemed to <u>take over</u> and she would move across the floor with incredible agility.
>
> Shortly before her first World Championships in Glasgow, Roisin's teacher <u>took</u> her <u>aside</u> during the lesson and reminded her that, whilst she had every confidence in her, the competition would be tough. Full of self-belief, Roisin took no notice and was convinced she would win. When she finished sixth, she was devastated and just couldn't <u>take in</u> the fact that she hadn't come first. She never did win a championship, but she eventually learnt to love dancing for itself rather than as a means to be the best. Then, three years ago Roisin's dancing career <u>took off</u> when she was <u>taken on</u> as a dancer with an Irish dance company that travels the world. There's no competing, only supporting – and she's never been happier.

3 Read the story again. Write the infinitive of each underlined phrasal verb next to its meaning below. The first one has been done for you.

1 start to like someone/something   *take to*
2 employ someone   take on
3 resemble someone   take after
4 move someone away from other people to talk   take aside
5 accept something as true   take in
6 gain control   take over
7 start doing something   take up
8 start to become successful   take off

Expressions with *take*

4 Complete each sentence (1–8) with an appropriate form of the verb *take*. The first one has been done for you.

A 1 A pair of shoes should last longer than two months. If I were you, I *would take* them back to the shop.
  2 My dad used to ___take___ me to school, but now I have to get the bus.
B 3 I lost money on that business deal! Of course I regret ___taking/having taken___ his advice!
  4 She criticises everybody else and refuses ___to take___ any of the blame herself.
C 5 If you ___took___ more interest in the children, they'd behave better!
  6 The stray cat was looking a lot healthier. It was clear that someone ___had taken/had been taking___ pity on it and given it something to eat.
D 7 It ___takes___ a great deal of courage to sing in front of an audience.
  8 Come on! I can't understand why you ___are taking/have taken___ so long to do this exercise.

5 Underline the expressions with *take* in Exercise 4.

A pair of shoes should last longer than two months. If I were you, I would <u>take</u> them <u>back to the shop</u>.

6 The expressions in Exercise 4 are organised into four groups, A, B, C and D. Match each of the following general meanings for *take* to an appropriate group.

1 to express what is needed or required _D_
2 to talk about the way people feel or react to others _C_
3 to talk about the movement of something/one from one place to another _A_
4 to accept _B_

7 Which group (A–D) in Exercise 4 do the following expressions belong to?

to take pride in something _C_   to be taken to hospital _A_   to take a joke _B_   to take the infinitive _D_

8 Now write a short story of your own using at least three expressions and three phrasal verbs with *take*.

4 A GOOD STORY

Reading and Use of English Part 6 Gapped text

1 **SPEAK** Do you find writing stories difficult? Why/Why not?

2 Read the article, ignoring the gaps. Decide which sentence (A–D) best summarises the writer's main idea.

A It takes natural talent to be a good storyteller.
B It is more useful to teach storytelling than grammar.
C Teachers need more training in how to teach storytelling.
D Children have the potential to be better storytellers than adults.

The art of storytelling...

 Writing stories is a craft that is crucial for life. And if the government insists, you can test it, measure it and use it in commerce, too

A report in *The Times* recently quoted a secondary school teacher who complained that their Year 7 intake no longer knew how to tell a story. 'They knew what a fronted adverbial was, and how to spot an internal clause, and even what a preposition was – but when I set them a task to write a story, they broke down and cried,' reported the teacher.

The fact that no importance is placed on storytelling makes me very frustrated not only because it puts so little value or emphasis on children's creativity, but also because storytelling is more than simply an art. **1 F** Politicians should know this better than anyone. What is "Vote for us and the country will be strong and stable" if not a story? Everything made of words is a story – from the stories we tell ourselves to the ones we watch on TV to the ones we relate to work colleagues at the water cooler.

2 C Contrary to the widely-held belief, creative writing is not just 'making stuff up'. Certainly, there are those who can do it instinctively. But what everyone on both sides of the debate seems to be missing is that storytelling *can* be taught *and* tested. I know that, because I teach it, albeit at an adult level.

People say children are natural storytellers, but this is not at all true, any more than it is of adults. Or rather, they are not naturally good storytellers. Most stories by children, although they may be charming, are boring because they are just one unconnected event after another. **3 E**

For stories to work, a whole array of measurable principles can be applied. We shouldn't be asking children about fronted adverbials, but about act structures, character arcs and the qualities of protagonists. What is the difference between real speech and fictional dialogue? What constitutes a dramatic event? **4 A** And all these features of the craft of storytelling can be taught and tested in the same way as grammar. This would be so much more valuable than parroting parts of speech.

5 G Let's instead tell them what they want to hear, and say, 'Yes, you can teach storytelling and you can test it and measure it and it's an immensely valuable tool, for commerce (if you're so obsessed with that) as much as anything else.'

Storytelling in its way can have just as much complexity as music or mathematics. That we don't really understand this craft – or that this *is* a craft – is partly because of the romantic myth of 'inspiration' put about by authors as much as anyone. It is taught in creative writing degrees. **6 B** Why, for instance, is the popular children's book *We're Going on a Bear Hunt* such a compelling story? And what has it got to do with stories like *Macbeth*? (And yes, it does have something in common – all stories do.)

This is a fascinating, fruitful subject, and to a large extent, quantifiable. We should incorporate it into the classroom in a way that will satisfy both sides of the debate. In this way, there can be a happy ending to what has so far been a very sad story.

Don't forget!

› For each answer, check that the whole sentence fits in with the meaning of the text before *and* after the gap.
› When you have finished, check your answers by reading through the whole text again to ensure that it makes sense.
› Check that the extra sentence does not fit into any of the gaps.

3 Six sentences have been removed from the extract. Choose from the sentences A–G the one which fit each gap (1–6). There is one extra sentence which you do not need to use.

A The list goes on and on.
B But it can be simplified enough to appear on the school curriculum as well.
C The reluctance to include story-writing on the school curriculum is because of a fundamental misunderstanding.
D It should be no more difficult than teaching grammar.
E In other words, they make no sense and have no direction or point.
F It is a crucial skill for life and commerce.
G So we should not be wasting our time accusing the government of wanting us all to be joyless grammar robots.

A GOOD STORY

Reading and Use of English

1 You could start the lesson with books closed and the question up on the board. After a minute, erase *writing* in the question and replace it with *telling*. After another minute, add *in English?* to the end of the question.

2 Students read the article for gist and then in pairs discuss which sentence best summarises the writer's main idea and why. Students have done this task type once before, but it might be worthwhile to revisit some of the tips covered in Unit 2. For example, they should look for connections between the article and the sentences removed from the text, such as pronouns, both personal (*he*, *she*) and demonstrative (*that*, *those*), as well as synonyms or other words from the same lexical field. Direct students to the **Don't forget!** box in the bottom left-hand corner.

3 With this reading task in particular, some students tend to finish much quicker than others, so it's a good idea to have a fast finisher task at hand. You could ask those that finish early to underline five new collocations in the text. Or you could check their answers, tell them if any are wrong and encourage them to correct themselves.

4 You could increase the difficulty of this task by assigning A and B roles to each pair. Students in the role of A disagree strongly with both statements, no matter their real opinions, while B students strongly agree.

READY FOR GRAMMAR
4 Past tenses and time linkers

Past Tenses

A The past simple is used to refer to:
1 completed actions which happened at a specific time.
   *I **went** to the cinema last night.*
2 completed actions and situations which happened over a specific period of time.
   *I **lived** and **worked** in Germany for 3 years.*
3 habitual actions or behaviour in the past.
   *We **played** football in the street when I was a child.*
4 a series of consecutive events in the past.
   *He **kissed** her, **said** goodbye and **closed** the door.*

B The past continuous is used to refer to:
1 temporary activities or situations in progress at a particular moment in the past.
   *Last week **we were sitting** on the beach.*
2 a past activity or situation already in progress when another action occurred (the activity or situation in progress may or may not continue).
   *I **was reading** to my son when the lights went out.*
3 activities or situations occurring at the same time.
   ***Ann was cutting** the grass while **I was cooking**.*
4 the background events in a narrative.
   ***It was snowing** heavily and a cold wind **was blowing**. My brother and I **were reading** in front of the fire. Suddenly there was a knock at the door.*

C The past perfect is used to:
1 show that a past action or situation occurred before another past action or situation.
   *When I saw Tim, **he had** just **passed** his test.*
2 We use the continuous form to emphasise the duration of the first past action or situation.
   ***She had been waiting** for over 2 hours when he phoned to say he couldn't come.*

Time linkers

1 The past perfect is often used with time linkers, e.g. *after, before, by the time, as soon as, once, when, until.*
   *I couldn't go out **until** I had done my homework.*

2 The past simple can be used if the order of events is clear:
   *He sold his house **before** he left the country.*
   or if the second event occurred as a result of the first.
   ***When** I realised what time it was, I ran outside.*

3 *After* is used to show the order of two or more events in the same sentence.
   ***After** he'd cleaned the house, he went shopping.*
   Afterwards means *after that*, and can go at the beginning or the end of a clause.
   *We had lunch and **afterwards** we went for a walk.*
   *They played tennis and had a coffee **afterwards**.*

4 *At last* suggests that something good happens after a long period of time or more than one attempt.
   *I've passed the First **at last**! I failed twice before!*
   In the end has a similar meaning and may also suggest there have been one or more changes or problems. The result may be good or bad.
   *The car broke down several times on the way but we got there **in the end**.*
   NB *eventually* can also be used in this sentence.
   At the end means at the point when something finishes.
   *Hand in your books **at the end** of the lesson.*

5 *As/when/while* can all be used with the past continuous to introduce an action which was already in progress when another action occurred.
   ***As/When/While** I was running, I saw a rabbit.*

6 *During/in/for* are all used as prepositions when referring to time, and are followed by a noun. *During* and *in* are used to say when something happened.
   *It rained a lot **during/in** the night.*
   For is used to say how long something took or lasted.
   *We went to Spain **for** two weeks **during** the summer.*

TB54

4 A GOOD STORY

Language focus

1-2 Alternatively, use a real story or anecdote from your own life. Prepare five similar sentences to 1–5 in Exercise 1 from your story. Make sure they include the same underlined grammatical tenses. Tell the story and give the students a gist question to answer. Then write or display your sentences on the board, and ask students to name the underlined past tenses.

3 Direct students to the **Ready for Grammar** section on page 212 (see TB54 and below). Tell students not to read the information about time linkers just yet. If your students have demonstrated a good understanding of the grammar so far, you could set the **Ready for Grammar** section for homework and move directly onto Exercise 4.

4 With stronger groups, you could ask students to work with a classmate and write two more pairs of sentences using the information from the Past Tenses section of the **Ready for Grammar** on page 212

(see TB54) for their classmates to discuss. Try to clear up any remaining doubts about the past tenses here before moving on to the time linkers.

5-7 Students work through the exercises in pairs. It may be helpful for students to underline *when* and *while* in the sentences in Exercise 4 before answering the questions in Exercise 5. In general, these exercises aim to raise students' awareness of common linking expressions that are often misused even by high-level learners. You will be doing students a big favour if you can get them using them correctly now!

8 Direct students to the **Ready for Grammar** section on page 212 (see TB54 and below).

9 Model the task yourself with a personal anecdote of your own. You could use this to elicit characteristics of anecdotes: they are brief, possibly exaggerated but true stories, usually happening in one place, contain only a few characters, often include dialogue, and end in an unexpected, humorous way.

READY FOR GRAMMAR

4 Past tenses and time linkers

1 A magazine for teenagers asked readers to write in with stories of their most embarrassing moments. Read these two stories and write the appropriate past form of each verb in brackets. There is an example at the beginning (0).

Bus blush

Something very embarrassing (0) _happened_ (happen) to me while I (1) _was travelling_ (travel) home from school on the bus one day. We (2) _were having_ (have) a laugh at the back of the bus when I (3) _saw_ (see) a friend from school. She (4) _was sitting_ (sit) at the front, so I (5) _ran_ (run) up and (6) _sat_ (sit) down behind her, pulling her ponytail and shouting, 'Hi there, Rebecca!' I felt so stupid when a man I (7) _had never seen_ (never/see) before turned round! 'Actually, my name's Andrew,' he (8) _smiled_ (smile). I (9) _didn't/did not stop_ (not/stop) blushing until I (10) _(had) got_ (get) home.

Face paint

My nephews (11) _had been asking_ (ask) me for days to take them somewhere, and eventually I (12) _agreed_ (agree) to go to the park with them. While they (13) _were playing_ (play) football, I (14) _fell_ (fall) (fall) asleep in the sun. Later, on our way to the shopping centre, where I (15) _had arranged_ (arrange) to meet my boyfriend, Paul, they (16) _kept_ (keep) telling me how beautiful I looked. As soon as Paul (17) _saw_ (see) me, he (18) _burst_ (burst) out laughing. 'Have you looked in a mirror?' he said. Catching my reflection in a shop window, I (19) _discovered_ (discover), to my horror, that my nephews (20) _had drawn_ (draw) a huge beard and moustache on my face with crayons. I nearly died of embarrassment.

Go back to **page 55**.

2 In sentences 1–6, underline the correct time linker.

1 She'd had it a week too long, and *after* / *during* / <u>*as*</u> she was taking **it** back, she realised she didn't have any money with her to pay the fine.

2 She took me aside *while* / <u>*during*</u> / *when* the break and asked why I hadn't handed **it** in.

3 Written by Prince, **it** was originally recorded by the funk band The Family in 1985, but **it** didn't take off <u>*until*</u> / *afterwards* / *eventually* **it** was released by Sinead O'Connor in 1990.

4 Unfortunately, *afterwards* / *after that* / <u>*after*</u> **it** flew at her and bit her on the nose, she took no further interest in **it**, and *at the end* / <u>*in the end*</u> / *at last* her parents reluctantly gave **it** to a friend, together with the cage.

5 Almost *eventually* / *while* / <u>*as soon as*</u> they'd taken **it** over, they got rid of the managing director.

3 What do you think 'it' might refer to in each sentence in Exercise 2?

1 a library book
2 a piece of homework
3 a song (specifically *Nothing Compares 2 U*)
4 a pet bird
5 a business

Go back to **page 55**.

TB55

A GOOD STORY

4 SPEAK Work in small groups. Discuss the following questions.
  1 Is too much emphasis placed on grammar teaching in your country?
  2 *Storytelling is a crucial skill for life and commerce.* Do you agree? Should it be taught in schools?

Language focus Past tenses and time linkers

Past tense review

1 Look at the following sentences from the beginning of a story and name the underlined past tenses. Choose from:

past continuous   past perfect continuous   past perfect simple   past simple

  1 It was a warm but cloudy summer's day and <u>my family and I were spending</u> the day in the mountains. <u>We were celebrating</u> my sister's birthday. past continuous
  2 <u>We had set off</u> from the city at 9 o'clock in glorious sunshine.   past perfect simple
  3 <u>We'd been playing</u> games and splashing about in the river all morning, but now it was time to eat.   past perfect continuous
  4 Just as <u>we were sitting down</u> at the picnic table, <u>it started</u> to pour down with rain.   past continuous + past simple
  5 As quickly as we could, <u>we picked up</u> all the plates and food, <u>put</u> everything back into the bags and <u>rushed</u>   past simple (x3)
     to the car.

2 In which sentence in Exercise 1 is the past tense or combination of tenses used to describe:
  a a series of actions or events following each other in chronological order?   5
  b a single event which occurred before the other past actions in the narrative?   2
  c an activity which continued until just before the main action of the narrative?   3
  d a situation which occurred over a period of time and which forms the background to the other past actions in the narrative?   1
  e an action which was in progress when another action occurred?   4

3 Go to **Ready for Grammar** on **page 212** for rules, explanations and further practice of past tenses.

4 SPEAK Work in pairs. Name the tenses in the following pairs of sentences and explain the difference in meaning between each pair.
                                                                        Past continuous, past simple
  1 a When he was having breakfast, he read the newspaper.   He read the newspaper *during* his breakfast.
    b When he'd had breakfast, he read the newspaper.   *Past perfect, past simple*   He read the newspaper *after* his breakfast.
                                                                        Past simple, past continuous
  2 a I heard about it when I was listening to the news on the radio.   I heard about it *while* I was listening to the news on the radio.
    b I listened to the news on the radio when I heard about it.   *Past simple, past simple*   I heard about it and as a *result* I listened to the news on the radio.
  3 a I lived in Oxford for six years.   *Past simple*   The speaker no longer lives in Oxford.
    b I had been living in Oxford for six years.   *Past perfect continuous*   This describes the situation before another situation or action occurred. We do not know whether the speaker still lives in Oxford or not.

Time linkers

5 In which of the sentences in Exercise 4 can *while* be used in place of *when*? In which sentences can *as soon as* be used in place of *when*? Do these words change the meaning of the sentences in any way?   *While* can be used in place of *when* in 1a and 2a. It emphasises that the two things happened at the same time, but does not change the meaning. *As soon as* can be used in place of *when* in 1b and 2b. It emphasises that the action in the main clause happened immediately after the action in the clause introduced by *as soon as*.

6 Complete each gap (1–3) with either *at the end*, *in the end* or *at last*.
  1 I'd like you to hand in your homework <u>at the end</u> of the class.
  2 We were going to catch a train but <u>in the end</u> we decided it would be cheaper to drive.
  3 We've found a house we like <u>at last</u>! We've been looking for nearly two years.

7 In which sentence in Exercise 6 could *eventually* be used without changing the meaning?
  In sentence 2, *eventually* can be used instead of *in the end.*

8 Go to **Ready for Grammar** on **page 212** for rules, explanations and further practice of time linkers.

9 SPEAK Work in pairs. Tell your partner about something embarrassing, unusual or exciting that happened to you. Use a variety of past tenses and time linkers.

55

4 A GOOD STORY

Writing Part 2 Report

1 **SPEAK** Work in pairs. Read the following Writing Part 2 Task. Choose one of the categories each and discuss with your partner what you could write about for your area.

Your local mayor wants to increase the number of visitors to your area. You have been asked to write a report for the mayor on **one** of the following:

- Cinemas, theatres and concert halls
- Sports facilities
- Transport facilities
- Parks and gardens
- Historic buildings and museums

The report should describe what your area offers visitors and make recommendations for improvements.

2 Read three possible introductions (A–C) to the report on *Cinemas, theatres and concert halls*. Complete each gap (1–8) with a word from the box, using the words in bold to help you. There is an example at the beginning (0).

aim   aims   contains   ~~looks~~   make   order   provide   terms   ways

A INTRODUCTION
This report **(0)** ___looks___ at some of the entertainment facilities that visitors to this town can find here. It also suggests **(1)** ___ways___ of improving these facilities **with the (2)** ___aim___ of attracting more visitors.

B INTRODUCTION
This report **(3)** ___aims___ **to** describe what our town offers visitors **in (4)** ___terms___ of cinemas, theatres and concert halls. It also **(5)** ___contains___ **recommendations** for improving these facilities so as to encourage more people to visit the town.

C INTRODUCTION
The purpose of this report is **to (6)** ___provide___ **an overview of** the town's cinemas, theatres and concert halls and **to (7)** ___make/provide___ **suggestions** on how to improve them **in (8)** ___order___ **to** attract more visitors.

56

A GOOD STORY 4

Note: if your class are taking the *B2 First for Schools* exam, please use the *B2 First for Schools writing lessons* on the Teacher's Resource Centre. Writing a report is not an option on this version of the exam.

Lead-in

Find a few pictures of interesting places to visit or activities to do in your own hometown that might be interesting to people visiting the area. If it's easier, you could also choose a major city in your home country. Before you show your students the pictures, tell them they must think of at least one question to ask you while you tell them about the places or activities. In small groups, students then tell each other about interesting places to visit or activities to do in their own hometowns. If mobile phones are allowed, ask students to find pictures to show their classmates. Finish the activity with a short discussion of what makes places or activities attractive to people visiting an area for the first time.

Alternatively, you may wish to use **Presenting a report** on the Teacher's Resource Centre at this point.

Writing

1 Students read the instructions and discuss one of the categories with a classmate. Alternatively, to extend this task you could ask students to discuss what they could write about for their area for all five categories.

2 This activity aims to show students how to write the introduction to a report not only appropriately, in terms of style, but also effectively, by demonstrating how to concisely inform the reader about the aim and content of the report. As shown in the examples, this can usually be done in one or two sentences.

Teaching tip

Use a feedback code when marking students' writing. Underline errors and simply write *T* for *tense*, *WW* for *wrong word*, etc. This will save you time, because you don't have to write out all the corrections yourself, but more importantly it will make feedback more interactive and encourage students to notice and correct their own mistakes. One word of warning: it's very important to make sure the students do in fact self-correct, and then make time yourself to check the students' self-corrections, or these errors might go uncorrected.

4 A GOOD STORY

3 Discuss the question in open class.

4 Once students have had the chance to discuss the questions in pairs, nominate three students from different pairs to tell the class about one of the paragraphs.

5 This question highlights a common error for B2 level students when writing reports or when using these verbs to give advice in other contexts. You could provide further practice creating a link with what the students talked about in Exercise 1, e.g. *What would you recommend doing at the weekend in your hometown?*

6 Give the students a few minutes to underline words or phrases and then compare with a partner. If you have the ability to project the text up on the board, students could come up and underline the words or phrases there. Remind students that it's perfectly fine for them to 'steal' as much useful language as they can from model texts and incorporate it into the practice writing they do during the course. That way on the day of the exam this appropriate lexis will naturally come to mind.

7 Direct students to the **How to go about it** box. Note that the information in this box could be adapted into a checklist to give the students for this writing task, e.g. *Does the report include headings?* Students should ideally plan their reports in class, thinking up ideas with their classmates and getting input on the plan from the teacher. You might also experiment with getting the students to write certain sections in class, i.e. just the introduction, or just one of the central paragraphs, either individually or together with another classmate.

Sample answer

Report about parks and gardens

Introduction

The aim of this report is to describe what our town offers visitors in terms of parks and gardens. It also makes recommendations for improving these facilities in order to encourage more people to visit the town.

Parks

This town has an excess of 70,000 habitants, but there are only two quite large parks where people can run and play. In addition, only one of the parks 'The Queen's Park', has sports facilities, for example football pitch or tennis court. Moreover, both parks, 'The Queen's Park' and 'The North's Park', are both in the north of the town, the south only has a small park.

Gardens

There are some small parks with flowers and trees that they are good for sitting and eating lunch if you are a worker. However, there is nothing in the town centre, where many people are, including business people and tourists.

Recommendations

I suggest puting sports facilities in the 'The North's Park' and make another park in the south. I also recommend to have a garden with flowers in the town centre where the people could enjoy and eat their lunch.

192 words

Examiner's comments

Content: The reader is only partly informed. The report begins well with a clear introduction, but thereafter, little mention is made of visitors. The writer aims the report at 'habitants', people in general and workers, and only briefly mentions tourists.

Communicative Achievement: The conventions of report writing are employed effectively, with good use of heading and sub-headings. The register is appropriately neutral, and the tone is generally objective, with one exception (*if you are a worker*). Straightforward ideas are communicated.

Organisation: The report is clearly organised in appropriate sections, thus helping to communicate the main points. A variety of appropriate linking words is used (e.g. *In addition; Moreover; However*). However, frequent repetition of the word 'parks' could be avoided in the second paragraph by using referencing (e.g. *In addition;, only one of these …; the one in the south*).

Language: There is an adequate range of vocabulary for report writing (*The aim of this report; improving these facilities*) and the topic (e.g. *sports facilities; football pitch; tennis court*). There are some errors with word formation and spelling (*(in)habitants; putting*) but these do not impede communication.

There is a range of simple and more complex grammatical forms (e.g. *The aim of this report is to describe what our town offers visitors in terms of parks and gardens*), though this is most successful in the more formulaic first paragraph.

The rest of the report contains some rather awkward use of language (e.g. *both parks … are both; where many people are*) and there are several non-impeding errors, such as the use or non-use of articles (*The North's Park (North Park); football pitch and tennis court; the people*), problems with verb patterns (*I suggest … make; I also recommend to have*) and other aspects of language (*that they are good for sitting; the people could enjoy (themselves)*).

Mark: Pass

A GOOD STORY

3 Read the continuation of the report from Exercise 2c. Is the style of the language in the report appropriate? Give reasons for your answer. *The report is for the local mayor and is written in an appropriately formal style.*

CINEMAS

There are three cinemas in the town centre, all of which are in poor condition and <u>create a bad impression on anyone visiting our town</u>. The buildings are old, the seats are uncomfortable and each cinema has just one screen, so <u>there is not much choice in terms of</u> films.

THEATRES AND CONCERT HALLS

<u>We are fortunate enough to have</u> two theatres and a large concert hall in our town. Unlike the cinemas, these buildings are well maintained and <u>offer</u> both residents and tourists <u>a wide variety of</u> plays and concerts. However, overseas <u>visitors comment on</u> the high prices of tickets and this prevents many from attending shows.

RECOMMENDATIONS

I recommend that the council should build a new multi-screen cinema complex, showing some original version films, <u>particularly for the benefit of</u> English-speaking tourists to our town. I also suggest offering special discounts on theatre and concert tickets for the many young foreign people who come here to study.

4 The question in Exercise 1 says that the report should consider visitors to the area. In the model answer, how does the writer show the relevance of the report to visitors in each paragraph?

Introduction: the writer says that suggestions will be made 'in order to attract more visitors'.

5 What structures are used after the verbs *recommend* and *suggest* in the final paragraph of the model answer report?
recommend + should + infinitive without to   suggest + gerund

6 Underline any other language in the model answer which could be used in the different reports for the question in Exercise 1. *See underlining in the model answer*

in poor condition

7 Now write your own answer for one of the other reports in the question in Exercise 1. Write your report in 140–190 words.

How to go about it

- Write a plan for your report.
  Note down positive and negative points about the facilities in your area. For each negative point, consider a recommendation you could make.
- In your plan you could have two or three central paragraphs after the introduction, with a final paragraph containing your recommendations. Alternatively, you could include a recommendation in each paragraph.
- Give each paragraph a short title.
- Follow the instructions in the question carefully.
  Remember to make your report relevant to visitors to your area.
- If you are not sure what to write about, you can invent information.
- Write your report in an appropriate style and use a range of language.
  In this report for the mayor, a formal style is appropriate.

For more information on writing reports, see **page 196**.

4 REVIEW

Reading and Use of English Part 4 Key word transformation

For questions 1–6, complete the second sentence so that it has a similar meaning to the first sentence, using the word given. Do not change the word given. You must use between two and five words, including the word given.

1 When the meeting was over, they went out for dinner.
   HAD
   As _soon as the meeting had_ finished, they went out for dinner.

2 When we eventually arrived at the party, all the food had been eaten.
   GOT
   By _the time we got to_ the party, all the food had been eaten.

3 He put everything back in its place before he left.
   UNTIL
   He did not _leave until he (had)_ put everything back in its place.

4 They decided against employing him, because of his age.
   TAKE
   They decided _not to take him on_, because of his age.

5 She is not at all interested in my work.
   INTEREST
   She does _not take/have/show any interest in_ my work.

6 This is the funniest book I've ever read.
   SUCH
   I've _never read such a funny_ book as this one.

Correcting mistakes

In each short text 1–5, there are two words which should not be there. Find these words and cross them out. The first one has been done for you.

1 At first we weren't sure whether we could afford to go on holiday, but in the end we ~~had~~ felt we ought to spend at least ~~during~~ a week on the coast.

2 I was extremely impressed with the special effects and some ~~part~~ of the action scenes. As for ~~as~~ the acting, though, I felt many amateurs could have done better.

3 Sophie was so ~~much~~ pleased after her last exam. 'At ~~the~~ last!' she cried. 'I've finished.'

4 When he ~~had~~ came home from work he ~~was~~ made himself a cup of tea and read the newspaper. It had been an exhausting day.

5 I'm so glad we took ~~to~~ your advice and went to the new Indian restaurant that's just opened. The service was marvellous and it was such ~~a~~ good food.

Vocabulary Films

Complete each gap with one word, the first letter of which has been given. You may need to use the plural form of a word.

1 The 2017 version of *Murder on the Orient Express* features **an all-star c**_ast_ including Kenneth Branagh, Penelope Cruz, Johnny Depp and Michelle Pfeiffer.

2 Brad Pitt won an Academy Award for Best Actor in **a Supporting R**_ole_ for his part in the 2019 film *Once Upon a Time in Hollywood*.

3 The novel was praised by **literary c**_ritics_ but the film had **poor r**_eviews_.

4 It's a well-written thriller, with convincing characters and **a gripping p**_lot_.

5 One ingredient of a good action film is an exciting and **memorable opening s**_cene_; some kind of chase involving cars or helicopters, for example.

REVIEW 4

Reading and Use of English Part 3 Word formation

1 Read the following text, ignoring the gaps for the moment. What is the purpose of the text?   to attract new students to the Storytime School of Storytelling

Storytime

The Storytime School of Storytelling offers a (0) __VARIETY__ of courses to anyone (1) __interested__ in the ancient art of storytelling. A wide range of people have studied with us, from tour guides to teachers, lawyers to (2) __librarians__ and bankers to business owners.

Their motives for attending our courses vary enormously. They may be keen to develop their (3) __confidence__ as public speakers, learn how to use stories in the classroom, or activate their (4) __creativity__ in a playful environment.

Whatever their reasons, participants usually find the experience absolutely (5) __fascinating__, as you can see from the enthusiastic testimonials on our website. Many of these point to the series of (6) __performances__ given to local schoolchildren as the highlight of their course. Others mention the supportive atmosphere in our school and the quality of the teaching.

Not (7) __surprisingly__, many people come back to Storytime again and again. We offer an almost (8) __unlimited/limitless__ number of courses ranging from *Animal tales* to *Using your voice* or *Creating your own stories*. Why not contact us? We're sure to have a course for you.

VARY
INTEREST

LIBRARY

CONFIDE
CREATIVE

FASCINATE
PERFORM

SURPRISE
LIMIT

2 Read the text again and use the word given in capitals at the end of some of the lines to form a word that fits in the space in the same line. There is an example at the beginning (0).

Writing Part 2 Review and Informal letter

Write an answer to one of the following in 140–190 words.

1 You recently saw this notice on an English-language website called *Game Plan*.

> **Reviews wanted!**
> **Game apps**
> Is there a game you play regularly on your phone?
> Write a review explaining the aim of the game, why you like playing it and who you would recommend it to.

Write your review.

For more information on writing reviews, see **page 197**.

2 This is part of a letter you have received from your English friend, Tanya.

> I'm not sure what to read next. What's the best book you've read recently? Tell me a little bit about the plot (not too much!) and say what you liked about it. If it sounds good, I'll see if I can get a copy in English.
>
> Thanks
>
> Tanya

Please go to the Teacher's Resource Centre for a Sample answer with Examiner comments for this Writing task.
Write your letter.

For more information on writing informal letters, see **page 193**.

59

4 A GOOD STORY

Pronunciation Silent consonants

1 ▶ 4.2 Compete the sentences with the missing words.
1 Did you ___know___ Mahershala Ali won an Academy Award for ___Moonlight___?
2 The book is a ___psychological___ thriller called ___Autumn___ in London.
3 For the role of the climate change ___campaigner___, the make-up department gave the actor ___wrinkles___ using prosthetics.
4 The ___muscle___-bound action hero ___climbed___ up the cliff in pursuit of the villain.

2 Each word you wrote in Exercise 1 contains at least one consonant which is not pronounced. Underline the silent consonants.

3 ▶ 4.3 Cross out the silent consonants in these words. Then listen to check.

ans~~w~~er   colum~~n~~   design   ech~~o~~   hal~~f~~   han~~d~~kerchief   ~~k~~nee   lam~~b~~   listen   receipt   s~~c~~ene

4 Read the short article about a book below. The silent consonants have been removed from the words in bold. Correct the spelling of the words in bold.

BOOK OF THE WEEK

Natasha Drake's bestselling fantasy epic ¹**Sords** (swords) and ²**casles** (castles) recounts the life of King Fabian and his ³**hansome** (handsome) but ⁴**disonest** (dishonest) sibling David, who is a constant source of problems for his brother. ⁵**Gosts** (Ghosts), goblins, elves and other fantastical creatures populate the ⁶**iland** (island) kingdom, but what really brings the book to life is the witty ⁷**rappor** (rapport) between the main characters as they deal with one disaster after another. The rather ⁸**solem** (solemn) ending left everyone guessing as to ⁹**wat** ¹⁰**woud** (whatwould) happen next. Well, the wait is finally over – the sequel is being released next ¹¹**Wenesday** (Wednesday). ¹²**Althou** (Although) some critics are already ¹³**douting** ¹⁴**wether** (doubting whether) it can match the success of the first instalment, all ¹⁵**sins** (signs) point to it topping the charts once more.

5 Work in pairs. Compare your answers to Exercise 4.

6 **SPEAK** Work in pairs. Play four in a row. Take a pencil and use the table below as your board. If you correctly cross out the one silent consonant in a word, you win the space. The aim of the game is to stop your partner winning four spaces in a row, and/or to win four spaces in a row before your partner. When you have finished one game, rub out your answers and play another.

whistle	plumber	~~h~~our	talk	debt	two
is~~l~~and	~~k~~nock	~~w~~rist	bomb	~~k~~not	cupboard
hi~~g~~h	could	aisle	~~w~~hole	light	doubt
sign	~~w~~rong	knife	salmon	mus~~c~~le	handsome
ballet	~~w~~rite	stomach	debut	sandwich	foreign

Pronunciation

1 ▶ 4.2 Go through the answers as a class.

2 To change the class dynamic, you could invite one student up to the front of the class, who then elicits the silent consonants from their classmates and underlines them on the board.

3 ▶ 4.3 Allow students to pair check before going over the answers as a class.

4-5 Students read the instructions and do the exercises.

6 To highlight student progress, finish the lesson by eliciting a few words from page 60 that the students did mispronounce, or likely would have mispronounced, before this lesson.

READY FOR READING

Introduction
In Parts 5 to 7 of the Reading and Use of English paper there are three extended texts, each accompanied by a different reading comprehension task.

Reading and Use of English Part 5 Multiple choice

1. Part 5 consists of a text followed by six multiple choice questions, each with four options. Before answering the questions, you should always read the text through quite quickly to get an idea of the overall meaning. Read *A Scottish wildlife safari* on page 62 and answer the following question.

   Which animals and birds does the writer say he and his family saw on the safari?
   seals, several interesting water birds (such as eider ducks and mergansers), an otter

2. In all of the reading tasks there will inevitably be words you do not know the meaning of. On many occasions, it is not essential for you to understand these words in order to complete the task, and you can ignore them. However, you may be able to use the context in which the word appears to help you work out the approximate meaning.

   Find the four words and phrases below in the second paragraph of the article, and then use the context and the clues you are given to work out the approximate meaning of each one.

   1. emblazoned — This clearly means 'written' in some way. How would you expect the name of the company to be written on the minibus?
      emblazoned: printed in a very noticeable way
   2. beaming — We are told that Ian has a 'cheerful, friendly manner'. So what might he be doing to give the impression that a part of his face goes 'from ear to ear'?
      beaming: smiling in a very obvious way
   3. hit it off — Would Ian's personality have a positive or negative effect on his relationship with the writer and his family?
      hit it off: like each other the first time you meet
   4. signed up for — In the next sentence, the writer says there are four empty seats. So what has 'no one else' done?
      signed up for: agreed to do; booked

3. Use context to work out the meanings of the words in bold in the third paragraph.
   stretch (n) = area (of water)
   skirts (v) = goes around or along the edge of
   clinging (v) = 'holding' onto tightly
   palpable (adj) = obvious, very easily noticed

READY FOR READING

Reading and Use of English

1. Reading the text first for gist is good habit for students to get into, but one common problem is that students slow down when trying to understand every sentence, or even every word. Make sure to always set a time limit for gist reading tasks like this one.

2–3. One common problem on the *B2 First* is candidates running out of time. One reason is because students get stuck on difficult words. Remind students they don't have to understand every word, but some less familiar words will be important to answer the questions. Allow the students to compare their ideas with a classmate before going over the meaning of words as a class. Check the pronunciation of *palpable* /ˈpælpəbl/.

READY FOR READING

A SCOTTISH WILDLIFE SAFARI

It's nearly one o'clock and I'm waiting expectantly with my wife and two daughters in a car park on the edge of the Scottish town of Fort William. We've arranged to meet Ian MacLeod, a local guide who'll be taking us on a half-day tour to see, we hope, some of the area's rich diversity of wildlife – seals, otters, sea birds and maybe even deer or an eagle. There's no guarantee, of course, as animals come and go as they please, but the numerous five-star reviews online have led us to believe that we will be in the best hands possible.

On the hour, a minibus with the words 'Wild West Safaris' emblazoned on its side pulls into the car park and out steps Ian, beaming from ear to ear. It's difficult not to warm to his cheerful, friendly manner and we all seem to hit it off with him from the start. This is particularly reassuring, since no one else has signed up for today's safari. It's just the five of us in the 9-seater minibus. 'I have to compete with a number of other attractions,' says Ian, by way of explanation. 'The Jacobite steam train, Loch Ness boat trips, the treetop rope course … A lot of families on holiday here opt for those things first.' So, probably, would we, I reflect silently, if the decision were left to my teenage daughters.

We set off. Not far from Fort William we take the car ferry across a narrow **stretch** of water to Corran, and then follow the road that **skirts** the waters of Loch Linnhe. 'The tide's not fully in yet, so we should see some seals along here,' Ian predicts. And sure enough, five minutes later we are rewarded with the sight of a dozen or so harbour seals, **clinging** resolutely to a small rock as the water rises slowly around them. It's a first for my daughters and their excitement is **palpable**. So too is their father's sense of relief and satisfaction – this was all his idea, after all.

We're soon back in the minibus and heading off further down the loch to look for otters. We park up in a small lay-by and while our guide boils up water on a camping stove for a cup of tea, we scan the loch for movement. 'If only it were,' he replies, when we ask him if this is his sole occupation, but he adds quickly, 'I really can't complain, though.' He explains that he also drives doctors out to patients in remote areas, a job which affords him plenty of quiet moments in which he can read up on the region's flora and fauna, local history and even geology, information he can pass on to his grateful safari customers.

And he really is a mine of information; we learn about the Ice Age in Scotland, the Jacobite Rebellions of the 18th century, the healing properties of the plants we see, the biting habits of midges (the west coast's ubiquitous mosquitos), and, to help us become independent wildlife observers, the ideal places to spot various Scottish animals in our own time. Which is a good job, because although we see several interesting water birds such as eider ducks and mergansers, the otter doesn't seem to want to show its face today.

Time's up, though – there's a ferry to catch and Ian's evening shift begins soon. We take the same road back to Corran, pleased at the day's results but slightly disappointed not to have seen our first ever wild otter. Suddenly, Ian glimpses something out of his side window. 'Otter!' he shouts and we scream to a halt. There's pure delight in his voice and for a brief moment, he's one of us. He's lived in the area for over thirty years, but he cannot hide his excitement at seeing this most elusive of creatures, as if for the first time. No wonder he loves his job.

---

4 Read the text again. For questions 1–6, choose the answer (A, B, C or D) which you think fits best according to the text.

1 In the first paragraph, the writer suggests that Ian
   - **A** has many satisfied customers. ✓
   - B has a very informative website.
   - C is not the most punctual of people.
   - D is not confident they will see much.

2 In the second paragraph, we learn that some visitors to the area
   - A do not turn up for tours they have booked.
   - B do not want to travel in a crowded minibus.
   - C do not find Ian very easy to get on with.
   - **D** do not consider a wildlife safari a priority. ✓

3 How did the writer feel when they saw the seals?
   - A impressed by the accuracy of Ian's predictions
   - **B** reassured that he had made the right choice of activity ✓
   - C surprised at how quickly they had spotted some wildlife
   - D pleased that his daughters had been the first to see them

4 What does Ian say about his work as a wildlife safari guide?
   - A It is not as profitable as his other job.
   - B It used to be his only source of income.
   - **C** He wishes he could dedicate himself full-time to it. ✓
   - D There are certain aspects of it that he doesn't like.

5 What does 'Which' refer to in line 56?
   - A an otter
   - B being a wildlife guide
   - C the writer's family holiday
   - **D** learning where to look for wildlife ✓

6 When the writer says 'he's one of us' in line 67 he means that Ian and the writer's family
   - A have never seen an otter in the wild before.
   - **B** react to seeing the otter in the same way. ✓
   - C watch the otter together from the roadside.
   - D are very noisy in the presence of the otter.

5 SPEAK Would you be interested in going on a wildlife tour with a guide? Why/Why not?

---

4 One exam strategy for multiple-choice questions is to first read the question or sentence stem, underline the key words, and then go look for the answer to the question or the information missing in the sentence. Once students have found the part of the text that contains the answer, then, and only then, do they read the four options and choose which says the same thing as the text. Students are much less likely to fall for distractors using this procedure.

5 Before doing this speaking activity, you could ask the students to identify the two animals in the pictures who the family were able to see on their tour (*seal, otter*). Get some feedback in open class after the students have discussed the question in pairs. You could ask a few follow-up questions, e.g. *Would you prefer to go on one in Scotland, or is there another place you'd be more interested in?*

READY FOR READING

Reading and Use of English Part 6 Gapped text

What to expect in the exam

Each correct answer in Parts 5 and 6 receives two marks; correct answers in Part 7 receive one mark each.

1 Part 6 consists of a text from which sentences have been removed and placed in a different order after the text. You have to decide which part of the text the sentences have been removed from. This task tests your understanding of the way texts are structured, so look carefully at the language both before and after the gap.

2 Read the headline and first paragraph of the newspaper article about the Siberian city of Yakutsk. What aspects of life in Yakutsk do you think might be mentioned in the article?

3 Read through the base text (the main text with the gaps). Are any of your ideas from Exercise 2 mentioned?

The coldest city on Earth
Shaun Walker enjoys a mini-break in deepest Siberia.

Yakutsk, in eastern Siberia (population 200 000), can convincingly claim to be the coldest city on earth. In January, the most freezing month, average 'highs' are around minus 40ºC; today the temperature is hovering around minus 43ºC, leaving the city covered in a blanket of freezing fog that restricts visibility to 10 metres. I have come here to find out for myself how people manage to survive in the world's coldest place.

Ex 4 C **Before venturing outdoors for the first time, I put on a suitcase's worth of clothes** to protect me against the cold, including a thermal undershirt, a long-sleeved T-shirt, a tight-fitting cashmere jumper, a padded winter coat with hood, two pairs of gloves and a woolly football hat. **1 C** The small part of my face that is naked to the elements definitely notices **the cold air**, but on the whole, **it feels fine**. As long as you're dressed right, I think, **this isn't too bad**.

After the gap, 'the cold air' tells us the writer is outside, so the missing sentence will probably serve as a transition from putting on the clothes to going outside.

Ex 4 G **2 G** The first place to suffer is the exposed skin on my face, which **experiences shooting pains and goes numb**. Then the cold penetrates the double layer of gloves and sets to work on **chilling my fingers**. The woolly hat and padded hood are no match for minus 43ºC either, and **my ears begin to sting**. Finally, I find myself with **severe pain all across my body** and have to return indoors.

In the previous paragraph the writer is untroubled by the cold: 'it feels fine'; 'this isn't too bad'. In this paragraph he begins to suffer. The missing sentence will probably refer to this contrast.

Despite the fact that the locals are stoically going about their business, and children are playing in the snow on the central square and laughing merrily, I realise that **I'll need a warm taxi to continue my exploration**. **3 A** **I collapse on the bed in the hotel room, and it takes half an hour for my body to feel normal again**. **Ex 4 A**

In the missing sentence the writer may refer to his planned exploration of Yakutsk and/or explain why he collapses on his hotel bed.

4 E **Workers continue working on building sites up to minus 50ºC, and children go to school unless it's below minus 55ºC**. 'Of course it's cold, but you get used to it,' says Nina, a Yakut woman who spends eight hours every day standing at her stall in the fish market. 'Human beings can get used to anything,' she says. **Ex 4 E**

Almost without exception, the women wear fur from head to toe. 'In Europe you have people who say it's not nice to wear fur because they love animals,' says Natasha, a Yakutsk resident, who is wearing a coat made of rabbit and a hat of arctic fox. 'They should come and live in Siberia for a couple of months and then see if they are still so worried about the animals. **You need to wear fur here to survive**. **5 F**' **Ex 4 F**

'For us, the winter is like the working week and the summer is like the weekend,' says local blogger Bolot Bochkarev. The short summer, when the temperature hits 30ºC or 35ºC for two or three weeks, is a time when **efforts are made to ensure that the region is ready for winter**. **6 D** **If they fail, those stuck without warmth risk death**. The whole region suffers harsh winters. A few hundred miles away is Oymyakon, known as 'The Pole of Cold'. It was here that the lowest ever temperature in an inhabited place was recorded – minus 71.2ºC. **Ex 4 D**

Reading and Use of English

1 Students read the information in Exercise 1 and the **What to expect in the exam** box. Ask them some simple questions to check their understanding of the task, e.g. *How many marks do you get for each correct answer?*

2–3 The aim here is to encourage students to make predictions about what they are about to read, a strategy that has been shown to be effective for improving reading comprehension. Point out that often the first paragraph of an article gives the reader a good idea of what it will be about. Titles and any accompanying photos can also help students make predictions. Elicit a few of their ideas in open class. Then, after they have skimmed the article, ask if any were mentioned.

READY FOR READING

READY FOR READING

4 Six sentences have been removed from the article. Choose from the sentences A–G the one which fits each gap (1–6). There is one extra sentence which you do not need to use.

How to go about it

- Before you read A–G, predict the general content of each of the six missing sentences.

  The comments in italics in the base text contain predictions about the general content of the missing sentences for gaps 1–3. Use the words in **bold** in the rest of the base text to make similar predictions about the missing sentences for gaps 4–6.
- Read sentences A–G. Use your predictions to help you choose the correct sentence for each gap 1–6.

  As you make your choices, underline words or phrases in sentences A–G which show links with the words in bold in the base text.
- Check your answers by reading through the whole article again to ensure that it makes sense. Check that the extra sentence does not fit into any of the gaps.

Note: In the exam, no help is given: you should make your own predictions and underline key words and phrases in both the base text and sentences A–G yourself.

A The thirteen minutes I have spent outside have left me out of breath and aching all over.
B Even wearing glasses gets tricky: the metal sticks to your cheeks and will tear off your skin when you remove them.
C I'm ready to face everything Yakutsk has to throw at me and I stride purposefully out of the hotel door.
D Heating pipes are examined and repaired.
E Locals are a little more skilled at dealing with the cold.
F Nothing else keeps you warm.
G Within a few minutes, however, the icy weather begins to make itself felt.

5 **SPEAK** If you had to live in either extreme heat or extreme cold, which would you choose and why?

4 Ask students to quickly discuss in pairs why parts of the text are in bold and how they might help them choose the correct missing sentences, but don't say why yet. Give students time to read through the instructions and **How to go about it** box. Then elicit if what they said about the parts of the text in bold was accurate. After the students have done the task, allow them time to check in pairs and justify their answers before correcting the exercise as a class.

5 To make this more dynamic, students could 'vote with their feet'. Everyone stands up. Those who prefer the extreme cold move to the right of the classroom; all those who prefer extreme heat, to the left. Students discuss the reasons for their choice with their classmates.

READY FOR READING

Reading and Use of English Part 7 Multiple matching

1 Part 7 consists of either one continuous text divided into sections, or a number of smaller texts. Ten questions or statements are placed before the text(s). For this task you are asked to find the specific information in the text(s) which matches the questions or statements.

2 **SPEAK** Look at the book titles on page 66 and discuss the following in pairs or small groups:
  1 Which, if any, of them have you read, either in English or your own language?
  2 Have you seen film versions of any of them?
  3 What do you know about the story and/or characters in each one?

3 You are going to read an article in which children's writer Leroy Hadley describes his five favourite classic works of children's literature. For questions 1–10, choose from the books (A–E). The books may be chosen more than once.

How to go about it

- Underline key words in the statements before the text.
  In the task below, numbers 1–4 have been done for you.
- Read each of the sections (A–E) looking for information which matches that contained in the statements.
  One of the answers (4) for A has been given, with the relevant part of the text underlined. There are two more statements which match A; find the statements and underline the relevant parts of the text. Then do the same for B–E.
- If there are any statements you have not matched, scan the text again looking for the information you need.

What to expect in the exam

- The words used in the statements (**1–10**) will not be the same as the words used in the relevant parts of the text, but they do express the same idea, e.g. **4 A**
- The information in a particular section could lead you to make the wrong choice, e.g. In section D 'My mother read this to me when I was ten' might lead you to match it to statement **1**, but later in section D we read: 'I read it on my own afterwards'.

Of which book does Leroy Hadley say the following?

I have still <u>not</u> actually <u>read it myself</u>.	1 A
<u>A lot of people</u> are <u>surprised</u> by one of its features.	2 D
The author shows his <u>main characters</u> in a <u>positive light</u>.	3 B
I have <u>not had it for very long</u>.	4 A
I read the <u>original version</u> of this story <u>as a child</u>.	5 C
It shows <u>a way of life</u> which <u>unfortunately</u> does <u>not exist now</u>.	6 B
It <u>reminds</u> me of a <u>certain period</u> of my life.	7 E
The story proved to be very <u>educational</u>.	8 A
Children will find it <u>easier to read</u> than the other books in this selection.	9 C
The <u>beginning</u> of the book <u>gave me ideas</u> for the <u>start of my latest work</u>.	10 E

4 **SPEAK** Tell each other about any other children's classics you have read, either English ones or ones originally written in your own language.

Reading and Use of English

1 This last reading task is different from the other two that come before in that it tests scanning (the ability to read a text quickly in order to find specific information), as opposed to skimming (reading for the general idea), which is tested in both Parts 5 and 6. Note that the **How to go about it** box suggests reading statements 1–10 before reading the text, the opposite approach recommended for Parts 5 and 6.

2 When students approach a reading text, they often bring with them useful background knowledge of the topic. The aim here is to encourage students to use what they already know about the books to help them make predictions.

READY FOR READING

3 Students read the instructions, the **How to go about it** and the **What to expect in the exam** boxes. Elicit how the task and exam strategies are similar or different to the other two reading tasks, e.g. *One similarity is that the part of the text which contains the answers won't use the same words as the statements. One thing that's different is that it can be made up of a number of smaller texts.* Students do the task and compare their answers with a classmate. In open class, ask students to justify their answers with a specific part of the text.

4 It's all right if students can't translate a title of a story in their own language(s) into English. Encourage them to just refer to it with the L1 title and tell their classmates as much as they can about it in English.

5 DOING WHAT YOU HAVE TO

This unit is concerned with obligations of different kinds — at home, school and work. The grammar and vocabulary, as well as the reading, writing, listening and speaking tasks, are related to this theme.

Read the unit objectives to the class.

KEY LANGUAGE
Obligation, necessity and permission
The world of work
en- prefix and *-en* suffix

PRONUNCIATION
Intrusive sounds /r/, /j/ and /w/

EXAM PRACTICE
Reading and Use of English Parts 1, 2, 3, 4 & 7
Writing Parts 1 & 2
Listening Parts 2 & 4
Speaking Parts 1, 2, 3 & 4

Speaking Part 1 Interview

Work with a partner. Discuss the questions.
1 What is/was your favourite subject at school? Why do/did you like it?
2 What do/did you like about your school?
3 Do you think you would be a good teacher?
4 What do you want to do when you leave school/university?
5 Would you prefer to do physical or mental work?
6 If a job interviewer asked about your personal strengths, what would you say?

SPEAKING Part 1 Interview

Focus students' attention on the images. Ask them if they are familiar with any of these signs. Lead an open class discussion by asking questions like: *In what kind of place might you find these signs? Do people pay more attention to some types of signs than others? Why?* Ask the students to close their books. Dictate the six questions in the Speaking Part 1 section using fast, natural pronunciation. Say each question twice only. Students then open their books to check. Highlight some of the features of connected speech introduced on page 14 and elicit any that made certain questions harder to copy down correctly. Put students in pairs to discuss the questions. Conduct brief feedback as a group. Board and discuss a few examples of emergent language.

ONLINE MATERIALS

Debate with mediator (**Teacher's Resource Centre**)
How to … (**Teacher's Resource Centre**)
Unit 5 Test (**Test Generator**)
Unit 5 Wordlist (**Teacher's Resource Centre**)
Unit 5 On-the-go-practice (**App**)

5 DOING WHAT YOU HAVE TO

Speaking Part 2 Long turn

1 Look at the photographs below. They show people doing different jobs.

Student A: Compare the photographs and say what you think the people might enjoy about doing these jobs.

Student B: When student A has finished, say which of these jobs you would prefer to do.

What you think the people might enjoy about doing these jobs?

2 Now change roles. Go to the **Additional materials** on **page 198** and do the Speaking Part 2 task.

Listening Part 2 Sentence completion

> **Don't forget!**
> - Write a word, number or phrase that you actually hear.
> - You do not need to write more than three words for each answer.
> - The words you read in the question may not be the same as those you hear in the recording.
> - You will hear distractors for many of the questions.

1 ▶ 5.1 You will hear a man called Mike Swift talking to a group of teenagers about the vocational courses offered by the college where he works. For questions 1–10, complete the sentences with a word or short phrase.

Before you listen to the recording, read through all the questions and try to predict the type of information you will hear for each one.

1 This is probably a number.

There are currently (1) __five/5__ different faculties at Mike's college.

Mike says that the (2) __television/TV__ studio in the Creative Skills faculty is unique for a college in the area.

Mike is particularly impressed that one former student of the college is already working as a (3) __radio producer__.

Increasing numbers of people are enrolling on courses in the (4) __Events/events__ Department.

Mike says that both the ability to work in an organised manner and good (5) __team management__ skills are important in a variety of jobs.

Some courses at Mike's college include a period of (6) __work experience__.

Most information technology courses are offered by the (7) __business__ faculty.

Mike says that applicants for the computer games development course need high marks in (8) __math(s)/mathematics__, as well as passes in other exams.

Mike says that guidance on what to study is available in the (9) __Study Options/study options__ section of the college website.

The (10) __evening__ courses at Mike's college normally last five months.

2 **SPEAK** Work in groups. Which, if any, of the courses and/or jobs mentioned in the listening would interest you? What would be your ideal job?

DOING WHAT YOU HAVE TO 5

Speaking

1 Put the students into groups of three. Student A turns to page 51; Student B, page 16; Student C, page 3. Give them a couple of minutes to read the information about Speaking Part 2 on their respective pages. They then take turns sharing what they read with their group members. Now reorganise the class in pairs for the Speaking Part 2 task. You may wish to check that the class know the name of the jobs the people are doing (gardener or topiarist; segway tour guide). Time the students or have them time themselves. Afterwards, elicit what advice they did or didn't follow from their initial discussion. If mobile phones are allowed, consider getting students to record themselves doing the task. They can listen to it afterwards to help improve their performance.

2 Ask students to swap roles and direct them to the Additional materials (see TB69).

Listening

1 ▶ 5.1 Students read the instructions and the **Don't forget!** box. Check the meaning of *vocational* and elicit some possible examples of courses offered at the college. Give them some time to read the task and make predictions about what type of word or phrase to listen for. Students could quickly compare their predictions before listening. Check the meaning of *faculty* and *enrol*. Write or display the answers on the board and encourage students to check any they got wrong in the Audioscript on page 238 (see below).

2 Students discuss the questions in small groups.

AUDIOSCRIPT

Listening Part 2 Sentence completion

▶ 5.1

M = Mike Swift

M: Hello, my name's Mike Swift and I'm here today to talk to you about the City College and the different vocational courses we run there.

Now, until fairly recently we had four different faculties at the college, but with the addition of the
Q1 Creative Skills faculty last year, there are now **five** altogether.

We're really proud of this new faculty. There are workshops for glass production, ceramics and textiles, as well as a state-of-the-art photography studio and the college's very own radio station, which broadcasts every weekday to the local area.
Q2 The star attraction, though, is the **television** studio – the only one of its kind in a further education college in this region.

I think it's worth mentioning that most of the first group of students who were on our media courses last year have already found jobs in the business. There's one working as a camerawoman, for example, quite a few sound or lighting engineers,
Q3 and even, in one case, a **radio producer** – which is pretty good going for a twenty-one-year-old! No presenters as yet, but you never know …

Now, the biggest building in the college is the Faculty of Leisure and Health, which offers over 200 courses in anything from sports coaching or alternative therapies to catering or cake decoration. But the fastest growing courses in this
Q4 faculty are those in the **Events** Department, with more and more students hoping to go into careers as exhibition organisers, concert promoters or wedding co-ordinators.

These are great courses, because if you decided to change careers at any point in the future, most of what you've learnt would still be useful to you.

Organisational skills, for example, are important
Q5 in a whole range of jobs, and so is good **team management** – knowing how to deal with a group of people who work under your supervision.

And there's something else about this type of course which makes it so attractive, and which is common to courses in some of the other faculties, too. During the
Q6 second term, the college organises **work experience** in local venues and businesses. You get a chance to find out what it's like to do the job for a few weeks – and you get paid, too, so that can't be bad!

Now, some of you, I'm sure, will be interested in working in IT. Well, we offer over eighty different information technology courses, some of them in the faculty of building and engineering – like CAAD, for example, which stands for 'computer-aided architectural design' – but the majority are taught in
Q7 the **business** faculty.

Computer games development is a popular choice and can lead to employment as a games developer working in design, programming, art or animation. But competition is high and the entry requirements are quite strict. We're looking for exam passes in at least five subjects, including English, and we
Q8 particularly want to see good grades in **maths**. Computer science is also a big advantage of course.

Incidentally, if you're not sure what course to take, the college does have a student support service, which will help you choose the right one. You can arrange for an interview with the careers advice team before you apply, or else you can go to our
Q9 online site and click on the **Study Options** heading for lots of helpful information and tips.

Now before I go on, I ought to mention that most of our courses last for just under a year – from September to June – and they're either full-time courses, meaning five days a week, or part-time, which are just one or two days a week. But we
Q10 do also have a number of **evening** courses, which usually run for five months.

And that brings me onto the different qualifications you can achieve on the various courses …

TB68

5 DOING WHAT YOU HAVE TO

Vocabulary

1 Students read the instructions and do the task on their own and then check their answers to Exercise 1 in the **Audioscript** on page 238 (see TB68).

2 Note that as students move towards a B2 level in English, they are expected to demonstrate an increasing awareness of collocation, as well as knowledge of how to express the same idea or message in more than one way.

3 After correcting the exercise, check understanding by nominating a stronger student to explain the difference in meaning among these ways of ending a job using their own words and examples.

4–5 Students do the exercise as suggested in pairs.

Suggested answers

1a to work part time – *when you are contracted to work fewer hours than the entire time appropriate, e.g. 21 hours per week* (a part-time job)

b to work full time – *when you are contracted to work the entire time appropriate to that job, e.g. 35 hours per week* (a full-time job)

2a to work overtime – *to work supplementary hours for which you are paid extra*

b to work long hours – *to work for many hours each day*

3a to work flexitime – *to work with a flexible timetable: within limits you decide when you start and when you finish, as long as you work the required total number of hours each month*

b to work shifts – *to work for a set period (e.g. 12 am to 8 am) before workers replace you for the next set period (e.g. 8 am to 4 pm)*

6 This can be done in open class. You may need to clarify the difference between *a cook* and *a cooker*. Note that *rubbish* is called *garbage* or *trash* in North America.

7 After students read the instructions, focus on the **Useful language** box. When describing the jobs, instruct students to start very general and move towards specifics: *This is a job you do outside. It's dangerous*, etc. You may want to model this yourself first. Divide the class into small groups. For stronger classes, tell them to describe other common jobs that don't appear in the pictures.

Extra activity

Set a web research task. Put students into small groups and assign them each one of the following jobs:

- professional skateboarder
- tour guide
- professional interpreter
- exterminator

or any other jobs you think your students might not be very familiar with.

Then, individually outside of the lesson, the students research their job, focusing on 1) important skills or knowledge, 2) qualifications/training, and 3) typical wages/salary. Also encourage students to make note of anything particularly interesting or surprising details they come across. This research could be done both in English and the students' first language(s). At the beginning of the next lesson, students discuss what they learnt with the other members of their group. Then each group prepares a brief presentation on their job.

UNIT 5

Speaking Part 2 Long turn

1 Look at the photographs below. They show people doing different jobs.

Student A: Compare the photographs and say what you think might be difficult for the people about doing these jobs.

Student B: When your partner has finished, say which of these jobs you would prefer to do.

What do you think might be difficult for the people about doing these jobs?

Go back to page 68.

DOING WHAT YOU HAVE TO 5

Vocabulary The world of work

1 In the following extracts from the listening, complete the collocations in bold with a verb. Then check your answers in the **Audioscript** on **page 238**.

1 ... with more and more students hoping to ___go___ **into careers** as exhibition organisers, concert promoters or wedding co-ordinators.

2 ... if you decided to ___change___ **careers** at any point in the future, most of what you've learnt would still be useful to you.

2 In 1–3, complete each collocation with two alternative verbs which have the same meaning. There is an example at the beginning (0).

> abandon ~~change~~ dedicate devote follow give up pursue ~~switch~~

0 After ten years as a teacher, I decided to ___change___ / ___switch___ **careers** and go into acting.

1 Eva intends to ___devote___ / ___dedicate___ **her career to** helping the homeless.

2 Luis was forced to ___abandon___ / ___give up___ **his career as** a pilot because of ill health.

3 After university, I hope to ___follow___ / ___pursue___ **a career in** journalism.

3 Complete each gap with a verb from the box. All the verbs describe ways of ending a job.

> made redundant   resigned   sacked

1 She sold her home, ___resigned___ from her job and moved abroad to teach English.

2 Ed was ___sacked___ from his last job for stealing, so no one will employ him now.

3 The economic crisis hit the company hard, and 50 workers had to be ___made redundant___.

4 Which of the following nouns is not normally used after the verb *to earn*?

a competition   *a good living*   *good money*   *a high salary*
a weekly wage   *earn a competition* is not possible

5 Explain the difference in meaning between the items in each pair (1–3).

1 a to work part time
   b to work full time

2 a to work overtime
   b to work long hours

3 a to work flexitime
   b to work shifts

6 Label the jobs in photographs a–e.   chef   hairdresser/barber   surgeon   dustman/rubbish collector   hotel receptionist

7 **SPEAK** Work in pairs. Take turns describing the jobs in Exercise 6 without naming them. Guess which job your partner is describing. Use some of the useful language in the box below.

Useful language

A Skills
You (don't) need good *telephone/computer/artistic/organisational/language* **skills** for this job.

B Adjectives for personal qualities
You (don't) need/have to be: *cheerful   confident   creative   fit   hard-working   patient   polite   talented*

C Adjectives for jobs
This is (not) a _____ job.
challenging   monotonous   responsible   rewarding   skilled   stressful   tiring   well-paid

a chef/cook

b hairdresser/barber

c surgeon

d dustman/rubbish collector/waste collector/refuse collector

e hotel receptionist

5 DOING WHAT YOU HAVE TO

> **Don't forget!**
> › Look at the words both before and after each gap, and consider the meaning of the whole sentence.

Reading and Use of English Part 2 Open cloze

1 **SPEAK** Work in pairs. You are going to read a short text which gives advice on how to write a job application letter. What do you think it will say?

2 Read the text quite quickly, ignoring the gaps. Are any of your ideas from Exercise 1 mentioned?

3 For questions 1–8, read the text again and think of the word which best fits each gap. Use only one word in each gap. There is an example at the beginning (0).

Writing a letter of application

Here are a **(0)** _few_ tips on how to write a formal application letter. Firstly, address your letter to the person mentioned in the job advertisement who deals **(1)** _with_ the applications. Use their surname only, after the words *Dear Mr*, *Dear Mrs* or *Dear Ms*. If, however, **(2)** _no_ name is given, *Dear Sir/Madam* is enough. Then, in the opening paragraph, which should **(3)** _be_ kept short, explain why you're **(4)** _getting_ in touch, and say where you saw the job advertised.

(5) _How_ you continue your letter will depend on the requirements of the position you're applying for. Typically, though, there are two or three paragraphs giving information about yourself, **(6)** _such_ as relevant skills, work experience and personal qualities, as **(7)** _well_ as reasons why you think you would be suitable for the job. Finally, **(8)** _after_ writing a short closing paragraph to indicate your interest in receiving a reply and thank your addressee, sign off using *Yours sincerely* if you know their name, or *Yours faithfully* if you do not.

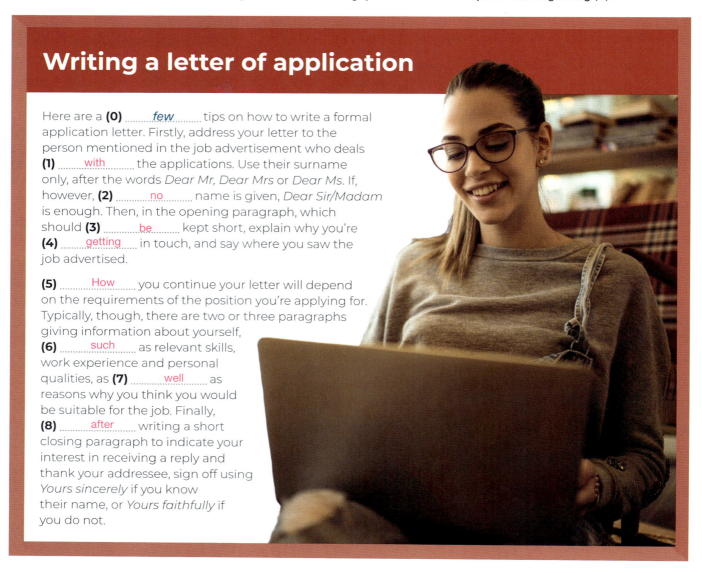

Writing Part 2 Letter of application

1 Read the following Writing Part 2 instructions.

You see the following advertisement in your local English-language newspaper.

> ### MUSICIANS AND DANCERS REQUIRED
>
> We need teaching assistants for the music and dance activities at our English-language summer school for young children.
>
> Write to the director, Mr Paul Beacon, giving details of:
> • your music and dancing skills
> • any relevant work experience you have had
> • why you would be suitable for the job.

DOING WHAT YOU HAVE TO

Lead-in

Put the students in pairs and ask them to imagine they are going to look for a new job. Ask: *What process would people normally go through?* Some groups, particularly those with younger students, may need some scaffolding for this task. You could board the following steps out of order and ask students to put them in the correct order: *look at job adverts, update your CV, write a letter of application/covering letter, go for an interview, accept a job offer*. Finish by eliciting a few things that might go wrong in this process that would prevent you from getting a job.

Reading and Use of English

1-2 Students discuss the question in pairs and then skim the text to check their answers. Get brief feedback.

3 Students read the instructions. Draw their attention to the **Don't forget!** box. Remind students that the type of gapped words are either grammatical (*prepositions, auxiliary verbs,* etc) or lexico-grammatical (*phrasal verbs, linkers,* etc). If you think your students will find this task difficult, you could give them the answers out of order. Finish by asking students if they learnt anything useful from the article.

Writing

1 This writing section continues with the topic of letters of application, introduced in the Part 2 Open cloze task. Ask students to read the task and think about what they would include in their letter. Conduct brief open class feedback.

Teaching tip

If possible, encourage your students to type up their writing and send it to you by email. This has a number of advantages. First of all, student writing is much harder to misplace – every teacher's nightmare! It also allows you to create an individual file on your computer for each student where you can save their corrected writing. This becomes a sort of writing portfolio that you can easily refer to and check in which areas each student is (or isn't) progressing. Finally, it makes the feedback process much smoother and faster, because students can easily respond to comments you've made in the document and send it back to you. Another good option is asking students to share a document with you via Google Docs or another similar programme.

Extra activity

Open cloze tasks are relatively simple for students to create themselves. For homework, ask students to find a short text on the internet related to the topic of work — about job interviews, for instance. Point out that it's OK to take a short section of a longer article. Give students a handout with a sample Part 2 task and a few simple rules:

- The text should be around 150 words.
- Take out eight individual words and number the gaps.
- Two words can't be gapped in a single sentence.
- Only gap words you could put back in yourself.
- Don't forget an answer key!

Have the students send their tasks to you by email. Print them out for the next lesson. These student-created tasks could be done in class periodically as warmers, fillers or fast finisher activities.

DOING WHAT YOU HAVE TO

2 Students read the model answer and think about the questions on their own before comparing their ideas with a classmate.

3 This exercise gives students useful practice distinguishing between formal and informal registers, as well as providing students with some useful language for formal letters. Point out that formal letters are highly formulaic, so when students write their own letter at home or in class, it's fine to borrow phrases from this model text or the one in the **Ready for Writing** section on 194–195.

4 Focus students' attention on the **How to go about it** box. Note this could be adapted into a checklist for the students to complete along with their writing, e.g. *Are the ideas organised into logical paragraphs? Is the letter written in a formal style?* When the students have chosen which task they would like to do, give them five minutes to plan their letters. Circulate and give advice as needed.

Sample answer

Dear Mr Kennedy

I have seen your advertisement in the last edition of 'English News' and I would like to apply for the post of volunteer at the pop and rock festival.

After reading the advertisement, I think I have the relevent experience to work at the festival. I am in my first year in the university where, I study music. I play guitar, violin and drums and I am also a member of a rock band that last year my friends and I created.

Furthermore, I have some experience to work with people because I used to have a job as waitress in a busy music café. I enjoyed meeting different people and helping the public in general, and I learned a lot in this position.

I would love to have the opportunity to volunteer at the pop and rock festival. I feel I would be well-suited to this role and I would like to help other people enjoy music as I do. Finally, I believe I would learn a lot from hearing different band stiles and this would benefit my study.

Thank you for your interest. I look forward to hearing from you.

Yours sincerely,

Claudia Diallo

199 words

Examiner comments

Content: All the content is relevant. The central paragraphs provide full information on the writer's relationship with music, relevant work experience and how she would benefit from volunteering.

Communicative achievement: The conventions of formal letters of application are used effectively. The register is appropriately formal for this application, and the letter would have a positive effect on the reader.

Organisation: *The letter is well organised with suitable paragraphs and an adequate range of cohesive devices, including linking words and expressions (After reading the advertisement; Furthermore; Finally), referencing (in this position; this would benefit my study) and substitution (as I do).*

Language: There is a good range of appropriate expressions and vocabulary for the task (e.g. *I would like to apply for the post of; I would love to have the opportunity to volunteer; I feel I would be well-suited to this role*). Punctuation and minor spelling mistakes do not distract the reader (*relevent; where, I study; stiles*) and grammatical errors do not obscure meaning (*I have some experience to work (of working) with people; work as (a) waitress; my study (studies)*)

Mark: Very good pass

DOING WHAT YOU HAVE TO 5

2 Read the letter of application for the job advertised in Exercise 1. Then answer the following questions.

1 Do you think the applicant would be suitable for the job? Why/Why not?
2 How well does the applicant follow the advice in the Open cloze text on page 70? What, if anything, should she change in her letter?

The applicant follows the advice well, except for the way she addresses the director and signs off. She should change Dear Mr Paul Beacon *to* Dear Mr Beacon, *and sign off with* Yours sincerely *instead of* Yours faithfully.

Dear Mr Paul Beacon

(1) ~~I've had a look at~~ [I have seen] your advertisement in the latest edition of 'English Weekly' and (2) ~~I want to ask~~ [I would like to apply] for a job as a music and dance teacher at your summer school.

I am a twenty-year-old music student in my second year at university and can play several instruments, including the piano, violin and clarinet. (3) ~~I've also been going to~~ [I have also been attending] a local dance academy for the past twelve years and am a member of a modern dance group called 'Pasos'.

Although (4) ~~I've never done any jobs~~ [I have no experience] working with groups of children, I teach piano and violin to (5) ~~quite a lot~~ [a number] of young private students. In addition, I choreograph many of the dances for 'Pasos' and teach the steps to the other members of the group.

I feel I would be (6) ~~really good at this job~~ [well-suited to], as I am a very calm and patient person. My whole life is devoted to music and dance and (7) ~~it'd be great to get~~ [I would love to have] the opportunity to pass on my skills to other people.

Thank you for taking the time to consider this application. (8) ~~Can't wait to hear~~ [I look forward to hearing] from you.

Yours faithfully

Sandra Agar

---

3 Replace the informal words and expressions (1–8) in Exercise 2 with the more formal equivalents in the box.

> a number   I have also been attending   I have no experience   I have seen
> I look forward to hearing   I would like to apply   I would love to have   well-suited to

4 Write an answer to one of the following Writing Part 2 questions in 140–190 words.

1 You see the following advertisement in your local English-language newspaper:

ARE YOU A MUSIC FAN?

We require English-speaking volunteers to help at a four-day international pop and rock music festival aimed at raising money for charity.

What relevant music-related interests do you have?
Do you have experience of working with people?
How would you benefit from helping at this event?

Write to Mr Liam Kennedy at *Music for Life* explaining why you would be suitable as a volunteer.

Write your letter of application in 140–190 words.

2 You see the following advertisement on your college noticeboard:
Write a letter to Ms Kate Rider, giving details of:
- your experience of working with animals
- why you would be suitable as a volunteer
- how you would benefit from this experience.

For more information on writing letters of application, see **pages 194–195**.

How to go about it

- Plan your answer, noting down any ideas which you could develop in your letter.
- Organise your ideas into logical paragraphs.
- Write your letter in a formal style, following the advice in the Open cloze text on page 70.
- Use a variety of linking devices.
- Check your work for grammar and spelling mistakes.

Brayton Animal Rescue Centre

Saving abandoned dogs and cats

We are looking for animal-loving volunteers to help out this summer in our busy rescue centre. Duties include cleaning cages, walking dogs and other general animal care tasks.

5 DOING WHAT YOU HAVE TO

Speaking Part 3 Collaborative task

Don't forget!
> Interact with your partner: ask them questions, respond to their answers and give your own opinions.
> In task 2 you do not have to agree with your partner.

1 **SPEAK** Here are some people who have to follow rules in certain situations and a question for you to discuss. Talk to each other about why it is important for the people in these situations to follow rules.

2 In which situation is it hardest to make sure the people follow the rules?

Useful language

It is important/essential/necessary for them to follow/obey the rules, otherwise …
The rules are designed/intended to …
If they break the rules, they will/might (not) …
Look again at the Useful language box on page 40.

3 Go to the Additional materials on page 199 and do the Speaking Part 4 task.

Reading and Use of English Part 7 Multiple matching

1 You are going to read an article in which four people talk about school rules. For questions 1–10, choose from the people (A–D). The people may be chosen more than once.

Which person states the following?

I fail to understand the reason for a rule at my child's school.	1 C
Something which was forbidden at the school before is actively encouraged now.	2 A
School rules serve to prepare young people for the future.	3 D
I disagree with the element of choice offered to my child.	4 B
I did not realise that I had accepted a rule at my child's school.	5 C
School rules were clearer and easier to understand when I was at school.	6 B
Some school rules affected my ability to study.	7 A
There has been a decline in standards of behaviour at my child's school.	8 D
I was angry at the way my child was made to feel.	9 C
I was discouraged from voicing my opinion on a rule at my child's school.	10 B

Don't forget!
- Read all the statements first, underlining key words.
- Read section A and match any statements you can. Underline the relevant parts of the text as you do so.
- Do the same for the other three sections.
- Scan the whole text again to find information which relates to any remaining statements you have not yet matched.

2 **SPEAK** Work in groups. Discuss these questions, giving reasons for your opinions.
1 Which of the school rules mentioned in the text do you find the most surprising?
2 Do you think pupils should be involved in deciding what the school rules are?
3 Should parents be asked to sign a school rules document?

DOING WHAT YOU HAVE TO 5

Speaking

1-2 Elicit what students remember about this task. Focus first on the **Don't forget!** box and then the **Useful language** one. Remind students that using this type of 'good' language will help them sound more natural — and improve their marks — on the day of the exam. Give the students time to write down a few sentences about the topic using the useful language, which they can then try to insert as naturally as possible into their conversations.

3 Direct students to the **Additional Materials** section on page 199 (see below).

Reading and Use of English

1 Put the students in groups and ask them to brainstorm some typical school rules. Elicit a few examples. Ask the students: *Do you think these are good rules? Why/Why not?* Students read the instructions and the **Don't forget!** box. Elicit the meaning of *lenient* in the title, as well as *forbidden* and *discouraged* in statements 2 and 10, respectively. Allow students time to check their answers in pairs and justify their answers. Go over the answers with the whole class.

2 Before discussing the questions, give students a couple of minutes in pairs to write at least one more question about the topic of school rules for another pair to discuss. While the students talk in pairs, circulate and make note of any examples of good language or common errors you would like to address later on the board.

UNIT 5

Speaking Part 4 Further discussion

SPEAK Following on from your discussion in the Part 3 task on page 72, discuss these questions with your partner. Give reasons for your answers.

1 Do/Did you disagree with any of the rules at your secondary school?
2 Should teachers be allowed to impose strict punishments on pupils who break the rules?
3 Some people think parents give teenagers too much freedom nowadays. Do you agree?
4 What should be done to reduce the number of accidents on the roads?
5 Do you think it is ever justified to break the rules?
6 Do you think sport would be more interesting to watch if there were fewer rules?

Go back to **page 72**.

5 DOING WHAT YOU HAVE TO

READY FOR GRAMMAR

5 Obligation, necessity and permission

Obligation and Necessity

1 *Must* is used:
   a for strong obligations imposed by the speaker (internal obligation). The speaker uses *must* to express his/her authority.
   *You **must be** here by 8 am. (manager to employee)*
   b to give strong advice.
   *It's a great film. You really **must go** and see it.*
   c to tell oneself what is necessary.
   *I **must remember** to phone Roger.*
   d in signs and notices indicating rules and laws.
   *Competition entries **must be submitted** by email.*

2 *Must not* or *mustn't* is used:
   a to talk about something that is not permitted.
   *Passengers **must not smoke** on the aircraft.*
   b to give strong advice.
   *You **mustn't work** too hard. You'll make yourself ill.*

3 *Must* does not have a past or future form. *Have to* is used instead.
   *We **had to write** a formal email in the exam.*
   *I don't have any money; I'**ll have to pay** you tomorrow.*

4 *Must* is possible in questions; *have to* is more common.
   ***Must you wear** that horrible dress?*
   *What do we **have to do** for homework?*

5 *Have to* can also be used to express obligation, particularly when this is imposed by someone else or by external circumstances (external obligation).
   *I **have to be** at work by 8 o'clock. The boss will get angry if I'm late. (employee to a friend)*
   *We **have to pull down** the window blinds in summer; otherwise it gets too hot in the flat.*
   Don't have to expresses a lack of obligation.
   *I'm glad I **don't have to wear** a suit. It's so hot today.*

6 *Need to* is used to express necessity.
   *Can we go to the baker's? I **need to get** some bread.*
   Don't need to/needn't express a lack of necessity.
   *We **don't need to/needn't** leave yet. It's only 2 o'clock.*
   Some speakers prefer to use *needn't* when giving permission not to do something (internal obligation):
   *You **needn't eat** the potatoes but you must eat the meat.*
   However, *don't need to* and *don't have to* are also possible here.
   To talk about general necessity (and not just one occasion) *don't need to* is preferred.
   *You **don't need to have** a degree to get a decent job.*
   A lack of necessity can also be expressed using the structure *there is/was no need (for someone)* + infinitive with *to*.
   ***There's no need (for you) to come** shopping with me; I can do it on my own.*

7 *Needn't have* + past participle is used to talk about an action which was unnecessary, but was performed.
   *I **needn't have prepared** so much food for the party; everyone had eaten before they came. (I prepared lots of food but realised afterwards that it wasn't necessary.)*
   Didn't need to + infinitive is also used to talk about an action which was unnecessary, but usually indicates that the action was not performed.
   *I **didn't need to prepare** much food for the party; everyone said they would bring something to eat. (I didn't prepare lots of food as I knew it wasn't necessary.)*

8 *Should* and *shouldn't* are used to express obligation or give advice. *Ought (not) to* has the same meaning.
   *You **ought to/should see** a doctor about your backache.*
   *If you're on a diet you **shouldn't eat** so much bread.*
   Should(n't) and *Ought (not) to* can also be used to say what we think is the right thing to do.
   *We **ought to/should do** more to help the environment.*
   In the negative, *I don't think you should* is more usual than *I think you shouldn't*.
   *I **don't think you should** buy that – it's too expensive.*

9 *Be supposed to* is used to talk about what should be done because of a rule or because it is expected.
   *Come on, it's 10 o' clock. You'**re supposed to be** in bed!*
   Had better + infinitive without *to* often implies a warning of possible negative consequences if the advice or precaution is not taken. The negative is *had better not*.
   *We'**d better not eat** it – it might be poisonous.*
   *You'**d better wear** a hat. I don't want you to get a cold.*

Permission

1 To express permission it is possible to use *can, may* (more formal) or *be allowed to*. In the negative these express lack of permission, or prohibition.
   *You **can have** a drink but you **can't have** any crisps.*
   *We **aren't allowed to go** out of school at lunchtime.*
   Could and *was/were allowed to* are possible for general permission in the past.
   *In my last job we **could wear** what we wanted to.*
   Could is not used when referring to a particular situation in the past. Only *was/were allowed to* is possible.
   *I **was allowed to stay** up late last night.*
   In the negative, however, *couldn't* is possible.
   *I **wasn't allowed to/couldn't stay** up late last night.*

2 *Let* and *make* are followed by the infinitive without *to*.
   Let is used to express permission or prohibition.
   *My dad doesn't/won't **let me watch** that programme.*
   Let is not normally used in the passive. *Be allowed to* is used instead.
   *I **wasn't allowed to go** to the party on my own.*
   Make is used to express obligation.
   *The teacher **made her do** some extra homework.*
   In the passive, *make* is followed by the infinitive with *to*.
   *He **was made to pay** for the window he had broken.*

HAVE SCHOOLS BECOME TOO LENIENT?

DOING WHAT YOU HAVE TO

We asked parents to compare their school rules with those of their children.

A SIMON

When I was at school – more years ago than I care to remember – far too much emphasis was placed on what we could and couldn't do, and sometimes this got in the way of learning. We had to wear our jacket and tie at all times, no matter what the temperature, and I remember sitting there in the height of summer, sweating profusely as I battled with algebra or struggled with French verb forms.

They didn't let us drink water in the classroom either. That would cause an outrage now. My daughter goes to the same school as I did, and we're asked to provide her with a refillable bottle, which she can take into class with her. They've realised that water improves concentration, so pupils almost *have* to drink it now.

B JENNY

At my son David's school, rule number one of their two-page Mobile Phone Policy states that 'pupils are strongly advised not to bring mobile phones to school'; then there are sixteen more rules describing situations in which they can and cannot be used. It's very confusing – it would be much simpler just to ban them altogether. That's what my old school would have done if mobile phones had been around then. Everything was black and white in those days, just like our school tie.

And that's another thing – David doesn't have to wear a tie if he doesn't want to, even though it's part of the uniform. That's just silly. I almost wrote to the school about it, but my son advised me against it. It seems that school rules are decided on jointly by students and teachers, and as a parent, I don't have any say in the matter.

C LUCY

My sixteen-year-old daughter isn't allowed to wear a nose stud to school on health and safety grounds. Can you believe it? According to the headteacher, in a busy school piercings present 'a very real risk of accidents'. I can't see why – they're no more dangerous than carrying a sharpened pencil in your pocket, and there's no rule against that, as far as I know. I used to wear earrings to school and never had any problems.

It seems I agreed to all this when I signed the school rules document at the beginning of last term, but I honestly wasn't aware of any ban on tiny metal objects in the nose. We were given a couple of warnings, but I was still furious when they made her take the stud out and sent her home for the day: they humiliated her in front of her classmates and there's no excuse for that.

D ANDREW

It's gone from one extreme to the other. When I was a lad, we weren't allowed to have shoulder-length hair at school. The headteacher cut it off in his office if we did, without so much as a phone call home. Now my boy mustn't have his hair cut too short, otherwise he'll be suspended until it grows back to 'a suitable length'. He thinks it's unfair, but ultimately all rules, whatever they are, help to maintain order and get children ready for the real world.

As a lawyer, I don't need to be convinced of their importance – they're part of my daily life. If anything, they should tighten the rules up a bit more at my son's place. Discipline there has gone downhill in the last few years and the kids seem to do what they want.

5 DOING WHAT YOU HAVE TO

Language focus Obligation, necessity and permission

1 Complete the second sentence so that it has a similar meaning to the first sentence, using the word in capital letters. Use between two and five words, including the word in capital letters, which you must not change.

1. It was compulsory to wear our jacket and tie at all times.
   HAD
   We _____*had to wear*_____ our jacket and tie at all times. (**A**)

2. We were not allowed to drink water in the classroom.
   LET
   They _____*didn't/did not let us drink*_____ water in the classroom. (**A**)

3. David is not obliged to wear a tie if he doesn't want to.
   HAVE
   David _____*doesn't/does not have to*_____ wear a tie if he doesn't want to. (**B**)

4. They don't let my sixteen-year-old daughter wear a nose stud to school.
   ALLOWED
   My sixteen-year-old daughter _____*isn't/is not allowed to wear*_____ a nose stud to school. (**C**)

5. She was made to remove the stud.
   TAKE
   They _____*made her take*_____ the stud out. (**C**)

6. I'm a lawyer, so it isn't necessary for anyone to convince me of their importance.
   NEED
   As a lawyer, I _____*don't/do not need to be*_____ convinced of their importance. (**D**)

2 Check your answers to Exercise 1 in *Have schools become too lenient?* The letters in brackets refer to the relevant sections of the text in which the answers can be found.

3 Correct the mistakes in the following sentences.
1. Children were ~~let~~ *allowed* to leave school at the age of twelve when my grandparents were younger.
2. My English teacher wears formal clothes in class, but she ~~mustn't~~ *doesn't have to* – she could wear jeans and a T-shirt if she wanted to.
3. When my parents were at school, they ~~must wore~~ *had to wear* a uniform, including a hat.
4. We ^*are* supposed to get homework after every English class, but it doesn't always happen.
5. Parents in my country ~~must~~ *have* to pay for their children's schoolbooks, but I don't think that's fair.
6. It's my view that schools should ~~to~~ provide all pupils with a tablet to use in class.
7. Children in schools used to be made ^*to* stand in the corner with a book on their head if they misbehaved.
8. I needn't ~~to~~ read the Grammar reference on page 214; I already know this area of grammar inside out.

4 SPEAK Work in pairs. Discuss how true the sentences in Exercise 3 are for you or the people mentioned.

5 Go to **Ready for Grammar** on **page 214** for rules, explanations and further practice.

6 SPEAK Talk about the things you *have to/are supposed to* do, or *ought to/should* do and those things you *don't have to* or *aren't allowed to* do at:
- home
- school/college/work
- the weekend.

I ought to tidy my room more often, but I never seem to find the time. I don't have to clean it, though. Either my mum or my dad does that for me.

DOING WHAT YOU HAVE TO   5

Language focus

1-2 Make a note of where students are weakest, and then focus on these aspects during the lesson.

3-4 When you correct this exercise as a class, elicit and/or teach the rules for how (semi-)modal verbs are used to express *obligation, necessity* and *permission* (see TB73).

5 Decide whether your students need more controlled practice with the grammar in the Ready for Grammar section on page 214 (see TB73 and below).

6 Monitor and provide on-the-spot error correction if students use the target language unsuccessfully.

READY FOR GRAMMAR

5 Obligation, necessity and permission

1 Complete the sentences with a pair of words from the box.

> can/can't   ~~can/must~~   can/should   can't/must
> needn't/must   shouldn't/must

0 A: Is it OK If I go to London with my friends at the weekend, Mum?
B: You __can__ go if you want to, but you __must__ phone me when you get there.

1 A: Are you sure it's OK to come in here?
B: Well, we __shouldn't__ really be here, but I __must__ just show you this.

2 A: Could I borrow an atlas?
B: Well, you __can__ certainly have a look at it here, but you __can't__ take it home with you, I'm afraid.

3 A: Do I have to write a date on this piece of work?
B: No, you __needn't__ write the date, but you __must__ remember to put your name.

4 A: Could I take the dog for a walk?
B: Yes, of course you __can__, but I think you __should__ wear your boots, don't you? It's very wet outside.

5 A: My parents won't let me go and see that film.
B: Well, if you __can't__ see it now, you __must__ try and see it when you're older.

2 Complete each gap with either *didn't need to* or *needn't have* and the correct form of the verb in brackets. There is an example at the beginning (0).

0 I wrote 250 words in my essay but realised later that the word limit was only 180.
I __needn't have written__ (write) so much.

1 What a waste of time! I __needn't have revised__ (revise) 16th-century European history; none of it appeared in the exam.

2 We __didn't need to pay__ (pay) for a babysitter for Zack last night; my parents looked after him at their house.

3 I was a bit concerned that my mum wouldn't like the earrings I'd bought her, but I __needn't have worried__ (worry) – she wears them every day.

4 I took an umbrella with me on holiday, but I __needn't have bothered__ (bother) – it didn't rain one single day.

5 It's a public holiday here today so I __didn't need to set__ (set) my alarm last night. I got up at 11.30 this morning!

3 Read the advertisement from an international magazine. Then complete Tim's email with the words in the box.

COMPETITION

Why not enter our exciting new writing competition?

The rules are simple: just write a story in no more than 600 words on any theme you like, and you could win a tablet.

Send us your entry* by email no later than 31st January. The winning story will appear in the March edition of *Your English*.

*Entrants must be at least 16 years old.

> better   don't have to   have to   mustn't
> need   ought   should   supposed to

To: Elisa
Sent: 6th January
Subject: Writing competition

Hi Elisa

Do you remember that writing competition I told you about? Well, my teacher suggested I (1) __should__ go in for it, so I think I will. I reckon the hardest thing for me will be the fact that you (2) __mustn't__ write more than 600 words. Once I start writing I just can't stop, so I'll (3) __need__ to control myself if I want to keep within the limit.

The good thing is you (4) __don't have to__ write about any specific topic – you can choose that yourself. But I think I (5) __ought__ to write about something I'm familiar with, don't you? I could base it around a fishing trip or a tennis match. The only problem is you're (6) __supposed to__ be at least sixteen to enter. My birthday's not until 4th February, but it would be a bit mean of them not to accept my entry, wouldn't it?

I (7) __have to__ send it in by the end of the month, so I'd (8) __better__ start writing soon, as I'm going skiing on the 19th.

Wish me luck!

Tim

Go back to **page 74**.

DOING WHAT YOU HAVE TO

Listening

1 Students discuss the question in pairs. Conduct brief open class feedback. Be careful not to be too judgemental or culturally insensitive if your students say they don't do any housework!

2 **5.1** Students read the instructions and the information in the **How to go about it** box. Circulate while the students read the questions and encourage them to underline key words. Elicit the meaning of *chore* (questions 6 and 7). In open class, you could quickly elicit the key words that students underlined for each item. Go over the answers in open class. (See answers highlighted in the **Audioscript** below)

3 During feedback, try to find at least one student who agrees and one who disagrees. Ask them to justify their opinions and respond to at least one of their classmate's points.

Extra activity

Elicit the chores in the photos in open class. In groups, students brainstorm 10 more. They then order them from the one they least mind doing to the one they absolutely hate doing, negotiating to reach a decision.

AUDIOSCRIPT

Listening Part 4 Multiple choice

5.2

I = Interviewer D = Deborah Chilton

I: Few of us would admit to actually enjoying doing the housework, so trying to ensure our teenage children do their fair share is no easy task. Deborah Chilton, the author of a new parenting book, *The Stress-Free Guide to Bringing up Teenagers*, is here to give us a few pointers. Deborah, where do we start?

D: Well, as you say, it's not easy, but being aware of what we're trying to achieve and why, is key in all this. [Ex 2 Q1] Getting teenagers to contribute to housework has so many benefits. It's an ideal way of teaching them what it means to belong to a family and a community. They also learn to take on more responsibility as they approach adulthood, and they pick up some useful skills on the way, too. Knowing all this motivates and encourages parents to see their goals through.

I: Right. And at what age should teenagers begin helping out with the housework?

D: Long before they reach adolescence. Teenagers are naturally resistant to being told what to do, and suddenly asking them at fourteen or fifteen to take on chores when they've never done anything to help before – well, let's just say it doesn't meet with a very positive reaction. [Ex 2 Q2] Parents often fail to take advantage of the fact that young children are quite happy to make their bed, tidy their room, lay the table or wash the dishes. So get them started early and you'll find it easier later on.

I: And what sort of things can teenagers do?

D: Cleaning, washing, ironing. Anything, really. Planning and cooking a meal each week is excellent training, and teaches teenagers how much time and effort goes into putting food on the table. Whatever they do, just [Ex 2 Q3] be sure to explain to them carefully how to do it first. My son once almost tried to wash the toaster in the sink while it was still plugged in!

I: Oh dear!

D: Yes. Teenagers will make mistakes, and that's part of the learning process. But it's best to try and avoid them before they actually happen.

I: Indeed. And what if your teenage son or daughter decides not to do a chore? What then?

D: Well, it's a good idea to make their contribution something that's important to *them* as well. That way, [Ex 2 Q4] if it's not done, they're the ones to suffer. So for example, if they don't do the washing, they won't have clean clothes for a party; if they don't do the shopping, they can't eat. They'll get the idea eventually.

I: So you wouldn't consider threatening them with punishments?

D: Only as a last resort. Punishments tend to cause bad feeling and resentment and can worsen the situation. If things don't get better, sit down together and [Ex 2 Q5] remind them of their duty to other family members and the need to work as a team. And for the same reasons, don't give financial rewards for completing chores. Housework is an obligation, rather than a choice, and no one gets paid for doing it.

I: Hmm. If only we did! So, housework has to be done, and that's it.

D: Yes, but there's still room for some negotiation. Understandably, teenagers like to feel they have at least some say in the matter. [Ex 2 Q6] So whilst the chore itself is not negotiable, when it is carried out might be. In fact, rather than say to your teenage child 'could you load the dishwasher?'– to which they could answer 'no' – ask them instead 'would you like to load the dishwasher before or after the film?' That way there's an element of choice, and the job gets done sooner or later.

I: Very clever. I like that.

D: Yes, and I would just like to say, that although domestic [Ex 2 Q7] duties can be a pain, they can also be a welcome distraction. Teenagers generally have a lot on their minds, whether it's schoolwork, friendship problems or boyfriend/girlfriend issues. Vacuuming the carpet, cutting the grass and cleaning the car provide an alternative focus and help take a teenager's mind off his or her daily concerns.

I: Certainly. And that's a very positive note to finish on.

DOING WHAT YOU HAVE TO 5

Listening Part 4 Multiple choice

1 **SPEAK** Work in groups. Do you think teenagers should be expected to help with the housework? Why/Why not?

2 ▶ 5.2 You will hear an interview with a writer called Deborah Chilton, who is talking about teenagers and housework. For questions 1–7, choose the best answer (A, B or C).

> **How to go about it**
> - As you read through the seven questions (or sentence beginnings), underline key words. This will help focus your attention on the relevant information when you listen to the recording. Questions **1** and **2** have been done for you.
> - The first time you listen to the interview, put a mark next to the option you think is correct. Listen carefully the second time before making your decision.

1 Deborah says it is <u>important</u> for <u>parents</u> to <u>understand</u>
   - (A) the different reasons for making teenagers do housework.
   - B how difficult it is to get teenagers to do housework.
   - C the advantages for the whole family of teenagers doing housework.

2 According to Deborah, what is the <u>mistake</u> that many <u>parents make</u>?
   - A They expect their children to do too many chores.
   - B They tell rather than ask their children to do chores.
   - (C) They wait too long before giving their children chores.

3 Deborah says that parents should give teenagers
   - A help when cooking a meal.
   - (B) clear instructions for tasks.
   - C more than one task a week.

4 According to Deborah, what should parents do if a teenager fails to do a chore?
   - A prevent the teenager from going out
   - B give the teenager extra chores to do
   - (C) let the teenager face the consequences

5 What does Deborah recommend parents should do if the situation does not improve?
   - (A) appeal to the teenager's sense of responsibility
   - B stop payment of the teenager's pocket money
   - C allow the teenager to choose an alternative chore

6 Which aspect of a chore does Deborah feel a teenager could decide?
   - A the type of chore
   - (B) the timing of the chore
   - C the method of doing the chore

7 Deborah says a positive feature of household chores is that
   - A they can be fun if they are done with help from other people.
   - (B) they give teenagers something different to think about.
   - C they are very varied.

3 **SPEAK** Work in pairs. Do you agree that teenagers should not be paid for doing household chores? Why/Why not?

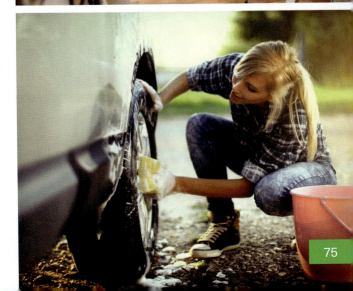

75

5 DOING WHAT YOU HAVE TO

Word formation *en-* prefix and *-en* suffix

1 Complete the extracts from the listening by adding the prefix *en-* or the suffix *-en* to the words in brackets to form verbs. Make any other necessary changes to the words.

   1 Trying to __ensure__ (*sure*) our teenage children do their fair share is no easy task.
   2 Knowing all this motivates and __encourages__ (*courage*) parents to see their goals through.
   3 So you wouldn't consider __threatening__ (*threat*) them with punishments?
   4 Punishments tend to cause bad feeling and resentment and can __worsen__ (*worse*) the situation.

2 Check your answers in the Audioscript on pages 238–239.

3 Write the verbs formed from the following adjectives. You will first need to form the noun before adding the *-en* suffix.

   a strong — strengthen
   b long — lengthen
   c high — heighten

4 In 1–5, use the word in brackets to form a word that fits the gap.

   1 Do you agree that travel __broadens__ (*broad*) **the mind** and __widens__ (*wide*) **our horizons**?
   2 Some people say that zoos are important because they __enable__ (*able*) us to learn about animals, and also help to protect __endangered__ (*danger*) **species**, those animals which might otherwise become extinct. What do you think?
   3 If you had to choose, would you __lengthen__ (*long*) **the working/school day** and go to work/school one day fewer each week, or __shorten__ (*short*) it and go one day more? Why?
   4 What do you think is the best way to __enlarge__ (*large*) your English vocabulary?
   5 Which of the following **problems** have __worsened__ (*worse*) in recent years in your country and which have improved? Is enough being done to solve them?
   football violence   crime   unemployment   pollution

5 **SPEAK** Work in groups. Discuss the questions in Exercise 4.

Writing Part 1 Essay

1 **SPEAK** Work in pairs. Read the following Writing Part 1 instructions. How would you answer the essay question and what could you say for each of the three 'Things to write about' in the Notes?

In your English class you have been talking about the world of work. Your English teacher has asked you to write an essay.

Write an essay using **all** the notes and giving reasons for your point of view.

It is better to work at home than in an office. Do you agree?
Notes
Things to write about:
1 contact with people
2 working hours
3 .... (your own idea)

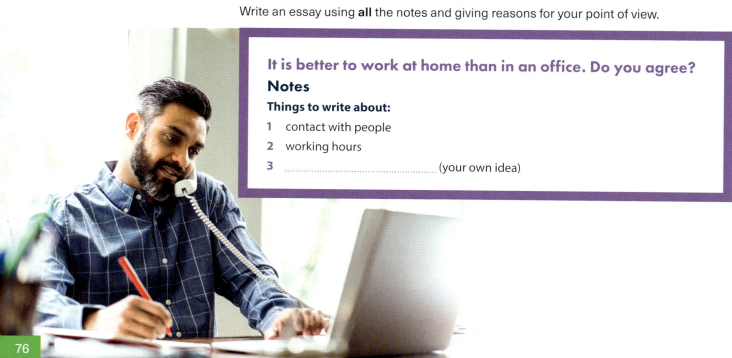

DOING WHAT YOU HAVE TO

Word formation

1 Note that *en-* as prefix is often added to verbs to make them transitive, as in the case of *ensure* and *encourage*. As a suffix, it often used to form verbs from adjectives, e.g. *worsen*, or from nouns, e.g. *strengthen*.

2 This could be made into a game by challenging pairs of students to find the sentences in the **Audioscript** on pages 238–239 (see TB75) and correct their answers as fast as they can. Once one pair of students finishes, everyone stops. The winning pair comes up to the board and corrects the exercise in open class.

3 This exercise demonstrates that, apart from adding affixes, word formation often involves making internal changes to words.

4-5 Make sure to leave time for the students to discuss the questions after they have been corrected. In general, students are much more likely to remember new words if they engage with them meaningfully, in this case by answering questions that include the new vocabulary.

Writing

1 You could turn the question, *Is it better to work at home or in an office?* into a lead-in by writing or projecting it on the board. After discussing some of their ideas in pairs, you could get a bit of feedback in open class before asking the students to look at the task and think about how to answer it.

Teaching tip

It's a good idea to raise students' awareness of the variety of words that can be formed from the same word stem, e.g. *compete, competition, competitor*, etc. A good fast finisher task (or filler) is to choose a few stem words from whatever exercise the students are doing in class and asking them to write down all of the different forms of the root word. Plurals and negatives count!

Extra activity

Particularly for essays, it is crucial to learn how to write effective topic sentences. Here are a couple of ideas for working on this important subskill.

1 Once students have come up with some ideas for their essay based on an exam task, such as the one in Exercise 4 on page 77, invite students to organise their ideas into paragraphs. They then try to summarise each paragraph in one sentence. These are topic sentences. Their ideas will be the examples in the paragraph, so a typical topic sentence might be: *There are a number of differences in the way young people are educated today than in the past.*

2 Another approach to topic sentences, from the opposite direction, is to erase them from a model answer to an essay, such as the ones found in the **Answer key** of *Ready for B2 First*. Tell students to read the rest of the paragraph and write a topic sentence. Remind the students that a topic sentence is a summary of the main ideas in the paragraph.

5 DOING WHAT YOU HAVE TO

2 Students read the instructions and discuss the questions in pairs. Note that this essay could be improved in a number of ways. Take the time to go through each issue and elicit ideas for specific improvements. If time allows, ask students to rewrite this essay together with a partner during the lesson.

3 Tell students that once they are finished with a piece of writing, they should take five minutes to proofread it in order to avoid problems with spelling and other silly little mistakes. Note that spelling is not specifically penalised on the *B2 First* exam, but spelling errors can sometimes confuse the reader and impede communication. Remind students that American spelling is perfectly acceptable, but they will need to be consistent and avoid spelling the same word more than one way.

4 Students read the instructions and the **Don't forget!** box. Note that this information could be adapted into a checklist, e.g. *Does the essay include a suitable introduction and conclusion?* The final writing could be done in class (timed, 40 minutes) or set for homework. Encourage the students to consult pages 189–191 in the **Ready for Writing** section for further advice on essay writing.

Sample answer

Is life harder for young people now than in the past?

The quality of young people's lives is much better than, for example, one hundred years ago, but these improvements have also brought complications.

On the one hand, today's younger generation has far more free time, during which there are numerous activities to choose from. What's more, in their holidays many young people travel abroad, something that earlier generations could only dream. In addition, not all children used to have access to education, and many left school with twelve or thirteen years, whereas nowadays, over half of school leavers go to university. Finally, regarding work, workers have more rights and technology has made many jobs much easier.

On the other hand, this technology has also caused that fewer people are needed for jobs which are now carried out by machines, so many young people only have more free time because they are unemployed. To make matters worse, because everyone has an education, there is more competition for these jobs, so it is even harder to find good, challenging work.

In my opinion, life was hard in the past for young people because they had fewer opportunities, but now the problems are different and life is more complicated.

207 words

Examiner's comments

Content: All content is relevant and the target reader is fully informed. Having established the time frame, comparing now with one hundred years ago, the writer presents a balanced argument. The essay focuses first on how life has improved in all three areas, namely, education, work, and the student's own idea, free time, and contrasts this with the negative effects of these improvements. The opinion in the final paragraph reflects this duality by suggesting that whilst there are more opportunities than in the past, life is consequently more complicated now.

Communicative achievement: The conventions of writing an essay are used successfully to hold the reader's attention. There is a clear essay structure with an opening statement, two paragraphs contrasting ways in which life is both easier and harder now than in the past, and a concluding paragraph expressing the writer's opinion.

Straightforward and more complex ideas are communicated, making a clear link between improvements made in society and corresponding hardships (e.g. *… because everyone has an education, there is more competition for these jobs, so it is even harder to find good, challenging work.*)

The essay is written in a consistently neutral register with some more formal language to introduce ideas (*On the one hand; On the other hand; In my opinion*).

Organisation: The essay is well organised and coherent. There is a clear overall structure and ideas are linked effectively both within and between paragraphs using a range of linking words and expressions (*What's more; In addition; To make matters worse*), relative clauses (*jobs which are now carried out by machines*) paraphrasing (*young people; today's younger generation; children; school leavers*), pronouns and determiners (*this technology; these jobs*).

Language: There is a range of vocabulary relevant to the topic (*today's younger generation; have access to education; workers have more rights; jobs … carried out by machines; competition for … jobs; challenging work; fewer opportunities*).

A range of simple and complex grammatical forms is used with a good degree of control, including passives (*fewer people are needed for jobs, which are now carried out by machines*), comparatives and infinitives (*during which there are numerous activities to choose from; it is even harder to find good, challenging work*).

Errors are minor and minimal, and usually occur when more ambitious language is attempted (*something that earlier generations could only dream; with twelve or thirteen years; has also caused that fewer people are needed*).

Mark: Very good pass.

DOING WHAT YOU HAVE TO 5

2 SPEAK Read the answer below to the essay question in Exercise 1 and discuss the following questions with your partner. Give examples from the answer.
a How well has the writer addressed the three points in the Notes?
b How varied is the writer's language?
c How appropriate is the style?
d Does the writer use appropriate linking devices?

> No, I don't agree. I'd prefer to work in an ~~ofice~~ [office].
> If you work at home you can't talk to anyone – ~~their's~~ [there's] only you and the computer. No one else. It's not very ~~helthy~~ [healthy] if you can't talk to people during the day. You don't hear other people's ideas and ~~oppinions~~ [opinions] and you get a bit ~~lonley~~ [lonely] with just the computer to talk to. You might talk to somebody on the phone but it's not the same.
> OK, if ~~your~~ [you're] at home and you don't have contact with ~~poople~~ [people], no one can talk to you and disturb you, so you do more work. So it's better to work at home if you just want to work all the time. But talking to people makes life more ~~intresting~~ [interesting] and it's pretty boring just working all the time. I think so, anyway.
> Anyway, maybe you don't ~~realy~~ [really] have many working hours at home, because you have loads of coffee ~~brakes~~ [breaks] and no one tells you, 'Come on, do some work'.
> So for all these reasons, my own idea is that it is better to work in an ofice than at home.

2
a The writer has dedicated most of the essay to the first point: *contact with people*. Little has been said about *working hours* and in the last paragraph, the writer has misinterpreted what is meant by *your own idea*: the third point in Writing Part 1 questions invites students to write about a third aspect of the essay question.

b The language is repetitive, with the result that some of the writer's ideas are not expressed very coherently. In the second paragraph alone, *talk to* is used four times; there are two more examples in the third paragraph, where *work(ing) all the time* is also repeated.

c The style is too informal, too conversational for an essay. As well as contractions (*I'd, can't, it's,* etc.) there are a number of informal words such as *OK, really, loads of, a bit (lonely)* and *pretty (boring)*. Short sentences such as *No one else* and *I think so, anyway* are also very conversational and an example of poor organisation of ideas.

d There is evidence of linking, but again this is often informal and limited to *if* (four times), *so* (three times), *but* (twice), *anyway* (twice) and even *OK*.

3 There are ten spelling mistakes in the answer above. Find the mistakes and correct them.

4 Now write an essay in 140–190 words on one of the following:
a Write your own answer to the question in **1** above.
(b) Write an answer to the following question.

In your English class you have been talking about the pressures that exist for young people nowadays. Your English teacher has asked you to write an essay.

Write an essay using **all** the notes and giving reasons for your point of view.

> **Life is harder for young people now than in the past.**
> **What do you think?**
> **Notes**
> **Things to write about:**
> 1 education
> 2 work
> 3 .... (your own idea)

Don't forget!
- Plan your essay. Consider all three points in the Notes.
- Write in a consistently formal or neutral style.
- Organise your ideas using paragraphs and linking devices.
- Include a suitable introduction and conclusion.
- Use a range of language and avoid repetition.
- Check your answer for accuracy.

For more information on writing essays, see **pages 189–191**.

5 REVIEW

Reading and Use of English Part 3 Word formation

For questions 1–8, read the text below. Use the word given in capitals at the end of some of the lines to form a word that fits in the space in the same line. There is an example at the beginning (0).

Boarding schools

Boarding schools are **(0)** _RESIDENTIAL_ schools that provide students with accommodation and food as well as education. The initial separation from the family can be a traumatic experience, and not **(1)** _surprisingly_, homesickness is a fairly common problem. However, **(2)** _supporters_ of boarding schools believe that this type of education **(3)** _encourages_ a sense of discipline and responsibility; children are taught to follow a strict daily routine and obey a clear set of rules, but they are also forced to make many **(4)** _decisions_ on their own, which leads to greater independence and increased self-confidence. In addition, spending long periods of time in the company of other boarders **(5)** _enables_ children to form close friendships and helps in the **(6)** _development_ of communication and social skills. Many parents also argue that boarding can **(7)** _strengthen_ family ties; living away from home often **(8)** _heightens_ a child's appreciation of precious time spent with the family, and teenage anger can be directed at teachers rather than parents.

RESIDENT
SURPRISE
SUPPORT
COURAGE

DECIDE

ABLE
DEVELOP
STRONG
HIGH

Reading and Use of English Part 1 Multiple-choice cloze

For questions 1–8, read the text below and decide which answer (A, B, C or D) best fits each gap. There is an example at the beginning (0).

Summer jobs FOR STUDENTS

Long summer holidays are an important **(0)** _C_ of any college or university **(1)** _D_ course. They provide you with an excellent opportunity to **(2)** _A_ practical experience in a working environment, enhance your CV and, of course, make some extra money to **(3)** _C_ a holiday or save for your future. There are numerous summer jobs available, some more satisfying than others, but most teaching valuable lessons about hard **(4)** _C_ and responsibility.

If you enjoy working with children, then you might be **(5)** _C_ to one of the many roles at a summer camp, including activity leaders, sports coaches or teachers. Food and accommodation are usually provided, so it's a great **(6)** _B_ to discover a new region, or even country. Stewarding and bar jobs at the many music festivals taking **(7)** _B_ in the summer may offer similar benefits, as well as free **(8)** _D_, so you can see your favourite bands and get paid, too.
Click here for information on a variety of vacancies, both in this country and abroad.

0	A piece	B area	C part	D section
1	A career	B title	C grade	D degree
2	A gain	B win	C earn	D reach
3	A pay	B spend	C fund	D cost
4	A task	B job	C work	D duty
5	A fitted	B applied	C suited	D employed
6	A plan	B way	C interest	D ability
7	A hold	B place	C stage	D show
8	A ticket	B pass	C permit	D entry

REVIEW 5

Language focus Obligation, necessity and permission

Underline the correct alternative to complete the sentences.

1 We won't be busy tomorrow, so you mustn't/can't/<u>needn't</u>/haven't come in to work if you don't want to.
2 I think we should/<u>ought</u>/must/could to phone Elisa and ask her if she wants to come.
3 I love the fact that I don't start work until ten, so I shouldn't/ought not/<u>don't have</u>/am not supposed to get up early.
4 On a 'Non-uniform Day' we're let/made/supposed/<u>allowed</u> to wear casual clothes to school if we want.
5 I'd prefer to walk to work today but I'd <u>better not</u>/rather not/ought not/cannot; I might get there late.
6 Where have you been? You were allowed/agreed/promised/<u>supposed</u> to be here half an hour ago!
7 The rules are very clear. You know you don't have to/don't need to/needn't/<u>mustn't</u> wear jewellery to school.
8 I was ill last Thursday so I could/<u>had to</u>/might/ought to hand in my homework the next day.

Reading and Use of English Part 4 Key word transformation

For questions 1–6, complete the second sentence so that it has a similar meaning to the first sentence, using the word given. Do not change the word given. You must use between two and five words, including the word given.

1 When I was younger I wasn't allowed to watch much television.
   LET
   When I was younger my parents <u>wouldn't/would not or didn't/did not let me watch</u> much television.

2 Paula had to wash up before she could go out.
   MADE
   Paula <u>was made to</u> wash up before she could go out.

3 Why can't we go to the party?
   ALLOWED
   Why <u>aren't we allowed to or are we not allowed to</u> go to the party?

4 You don't need to hand in the homework until next week.
   NEED
   There is <u>no need for you to</u> hand in the homework until next week.

5 I think you should see a doctor.
   BETTER
   I think you <u>had/'d better see</u> a doctor.

6 Do you know what our homework is?
   SUPPOSED
   Do you know what <u>we are/we're supposed to</u> do for homework?

Writing Part 2 Report

The school where you learn English has decided to improve its language learning facilities. You have been asked to write a report for the Principal, describing the current facilities and making suggestions for improvements. Report on the classrooms and the library and anything else you think is important.

Write your report in 140–190 words.

For more information on writing reports, see **page 196**.
Please go to the Teacher's Resource Centre for a Sample answer with Examiner comments for this Writing task.

5 DOING WHAT YOU HAVE TO

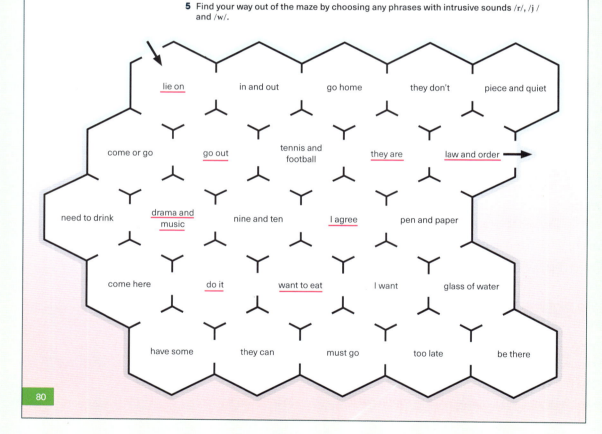

Pronunciation

1-2 ▶ **5.3** Note that in most of England, Wales, Australia and New Zealand, people don't pronounce the /r/ after vowels at the end of words like *car* or *chore*. But if you always pronounce the /r/ sound in such words, as people do in most parts of Ireland, Scotland and North America, /r/ is always present and therefore not intrusive.

3 Students do the exercise individually and then check in pairs.

4 ▶ **5.4** Suggest first practising the two words with the intrusive sound in isolation before practising the whole sentence.

5 Organise the students into groups for this last activity. Monitor their pronunciation of the intrusive sounds.

6 RELATIVE RELATIONSHIPS

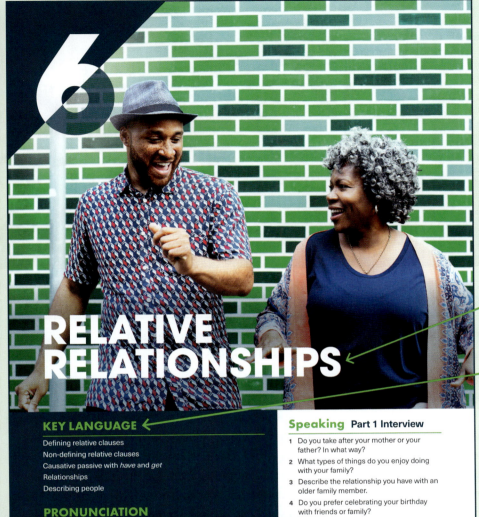

KEY LANGUAGE

Defining relative clauses
Non-defining relative clauses
Causative passive with *have* and *get*
Relationships
Describing people

PRONUNCIATION

Connected speech: final consonant and initial vowel

EXAM PRACTICE

Reading and Use of English Parts 1, 3, 4 & 5
Writing Part 2
Listening Parts 1 & 3
Speaking Parts 1, 3 & 4

Speaking Part 1 Interview

1. Do you take after your mother or your father? In what way?
2. What types of things do you enjoy doing with your family?
3. Describe the relationship you have with an older family member.
4. Do you prefer celebrating your birthday with friends or family?
5. Do you spend most of your free time on your own or with friends?
6. What do you like most about your best friend?

This unit is about our relationships with our friends and family, and the reading, writing, listening and speaking tasks all touch on different aspects of this topic. Students will also look at vocabulary related to describing people.

Read the unit objectives to the class.

SPEAKING Part 1 Interview

Focus students on the photo and ask: *What do you think the relationship is between these people? Why?* Have the students imagine these two people are their friends or family members. In pairs, ask them to discuss how they would describe the two people in terms of their personality and physical appearance to someone who has never met them before.

For Speaking Part 1, remind the students to 'show what you know'— that is, use more interesting or more sophisticated language when the opportunity arises. Give two example responses to the first question:

a) *Both my mother and I are tall. We have dark hair.*
b) *I would say I resemble my mother more than my father. We are both quite tall and have wavy, dark hair, though my mother is starting to go grey.*

Check the meaning of *take after* before inviting students to discuss the questions with a classmate. Circulate and make note of any good examples of interesting or sophisticated language used by the students during their conversations. Then share these examples in open class and elicit anything else the students said that they were particularly proud of.

ONLINE MATERIALS

Useful phrases cards (**Teacher's Resource Centre**)
Definitions (**Teacher's Resource Centre**)
Unit 6 Test (**Test Generator**)
Unit 6 Wordlist (**Teacher's Resource Centre**)
Unit 6 On-the-go-practice (**App**)

6 RELATIVE RELATIONSHIPS

Vocabulary Relationships

1 SPEAK Work in pairs. What do you think are the key ingredients of:
  a a good friendship?   b a successful marriage?

2 Look at these sentences about a woman called Amy. Match a sentence beginning 1–6 with an ending a–f.

1 Nobody in the office **gets** — a **out of** patience with her, too, and wants to move out.
2 Even Joe, the cleaner, **fell** — b **up** trying to be friendly; Amy hardly speaks to her.
3 Her flatmate, Mia, has **run** — c **on with** Amy. She's just so unpleasant to work with.
4 Mia told me she had **given** — d **out** their problems, but they'll argue just as much.
5 And her boyfriend's **split** — e **out with** her. Amy said he always left her desk untidy.
6 They'll say they've **sorted** — f **up with** her again – but they'll get back together soon.

3 Write the infinitive of each of the phrasal verbs from Exercise 2 next to its meaning.

1 end a romantic relationship with someone   _split up with_
2 have a good relationship with someone   _get on with_
3 stop doing something you are trying hard to do   _give up_
4 use all of something and not have any left   _run out of_
5 deal with a problem successfully   _sort out_
6 stop being friendly with someone after a disagreement   _fall out with_

4 SPEAK Study the sentences in Exercise 2 then cover up the endings a–f. Take turns with your partner to read out the beginnings 1–6 and complete the sentences from memory.

5 Use the context in these sentences to help you work out the meaning of the phrasal verbs in bold.

1 After Leo's parents died, his aunt **brought** him **up** as if he were her own son.
2 I was born in England but I **grew up** in France; I lived in Paris until I was 18.
3 Parents need great patience to be able to **put up with** teenagers' changing moods.
4 Amy cried when her dad **told** her **off** for breaking a glass; he sounded very angry.
5 My mum is my role model. I **look up to** her because of her kindness and tolerance.
6 Tim's parents felt he had **let** them **down**. He'd repaid their generosity by stealing from them.

6 Write five sentences, each containing one of the phrasal verbs from Exercises 2 and 5. Leave spaces where the phrasal verbs should be.

7 Ask your partner to complete the sentences with the correct phrasal verbs.

RELATIVE RELATIONSHIPS 6

Lead-in

Invite students to write a poem of at least five lines with the title 'A Good Friend'. (Note that in English everything except for prepositions, articles and coordinating conjunctions is capitalised in titles, which may not be the case in the students' L1.) Each line of the poem starts with *A good friend …* The lines don't have to rhyme. Model a couple of lines on the board. For example:

A Good Friend

A good friend always calls you on your birthday.

A good friend is someone who you can trust.

…

Tell the students not to copy your sentences! They work on their poems individually. Stop them when everyone has written five or more lines. Then put students into small groups and have them share their poems. In open class, elicit a few of the lines they liked best.

Vocabulary

1 If you do the lead-in above, focus the students on the key ingredients of a successful marriage. Get brief feedback.

2–3 Tell students they are going to look at some common phrasal verbs related to relationships. Students do the matching individually and then compare their answers with a partner. You could correct this by asking one pair to read the full sentence, with Student A reading the first half and Student B reading the second half. Exercise 3 could be done in open class or in pairs. Remind the students about the pronunciation rule for phrasal verbs (see the **Teaching tip** on TB8).

4 Students do the activity as suggested.

5 Give the students a minute to read the sentences on their own before discussing them with a classmate. In open class, elicit the meaning of the phrasal verbs and put synonyms or short definitions for each on the board. Alternatively, you could have students look up the words in monolingual dictionaries or on *www.macmillandictionary.com* if mobile phones are allowed.

Answers

1 take care of a child until he or she becomes an adult
2 change from being a baby or young child to being an older child or adult
3 tolerate or accept unpleasant behaviour by someone without complaining
4 criticise someone angrily for doing something wrong
5 admire and respect someone
6 make someone disappointed

6–7 Make sure to check the students' sentences for accuracy in general, and for appropriate use of the phrasal verbs in particular, before they exchange them. The sentences could also be written together in pairs and then exchanged with another pair.

Teaching tip

Phrasal verbs can be daunting for students to learn and use for a couple reasons. First, their lexical meaning is often idiomatic. Second, their grammatical form can be complex, as shown in the extra activity below. So, what is important for students trying to learn and remember phrasal verbs? Here's list of best practices:

- Learn and record them by topic
- Identify context
- Learn and record them in full sentences
- Learn and study them as a single unit of meaning
- If possible, remember them with images, stories or by making a personal connection

Extra activity

Phrasal verbs can be separable or inseparable. With a separable phrasal verb, you can split the verb and the particle and put the direct object in the middle, e.g. *His aunt brought him up.* With inseparable phrasal verbs like *run out of*, you can't do this. Tell the students to find three examples of separable phrasal verbs in Exercise 5 (*bring up, tell off, let down*). Note that when the direct object is a noun, it can go after the phrasal verb or in the middle. But if it's a pronoun, it has to go in the middle. Board the following three sentences and elicit the rules:

- The teacher told the student off.
- The teacher told off the student.
- The teacher told her off.

TB82

RELATIVE RELATIONSHIPS

Speaking

1-3 Ask the students: *What are some common problems people have with their friends and family? What causes them?* Discuss in open class. These tasks could be done either in pairs or in groups of three. Circulate and make note of any interesting emergent language to board and analyse after the activity. You may wish to use the **Useful phrases cards** on the Teacher's Resource Centre as a lead-in or as an extension to this section.

Listening

1 ▶ 6.1 Students read the task instructions and the **Don't forget!** box. Encourage your students to try listening for the cause of the problem, and once they hear it, choosing the closest option, instead of trying to keep all of the options in mind while they listen.

2 Students discuss the question in groups.

Speaking Part 4 Further discussion

SPEAK Following on from your discussion in the Part 3 task on page 83, discuss these questions with your partner. Give reasons for your answers.

1 Would you prefer to share a flat with friends, or live with your parents?
2 What do you think is the ideal number of brothers and sisters to have?
3 Is it possible to get on well with people who have very different opinions from us?
4 Some people say that being a parent is the hardest job in the world. Do you agree?
5 Should all schools be mixed-gender, with both boys and girls, or is single-sex education better?
6 Some companies allow their employees to work at home on one or more days of the week. Do you think this is a good idea?

Go back to **page 83**.

AUDIOSCRIPT

Listening Part 3 Multiple matching

 6.1

Speaker 1 Before Paul started school, he used to come round to us every morning while his mother, Lynda – my daughter-in-law – was at work. He had almost limitless energy and at times he was rather difficult to control. We only had to look after him for four hours each day, but it completely wore us out. His mother would tell us off for letting him watch too much television – she said Paul needed to work his energy off in the park or on long walks. Easy for her to say, but we weren't getting any younger and watching television was a useful survival strategy. I remember arguing with Lynda on more than one occasion about this.

Ex 1 C

Speaker 2 I shared a flat once with someone who used to get annoyed about the silliest of things. We got on fine at the beginning, probably because we hardly ever saw each other – he had an evening job in a bar and I worked during the day in a supermarket. When I got to know him better, though, I realised just how difficult he could be. Things had to be done his way and his way alone. He was obsessive about tidiness and he couldn't bear it if I left anything lying on the floor. He'd also tell me off for cooking food that made the house smell. I had to move out in the end. I couldn't stand it.

Ex 1 B

Speaker 3 Julie was a friend as well as a colleague. I looked up to her and admired her self-belief and quiet determination. It came as no surprise when she was promoted to senior manager and I wasn't. I didn't think it was unfair or anything. She deserved it. Of course I was disappointed, but I got over it quickly enough. But Julie was now my boss and it soon became clear that she wasn't good at managing people. She bullied and shouted, and upset most people in the department, including me. To her credit, she realised she wasn't suited to the job and she asked for a transfer. But I haven't spoken to her since she left.

Ex 1 F

Speaker 4 My brother, Phil, and I always used to get on very well, despite having very different ideas and opinions about things. Recently, though, something's come between us that's changed all that. The money we inherited from our grandmother wasn't divided equally between us. She left me more because I'm married with two children and Phil's single. At least that's what she said in her will. Understandably, I suppose, Phil thinks it's a bit unfair and feels hard done by. We haven't exactly fallen out with each other, but there's certainly a tension between us that wasn't there before.

Ex 1 H

Speaker 5 We split up around about this time last year, just before he went off to India. I'd always been very tolerant and understanding – I knew how much John's work meant to him and I'd put up with the situation for as long as I could. But we both realised these long periods of separation weren't good for the relationship. Not being able to make any plans for the future inevitably caused friction, so we decided to end it. We still see each other from time to time, and it's good because there's not the same tension between us that there used to be.

Ex 1 E

RELATIVE RELATIONSHIPS

Speaking Part 3 Collaborative task

1 **SPEAK** Work in pairs. Complete the speaking tasks below. Use the Useful language box to help you. Imagine that a magazine for teenagers and young adults is going to publish a series of articles giving advice about relationships. Below are some of the relationships they want to include.

Talk to each other about what problems might arise in these relationships.

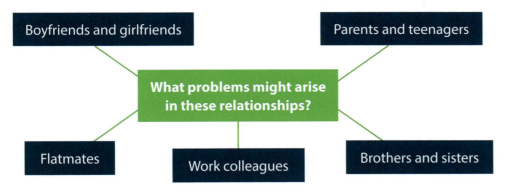

2 Now decide which two relationships teenagers and young adults would be most interested to receive advice on.

Useful language

Task 1

1 Try to use some of the phrasal verbs from the Vocabulary section on page 82.
2 **Expressions for changing topic**
Let's talk about … first/next.
Shall we move on to … now?

Task 2
This relationship is far more/less relevant to (young adults) than that one.
(Teenagers) would have great/little/no interest in reading about that.
This one would have great/limited/no appeal to (teenagers).

3 Go to the **Additional materials** on **page 199** and do the Speaking Part 4 task.

Listening Part 3 Multiple matching

1 ◯ **6.1** You will hear five short extracts in which people are talking about problems in their relationships with other people. For questions 1–5, choose from the list (A–H) what each speaker says was the cause of the problem. Use the letters only once. There are three extra letters which you do not need to use.

A the stress of working long hours
B the other person's general lack of tolerance
C having different ideas about how to keep someone occupied
D the other person's lack of self-confidence
E not having enough time together
F the other person's inability to adapt to a new role
G never having enough money
H the other person's sense of injustice

Speaker 1 **C** 1
Speaker 2 **B** 2
Speaker 3 **F** 3
Speaker 4 **H** 4
Speaker 5 **E** 5

A, D and G not used

> **Don't forget!**
> › Underline key words and phrases in the eight options.
> › Listen carefully both times before making your final decision.

2 **SPEAK** Work in groups. Which of the five speakers do you have most sympathy for? Why?

6 RELATIVE RELATIONSHIPS

Language focus Defining relative clauses

Defining relative clauses contain information which is essential for our understanding of the whole sentence.

1 Read the extract from the listening exercise and answer the questions.

*I shared a flat once with someone **who** used to get annoyed about the silliest of things. He'd also tell me off for cooking food **that** made the house smell.*

1 The words in bold are relative pronouns. What alternative pronouns can be used?
in the first sentence – *that*; in the second sentence – *which*
2 Can the relative pronoun be omitted from these two sentences? Why/Why not?
They cannot be omitted because they are the subject of the verb in the relative clause.

2 A relative pronoun has been omitted from the following sentence. Where could it be inserted and which one(s) could be used?

The money we inherited from our grandmother wasn't divided equally between us.

1 Which relative pronoun has been omitted from the extract? Where could it be inserted?
The money (that/which) we inherited from our grandmother wasn't divided equally between us.

In this sentence, the subject in the relative clause is *we*: the underlined relative pronouns (*that/which*) are the object of the verb in the relative clause. They can be omitted.

2 Why is it possible to leave the pronoun out in this case?

3 Which of these two sentences is more formal? Can the relative pronoun be omitted in either of them? The first sentence is more formal. The relative pronoun can be omitted in the second sentence but not the first.

1 The woman **to whom** I spoke had no idea what was going on.
2 The woman **who** I spoke **to** had no idea what was going on.

4 Go to Ready for Grammar on page 216 for rules, explanations and further practice.

5 Complete each of the gaps below with an appropriate relative pronoun or relative adverb. Decide if there is more than one possibility for a particular gap and whether the word(s) can be left out.

DO YOU KNOW THE NAME OF …

1 the French island __where__ Napoleon Bonaparte was born and __whose__ largest town is Ajaccio? Corsica
2 the Italian town __which/that__ is famous for its leaning tower? Pisa
3 the former Hollywood actor __who/that__ became the 40th President of the United States of America in 1981? Ronald Reagan
4 the first book __which/that/–__ JK Rowling wrote for the *Harry Potter* series? Harry Potter and the Philosopher's Stone
5 the English author __who/that__ wrote *Animal Farm* and *1984* and __whose__ real name was Eric Arthur Blair? George Orwell
6 the musical film __which/that/–__ Emma Stone starred in alongside Ryan Gosling and for __which__ she won an Oscar in 2017? La La Land
7 the celebration at the end of October during __which__ children in a number of countries dress up as creatures such as witches, ghosts and zombies? Hallow'en
8 the English singer __who/that__ has had chart success with singles such as *Castle on the Hill* and *Shape of you*, and __whose__ albums are named after mathematical symbols? Ed Sheeran

6 SPEAK Work in groups. Answer as many of the questions in Exercise 5 as you can.

7 Complete the following sentences with your own ideas.

1 A good friend is someone who …
2 I don't like people that …
3 I'd like to have a job which …
4 I'll never forget the time when …
5 I wouldn't like to live in a country where …

8 SPEAK Work in pairs. Compare your sentences from Exercise 7. Ask each other questions about what you have written.

RELATIVE RELATIONSHIPS

Language focus

1–3 Let the students work in pairs or on their own.

You could link Exercise 3 to writing by asking the students in which types of writing tested on the *B2 First* exam would you be more likely to use *to whom* (essay, report, formal letter).

4 Direct students to the **Ready for Grammar** section on pages 216–217 (see below). Use your judgment on how much time needs to be spent here before returning to page 84. Anything that isn't done in class can be set for homework or saved for revision.

5–6 If possible, project the text on the board and invite students to come up and write the answers there. The answers to the quiz could be elicited in open class. If time allows, students could be given a few minutes to find any answers they didn't know using their mobile phones, if allowed.

7–8 During this semi-free practice activity, circulate and provide on-the-spot error correction for the target language, but any other common errors can be written down and addressed in a corrective feedback stage afterwards.

You may wish to finish this section with a game of **Definitions** which can be found on the **Teacher's Resource Centre**.

READY FOR GRAMMAR

6 Defining relative clauses

Defining relative clauses contain information which is essential for our understanding of the whole sentence.

Person	who/that	The man **who/that normally comes to clean our windows** is on holiday this month.
Thing	which/that	There's only one clock **which/that works properly in this flat**!
Possession	whose	A widow is a woman **whose husband has died**.
Place	where	We bought this table in the shop **where Sam works**.
Time	when	May is the month **when most tourists visit the island**.
Reason	why	This documentary explores the reasons **why birds migrate**.

- The relative clause identifies which person, thing, place, etc. is being talked about.
- No commas are required either at the beginning or the end of the relative clause.
- *That* can be used instead of *who* for people and *which* for things, particularly in spoken English.
- *Whom* can be used instead of *who* when it is the object of a verb or comes after a preposition. It is more formal than *who*.
  *Students **for whom** English is a second language should consider taking the course.*
- The relative pronouns *who, that* and *which* can be omitted if it is the object of the verb in the relative clause.
  *I'm enjoying the book **(which/that)** you lent me.*
- The relative pronouns *who, that* and *which* cannot be omitted if it is the subject of the verb in the relative clause.
  *That's the waiter **who/that** served us last time.*
- The relative adverb *where* has the meaning 'in/at which'.
  *He lives above the shop **where** I work.*
- *When* has the meaning 'on/in which' and can be omitted or replaced by *that* in defining relative clauses.
  *Do you remember that day **(when/that)** we went to Rhyl and it snowed?*
- *Why* has the meaning 'for which' and can be omitted or replaced by *that* in defining relative clauses.
  *The reason **(why/that)** I'm phoning is to ask you for Tina's address.*

6 Defining relative clauses

1 Complete these sentences using *when, where, why* or *whose*.

1. What's the name of the place ___where___ we had that accident last year?
2. One of the reasons ___why___ people from Mediterranean countries live so long is because they eat so well.
3. I'll always remember the day ___when___ I started my first job.
4. That's the woman ___whose___ husband you spoke to on the phone.

2 Choose the correct options. Sometimes more than one option is possible.

1. Last summer, I visited a friend *she* / <u>who</u> / <u>–</u> / <u>where</u> lives in New York.
2. There's the new shop <u>where</u> / <u>–</u> / *what* / <u>which</u> I was telling you about.
3. The man *his* / <u>whose</u> / *–* / <u>who</u> house we stayed in was the local mayor.
4. I've had one of those days *which* / <u>when</u> / <u>–</u> / <u>that</u> everything goes wrong.
5. The village *which* / <u>in which</u> / <u>where</u> / *that* she grew up is now abandoned.
6. Liam is finally doing a job <u>that</u> / <u>which</u> / <u>–</u> / *where* he really enjoys.
7. There's a person in our block of flats *where* / *which* / <u>–</u> / <u>who</u> plays the violin.
8. Name a song <u>that</u> / <u>–</u> / <u>which</u> / *whose* doesn't have the word 'love' in its lyrics.

Go back to **page 84**.

6 RELATIVE RELATIONSHIPS

Reading and Use of English

1-2 Students discuss the questions and then quickly read the text. In open class, ask if any of their ideas are mentioned.

3 Allow the students time to read the instructions. Check that they understand the explanation of why *plenty* is the only correct option for the example (0). Focus their attention on the **How to go about it** box. Note that students should refer to the advice given here for items 4 and 5 while doing the task.

Extra activity

One problem with multiple-choice cloze exercises is that students are exposed to more incorrect language than correct language. After all, 75 percent of the words in the options are wrong. This can be turned into an advantage, however, by asking students to rewrite some of the sentences from the text to make the wrong answers right. This way students not only learn how to use the word in the right option better, but also how to use the three words in the wrong options as well. Here are some rewritten sentences for example gap (0):

There are a <u>number</u> of reasons why you might want to use …

There are <u>various</u> reasons why you might want to use …

There are <u>several</u> reasons why you might want to use …

Teaching tip

One good way to bring a Reading and Use of English task to life is by simply googling the topic and reading up on it a bit before the lesson. For example, when you search for 'friendship apps' you will find that there are a number of popular ones, each with a slightly different focus. One connects you with your neighbours, while another helps new mothers meet other mothers. Sharing what you learnt with your students can lead to interesting discussions. Alternatively, have the students research the topic of next class's task at home before the lesson and discuss what they learnt in class before doing the task.

RELATIVE RELATIONSHIPS

Reading and Use of English Part 1 Multiple-choice cloze

1 **SPEAK** Work in pairs. You are going to read a text about friendship apps, which put people in touch with others who want to make new friends. Why do you think increasing numbers of people are using these apps?

2 Read the text, ignoring the gaps. Which, if any, of the reasons you gave in Exercise 1 are mentioned?

3 For questions 1–8, read the text again and decide which answer (A, B, C or D) best fits each gap. There is an example at the beginning (0).

0 A various   B several   C <u>plenty</u>   D number

All four words express the idea of *more than a few*, but only *plenty* fits grammatically. Neither *various* nor *several* are followed by the preposition *of*, and whilst *a number of reasons*, with the indefinite article *a*, would be correct, *number of reasons* is not.

How to go about it

- Read through the whole text first, ignoring the gaps, to get a general idea of the content.
- When choosing an answer, look carefully at the whole sentence, not just the words immediately before and after the gap.
  This is particularly important in a question like number 5 below, where the gap requires a linking word.
- Think about meaning, grammar and collocation when making your decisions. Sometimes, two or all three of these areas will be important for a particular answer.
  For number 4 below, all three areas should be considered. For number 5, both meaning and grammar are important.

FRIENDSHIP APPS

There are **(0)** ...**C**... of reasons why you might want to use one of the many friendship apps currently **(1)** ...**B**... . You may, for example, have moved to a new city, where there is **(2)** ...**A**... nobody you know. Perhaps you're the only single person in your group and you'd **(3)** ...**C**... go to a concert with someone than spend the evening at a dinner party with cosy couples. Or maybe you just want to **(4)** ...**A**... your circle of friends – friends you actually meet up with, as opposed to those you know online.

For **(5)** ...**D**... we may have hundreds of virtual friends, many of us have just a handful of real-life ones. Whilst social media should arguably **(6)** ...**C**... some of the blame for this, supposedly causing us to lose our ability to communicate face to face, there are other factors. We're working **(7)** ...**C**... hours than ever before, with little time left over for socialising, and we're also spending more time living alone, **(8)** ...**B**... marriage in favour of the single life. No wonder friendship apps are increasingly in demand.

1 A disposable   B <u>available</u>   C enjoyable   D suitable
2 A <u>absolutely</u>   B completely   C perfectly   D entirely
3 A prefer   B better   C <u>rather</u>   D happier
4 A <u>widen</u>   B rise   C grow   D spread
5 A despite   B instead   C unless   D <u>although</u>
6 A catch   B stand   C <u>take</u>   D meet
7 A greater   B further   C <u>longer</u> D higher
8 A waiting   B <u>delaying</u> C pausing   D holding

4 **SPEAK** Work in groups. Do you agree that social media is 'causing us to lose our ability to communicate face to face'? Why/Why not?

85

RELATIVE RELATIONSHIPS

SISTERS

Clara and Silvia Petrosillo were eight and six respectively when they moved into the house next door to ours one cold December morning. I watched from the warmth of our lounge as the sisters helped their parents carry a number of items into their new home from the family car. They worked in unison, each holding on to the same box or object, moving perfectly in step with one another towards the front door without ever exchanging a single word, like a well-rehearsed dance duo. They seemed at ease in each other's company and I imagined they must spend a great deal of time together. I wasn't wrong.

At first, I was reluctant to approach the sisters, whose expressionless faces and wild, unruly hair did not particularly invite friendly overtures. And anyway, they preferred to stay in the house most of the time, so I would only really see them when Mr Petrosillo bundled them into the car in the morning to take them to school. When the evenings grew lighter, they were persuaded to play outside, but to begin with, they seemed fearful of leaving the safety of their back garden, and shyly avoided eye contact with me as I watched them from my own.

Eventually, though, the sisters showed signs of coming out of their shells. They began to venture out into the park across the road, and I seized on the opportunity to speak to them. They allowed me to join in their games, but they would converse together in earnest whispers, which made me feel excluded, and they laughed very little. To be honest, the only time they looked truly happy was when they were on their roller-skates, sailing hand-in-hand down the road, with Clara, who seemed more confident, shouting at the younger Silvia to bend her knees or straighten her back. As for me, and despite my best efforts, the Petrosillo sisters never really allowed me to get close to them. They preferred to keep themselves to themselves and do everything together, alone.

Until, that is, Harry Reynolds appeared on the scene; Clara's scene. She was seventeen, and he was seven years older, with a car, and a well-paid job in a life assurance company. Silvia appeared untroubled by this. Her face, at least, gave nothing away; but then, it never did. Clearly, though, it was the beginning of a new reality, one which quickly drove the sisters apart, and when Clara went off to study law a year later, the distance between them grew. Silvia, who left school at sixteen, took a job as a gardener with the Council, had her head shaved and acquired a large tattoo on her back. She continued to live with her parents. Meanwhile, Clara graduated and moved to London, where she eventually became a partner in an international law firm. My parents told me that the sisters spent very little time together whenever Clara came to visit.

One day last summer, Clara turned up driving a two-seater convertible. The Petrosillos' house was up for sale and she'd come to clear her old things out. I was back home as well, visiting my parents, and happened to be looking out of the lounge window, from where I could see Silvia taking out the rubbish. When she saw her sister parking, Silvia paused as though she might go out into the street to greet her. But then she turned around and went quietly back into the house.

Then one afternoon, I saw the sisters sitting on the front doorstep in what looked like embarrassed silence, putting on their old roller-skates. They skated slowly around the driveway a few times before finally going out through the front gate. They exchanged an awkward glance, then moved off down the road, gradually gathering speed. At one point, Silvia wobbled, and it looked as if she was going to fall over. But Clara held out her hand, and Silvia, after a brief hesitation, took it. As they skated on, it was, for a moment, as though nothing had changed, and the sisters were who they had once been, before life came between them.

RELATIVE RELATIONSHIPS

Lead-in

Start this lesson with a live listening activity. Tell the students about a relationship with a family member or friend that has changed over the years. (It might be nice to focus on one that has changed for the better.) Put five details from the story on the board, for example, a number, a place name, an adjective, etc. While you talk, the students listen for the words and take note of what significance they have in the story. Check in open class. Note that students often find this type of authentic listening activity very engaging. What's more, it gives students useful exposure to natural, unrehearsed spoken language.

Teaching tip

For Part 5, students should get in the habit of reading the text quickly for gist. This is an important preparatory strategy, which gets students ready for the deeper understanding of the text required to answer the multiple-choice questions correctly. It is also helpful for answering questions that require a global understanding of the text. However, a common problem is that students slow down and start trying to understand each sentence — or even every word.

You can train your students to read faster by setting strict time limits for gist reading tasks and then slowly reducing them over the course of the year. By the day of the exam, students should ideally be able to skim read at about 300 words per minute, which translates into around two minutes for a typical *B2 First* reading task. For the story on page 86, you could give them three or four minutes and see how they do.

Extra activity

Raise your students' awareness of how distractors are designed and written with the following activity. Put the following categories on the board:

i) The option contains words from the text that are near to where the answer is.
ii) They contain words that are in the text, but the overall meaning is different.
iii) The option says something that may be true but is not stated in the text.
iv) A word is used with one meaning in the text and then a different meaning in the option.

Students answer the questions in the usual way but label the wrong answers by which kind of distractor is employed (i, ii, iii, iv). Note that not every wrong answer involves a distractor. For example, the correct answer to question 1 is B. Option A could be labelled as iii; Option D, ii.

Answers

1 *A iii, D ii*
2 *A ii, D ii*
3 *A iii*
4 *A ii, D iii*
5 *A iii, B i, C i*
6 *B ii, D iii*

6 RELATIVE RELATIONSHIPS

Reading and Use of English

1 The live listening activity on TB86 would provide a good model for this task and naturally transition into it. Alternatively, you could say that you have been discussing the topic of relationships in this unit and now you'd like the students to talk specifically about one of their own.

Give the students some time to prepare. When they are ready to go, give them another minute to silently rehearse their descriptions in their heads before speaking to their partners. This will get the students thinking about not only what they want to say but how they want to say it.

2 Students read the instructions and the **Don't forget!** box. Stress the fact that they should always put down an answer, even if they have no clue. There is still a 25% chance of getting the answer right!

3 Students discuss the question in small groups.

READY FOR GRAMMAR

6 Non-defining relative clauses

Non-defining relative clauses contain information which is not essential for our understanding of the sentence. We can identify which person or thing is being talked about without the information in the relative clause.

*Their new house, **which has five bedrooms and a games room**, is much larger than their previous one.*

Commas are required both at the beginning and the end of the relative clause (except when the end of the relative clause is also the end of the sentence). *That* cannot be used in place of *who* or *which*.

- Relative pronouns and relative adverbs cannot be omitted from non-defining relative clauses.

  *Her maths teacher, **who/whom** everyone in the class adored, announced that he was leaving the school.*

- Non-defining relative clauses are more common in written English.

- *Which* can be used in non-defining relative clauses to refer to the whole of the main clause.

  *No one phoned him on his birthday, **which** made him feel rather depressed.*

Defining & non-defining relative clauses

Note the difference in meaning between the following pairs of sentences.

Non-defining: Hospital doctors, who work long hours, are well paid. (= All hospital doctors work long hours and all of them are well paid.)

Defining: Hospital doctors who work long hours are well paid. (= Only those hospital doctors who work long hours are well paid.)

Non-defining: My sister, who lives in Rye, has two sons. (= I have one sister. She lives in Rye and she has two sons.)

Defining: My sister who lives in Rye has two sons. (= I have more than one sister. The one who lives in Rye has two sons.)

Relative clauses and prepositions

1 Prepositions usually come at the end of defining and non-defining relative clauses.

   In defining relative clauses the relative pronoun is usually omitted.

   *The town I grew up **in** has changed a lot since I left.*

   In non-defining relative clauses the relative pronoun is never omitted.

   *Keith Rolf, **who** I used to work with, lives in Paris now.*

2 In more formal English, prepositions often come before the relative pronouns *whom* for people and *which* for things (in which case the pronoun cannot be omitted).

   *We shall be visiting the room **in which** Turner painted some of his greatest works.*

   *The head waiter, **to whom** we addressed our complaint, was not particularly helpful.*

RELATIVE RELATIONSHIPS

Reading and Use of English Part 5 Multiple choice

1 **SPEAK** Work in pairs. Describe a relationship with a family member or friend which has changed over the years.

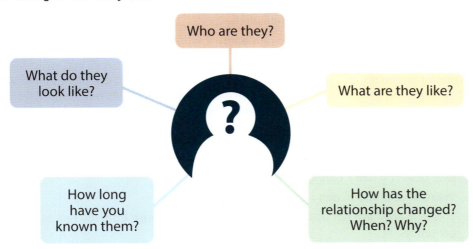

- Who are they?
- What do they look like?
- What are they like?
- How long have you known them?
- How has the relationship changed? When? Why?

2 You are going to read a short story about two sisters. For questions 1–6, choose the answer (A, B, C or D) which you think fits best according to the text.

1 What point does the writer make about the sisters in the first paragraph?
  - A They preferred not to speak to each other.
  - **B The closeness of their relationship was apparent.**
  - C They enjoyed doing the task they had been given.
  - D This was not the first time they had moved house.

2 In the second paragraph, the writer says that she
  - A was discouraged by Mr Petrosillo from playing with the sisters.
  - B was not allowed to go next door to the sisters' house.
  - **C was initially put off by the appearance of the sisters.**
  - D was nervous about inviting the sisters into her garden.

3 What is meant by 'the sisters showed signs of coming out of their shells' in lines 20–21?
  - A They looked older and more mature.
  - **B They appeared to be growing in confidence.**
  - C They made it clear that they wanted to play.
  - D They indicated that they were allowed to leave their house.

4 In the third paragraph the writer says that the Petrosillo sisters
  - A refused to let her go roller-skating with them.
  - B said some unpleasant things about her to each other.
  - **C showed little interest in her attempts at friendship.**
  - D deliberately tried to make her feel unwelcome.

5 What does *this* refer to in line 36?
  - A the age difference between Harry and Clara
  - B the fact that Harry was successful
  - C the nature of Harry's work
  - **D the fact that Clara had a boyfriend**

6 When Clara returned to her parents' house last summer, the sisters
  - **A appeared uncomfortable in each other's company.**
  - B were noticeably less proficient at roller skating.
  - C were no longer on speaking terms with each other.
  - D had trouble throwing away their old possessions.

3 **SPEAK** How do you think your life will change in the next ten years?

Don't forget!
- Read the whole story first for an overall understanding.
- For each question, eliminate the options which are clearly wrong, then check the option or options you have not eliminated.
- If you still cannot decide, choose one of the options.

RELATIVE RELATIONSHIPS

Language focus Non-defining relative clauses

1 Look at the following sentence from *Sisters*.

Silvia, who left school at sixteen, took a job as a gardener ...

This sentence contains two separate ideas.

Main idea: Silvia took a job as a gardener.

Second idea: Silvia left school at sixteen.

The information contained in the second idea is not essential to our understanding of the meaning of the main idea. A relative clause which contains non-essential information is called a non-defining relative clause.

2 Choose the correct options to complete the rules for non-defining relative clauses.

In non-defining relative clauses:

a *who* or *which* **can** / **cannot** be replaced by *that*.

b the relative pronoun **can** / **cannot** be omitted.

c commas **are** / **are not** used to separate the relative clause from the rest of the sentence.

3 Go to **Ready for Grammar** on **page 216** for rules, explanations and further practice.

Open cloze Relative clauses

1 **SPEAK** Work in pairs. How well do you know your neighbours? How often do you speak to them?

2 For questions 1–12 read the text below. Complete each of the gaps with either a relative pronoun (*who, which, that, whose*) or a relative adverb (*when, where*). If there is more than one possibility, or the word can be left out, you should also indicate this. There is an example at the beginning (0).

How well do you know the people (0) __who/that__ live in the same street, or even the same block of flats as you? Perhaps like me, you live in a large city, (1) __where__ it's easy to go unnoticed and sometimes difficult to get to know even your closest neighbours. If you do, it's very likely there's a social media site (2) __which/that__ can help.

When I moved to the area in (3) __which__ I currently live, I signed up to a website (4) __whose__ main aim is to bring communities together, to get people (5) __who/that__ live in the same neighbourhood interacting more. Thanks to this website, (6) __which__ has over one thousand users in my part of the city alone, I found a neighbour (7) __who/that/–__ I could go running with at weekends. I also got to know the recently retired owner of the local bookshop, (8) __who__ answered my request for someone to look after my dog last July, (9) __when__ I turned thirty and had a holiday abroad to celebrate.

You can also use the site to sell that bike (10) __which/that/–__ you no longer ride, advertise your services as a babysitter, announce events (11) __which/that__ are being held locally, or organise your own activities with other neighbours, like museum trips or countryside walks. You're also encouraged to share your possessions, to lend people things like ladders or tools, (12) __which__ may be expensive to buy and used only very occasionally.

3 **SPEAK** Work in groups. Do/Would you use a website like this? Why/Why not?

RELATIVE RELATIONSHIPS 6

Language focus

1. Books closed. Put the two sentences up on the board and ask concept questions to elicit the information in Exercise 1, e.g. *Does this sentence contain one or two pieces of information?* (Two) *Which is the main idea?* (That she took a job as a gardener) *Does the sentence still make sense if we take out the second piece of information?* (Yes). Note that adding a picture of a girl gardening would help bring this presentation to life.

2. You could either ask the students to open their books and answer the questions in Exercise 2 or simply continue asking questions in open class with books closed, e.g. *Can we replace this 'who' with 'that'?* (No).

3. Direct the students to the **Ready for Grammar** section on page 216 (see TB87 and below). If your students demonstrate a good understanding of the grammar by this point, you could set the **Ready for Grammar** section for homework and move onto the cloze task.

Open cloze Relative clauses

1. You may need to check the meaning of *neighbour* before asking the students to discuss the question in pairs. Conduct brief feedback. Note that students are often exposed to both British and American spelling but don't always know which one is which. Point out that for words like *neighbour*, *colour*, *humour*, *flavour*, etc. the American spelling is the shorter one without 'u'.

2. This exercise aims to give students further practice with relative pronouns in an exam task where they are quite often tested, Reading and Use of English Part 2.

3. Students discuss the question in pairs. You could link this to the prior discussion of friendship apps on page 85.

READY FOR GRAMMAR

6 Non-defining relative clauses

1. For 1–5, link the ideas contained in the two sentences to form one sentence. Use an appropriate relative pronoun (*who*, *which*, *whose*) or relative adverb (*when*, *where*) and make any other necessary changes. Don't forget to add commas.

    0. Main idea: This photograph shows the royal family on the palace balcony.
       Second idea: This photograph was taken in 1919.
       This photograph, which was taken in 1919, shows the royal family on the palace balcony.

    1. Main idea: We spent the weekend in York.
       Second idea: My mother was born in York.
       We spent the weekend in York, where my mother was born.

    2. Main idea: My best friend has just got married.
       Second idea: My best friend always said she wanted to stay single.
       My best friend, who always said she wanted to stay single, has just got married.

    3. Main idea: My oldest sister lives in Munich.
       Second idea: My oldest sister's husband is German.
       My oldest sister, whose husband is German, lives in Munich.

    4. Main idea: The best time to visit Iceland is in summer.
       Second idea: The average temperature in Iceland in summer is around ten degrees.
       The best time to visit Iceland is in summer, when the average temperature is around ten degrees.

    5. Main idea: He has to work on Saturdays.
       Second idea: He isn't very happy about the fact that he has to work on Saturdays.
       He has to work on Saturdays, which he isn't very happy about.

2. Decide whether the relative clause in each of the following sentences is defining or non-defining. If the relative clause is non-defining, add commas in the appropriate place(s). If it is defining, say whether the relative pronoun or adverb can be omitted or not. There are two examples at the beginning (0 and 00).

    0. My father who works in a chocolate factory never eats sweet things.
       My father, who works in a chocolate factory, never eats sweet things. Non-defining.

    00. There'll be a prize for the student who tells the most jokes in 5 minutes.
        Defining – the relative pronoun who *cannot be omitted.*

    1. Lady Gaga, whose real name is Stefani Joanne Angelina Germanotta, was born on March 28 1986.
       Non-defining (the name itself defines the person)

    2. What's the name of the village where you got married?
       Defining – *where* cannot be omitted

    3. He hasn't given me back the book that I lent him.
       Defining – *that* can be omitted

    4. She told me that Vasilis had failed his driving test, which didn't surprise me at all.
       Non-defining – *which* refers to the whole clause

    5. That song always reminds me of the time when I was working in Brazil.
       Defining – *when* can be omitted

    6. He's the only person in this class whose first name begins with 'Z'.
       Defining – *whose* cannot be omitted

    7. Emma received a phone call from her Managing Director, who had been impressed by her sales performance. Non-defining – she has, we assume, only one Managing Director

    8. Few written records have survived so it is a period of history about which we know very little.
       Defining – *which* cannot be omitted as it follows a preposition. The sentence could be changed to: *Few written records have survived so it is a period of history which we know very little about.* In this case, *which* could be omitted

    Go back to **page 88**.

RELATIVE RELATIONSHIPS

Lead-in

Show the class a photo of a friend or family member. Ask the students to speculate about his or her personality. Then say what the person is really like, using at least a couple of the personality adjectives from Exercise 1, e.g. *He is a bit stubborn. It's hard to convince him to change his mind about anything.*

Vocabulary

1 Check the pronunciation of *reserved* /rɪˈzɜːvd/, *enthusiastic* /ɪnˌθjuːziˈæstɪk/ and *passionate* /ˈpæʃənət/. Note that the pairs of adjectives in this exercise don't sound quite right the other way around. Collocating word pairs like these are common in English: *black and white*, *kind and helpful*, *nice and easy*, etc.

2-3 This could be done in pairs or up on the board in open class. Check the pronunciation of *patient* /ˈpeɪʃnt/ and *sociable* /ˈsəʊʃəbl/. Note that *mature* has two common pronunciations: /məˈtʃʊə(r)/ and /məˈtjʊə(r)/. In these cases, teach the one that sounds most natural to you. Be careful with *sensitive*, which is a false friend in several European languages. Note that this exercise is a revision of words the students have seen in the Word formation section on page 24.

It's also worth mentioning here that prefixes are not usually stressed unless to express contrast, e.g. *I wouldn't call him a patient person. I think he's pretty IMpatient, actually.*

4 Monitor the students' use and pronunciation of the target language, providing on-the-spot error correction.

5 Pre-teach *complexion*. While going over the answers with the class, take a bit of extra time and explain how the odd word out is used, e.g. *We wouldn't say someone has bald hair. We would just say he's bald.*

6 At B2 level, it's good to start raising students' awareness of the positive or negative connotations of certain words.

Answers

1 All the adjectives describe weighing too much.
Fat has negative connotations in many parts of the world.
Plump is more positive and can mean either weighing a little too much or can be used as a 'polite' way of describing someone who is fat.
Overweight is descriptive and of the three, is the most neutral.

2 All of the adjectives describe not weighing too much.
Thin means having little fat on the body; it is descriptive and neutral.
Slim means being attractively thin and has positive connotations.
Skinny means being unattractively thin and has negative connotations.

7 While students describe the pictures, monitor their use and pronunciation of the vocabulary for describing people.

Extra activity

Backs to the Board is classic game in ELT for good reason. It's not only fun and effective in terms of practising vocabulary, but it also requires students to produce a lot of language.

The game is usually played by having one student sit with their back to board, hence the name. The other students explain a word or phrase written on the board that the student in the chair can't see. However, there are lots of other variations. For example, it can be done in teams, with more than one student guessing the same word or two different words (so they can't copy each other). Or in reverse, with two or three students describing a word that the rest of class has to guess. Or with all the words on the board and the students playing in pairs (the student guessing has to turn their chair around so they can't look).

There are lots of ways to tweak familiar activities in order to keep them fresh.

AUDIOSCRIPT

Listening Part 1 Multiple choice

▶ 6.2

W = Woman   M = Man   G = Girl

1 You hear a woman on the radio talking about her father.
W: I always got on very well with my mother. I felt I could turn to her for advice, share confidences with her, because she understood my problems. With my father it was different. I found it difficult to talk to him, and when we did speak you could feel the tension between us. I think it was partly because [Ex 1 Q1] I take after him so much – I inherited my lack of confidence from him for one thing – and I blamed him for my own weaknesses.

2 You overhear a man talking about a former teacher.
M: After the first lesson we all thought he was a bit mad. But he was just different. Most of the other teachers in the school were really serious and uninspiring. They'd speak, we'd take notes and that was about it. It was deadly dull. But Hilton-Dennis would jump around the room, waving his arms about and jabbering away in Italian at us. He seemed to really enjoy what he was doing, and [Ex 1 Q2] I took to him almost straight away. He managed to communicate his passion for the subject and he got a lot of people interested in learning the language.

3 You hear a woman complaining about one of her employees.
W: I'm going to have to have a word with Simon again. If it's not one thing, it's another.
M: Is Simon the scruffy one?

TB89

RELATIVE RELATIONSHIPS

Vocabulary Describing people

1 Some adjectives for describing personality are often used in combination with others which have a similar or related meaning. Complete the combinations in sentences 1–8 with the words from the box.

cheerful enthusiastic generous inconsiderate reserved respectful ~~sincere~~ stubborn

1. An **honest and** _sincere_ politician, Ruth Jackson says what she means and means what she says.
2. Make it clear to the interviewer that you are **passionate and** _enthusiastic_ about the job, that you couldn't imagine doing anything else.
3. Our upstairs neighbours are **selfish and** _inconsiderate_. They play loud music late into the night without a thought for anyone else.
4. We place a high value on good manners at this school, and expect pupils to be **polite and** _respectful_ towards each other at all times.
5. Lily is always so **friendly and** _cheerful_; she has a permanent smile on her face when she talks to you.
6. They were such a **kind and** _generous_ host family; they took me everywhere and paid for everything.
7. There's nothing wrong with being **shy and** _reserved_; introverts are just as important as extroverts.
8. This is the tale of a **proud and** _stubborn_ king, who would listen to no one's advice but his own.

2 Put the words in the box below in the correct column (*im-*, *in-* or *un-*) in the table to form negative adjectives. Then check your answers in Exercise 3 on page 24.

~~ambitious~~ decisive mature patient reliable tolerant

im-	in-	un-
immature	indecisive	*unambitious*
impatient	intolerant	unreliable
immodest	insensitive	unimaginative
impolite	insincere	unsociable

3 Now add these words to the table in Exercise 2.

imaginative modest polite sociable sensitive sincere

4 **SPEAK** Work in pairs. Think of two people you know, for example a relative and a friend, and describe what these people are like, using the adjectives you have just studied to help you.

5 One adjective in each group is not normally used before the noun in capital letters. Cross out the adjective which does not fit.

1. flowing   scruffy   ~~bald~~*   shoulder-length   straight   curly   **HAIR**
2. dark   hazel   sparkling almond-shaped   piercing   ~~pierced~~ **EYES**
3. wrinkled freckled ~~thinning~~ round   tanned   expressive **FACE**
4. smooth   pale   dark   healthy   ~~well-built~~ spotty **COMPLEXION**

* We can say *he is bald* but not *he has bald hair*.

6 What is the difference between the words in each of the following groups?

1. fat / plump / overweight   2. thin / slim / skinny

7 **SPEAK** Work in pairs. Take it in turns to compare two people in the photographs and say which you would prefer to meet and why. As well as describing their physical appearance and clothes, you should also speculate about their personality.

6 RELATIVE RELATIONSHIPS

Listening Part 1 Multiple choice

▶ **6.2** You will hear people talking in eight different situations. For questions 1–8, choose the best answer (A, B or C).

1 You hear a woman on the radio talking about her father.
   What does she say about him?
   A He was not very talkative.
   (B) He was very similar to her.
   C He was very sure of himself.

2 You overhear a man talking about a former teacher.
   What does the man say about the teacher?
   A His teaching style was boring.
   B His behaviour was distracting.
   (C) His enthusiasm was contagious.

3 You hear a woman complaining about one of her employees.
   What is she complaining about?
   A his untidy appearance
   (B) his poor punctuality
   C his impolite behaviour

4 You hear part of a radio programme in which a man is giving advice.
   Who is he giving advice to?
   (A) parents
   B teachers
   C teenagers

5 You hear two people talking about a friend. What do they agree about her?
   A She is impatient.
   (B) She is indecisive.
   C She is bad-tempered.

6 You hear a girl talking about her tennis coach.
   How does she feel about his coaching methods?
   A pleased with the importance he gives to fitness
   B impressed by the encouragement he gives to players
   (C) grateful for the individual attention he gives to her

7 You hear a man and a woman talking about a person in a photograph.
   Who is the person in the photograph?
   (A) the man's sister
   B the man's mother
   C the man's daughter

8 You hear an elderly woman talking to a man about her new neighbours.
   What does she like about them?
   A They are often away at weekends.
   (B) They have been very friendly.
   C They look after their garden.

Language focus Causative passive with *have* and *get*

1 Complete the extracts from the listening with the correct form of the verb in brackets.

   Extract 4: ... they want **to have their nose** ___pierced___ (*pierce*) or **get a tattoo** ___done___ (*do*).

   Extract 7: She**'s had it** ___framed___ (*frame*) and it's up on the wall in her living room.

2 Check your answers in the relevant extracts of the **Audioscript** on **pages 239–240**. What form of the verb does each of your answers have? *the past participle*

3 In 1 and 2 explain the difference in meaning between the two sentences a and b.
   1 a He's repaired the car. *He repaired the car himself.*
      b He's had the car repaired. *Someone/A mechanic repaired it for him.*
   2 a He cut his hair. *He cut his own hair.*
      b He got his hair cut. *Someone/A hairdresser cut it for him.*

4 Go to **Ready for Grammar** on **page 218** for rules, explanations and further practice.

RELATIVE RELATIONSHIPS

Listening

▶ **6.2** Start by having students describe the photos in pairs. Then, while reading the questions, ask them to associate the question with one or more of the pictures. Get brief feedback. Remind the students about a few of the tips from the **What to expect in the exam** box on page 52. Encourage them to underline key words in the question or stem.

Language focus

1-2 If you have the students check their answers in the Audioscript (see TB89 and below), remind them they only need to read 4 and 7.

3 Draw a stick figure of a man and a car, or display a picture, to help bring the presentation to life. Ask concept questions, e.g. *Is the car fixed in both sentences?* (Yes) *Who actually did the work on the car in a?* (The man) *And in b?* (Probably a mechanic) *Did the man arrange with the garage to have them fix the car?* (Most likely yes).

4 Direct the students to the **Ready for Grammar** section on page 218 (see TB91). If your students have demonstrated a good grasp of the grammar, set Exercise 1 for homework and go directly to Exercise 2.

AUDIOSCRIPT continued

W: Yes, he is. That's not what worries me, though. He doesn't have any contact with the public, so I don't mind what he looks like.

M: So has he been rude again?

W: No, we managed to sort that one out. I took him aside a couple of months ago and had a long talk with him. He's been quite pleasant since then. But **Ex 1 Q3** I need reliable people who turn up on time and he's been late for work three times this last fortnight. I'm beginning to regret taking him on.

4 You hear part of a radio programme in which a man is giving advice.

M: Unfortunately, there's not always a direct relationship between hard work and good performance at school. Think how demotivating it must be for a young person to spend hours on homework and then get low marks for their trouble. Something like that can seriously affect their self-esteem and their confidence. So they may look for other ways to feel good about themselves. Let's **Ex 1 Q4** imagine they come to you and say they want to have their nose pierced or get a tattoo done. Would you let them? Maybe not, but perhaps you should at least consider their motives for wanting to do so.

5 You hear two people talking about a friend.

W: I've asked Lucy to choose a restaurant to go to for her birthday.

M: Oof! Good luck with that. You know how long it **Ex 1 Q5** takes her to come to a decision on anything.

W: I know. She never seems to be able to make up her mind. And then she wonders why we all lose our patience with her.

M: It might be better just to book a place yourself and tell her where we're going.

W: Well, yeah, but that's a bit unfair. It's her birthday, after all. She might get upset.

M: Lucy? No. When have you ever seen her in a bad mood?

W: True. Perhaps you're right.

6 You hear a girl talking about her tennis coach.

G: Like all coaches, he's got his good and bad points. **Ex 1 Q6** I like the fact that he comes over and corrects me if he sees I'm doing something wrong, like the way I hold the racket or hit the ball. I appreciate that, it's really helpful. But I guess he can come across as a bit aggressive sometimes. He gets angry and shouts a lot if he thinks you're not trying. That doesn't bother me too much – he just wants to get the best out of us. But I don't see why we have to spend ten minutes at the beginning of each session running round the tennis court. It's important to be fit, but we could do all that in our own time.

7 You hear a man and a woman talking about a person in a photograph.

W: It's a lovely photo. She looks so relaxed and cheerful – as if she's really enjoying it all.

Ex 1 Q7 M: Yeah, it's my mum's favourite. She's had it framed and it's up on the wall in her living room. She was starting to think she might never see her daughter in a wedding dress, so it's got pride of place above the telly. Beth doesn't like it though.

W: Why not?

M: She says you can see all her wrinkles. She's a bit sensitive about her age.

W: Oh dear. So, anyway, do you think there'll be a photo of you above your mum's telly one day? Little brother in a wedding suit?

M: Don't you start!

8 You hear an elderly woman talking to a man about her new neighbours.

M: So how are the new neighbours?

W: Well, I must say I'm quite pleased so far. It's early days, of course – they've only been there for a couple of weeks. But they do seem better than the last ones. All those weekend parties. Such an unpleasant family.

M: Have you invited them round yet?

Ex 1 Q8 W: Well, no, I haven't had a chance. You see, they've asked me to go to their house on two occasions already – and one of those was for lunch.

M: That's very sociable of them.

W: Yes, it is, isn't it? As I say, I'm rather pleased. They've even offered to come and cut my grass for me.

TB90

6 RELATIVE RELATIONSHIPS

Writing

1 Books closed. Board the two questions from the notice and get the students to discuss them in pairs. Nominate a few students to tell you what they talked about with their partners. Tell students that at the end of the lesson they will write an article about a person that influenced them. Give the students a moment to look at the writing task.

2 Students read the model answer and decide which person in the photos is described. Tell them to ignore the errors for now. Did they like the article?

3 In pairs or individually, students find the errors and correct them. Circulate and offer help as necessary. If possible, correct by projecting the text on the board.

4-5 Students do the activities in pairs.

Answers

a She has a straight back and a determined look on her face. She's always cheerful and I've never seen her in a bad temper … she's nearly half my size and so small that she sometimes wears children's clothes

b turn out, fallen out with, sort … out, look up to

c And, So, And although, But despite this, So even though

6 Students read the instructions. Then focus on the **Don't forget!** box. Note that this information could be adapted into a checklist, e.g. *Does the article include a range of descriptive language?* Remind the students that it's perfectly fine to borrow ideas (for example, how to start or finish their articles) from the model text in Exercise 2 or from the one on page 192 in the **Ready for Writing** section. The final writing could be done in class (timed, 40 minutes) or set for homework.

READY FOR GRAMMAR

6 Causative passive with *have* and *get*

1 The structure *have/get* + object + past participle to indicate that the action is done for the subject by someone else and not by the subject. The subject causes the action to be done.

Compare the following:

I repainted the windows.   (= I did it myself)

I had the windows repainted.   (= someone did it for me)

Get can be used instead of *have*. It is more informal.

Where **did** you **get** your photos **developed**?

All tenses of *have* and *get* are possible.

We've just **had** our washing machine **repaired**.

I'm **getting** my hair **done** tomorrow.

2 The same structure can also be used for events (usually unpleasant) which are outside of the speaker's control.

John **had** his house **broken into** last week.

---

6 Causative passive with *have* and *get*

1 In questions 1–6, write a suitable form of *have* in the first gap and the correct form of the verb in brackets in the second. The first one has been done for you.

1 Would you like __to have__ any part of your body __pierced__ (*pierce*)?
2 What are the advantages and disadvantages of __having__ your head __shaved__ (*shave*)?
3 If you could __have__ your photo __taken__ (*take*) with someone famous, who would you choose?
4 When was the last time you __had__ a tooth __filled__ (*fill*)?
5 Have you ever considered __having__ your hair __restyled__ (*restyle*)?
6 Do you know anyone who __has had__ something __stolen__ (*steal*) from them?

2 **SPEAK** Work in pairs. Ask and answer questions 1–6 in Exercise 1. Develop your answers.

A: Would you like to have any part of your body pierced?

B: I wouldn't mind, but I'm a hotel receptionist and I don't think my boss would be very happy if I went into work with a nose stud or a tongue piercing.

Go back to **page 90**.

RELATIVE RELATIONSHIPS

Writing Part 2 Article

1 Read the following Writing Part 2 instructions.

You see this notice on your school noticeboard.

> **Articles wanted**
> INFLUENCES
> - Which person has had a big influence on you?
> - How has this person influenced you?
>
> Write us an article for the school magazine describing the person and saying how he or she has influenced you.

a

2 Read the sample answer below. Which of the three people in the photographs is most similar to the one described in the answer? c

> ### 'Cheer up, chicken!'
>
> That's what my grandmother, my Nana, ~~says me~~ *says to me/tells me* when things aren't going well. Then she tells me, 'It'll turn out alright ~~at~~ *in* the end, you'll see.' And she's nearly always right.
>
> So when I'm ill, or I've ~~fell~~ *fallen* out with a friend or I'm just feeling down, I imagine Nana, with her wrinkled, but smiling face and sparkling blue eyes, saying her words of encouragement to me. And although my problems ~~they~~ don't just magically disappear, they don't seem so bad anymore and I'm in ^a better mood to sort them out.
>
> Nana has taught me to be positive in difficult moments. She's had many of them in her long and hard life. But despite this, she has a straight back and a determined look on her face. ~~Always she is~~ *She is always* cheerful and I've never seen her in a bad temper.
>
> So even though she's nearly half my size and ~~such~~ *so* small that she sometimes wears children's clothes, she's the person I most look up ~~at~~ *to* in my family. She's a little lady with a big influence.

b

c

3 The sample answer contains eight mistakes. Read the article again and correct the mistakes.

4 What techniques does the writer use:

a to attract and interest the reader at the beginning of the article?
First sentence follows on directly from a catchy title. The use of direct speech also adds colour.
b to leave the reader something to think about at the end of the article?
Writer plays with the meaning of look up to and ends by comparing her small size and big influence.

5 Find examples in the sample answer of the following features:

a language of description, e.g. *her wrinkled, but smiling face and sparkling blue eyes*
b phrasal verbs, e.g. *cheer up*
c linking words, e.g. *Then*

6 Now write your own answer to the question in Exercise 1 in 140–190 words.

For more information on writing articles, see **page 192**.

> **Don't forget!**
>
> › Begin with an interesting opening paragraph.
> › Include direct questions and/or direct speech for a lively article.
> › Use contractions and phrasal verbs for an informal style.
> › Include a range of descriptive language and linking words.
> › Leave the reader something to think about at the end.
> › Give your article a catchy title.

6 REVIEW

Language focus Relative clauses

The following sentences contain both defining and non-defining relative clauses. Complete the sentences with appropriate relative pronouns, giving alternatives where more than one answer is possible. Add commas if necessary.

1 Mr Jones, __who__ has taught here for 15 years, will be leaving the school at the end of term. He has accepted the post of headteacher at St Mary's, the school in __which__ he began his teaching career in 1990.

2 **A:** Yesterday I spoke to the boy __who/that__ has just moved into the house on the corner.
  B: Do you mean the one __whose__ mum looks like Meryl Streep?

3 **A:** Do you know a good place __where__ we could go for an Indian meal?
  B: Yes, we could go to that restaurant __which/that__ has just opened in Farndale Street.

4 The reason __why/that__ we're going skiing in March is because it's much cheaper then. Obviously we'd prefer to go in January, __when__ the snow's better, but we can't afford it.

5 The fox, __which__ is normally a very shy animal, can often be seen in city centres. It tends to keep to residential areas, __where__ food is usually easy to find.

6 You're the only student __who/that__ hasn't written the essay. What's more, it's the third piece of homework in a row __which/that__ you haven't done.

7 I lost that necklace __which/that__ I was wearing on Friday, __which__ made me very unpopular at home. It belonged to my eldest sister, __whose__ boyfriend gave it to her for her birthday.

Don't forget!
Check the spelling of the words you write. No marks will be awarded for a misspelt answer.

Reading and Use of English Part 3 Word formation

For questions 1–8, read the text below. Use the word given in capitals at the end of some of the lines to form a word that fits in the space in the same line. There is an example at the beginning (0).

Home | Wanted | Available | Contact

WANTED: Flatshare in the Hove area

I'm 22 and looking for a place to live within walking (0) __DISTANCE__ of Hove station. A double bedroom in shared (1) __accommodation__ would be ideal, and I can pay up to five hundred pounds a month. I'm a clean, (2) __reliable__ flatmate, who always pays his rent on time. Those who already know me like my relaxed, easy-going (3) __personality__ and the fact that I'm usually (4) __cheerful__ and rarely in a bad mood. Like most people, I enjoy spending time on my own now and again, but that certainly doesn't mean I'm (5) __unsociable__. On the contrary, I'm very (6) __excited__ at the prospect of meeting new people who would happily go out with their flatmate once in a while, and (7) __occasionally__ cook a meal together in the flat. (I'm pretty useful in the kitchen, by the way!) I'm a newly-qualified civil (8) __engineer__ and I'd be out until quite late, so you wouldn't have to put up with me much during the day!

DISTANT
ACCOMMODATE

RELY

PERSON
CHEER

SOCIABLE
EXCITE

OCCASION

ENGINE

REVIEW

Vocabulary Relationships

In sentences 1–8, complete the first gap with the correct form of an appropriate verb from box A, and the second gap with the correct particle from box B.

A bring fall give get let look sort ~~tell~~

B down ~~off~~ on out out to up up

1 He was ___told___ ___off___ for hitting his sister and made to apologise to her.
2 I've ___given___ ___up___ trying to keep the flat tidy; the people I share with make no effort to help at all.
3 My parents worked hard to pay for my education, so when I kept getting into trouble at school, they felt I had ___let___ them ___down___.
4 I don't ___get___ ___on___ very well with my boss; we have a mutual dislike for each other.
5 I was ___brought___ ___up___ by my parents to believe that honesty is the best policy.
6 I was upset when I found out my uncle had spent time in prison: I had always ___looked___ up ___to___ him and considered him a role model.
7 My two girls are always ___falling___ ___out___ over the silliest of things; they'll go for days without talking to each other.
8 We've had our problems, but we've always managed to ___sort___ them ___out___.

Reading and Use of English Part 4 Key word transformation

For questions 1–6, complete the second sentence so that it has a similar meaning to the first sentence, using the word given. Do not change the word given. You must use between two and five words, including the word given.

1 I won't tolerate your bad behaviour any longer.
  PUT
  I refuse ___to **put** up with___ your bad behaviour any longer.

2 We can't make an omelette because we don't have any eggs left.
  RUN
  We can't make an omelette because we ___have/'ve **run** out of___ eggs.

3 You shouldn't follow Petra's example.
  SHOULD
  Petra is not a person ___whose example you **should**___ follow.

4 His enthusiasm for the job impressed us a great deal.
  HOW
  We were greatly impressed ___at/by/with **how** enthusiastic he was/is___ about the job.

5 A friend is coming to repair our roof next week.
  GETTING
  We ___are **getting** our roof repaired___ by a friend next week.

6 We don't want a complete stranger to do it.
  HAVE
  We don't want ___to **have** it done by___ a complete stranger.

Writing Part 2 Informal email

This summer you are going to spend one month studying English in an English-speaking country. Read this part of an email you received from your host family and write your reply to them.

Write your email in 140–190 words.

For more information on writing informal emails, see **page 193**.

See the Teacher's Resource Centre for a Sample answer with Examiner's comments for this task.

From: Kate and Andy Newson

We have your personal details but perhaps you could tell us a little more about yourself. How would you describe your personality and what sorts of things would you like to do when you're here?

Thanks

Kate and Andy Newson

Don't forget!
You may write a formal or an informal reply, but the style of your email should be consistent.

6 RELATIVE RELATIONSHIPS

6 RELATIVE RELATIONSHIPS

Pronunciation Connected speech: consonant-vowel linking

1 ▶ 6.3 In connected speech, when one word ends with a consonant sound and the next word begins with a vowel sound, the two sounds are often linked together without a noticeable pause between them.

Look at this example from the listening on page 90, then listen and repeat.

She's had‿it framed, and‿it's‿up‿on the wall‿in her living room.

2 Draw (‿) to predict which words are connected in sentences 1–5.
   1 Ask‿Alan‿if he can come‿on Friday.
   2 We live‿in‿a flat‿on the edge‿of town.
   3 Pick‿it‿up and put‿it‿on the table.
   4 I found‿a box‿of sweets‿in your room.
   5 This town‿isn't big‿enough for both‿of‿us.

3 ▶ 6.4 Listen to the sentences from Exercise 2 to check your answers.

4 **SPEAK** Work in groups of three. Practise saying sentences 1–6 using consonant-vowel linking. Then time each other to see who can say all six sentences without stopping in the shortest amount of time.

   1 Can I have an egg?
   2 Can I have a box of eggs?
   3 Can I have a box of eggs and an apple?
   4 Can I have a box of eggs and a bag of apples?
   5 Can I have half a box of eggs and a bag of apples?
   6 Can I have eight and a half boxes of eggs and a bag of apples?

Pronunciation

1 ▶ 6.3 You could start by boarding the sentence in Exercise 1. Say it once slowly and carefully. Then say it again at a fluent, normal speed, linking words together where appropriate. Elicit what's happening when you say it faster. If needed, isolate and repeat shorter sections, e.g. *She's had it*, to more easily elicit the consonant-vowel linking rule. Students open their books. In pairs, they practice saying the full sentence in Exercise 1, linking the words as indicated.

2–3 ▶ 6.4 Together with a classmate, students apply the rule to predict where consonant-vowel linking will occur and then check with the recording.

4 Students do the activity in groups as suggested. Monitor the students' use of consonant-vowel linking.

READY FOR LISTENING

Listening Part 1 Multiple choice

1 Part 1 contains eight short unrelated extracts with multiple-choice questions. In each extract you will hear either a monologue or a conversation.

Here is a typical question from Part 1.
You hear two people talking about the twice-weekly fitness class they both attend.
What do they agree about it?
A There is not much variety.
B There are too many students.
C There is not enough equipment.

> **What to expect in the exam**
>
> One or more of the eight multiple-choice questions may require you to recognise what the speakers agree about, as in the example in Exercise 1.
>
> See also questions 4, 7 and 8 on page 96.

2 You should not choose an answer simply because a word or phrase that you hear appears in one of the options (A–C). These words and phrases could be distractors. In addition, for questions like the one above, make sure both speakers share the opinion.

In the following extracts, the sections in bold would be distractors for each option (A–C) in the question above. Say why each answer would not be correct.

> A There is not much variety.
> Man: Last year was so boring. There was **hardly any variety in the classes**.
> Woman: **Yeah**. This new teacher's a real improvement – every lesson is different.
> B There are too many students.
> Man: I can never hear her instructions. **There are always too many people talking**.
> Woman: **I know. It's annoying**. And it's always the same four or five students.
> C There is not enough equipment.
> Man: **They should get some more equipment**. That'd make the classes more fun.
> Woman: I'm not sure **I agree with you**. I think the teacher's the problem.

A Both speakers agree that there was not much variety last year, but this year, the woman says, the situation is much better.
B Both speakers agree that too many people talk over the teacher's instructions, but not that there are too many students in the class.
C The man suggests that there is not enough equipment, but the woman does not agree with him.

3 Read the actual script for the question in Exercise 1 and answer these questions.
1 What is the answer and which language helped you decide? **C**
2 Which language is used to create distractors?

> Woman: I wonder what we'll do today? Aerobics, body-pump, circuit training, salsa ...?
> Man: Maybe basketball. We haven't done any sport for a while. I know what we *will* be doing, though – the <u>same old</u> warm-up exercises at the beginning. It <u>never changes</u>. **1 A**
> Woman: Oh, come on, don't exaggerate. She's a great teacher and she does really well, despite <u>the poor facilities</u>. **1 C**
> Man: Yeah, the place could really do with a few more of the basics, like weights, balls, mats ...
> Woman: ... or steps – we're always having to share those. <u>And it's not as if we're a big class with loads of students</u>. **1 B**
> Man: <u>We're all here today, though, by the looks of it. A full house again</u> – that's good.

B, E and G are not used

READY FOR LISTENING

Listening

1 Students read the instructions, the example extract and the **What to expect in the exam** box. Check the meaning of *fitness*; students may be more familiar with the collocation *be/stay fit*. Elicit what *it* refers to in the question, *What do they agree about it?* (the fitness class). Note that students will be able to identify this type of question, where you have to listen for what people agree on, because they nearly always contain the word *agree* and/or the word *both*.

2 Students discuss the distractors in pairs.

3 Give students a minute to read the audioscript on their own before comparing their ideas with a classmate. Conduct brief feedback as a class.

4 ▶ 0.1 Play the recording twice and get the students to check their answers in pairs. It would be a good idea have the students use the **Audioscript** (see **Teacher's Resource Centre**) to check any answers they got wrong.

TB95

READY FOR LISTENING

4 ▶ 0.1 You will hear people talking in eight different situations. For questions 1–8, choose the best answer (A, B or C).

1 You hear a man talking about the use of mobile phones in restaurants.
   What point is he making?
   A Mobile phones can cause waiters to be distracted from their work.
   B The use of mobile phones has had an effect on food presentation.
   C Chefs are annoyed at the overuse of mobile phones in restaurants.

2 You hear two friends talking about a concert they went to.
   How does the woman feel about it?
   A critical of the performer's selection of songs
   B upset at being unable to see the performer very well
   C disappointed with the performer's relationship with his audience

3 You hear a man talking on the radio about a sport called pickleball.
   What is the speaker's main purpose?
   A to outline the basic rules of the sport
   B to encourage people to take up the sport
   C to explain why he became interested in the sport

4 You overhear two students talking about the temporary job they are both doing in a factory.
   What do they agree about?
   A how low the pay is
   B how boring the job is
   C how long the working day is

5 You hear a woman reviewing a biography on the radio.
   Who is the subject of the book?
   A an actor
   B a sportsman
   C a businessman

6 You hear a man talking about his new doctor.
   The man thinks she should
   A refuse to see patients who don't arrive on time.
   B spend more time with each patient.
   C keep to appointment times.

7 You hear two people talking about their local supermarket.
   What do they both like about it?
   A the wide range of goods
   B the reasonable prices
   C the friendly staff

8 You hear two people talking about a foreign language film they have just seen with subtitles.
   What do they agree was bad about the subtitles?
   A their size
   B their speed
   C their inaccuracy

Listening Part 2 Sentence completion

1 ▶ 0.2 You will hear a woman called Helen Wells talking about her job in a zoo.

Before you listen, predict the type of information you might hear for questions 1–10.

1 This will be a noun, or an adjective plus noun, possibly with a similar meaning to the word 'display'.

> **What to expect in the exam**
>
> › You will hear distractors for many of the questions.
>   *For number 1, for example, you will hear two different nouns which are used to refer to the display; only one of them is correct here. And for number 2, you will need to choose between two different threats faced by the birds.*
>
> › The words and sentence structure in the question may not be the same as those used in the recording.
>   *For question 3, for example, instead of ... in this year's shows, audiences enjoyed watching ... , you will hear: A popular part of this year's shows was when ...*

96

Listening

1 In pairs, ask the students to think of a few possible duties of someone who works at the zoo, e.g. feeding the animals, selling tickets, etc. Students then look through the task and make predictions about what types of word(s) might fit in the gaps. Feedback in open class. Then focus on the **What to expect in the exam** box. Stress the fact that the sentences in the task contain the same information as what they will hear in the recording but are phrased differently. Ask the students: *Will you hear only one person talking in this exercise?* (Yes, Part 2 is always a monologue) *Will the information in the recording be in the same or a different order as the questions?* (The same order). Remind students they can only write up to three words and that minor spelling errors are not penalised, as long as it's very clear what word they wanted to write.

2 ▶ 0.2 Play the recording twice. You could elicit the answers in open class or ask the student to find them in the **Audioscripts** (see **Teacher's Resource Centre**).

READY FOR LISTENING

2 ▶ 0.2 For questions 1–10, complete the sentences with a word or short phrase.

Helen says that the zoo refers to the display of exotic birds as a (1) **demonstration**.

Helen suggests the biggest threat to the birds is (2) **habitat loss / loss of habitat**.

Helen says that in this year's shows, audiences enjoyed watching a toucan catch a (3) **grape** in mid-air.

According to Helen, children don't usually mind having a macaw sitting on their (4) **arm(s)**.

Helen thinks that trainers need to be quite (5) **sociable** people.

Helen says that good (6) **team work / teamwork** is an important part of the job.

During a show this year, a cockatoo flew away and landed on a (7) **fountain**.

The trainers check the birds' (8) **weight** daily, to ensure there are no health problems.

Helen says that cleaning out the bird cages is often (9) **entertaining** work.

Helen says she didn't like the fact she frequently had to work (10) **overtime** this summer.

Listening Part 3 Multiple matching

1 You will hear five short extracts in which people are talking about summer jobs they once did.

Before you listen, read the following example of the kind of extract you will hear. Then answer questions 1–3 below.

1. What did the speaker like most about the job? Choose from the list **A–H** in Exercise 2.
2. Which part or parts of the script give(s) you the answer?
3. In the underlined parts of the script, the speaker makes reference to the following: responsibility   earning good money   socialising
Why are options D, G and H not correct here?

Example extract

My dad knew someone who had some kind of position of responsibility with a big supermarket chain, and he once got me a summer job working part-time in one of their stores. That was the main plus point, actually - just doing mornings and having the rest of the day to myself. Of course, I didn't make as much money as I could have done, but it was enough to fund my social life for the holidays. In fact, sometimes I'd go out in the evening with some of the people from the supermarket – I got on well with nearly everyone there.

1 E

2 *… working part time … That was the main plus point, actually – just doing mornings and having the rest of the day to myself.*

3 The speaker was not given responsibility. The person who found them the job had a position of responsibility.

The speaker says I didn't make as much money as I could have done. He or she does not say they earned good money.

The speaker socialised with people from the supermarket after work, not during the breaks.

2 ▶ 0.3 For questions 1–5, choose from the list (A–H) what each speaker says they liked most about the job. Use the letters only once. There are three extra letters which you do not need to use.

A being appreciated for their work
B practising a foreign language
C having time to do tourism
D being given responsibility
E not working long hours
F being able to develop a skill
G earning good money
H socialising during the breaks

Speaker 1 **D** 1
Speaker 2 **A** 2
Speaker 3 **F** 3
Speaker 4 **H** 4
Speaker 5 **C** 5

What to expect in the exam

› Each extract lasts about 30 seconds.
› The speakers will not use exactly the same words that appear in options **A–H**.
› You will usually hear distractors in all five extracts.

97

Listening

1 In open class, elicit a few jobs young people might typically do during the summer. Ask if any of the students have ever had a summer job. Exercise 1 aims to raise students' awareness of key features of Listening Part 3, including the type of distractors that are likely to be included. Get brief feedback. Note that students might find it helpful to listen for what each speaker liked most about the job, and then look down at the options and choose the one most similar to what they heard, rather than trying to keep all the options in mind while they listen.

2 ▶ 0.3 Play the recording twice. Allow students to check their answers after the first and second time they listen. If many of the students answered a particular question incorrectly, have them check the **Audioscripts** (see **Teacher's Resource Centre**). Make sure they not only understand why the right answer is right, but also why their wrong answer is wrong. To round off the activity, ask the students to discuss which summer jobs from the listening task they would or wouldn't mind doing and why.

TB97

READY FOR LISTENING

READY FOR LISTENING

Listening Part 4 Multiple choice

1 You will hear part of an interview with a roller-coaster enthusiast called Steve Muir.

Read question 1 and the extract from the recording. Decide on the correct answer, underlining the part or parts of the text which justify your choice.

1 What impressed Steve most when he first saw a roller coaster as a child?
- **A** the sounds associated with the ride
- B the shape of the wooden structure
- C the speed of the train

Interviewer:	I'm talking today to Steve Muir, who's passionate about roller coasters. Steve, tell us what first got you interested.
Steve Muir:	Well, I remember as a small boy, looking up at this huge wooden construction shaped like a wave, hearing <u>the clicking of the chain</u> as it pulled the cars to the top of the lift hill, then <u>the riders screaming</u> their heads off as they hurtled round, and <u>the whooshing noise of the train</u> as it hurried by. <u>There was a kind of music to it all, and it made me think, 'I want to do that one day.'</u>

Both B, the shape of the wooden structure (shaped like a wave), and C, the speed of the train (they hurtled round … it hurried by), are mentioned, but it was the sounds (a kind of music to it all) that impressed him most and made him want to try it himself.

2 **SPEAK** With your partner, explain with reference to the text why the other options are wrong.

3 ▶ 0.4 For questions 2–7, choose the best answer (A, B or C).

What to expect in the exam

- You are given one minute to read the seven questions, together with their alternative answers (**A**, **B** and **C**), before you hear the recording. One possible approach is to read all seven questions (*see 2, 4, 5 and 6 below*) and sentence beginnings (*see 3 and 7 below*) before you read the alternative answers. This will quickly give you a general idea of the content of the listening.
- A Part 4 listening script usually consists of a series of seven exchanges: a question, or comment from the interviewer followed by an extended response from the interviewee.

    This is the case in this particular listening, with the only exception of question 2, where Steve's response to the question 'what is it about roller coasters that gives you your biggest thrill?' is interrupted by a brief reaction from the interviewer.

2 What is the main cause of excitement now for Steve about roller coasters?
- A the anticipation of the ride
- **B** the sensation of floating
- C the feeling of fear

3 Steve says that when a place became available on the United States coach tour
- A his application was initially rejected.
- **B** he had to make a quick decision.
- C a friend put forward Steve's name.

4 What does Steve say about the first theme park they went to on the tour?
- A They had to travel a long distance to get there.
- B They spent more time there than in any other park.
- **C** They were given exclusive access to the roller coasters.

5 What did Steve particularly enjoy about the *El Toro* roller coaster?
- **A** He rode it in near darkness.
- B Many of the seats were unoccupied.
- C It was the fastest roller coaster he had been on.

6 What does Steve say about the *Maverick* roller coaster?
- **A** His enjoyment of it increased with each ride.
- B It maintained the same speed throughout.
- C He was disappointed by its height.

7 The last time Steve went to the theme park in Abu Dhabi
- A he suffered from the heat.
- B he had to queue for a long time.
- **C** he spent longer there than intended.

4 Look at the Audioscript on pages 248–249 and for questions 2–7 follow the same procedure as in Exercises 1 and 2 above.

Listening

1–2 Start by asking if the students enjoy going on roller coasters. Students then read the instructions. Encourage students to listen for the answer and then decide which option corresponds most closely to their own answer. If you listen for the options, you are far more likely to fall for distractors. Students could practise this strategy here by first reading the text and finding what seemed to impress Steve the most about roller coasters. They could then discuss their answers in pairs and decide on a correct option together.

3 ▶ 0.4 Focus the students on the **What to expect in the exam** box. Play the recording twice. Stress the fact that students will not have enough time to carefully read through all the options, so it's best to focus on the questions.

4 In pairs, students underline the part of the Audioscript (see Teacher's Resource Centre) that contains the correct answers. Encourage them to discuss why the incorrect answers are incorrect.

7 VALUE FOR MONEY

This unit explores the topic of shopping as well as city and village life. Students will practise writing formal and informal emails. The skill of paraphrasing, which is relevant in all parts of the *B2 First* exam, is also developed.

Read the unit objectives to the class.

KEY LANGUAGE
Present perfect simple
Present perfect continuous
Shopping
Paraphrasing and recording
Towns and villages

PRONUNCIATION
Contrastive stress

EXAM PRACTICE
Reading and Use of English Parts 2, 4 & 6
Writing Parts 1 & 2
Listening Parts 2 & 4
Speaking Parts 1 & 2

Speaking Part 1 Interview
1. What are the good points about living in your area?
2. Is there anything you don't like about it?
3. What changes have there been in your local area in recent years?
4. Do you think you will always live in the same area?
5. If you could choose, where would you most like to live?

SPEAKING Part 1 Interview

Focus the students on the picture. Ask them to speculate about what the women are doing. Ask the students what they would look for in a house or flat they were planning to buy or rent.

Before they discuss the questions, it's worth mentioning to your students that while the idea of Speaking Part 1 is for candidates to give personal information about themselves, the actual personal information they share with examiner is 100% their choice. Particularly for adults, even questions that are designed to be innocuous might inadvertently provoke strong emotions. To give an example, for most people the question *What changes have there been in your local area in recent years?* would be harmless, but if the place where a candidate lives had been particularly hard hit by a financial crisis — or a natural disaster like an earthquake or flood — this question could be potentially quite upsetting to answer. Remind students that they are not required to tell the examiner anything they don't want to. In fact, they are not even required to tell the truth!

ONLINE MATERIALS

Which property? (**Teacher's Resource Centre**)
Guessing game (**Teacher's Resource Centre**)
Unit 7 Test (**Test Generator**)
Unit 7 Wordlist (**Teacher's Resource Centre**)
Unit 7 On-the-go-practice (**App**)

7 VALUE FOR MONEY

Why have the people decided to go shopping in these different places?

Speaking Part 2 Long turn

1 Look at the photographs 1 and 2. They show people shopping in different places.

Student A: Compare the photographs and say why you think the people have decided to go shopping in these different places.

Student B: When your partner has finished, say which of these places you would rather shop in.

2 Now change roles. Go to the **Additional materials** on **page 200** and do the Speaking Part 2 task.

Vocabulary Shopping

1 Complete each gap with a word from the box. The first one has been done for you.

centres   charge   discount   ~~make~~   order
price   purchase   stock   value   worth

Home | Blog | Archives

A REAL BARGAIN!

I tried to get a speaker for my sister's birthday in town, but none of the shops had the (1) _make_ that she wanted in (2) _stock_. I hate going to huge shopping (3) _centres_, so I decided to (4) _order/purchase_ one direct from a major retailer's website. The (5) _price_ was reasonable, so I bought another one for myself. And because the total cost was over a certain amount, delivery was free of (6) _charge_, plus I was offered 20% (7) _discount_ off my next (8) _purchase/order_. The speakers turned out to be very good (9) _value_ for money – they're great quality and (10) _worth_ every penny I spent.

VALUE FOR MONEY

Lead-in

Board the places to shop listed below. Individually, students rank them from where they most like to shop (top of the list) to where they least like to shop (bottom of the list). They then compare their lists in pairs or small groups, explaining why they put particular places towards the top or bottom. In open class, ask the students to comment on any notable similarities or differences.

shopping centres, big-box stores, chain stores, small local shops, boutiques, charity shops, department stores, street markets, pound shops

You may need to check the meaning of *pound shop*, *department store* and *big-box store*.

Speaking

1-2 To get students comfortable with the exam, it's good to start replicating exam conditions as much as possible at this point in the course. For this Part 2 task, put the students in groups and assign one to be the speaking examiner, who keeps the time. Tell students in the role of examiner to be strict with the timing and to stop the candidates with a polite but firm 'thank you', just as a real examiner would. Put the official instructions on the board or a handout for the examiner to read:

In this part of the test, I'm going to give you two photographs. I'd like you to talk about your photographs on your own for about a minute, and also to answer a short question about your partner's photograph. (Candidate A) it's your turn first. Here are your photographs. They show people shopping. I'd like you to compare the photographs and say why you think the people have decided to go shopping in these different places. All right? (1 minute) Thank you. (Ask follow-up question, 30 seconds). Now (Candidate B), here are your photographs. They show …

Vocabulary

1 Before students do the exercise, check the meaning of *bargain* in the title. Note that *shopping centres* are called *shopping malls* in North America. During feedback, you may want to contrast how *ask* and *order* are used in English, as in other languages one word is often used for both. For the exercises in this vocabulary section, encourage students to create a new page in their vocabulary notebooks for the topic of *shopping* and record any new words or collocations.

UNIT 7

Speaking Part 2 Long turn

Look at the photographs. They show people shopping in different places.

Student A: Compare the photographs and say why you think the people have decided to go shopping in these different places.

Student B: When your partner has finished, say whether you like shopping for clothes.

Why have the people decided to go shopping in these different places?

Go back to **page 100**.

7 VALUE FOR MONEY

2 Elicit the pronunciation of *receipt* /rɪˈsiːt/. If time allows, invite the students to write their own short blog post about something they bought that they were very happy or unhappy with. Students must use at least five words or phrases from Exercises 1 and 2. When finished, put them up around the room. Students then circulate and read each other's accounts.

3 Note that these are typical questions for Speaking Part 1. Encourage the students to 'show what they know' and use as much good vocabulary from Exercises 1 and 2 as possible. Monitor the students' use of the target language, providing on-the-spot error correction as necessary. For any other common errors, write them down and discuss them after the activity.

Listening

1 After the students discuss the question in pairs, get some brief feedback from the class.

2 ▶ 7.1 Students read the instructions. Focus on the **Don't forget!** box. Note that on the *B2 First*, students have precious little time to look at the task before the recording starts. Train students to read the questions quickly by setting strict time limits. For Part 2, students will have only 45 seconds on the exam, but to start give them around twice as long and then slowly reduce the timing to the official one. (See answers highlighted in the **Audioscript** below.)

3 Students discuss the questions in pairs. In open class, nominate a few students to share their thoughts on the future of bookshops. Ask whether the rest of the class agrees with their predictions.

AUDIOSCRIPT

Listening Part 2 Sentence completion

▶ 7.1

Hello, my name's Joy Townsend and I'm here to tell you about the bookshop called *More than books*, which my husband and I started up recently. We had originally planned to open it in June, but we had to get the builders in, and they didn't start work till the end of May, so it wasn't until the middle of **Ex 2 Q1** July that we were actually able to welcome our first customers.

We're in a main shopping street, on the ground floor below a lawyer's office, and to give you an idea of the size of our premises, let me just say there's enough room to fit a small supermarket in there, **Ex 2 Q2** although before us it was actually a shoe shop. Unfortunately, they had trouble meeting the cost of the rent and decided to close the business.

Anyway, the point is, we have the space to do more than just sell books. Towards the front of the shop, for example, is a small café area, which I'll tell you about in a minute, and at the far end we've had a **Ex 2 Q3** little stage set up, for which we've got a programme of events and activities planned. Again, more about that later.

As a bookshop, we want to appeal to all types of readers, so we sell a wide range of books, both fiction and non-fiction, including an impressive selection of children's books. And in the shop window, rather than having recently published **Ex 2 Q4** books on show, we display some of our bargain books – ones that we're offering at a discount or that belong in our 'three for the price of two' deal. The idea, of course, is to catch the attention of shoppers and encourage them to come in.

Once they're in, they're usually captivated by the smell of coffee coming from the café area, and in **Ex 2 Q5** particular, by the sight of our homemade cakes, which have become the talk of the neighbourhood, by all accounts. People are hearing good things about them, and coming in to try them for themselves. We're now also thinking about offering a range of fresh salads, which could be an attractive option for office workers during the lunch period.

As I mentioned, we have a number of events and activities programmed. Coming up the week after **Ex 2 Q6** next, for example, is jazz guitarist, Dave Simmons, who lives in the area and has kindly offered to play a set for us free of charge. Then two weeks after that, folk singer Angie Davies, a personal friend of mine, is coming all the way from her home town of Bristol to perform for us.

Ex 2 Q7 We've already had a poetry reading, which was very well attended. In fact, it caught us by surprise and we didn't have enough seats for everyone. That was last week, and we're hoping that just as many people come to the book presentation at the end of *this* week.

Our most successful events so far, though, have been the storytelling sessions for children. We **Ex 2 Q8** pay a professional group called *Magic Words* to come in every now and again to entertain the kids. The sessions are not cheap, but the shop is always full, and the mums and dads buy lots of books.

And finally, we've set up a reading group, which meets on the first Tuesday of every month. The theme for discussion since September has **Ex 2 Q9** been 'loneliness', but that will change in January to a topic of the group's choice. A total of three books are suggested for each topic, and they can be purchased from us at a reduced price.

All of this, then, is helping us to attract customers, but we've also decided to advertise. We couldn't afford to pay for radio advertising, and we weren't convinced a leaflet campaign would be very **Ex 2 Q10** effective, so we've taken out an ad in the local newspaper. It wasn't cheap, but we're hoping it will turn out to be money well spent. We'll see.

VALUE FOR MONEY 7

2 Complete each gap with a word from the box. The first one has been done for you.

> back back bargains fit for mind on ~~on~~ out
> price receipt refund sales till up

HOME   BLOG   ARCHIVES

BIRTHDAY JEANS
POSTED 24 APRIL

I got some money for my birthday in July, and decided to **spend** it (1) __on__ some new clothes in the summer (2) __sales__. I was hoping I might **pick** (3) __up__ a few (4) __bargains__. In one shop, they were selling some really good jeans at half (5) __price__. Unfortunately, they had **sold** (6) __out__ of my size, but I **tried** (7) __on__ a smaller pair just in case, to see if they would (8) __fit__. They didn't really – they were a bit tight, but they were cheap and I liked them, so I **paid** (9) __for__ them at the (10) __till__ and went off to look for something else. However, after a few days, I changed my (11) __mind__ about the jeans and decided to **take** them (12) __back__ to the shop and ask for a (13) __refund__. I couldn't find the (14) __receipt__, though, and the assistant wouldn't **give** me my money (15) __back__ without it.

3 SPEAK Work in pairs. Discuss the questions.
1 Do you like going to large shopping centres? Why/Why not?
2 Is it better to go shopping with friends, family or alone? Why?
3 What types of things do you buy online and why?

Listening Part 2 Sentence completion

1 SPEAK Work in pairs. Imagine you want to open a new bookshop. Discuss what you would do to attract customers and to make your bookshop better than any others in your area.

2 ▶ **7.1** You will hear a woman called Joy Townsend talking about a bookshop called *More than books*, which she and her husband have just opened. For questions 1–10, complete the sentences with a word or short phrase.

Joy and her husband opened their bookshop in the month of (1) __July__.
Joy says the bookshop used to be a (2) __shoe shop__.
At the back of the shop, Joy and her husband have had a small (3) __stage__ built.
In the window of the shop there is a selection of (4) __bargain__ books.
Joy says that the (5) __(homemade) cakes__ in the café area are attracting new customers.
A local (6) __jazz guitarist__ will be performing in the bookshop in two weeks' time.
Joy says that more people came to the (7) __poetry reading__ in the shop last week than they were expecting.
Joy says they sometimes hire a group of storytellers called (8) '__Magic Words__'.
The reading group is currently discussing the topic of (9) __loneliness__.
Joy says they have paid for a (10) __(local) newspaper__ advertisement.

> **Don't forget!**
>
> In the exam you have 45 seconds to read the Part 2 questions. Use this time to try to predict the type of information you might hear.

3 SPEAK Work in pairs. Did Joy mention any of the ideas you discussed in Exercise 1? Do you think bookshops have a future? Why/Why not?

7 VALUE FOR MONEY

Reading and Use of English Part 6 Gapped text

1 **SPEAK** Work in pairs. What happens in some countries on Black Friday? What do you think is the origin of the term 'Black Friday'?

2 Read the base text (the text without the missing sentences) about Black Friday to check your ideas.

3 Six sentences have been removed from the article. Choose from the sentences A–G the one which fits each gap (1–6). There is one extra sentence which you do not need to use.

BLACK FRIDAY

Retail's biggest day of the year is known for in-store chaos but has proven itself an unstoppable commercial force.

Black Friday, the annual scramble for discount presents for the upcoming holidays, takes place each year in shopping centres around the world towards the end of November. A media favourite because of the outbreaks of chaos that commonly erupt in the shopping aisles as bargain-hunters squabble over flat-screen TVs and step over people to grab a cut-price Xbox, the day unofficially marks the beginning of the festive retail season.

Whatever you think of it, Black Friday has become an annual fixture and looks here to stay. **1 G** Perhaps the most famous example of **this** is the Black Friday of 25th October 1929, following Black Thursday, when the New York Stock Exchange collapsed, bringing about the Great Depression. One explanation for why the modern discount bonanza has been given the same sinister name is that it always takes place the day after the Thursday of Thanksgiving, when workers would frequently call in sick in order to enjoy a four-day weekend, a disaster for the US economy. **2 E** The first recorded use of the term to identify this annual phenomenon appeared in the November 1951 issue of the industrial trade journal *Factory Management and Maintenance*. **3 D** By November 1975, the phrase was being used by *The New York Times* to refer to the atrocious traffic congestion seen in Philadelphia as shoppers raced out for bargains in the hope of spreading the cost of Christmas over a longer period.

An alternative explanation offered by accountants is that the day is the moment at which stores make so much money they cease operating at a loss and move from the red into the black. **4 A** During **this** period, retailers have become more strategic about their approach to the day, offering major sales promotions and extending their opening hours, often to midnight.

Amazon has been credited with bringing this very American event to the UK since it first began offering Black Friday deals in 2010. Asda, owned by US giant Walmart, followed suit in 2013 and the craze has snowballed from there. Some UK chains have moved to distance themselves from Black Friday as a result of the particularly unruly scenes that unfolded in 2014. **5 F**

The day has been criticised in the US for the strain it places on staff at the big stores, the safety risks associated with large-scale crowd management and the occasional dishonest business practices involved. **6 B** The madness has nevertheless spread around the world. France, Italy, Spain, the Netherlands, Norway, Denmark, Sweden, Brazil, Nigeria and South Africa have all embraced the mania in recent years.

102

VALUE FOR MONEY 7

Reading and Use of English

1-2 Students discuss the questions in pairs and then quickly read the article to check their answers. Set a time limit of no more than three minutes for this skimming task. Tell them to ignore the missing sentences for now. In open class, ask if any of their ideas are mentioned in the article.

3 Students read the instructions. Focus their attention on the words in bold in the text and the removed sentences. Ask the students: *What kind of words are these? Why is it important to focus on this type of word in this reading task?* Then direct them to the **Don't forget!** box. Before checking the answers as a class, allow the students some time to check their answers in pairs, justifying their answers (when appropriate) with reference to the grammatical words in bold.

4 If time allows, adapt this into a class debate, with half of the class on one side and the other half on another. Give them time to think of three or four good points to make. Students should defend their side no matter their real opinion.

Extra activity

One unfortunate aspect of the paper-based exam is that for the Part 6 reading task the sentences removed from the text always appear on a separate page, as they do on page 103 in the coursebook. This means that students have to keep looking back and forth between the two pages while they do the task. To temporarily reduce this difficulty, make a copy of the missing sentences and cut them up into individual slips of paper, which can then be moved across the text. Make a set for each student.

Teaching tip

By this point in the course, students will have had sufficient practice with *B2 First* exam tasks to have an idea of where their strengths and weaknesses lie. Set aside 10 minutes one day in class and have the students create a new page in their vocabulary notebooks entitled '(Almost) Ready for B2 First'. Divide the page in two. Label one half 'Ready' and the other 'Almost ready'. Students open their books to page IV (TBVI). Using the information there, they write each part of each paper in 'Ready' or 'Almost ready' based on how confident they feel with them. In groups, ask the students to compare their lists and discuss what makes certain parts more challenging than others. Monitor and make notes, as this will help you focus your lessons on the students' needs. Throughout the course, revisit this page from time to time and encourage students to move tasks from 'Almost ready' to 'Ready' as they gain more confidence. This allows students (and the teacher) to see progress.

7 VALUE FOR MONEY

Language focus

1. The presentation of this grammar could be made more dynamic by putting the rules and examples on different slips of paper. Give the students the examples first and they discuss why the present perfect is used in the sentences. Then give students the slips of paper with rules to match to the examples. Note that there may be some overlap in these rules, since all the sentences illustrate some connection between the past and the present. Rule number 1, for example, could also apply to the example sentence for rule number 3. This can be discussed during feedback.

2. This exercise could be done individually or in pairs.

3. Direct the students to the **Ready for Grammar** section on page 218 (see below and TB104). Students will need to do Exercise 1 about time expressions in class, but if your students have demonstrated a good understanding of rules 1–5, Exercise 2 in the **Ready for Grammar** section could be set for homework or saved for a revision lesson later on in the course.

4–5 These activities give students the opportunity to personalise the grammar and practise it in a less controlled way. Students write their sentences individually and then discuss in pairs. Alternatively, students could write three sentences about themselves in the present perfect – two true and one a lie. Encourage them to use time expressions. Then, in groups, students take turns reading out their three sentences and guessing which of their partners' sentences are lies. To do this, they should ask questions for more information, most of which will be in the past simple, e.g. *When did you start doing …?*

READY FOR GRAMMAR

7 Present perfect simple

The present perfect links past events and situations with the present.
The present perfect is used:

1. to describe something that started in the **past** and continues to the **present**.
   We have lived in this house ever since we got married.

2. to describe events which occurred at some time between the **past** and the **present**. Exactly when they happened is not known or not important.
   I've been to Poland three or four times.

3. to talk about something which occurred in the past, but in an unfinished time period which includes the present.
   Judy's boyfriend has phoned her three times this morning – and it's not even 11 o'clock!

4. to give news of recent **past** events which have some relevance to the **present**.
   Lisa has had an accident: she's in hospital but she's OK.

5. after the expression *it/this/that* is the *first/second/third*, etc. *time*
   This is the first time **I've seen** this programme.

The present perfect is <u>not</u> used to refer to past events if the specific time at which they occurred is mentioned. In this case, the past simple is used.
Compare:

Present perfect: You**'ve told** me that joke before. (when exactly is not important here)

Past simple: You **told** me that joke last week. (the specific time is mentioned)

For more information on the use of the past simple, see Unit 4.

Time Expressions

1. The present perfect is commonly used with *ever, never, just, recently, so far, still, yet* and *already* when referring to a time period up to now.
   They haven't booked their holiday **yet**.
   We've only lost one game **so far** *this season.*

2. *For* is used with periods of time to show how long something has lasted.
   I've known Eric **for** *twenty years.*
   Since is used with points in time to show when something started.
   I've had this watch **since** *1984.*

VALUE FOR MONEY 7

A Whichever of **these** reasons is correct, 'Black Friday' has only really caught on as a label within the last twenty years.

B **These** might include stores artificially inflating prices on goods in advance, only to then 'slash' the cost back down to its original value, or temporarily selling inferior products just to meet demand.

C In the last few years, there has been a trend towards offering bargains up to a week before Black Friday.

D So Black Friday as we understand it today can be traced back at least **that far**.

E The impact of **this** was only reduced if families used their additional leisure time to go to the stores.

F **These** led to in-store security finding themselves unable to cope and the police having to intervene.

G The phrase 'Black Friday' has been used around the world since at least the mid-19th century to refer to days of national disaster.

> **Don't forget!**
>
> Look for connections between the language in the missing sentences and the language in the text.
>
> *To help you, some grammatical words* (this, these *and* that far) *are written in* **bold** *in both the base text and the missing sentences A–G.*

4 SPEAK Work in groups. 'An excellent opportunity to pick up bargains' or 'the worst example of unchecked consumerism': what do you think of Black Friday?

Language focus Present perfect simple

1 The present perfect is used:

1 to describe something that started in the **past** and continues until the **present**

   People **have used** *the phrase 'Black Friday' since the mid-19th century to refer to days of national disaster.*

2 to describe events which occurred at some time between the **past** and the **present** (exactly when they happened is not important)

   Many **have criticised** *the day in the US for the strain it places on staff at the big stores.*

3 to talk about something which occurred in the **past** but in an unfinished time period which includes the **present**

   I've already **picked up** *several bargains this morning. (It is still the morning and I may pick up more bargains.)*

4 to talk about recent **past** events with some relevance to the **present**

   Black Friday **has spread** *around the world; it now takes place in countries such as Spain, Brazil and South Africa.*

5 to talk about the first, second, third etc., time something has occurred between the **past** and the **present**.

   I can't believe this is the first time you've **heard** *of Black Friday!*

2 Which of the five descriptions above can be used to explain the use of the present perfect simple in these sentences?

   a Your parents have just arrived. I can hear their car.   4
   b I've known Keith since we started school together.   1
   c Sue has worked in a number of different countries.   2
   d That must be the tenth time you've told me that joke!   5
   e Ben's already sent me fifteen text messages this week.   3
   f Mrs Avery has lived in that house for over sixty years.   1
   g This film's very familiar – I think I've seen it before.   2
   h I've lost my glasses. Can you help me look for them?   4

3 Go to **Ready for Grammar** on **page 218** for rules, explanations and further practice.

4 Write four true sentences about yourself using the present perfect, and four using the past simple. Include a different time expression in each sentence.

   So far today I've had three cups of coffee.   I went to the zoo on my 11th birthday.

5 SPEAK Work in pairs. Compare your sentences with your partner's. Ask each other questions about what you have written.

   Have you eaten anything?   What memories do you have of your day at the zoo?

7 VALUE FOR MONEY

Vocabulary Paraphrasing and recording

If you paraphrase a sentence, you use different words to express the same meaning.

1 In 1–8 below, complete each gap with one word so that the second sentence has the same meaning as the first. The second sentence is taken from *Black Friday* on page 102. There is an example at the beginning (0). Do the exercise without looking back at the reading text.

> **What to expect in the exam**
>
> Paraphrasing is relevant in all areas of the *First* exam.
> - In the **Reading** and **Listening** tasks, multiple-choice and multiple-matching questions often paraphrase what is written in the text or said in the recording.
> - In the **Writing** and **Speaking** papers, you should avoid repeating the same language and use a wide range of vocabulary and structures.
> - In Part 4 of the **Reading and Use of English** paper, the transformations test your ability to paraphrase.

0 People associate the biggest shopping day of the year with chaos in shops.
Retail's biggest day of the year **is** _known_ **for** in-store chaos.

1 The press love it because of the chaotic scenes that usually occur in the shopping aisles.
[It is] **a media** _favourite_ **because of the** _outbreaks_ **of chaos** that commonly **erupt** in the shopping aisles. **(3–4)**

2 The New York Stock Exchange collapsed, causing the Great Depression.
The New York Stock Exchange collapsed, _bringing_ **about** the Great Depression. **(9–10)**

3 The day has been criticised in the US because of the stress it causes staff at the big stores.
The day has been criticised in the US for **the strain it** _places_ **on** staff at the big stores. **(36–37)**

4 'Black Friday' has only really become popular as a label within the last 20 years.
'Black Friday' has only really **caught** _on_ as a label within the last 20 years. **(A)**

5 These practices might include stores artificially increasing the price of goods beforehand.
These [practices] might include stores artificially inflating prices on goods **in** _advance_ ... **(B)**

6 ... or temporarily selling inferior products just to ensure they have enough to sell.
... or temporarily selling inferior products just to _meet_ **demand. (B)**

7 We know that the current use of Black Friday originated at least as long ago as that.
Black Friday as we understand it today **can be traced** _back_ **at least that** _far_. **(D)**

8 These events resulted in in-store security finding themselves unable to cope.
These [scenes] _led_ **to** in-store security finding themselves unable to cope. **(F)**

2 Check your answers in *Black Friday* on page 103. The numbers in brackets in 1–3 refer to the lines in the text; the letters in 4–8 refer to sentences A–G.

3 Paraphrasing is a useful way to record vocabulary. Paraphrase the following sentences from the article and record both sentences in your vocabulary notebook. You do not need to change every word in the sentence. The first one has been done for you.

1 Black Friday takes place each year towards the end of November. (1–3)
  Black Friday occurs every year near the end of November.

2 ... Black Friday has become an annual fixture and looks here to stay. (7–8)
  ... Black Friday now takes place every year and it looks as if it will continue to do so in the future.

3 ... workers would frequently call in sick ... (13)
  ... employees would often phone their workplace to say they were ill.

4 ... and extending their opening hours, often to midnight. (27–28)
  ... and increasing the number of hours they stay open, often to midnight.

5 Amazon has been credited with bringing this very American event to the UK. (29–30)
  Some people say that Amazon is responsible for bringing this very American event to the UK.

VALUE FOR MONEY 7

Vocabulary

1-2 An alternative introduction is to put the example (0) up on the board and ask the students if the two sentences have the same meaning. Tell the students that this is called paraphrasing and then ask: *In which parts of the exam is paraphrasing particularly relevant?* Elicit or explain that this is tested most directly in key word transformations, but, as explained in the **What to expect in the exam** box, paraphrasing is important in both the receptive and productive parts of the exam. It might be useful for students to work through sentences 1–8 in pairs so they can help each other. Direct the students to the article on pages 102–103 to check their answers. Fast finishers could choose a few of the sentences to study and then test each other on them, providing the second paraphrased sentence from memory.

3 Explain to students that paraphrasing is so important on the exam that it should be kept in mind while recording new language in their vocabulary notebooks. Stress that improving your English does not consist of simply learning a new word in order to say something you don't know how to say yet, but also learning new ways of saying the same thing.

READY FOR GRAMMAR

7 Present perfect simple

1 Complete sentences 1–10 with an appropriate word or phrase from the box. Use the verb tenses and the words in bold to help you. The first one has been done for you.

> far today   it got dark   I was younger   months ago
> my 11th birthday   ~~the last few days~~   this month
> week   were both three   years

1 I've had loads of homework **in** _the last few days_.
2 I wanted to get home **before** _it got dark_.
3 We went to see a musical **on** _my 11th birthday_.
4 I've drunk three cups of tea **so** _far today_.
5 I didn't like mushrooms **when** _I was younger_.
6 We've had three storms **already** _this month_.
7 I last saw Angelina about **three** _months ago_.
8 Lou and I have been friends **since we** _were both three_.
9 I've known Tony and Sue **for several** _years_.
10 We finally won our first match **last** _week_.

2 Complete the gaps in this phone conversation with the past simple or the present perfect simple of the verbs in brackets.

Alison: Hi Sam, it's Alison. I hear that you and Nieves are getting married next May. How long **(1)** _have you been_ (*you/be*) engaged?

Sam: About six months. I **(2)** _proposed_ (*propose*) to her when we were on holiday in Fiji. We **(3)** _kept_ (*keep*) it secret for about a month or so after that, just until we **(4)** _were_ (*be*) sure of the date for the wedding.

Alison: So **(5)** _have_ you _made_ (*make*) all the arrangements yet?

Sam: Well, some of them. We **(6)** _have/'ve agreed_ (*agree*) on who to invite and we **(7)** _have/'ve drawn_ (*draw*) up a guest list. Don't worry, you're on it! We just **(8)** _haven't sent_ (*not/send*) the invitations out yet. And last week we **(9)** _booked_ (*book*) a place for the reception.

Alison: And **(10)** _have_ you _decided_ (*decide*) where you're going to live?

Sam: Yes. We **(11)** _have/'ve saved_ (*save*) up enough money for a deposit on a flat we like near the centre. We're going into town to pay that tomorrow. We **(12)** _fell_ (*fall*) in love with the idea as soon as we **(13)** _saw_ (*see*) the plans. They **(14)** _haven't finished_ (*not/finish*) building it, but we **(15)** _spoke_ (*speak*) to the estate agent last week and she **(16)** _told_ (*tell*) us it should be ready by May. We're so excited!

Go back to **page 103**.

VALUE FOR MONEY

Listening

1. For this **SPEAK** activity, it would be worth revisiting the *Preferences on specific occasions* section on page 206 (TB19) in **Ready for Grammar**. This could be done before, to prime the students to use the language during the task, or afterwards in a focus on form stage, where you could revise the grammar while correcting or upgrading examples of the students' language collected during the speaking activity.

2. ▶ 7.2 After the students have read the instructions, focus their attention on the **Don't forget!** box. Check the meaning of *commuter* (question 3) and *encourage* (question 5). Note that on the *B2 First* exam, students will have only a minute to read the questions in Part 4. Therefore, for the reasons explained on TB100, it would be useful to begin setting time limits at this point in the course.

3. Direct students to the **Audioscript** on pages 240–241 (see below). They discuss the meaning of the phrasal verbs in pairs. Feedback in open class.

4. Organise the students into new groups, preferably with students they have not yet worked with during the lesson. Before they begin speaking, nominate a student from each group to be the one to share the most important points from their discussion with the class afterwards. Encourage them to take notes.

AUDIOSCRIPT

Listening Part 4 Multiple choice

▶ 7.2

I = Interviewer H = Holly

I: With me today is Holly Ridge, who's writing a book about village life in the modern age. *(Ex 2 Q1)* **What's the title of your book, Holly?**

H: If only I knew! **I just can't seem to come up with one which will both reflect the content, and encourage people to buy the book.** My editor suggested *Twenty-first-century village life*, but that didn't sound very inspiring. We'll need to agree on one soon, because the publisher is currently **putting together** its autumn catalogue, well in advance of the publication date.

I: So what for you is a typical village, Holly?

H: Well, I'm not sure there is one. People usually imagine a pleasant square or green, with a pretty church, picturesque old cottages and a slow pace of life. *(Ex 2 Q2)* **This is not entirely wrong and does go some way to describing villages.** But it doesn't take account of what **goes on** in each one. What you see are just the stages or film sets, but the stories played out on them are all very different. Each village has its own personality, its own peculiarities, and functions in its own particular way.

I: But there are certain types of village, aren't there? Commuter villages, for example.

H: Yes, that's right. People who work in large cities are bound to be attracted to villages which are within reasonable travelling distance. Some locals will tell you that a large influx of commuters has changed the appearance and nature of their village, **turning** it **into** a small town. 'Commuters have different priorities,' they say. 'They don't contribute to the life of the village.' This may or may not be true, but *(Ex 2 Q3)* more worrying is **the fact that their arrival pushes up house prices, which become so expensive that the original inhabitants, young families in particular, have to move away.**

I: And that's also a problem with second-home ownership, isn't it?

H: Well, yes, the buying of houses for use as second homes can have a more devastating effect on some villages. They might be lively, busy places at weekends and in the holidays, but they'll be empty the rest of the time – almost like ghost towns. *(Ex 2 Q4)* **Only the older residents remain, so there is no longer that mix of generations,** which is so beneficial for the life of the village. And shops, health centres, libraries and village schools are forced to close.

I: And are there any ways of preventing this?

H: I think there are, yes. Let's not forget that villages are places for people to live in, so the important thing is to make people want to come and live in them. And to attract a range of people, you need a range of housing, from the picturesque old cottages I mentioned before, to more affordable, modern houses. *(Ex 2 Q5)* **That might change the look of a place, make it less appealing to the eye,** but it will help to keep it alive, so it's a price worth paying.

I: The Localism Act could help with all of this, couldn't it?

H: Certainly, yes. *(Ex 2 Q6)* **The Localism Act makes it possible for ordinary people to bring about improvements in their community.** It gives them legal powers to get more homes built, provide better local services or stop a school closing. It's a lengthy and complex process, but basically, residents **draw up** a Neighbourhood Plan of what they want to accomplish, and submit it to the local council. The council can either **turn** it **down**, or approve it, in which case it goes to a referendum for all the residents to vote on. And if at least 50% vote in favour, the plan is activated.

I: Very interesting. Now, I know you live in a village, Holly. Is it doing well?

H: Yes, it is. It's in very good health. It's just outside the commuter belt, but we have both a primary and a secondary school and one or two shops and cafés. *(Ex 2 Q7)* **I enjoy living there.** It helps that I've **set up** a small gardening business, so that puts me in contact with others, and **I know most people in the village, at least to say hello to. I'm on friendly terms with everyone.**

I: Sounds ideal.

7 VALUE FOR MONEY

Listening Part 4 Multiple choice

1 **SPEAK** Work in pairs. Discuss the advantages and disadvantages of living in a village and living in a city. Which would you prefer?

2 ▶ 7.2 You will hear part of a radio interview with a woman called Holly Ridge, who is writing a book about villages. For questions 1–7, choose the best answer (A, B or C).

1 What does Holly say about the title of her book?
   A The publisher did not like her suggestion.
   (B) She has not been able to think of a suitable one.
   C It will only be revealed when the book is published.

2 Holly says that common perceptions of the typical village
   A are old-fashioned.
   (B) have an element of truth in them.
   C are influenced by what people see in films.

3 What is Holly's main concern about commuter villages?
   A Villages lose their original character.
   B Commuters do not integrate into village life.
   (C) Local people can no longer afford to live in them.

4 What does Holly say about some villages where people buy second homes?
   (A) They do not have a balance of age groups.
   B They can be frightening places to live in.
   C They have good services and amenities.

5 Holly says that a possible result of encouraging people to live in villages is that
   (A) the appearance of villages may be sacrificed.
   B the cost of housing in villages may increase.
   C new houses may outnumber old houses in villages.

6 Holly says that the Localism Act is a law which enables communities to
   A organise their own local elections.
   (B) achieve changes in their local area.
   C reject new members of their local council.

7 What does Holly say she likes about the village where she lives?
   (A) the good relations she has with other villagers
   B the quality of local healthcare services
   C the large number of small businesses

3 Look at the **Audioscript** on **pages 240–241** and use context to help you work out the approximate meanings of the phrasal verbs in bold.

4 **SPEAK** Work in groups. What are villages like in your country? How similar are they to those described by Holly in the listening?

Don't forget!
› Underline key words in the questions or sentence beginnings.
› For each question you will hear distractors.
› Listen carefully both times before making your final choices.

3 Suggested answers
come up with = think of
put together = produce (by combining several different things)
go on = happen
turn into = make something change into something different
push up = make something increase
bring about = cause (changes) to happen
draw up = prepare and write (a plan)
turn down = reject
set up = start (a business)

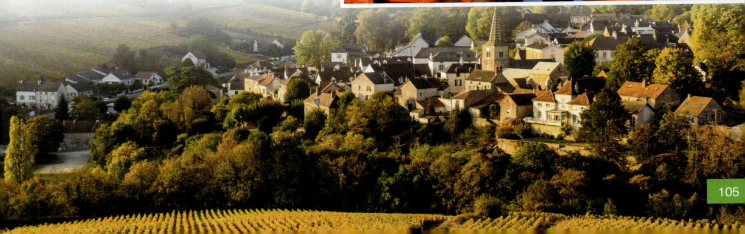

105

7 VALUE FOR MONEY

Vocabulary   Towns and villages

1 Complete each gap with a word from the box to form places you might find in a village, town or city. The first one has been done for you.

building   flats   housing   industrial   office   pedestrian   ~~residential~~   shopping

1 This charming three-bedroomed villa is located in a quiet _residential_ **area**
2 You can't drive down Bromley Way anymore – it's a _pedestrian_ **street** now.
3 My uncle lives on the fifteenth floor of a huge **block of** _flats_.
4 I usually buy my clothes at the **indoor** _shopping_ **centre** on the edge of town: there's so much choice under one roof.
5 Most of the _office_ **blocks** here are occupied by insurance companies and law firms.
6 Property prices fell and all construction stopped, leaving a number of abandoned _building_ **sites** around the town.
7 They knocked down all the houses and built an _industrial_ **estate** for small manufacturing businesses.
8 It's easy to get lost on the _housing_ **estate** where I live: all the properties look exactly the same.

2 SPEAK Work in pairs. Can you think of an example for each of the places in Exercise 1 in the area where you live? For each place, answer the following questions:

a Is it *on the outskirts* of your town or village or *in the centre*?
b Is it *within easy walking distance* of your home?

3 In 1–6, write down the pair of adjectives which could be used to describe each place.

boring/dull   green/leafy   lively/vibrant   neglected/run-down
pretty/picturesque   prosperous/thriving

1 A village with narrow streets and attractive 17th-century cottages.   _pretty/picturesque_
2 A city with an exciting atmosphere and plenty going on all the time.   _lively/vibrant_
3 A place where there's very little to do and nothing ever happens.   _boring/dull_
4 An urban area in bad condition that has had no money spent on it.   _neglected/run-down_
5 A town with successful businesses and a high standard of living.   _prosperous/thriving_
6 A suburb with quiet, tree-lined streets and gardens full of plants.   _green/leafy_

4 SPEAK Work in pairs. Which adjectives in Exercise 3 would you use to describe the area where you live? Give reasons for your choices.

VALUE FOR MONEY

Vocabulary

1 This vocabulary section continues with the topic of villages introduced in the listening on page 105. Note that students are often asked to talk or write about the places where people live in the *B2 First* exam; this vocabulary section aims to help them do so with more sophistication. You may wish to use **Which property?** on the Teacher's Resource Centre as a lead-in or extension to the lesson.

Check the pronunciation (particularly the word stress) of *industrial* /ɪnˈdʌstriəl/, *pedestrian* /pəˈdestriən/ and *residential* /ˌrezɪˈdenʃl/. To change the dynamic, you could put a couple of corrected versions of this exercise on the walls of the classroom and ask students to get up and check their answers when they are ready. Fast finishers could study the exercise for a minute, and then close their books and write down as many of the collocations as they can remember.

2 If mobile phones are allowed, encourage students to search for the place names in Google images to show their partners. This will help link each collocation with an image in their memories.

3 Check the pronunciation (again, particularly word stress) of *picturesque* /ˌpɪktʃəˈresk/ and *prosperous* /ˈprɒspərəs/. Check the meaning and pronunciation of *cottage* /ˈkɒtɪdʒ/. Ask the students if they know any places that fit the descriptions. In pairs, ask the students to quickly quiz each other by covering the column on the right and trying to remember the missing words.

4 Give the students a few minutes to quietly prepare on their own before speaking to a classmate. If all of your students live in the same city, you could suggest they describe a place where they lived in the past, or where they spend their holidays, to avoid too much overlap in the students' descriptions. Note that this **SPEAK** activity lends itself to task repetition (see **Teaching tip** on TB16).

READY FOR GRAMMAR

7 Present perfect continuous

1 The present perfect continuous can be used to talk about an activity which started in the past and continues to the present, or a point just before the present.

*Sorry I'm late. **I've** just **been playing** tennis with Joe.* (recently finished)

***I've been studying** all morning. I'm going to stop soon.* (still continuing)

To emphasise that an activity has been completed, the present perfect simple is used instead of the continuous.

Compare:

***We've been painting** the lounge. There's still a bit more to do, but we're going to carry on after lunch.* (not completed)

***We've** just **painted** the lounge – it looks so much better now.* (completed)

2 Like the present perfect simple, the continuous form can be used to talk about <u>the effects in the present</u> of something that happened in the past.

Compare:

<u>Your new shoes are ruined!</u> ***You've been playing** football in them, haven't you?* (an activity)

<u>I can't do any sport for a few weeks</u>; ***I've broken** my arm.* (a single action)

3 The present perfect continuous is often used to suggest that a situation or activity is **temporary**.

Compare:

*We're decorating Ali's room, so **she's been sleeping** on the sofa.* (temporary)

*She's always **slept** badly, ever since she was a child.* (permanent)

4 It can also be used to talk about an action or activity that is **repeated**.

Compare:

***I've been trying** to phone Tim all day, but there's no reply.* (repeated action)

***I've phoned** Amy. She said she'll be here in a minute.* (single action)

5 The continuous form is not used if we talk about the number of things that have been completed or the number of times a thing has been done.

***I've been ironing** shirts all morning.* (focus on the activity)

***I've ironed** over twenty shirts this morning.* (focus on the completed actions)

6 Stative verbs such as *have* (to possess/own), *think* (to have an opinion), *be*, *like*, *believe*, *understand* and *know* are not normally used in the continuous form.

***We've known** each other for a long time.* ✔
We've been knowing each other for a long time. ✘

7 VALUE FOR MONEY

Language focus

1-2 This exercise gives students the chance to show how much they know about differences between the present perfect simple, which they explored on page 103, and the present perfect continuous. Ask students to discuss the sentences in pairs and then direct them to the **Ready for Grammar** section on page 220 (see TB106 and below). They read the grammar rules to check. In open class, go through each pair of sentences together, asking students to explain the differences between the sentences based on what they have read. Try to resolve any doubts during this teaching stage before moving students onto the controlled practice activities.

Alternatively, you could project the pairs of sentences on the board one by one. In open class, elicit the differences and underlying rules from the students with concept questions, e.g. *Has he finished the book?* Use the explanations in the **Ready for Grammar** section to help you. Note that if students have demonstrated a good grasp of the grammar by this stage, it may not be necessary to do the two practice exercises in the **Ready for Grammar** section. These could be set for homework or saved for revision. You could instead use the **Guessing game** on the **Teacher's Resource Centre** that allows for freer practice of the grammar point.

3 Students do the exercise individually and then check in pairs. Go over the answers in open class.

4 This activity allows the students to practise the grammar in a less controlled way. Check the meaning of *castaways* and *shelter*. Divide the class into two groups: journalists and castaways. Give them time to discuss either the questions or answers with their group members. Then pair up the castaways and journalists. They roleplay the interview. Monitor and provide on-the-spot correction of the target language. For any other common errors, note them down to address later in a corrective feedback stage.

READY FOR GRAMMAR

7 Present perfect continuous

1 Underline the correct alternative in each sentence.

1. Crime writer Ian Rankin has *written* / *been writing* more than twenty novels featuring Inspector John Rebus.
2. We've just got back from holiday, so I've *washed* / *been washing* our clothes. I'm just going to put some more in the washing machine now.
3. Come on, hurry up! You haven't even *had* / *been having* a shower yet, have you?
4. Pablo *is playing* / *has been playing* on his phone since he got up this morning.
5. I've just *repaired* / *been repairing* the garden wall, but it's just started to rain, so I'll have to finish it tomorrow.
6. The Carruthers family has *owned* / *been owning* this house for over two hundred years.

2 Correct the mistakes in the following sentences.

1. My mother's ~~been worked~~ [been working / worked] as a postwoman for just over a year.
2. Mario has ~~been breaking~~ [broken] his leg three times in the last three years.
3. I've ~~being~~ [been] helping my sister with her wedding preparations this morning; we've had a nice time together.
4. We've been thinking about our summer holiday; we haven't ~~been making~~ [made] a decision about where to go yet.
5. Do you realise how long ~~time~~ I've been waiting for you here?
6. We've ~~been having~~ [had] our dog for three days now and we still haven't come up with a name for it.
7. Moreno's been playing in this team for four years and that's the first time he's ~~been scoring~~ [scored] a goal.
8. I can't remember the last time ~~I've been going~~ [I went] to the cinema. It was about three years ago, I think.

Go back to **page 107**.

VALUE FOR MONEY

7

Language focus Present perfect continuous

1 **SPEAK** Work in pairs. For questions 1–4, compare the two sentences a and b, and discuss why the present perfect simple or continuous is used in each case.

1 a I've just been reading that book I bought on holiday. I can't put it down.
   The speaker has not finished the book yet.
   b I've just read that book I bought on holiday. I really enjoyed it.
   The speaker has finished the book.
2 a He's been going to that new supermarket to do his shopping recently.
   A repeated action; he has been doing it on a regular basis. (We do not know if he is shopping there now or not.)
   b He's gone to that new supermarket to do his shopping. He'll be back soon.
   A single action; he is at the supermarket (or on his way home) now.
3 a I'm moving soon. I've been looking at flats all day.
   A focus on the activity of looking at flats. It is not clear whether they will continue to look today or not.
   b I'm moving soon. I've looked at three flats so far today.
   A focus on the actions which have been completed, the number of flats which have been looked at. Suggests they will continue to look today.
4 a She's been living with her parents since May, just until she finds a place of her own.
   A temporary situation; she is not living with them on a permanent basis.
   b She's lived with her parents all her life.
   A long term, possibly permanent situation.

2 Go to **Ready for Grammar** on **page 220** to check your answers to Exercise 1 and for further practice.

3 Complete the gaps in the following text with either the past simple, the present perfect simple or the present perfect continuous form of the verbs in brackets. The first three have been done for you.

We (1) ___bought___ (buy) our car just after we got married, so we (2) ___have had___ (have) it for over ten years now. Unfortunately, just recently it (3) ___has been giving___ (give) us problems. I (4) ___have/'ve taken___ (take) it to the garage for repairs twice this year already (last month I (5) ___had___ (have) to pay for a new gear box), and for the last few weeks the engine (6) ___has/'s been making___ (make) a strange noise, especially when the car turns a corner. As a result, (7) ___have/'ve been travelling___ (travel) to work by bus, because I'm not sure the car will get me there safely. I (8) ___even walked___ (even/walk) a couple of times last week. The thing is, we (9) ___have/'ve been saving___ (save) to buy a new car, but my husband (10) ___has/'s just lost___ (just/lose) his job, so we'll probably have to get a second-hand one instead, with the money we (11) ___have/'ve put___ (put) aside so far. For the past week or so, I (12) ___have/'ve been looking___ (look) online, and my husband (13) ___has/'s been going___ (go) to second-hand car showrooms. We (14) ___have not/haven't found___ (not/find) anything we like yet – or that we can afford – but my brother (15) ___phoned___ (phone) just a few minutes ago to say he might have something for us.

4 **SPEAK** Work in pairs. Read the following scenario then do the role play below.

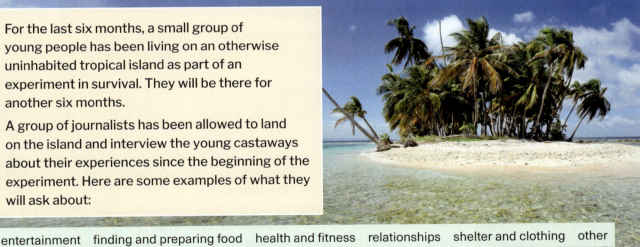

For the last six months, a small group of young people has been living on an otherwise uninhabited tropical island as part of an experiment in survival. They will be there for another six months.

A group of journalists has been allowed to land on the island and interview the young castaways about their experiences since the beginning of the experiment. Here are some examples of what they will ask about:

entertainment   finding and preparing food   health and fitness   relationships   shelter and clothing   other

Student A

You are a journalist. You should prepare your questions for the interview.

For each of the above categories write questions which focus on:

1 **Activities:** e.g. *What have you been using to hunt animals?*
2 **Completed actions:** e.g. *Have you caught many fish?*

Student B

You are a castaway. You should prepare some answers for the interview.

For each of the above categories write sentences on:

1 **Activities:** e.g. *I've been eating fruit from the bushes and trees.*
2 **Completed actions:** e.g. *We've built a very basic kitchen.*

Now roleplay the interview.

107

7 VALUE FOR MONEY

Writing Part 2 Formal and Informal email

What to expect in the exam

In Part 2 of the Writing paper, one of the options might be a letter or an email. The requirements for emails are similar to those of letters. Answers must be grammatically correct with accurate spelling and punctuation, and written in a style which is relevant to the target reader and the situation. The abbreviated language of text messages is not appropriate.

1 Would a formal or informal style be more appropriate for each of the following Writing Part 2 tasks? Why?

A You have been asked to reply to the following email from the new English director of the language school where you study. *A formal style would be appropriate. The target reader is the director of a school. The style of the language in his email is also formal.*

I plan to arrive on August 6th in order to find some temporary rented accommodation. I would not require anything too expensive, preferably somewhere with good shopping facilities nearby and not too far from the school. Could you recommend two possible areas?

Best regards

John Simpson

Write your email in 140–190 words.

B This is part of an email you have received from your English friend, Rob.

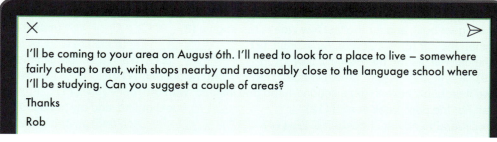

I'll be coming to your area on August 6th. I'll need to look for a place to live – somewhere fairly cheap to rent, with shops nearby and reasonably close to the language school where I'll be studying. Can you suggest a couple of areas?

Thanks

Rob

Write your email in 140–190 words. *An informal style would be appropriate. The target reader is a friend. The style of the language in his email is also informal.*

2 Read the following answer to writing task A in Exercise 1, ignoring the numbered words, and answer these questions.

a Is the style appropriate and consistent?
  Yes, it is consistently formal.
b Has the writer addressed all the points in John Simpson's email?
  Yes, she mentions cost, shops and proximity to the school.

A

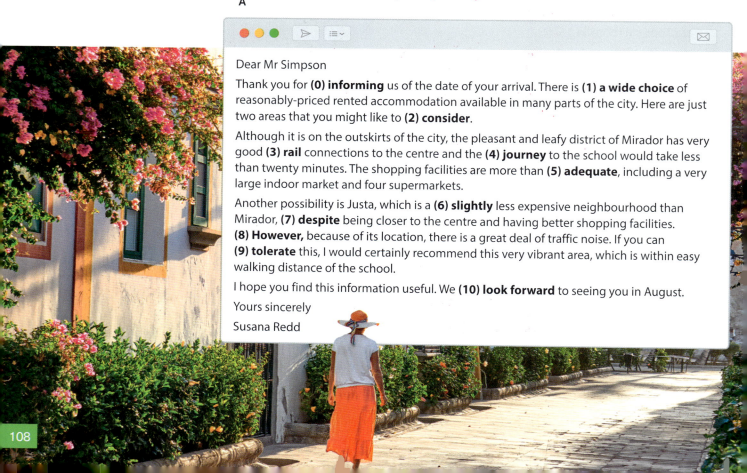

Dear Mr Simpson

Thank you for **(0) informing** us of the date of your arrival. There is **(1) a wide choice** of reasonably-priced rented accommodation available in many parts of the city. Here are just two areas that you might like to **(2) consider**.

Although it is on the outskirts of the city, the pleasant and leafy district of Mirador has very good **(3) rail** connections to the centre and the **(4) journey** to the school would take less than twenty minutes. The shopping facilities are more than **(5) adequate**, including a very large indoor market and four supermarkets.

Another possibility is Justa, which is a **(6) slightly** less expensive neighbourhood than Mirador, **(7) despite** being closer to the centre and having better shopping facilities. **(8) However,** because of its location, there is a great deal of traffic noise. If you can **(9) tolerate** this, I would certainly recommend this very vibrant area, which is within easy walking distance of the school.

I hope you find this information useful. We **(10) look forward** to seeing you in August.

Yours sincerely

Susana Redd

VALUE FOR MONEY 7

Lead-in

In pairs, ask the students to think of reasons or situations in which they would write either formal or informal emails. Challenge them to think of at least five reasons/situations for each. Elicit their ideas to the board in open class. Ask the students: *Why do we need to write in a more formal style sometimes? What happens if we write too informally in these situations? When you look at an email, how can you immediately tell whether it's a formal or informal one?*

Writing

1. Students read the instructions and the exam tasks. In open class, discuss the reasons why task A would require a more formal response than task B. Ask the students: *What would happen if you responded too formally to Rob?* Point out that these two exam tasks are very similar to the ones they may encounter on the *B2 First* exam.

2–3 These exercises provide students with two good model answers, giving them a clear idea of what formal and informal emails written for the *B2 First* are supposed to look and sound like. It also gives them some useful practice with distinguishing between formal and informal registers, an area where students at this level will still lack full awareness and sensitivity.

Extra activity

Often when we ask students to write something in class, no matter what type of writing it may be, the only real audience is the teacher, because that's the only person who is ever expected to read it. Try to create opportunities for students to read each other's writing — or even write to each other. For example, when you ask your students to write their emails in response to the task on page 109, instead of sending the email to the teacher as an attachment, students could send it as a real email to a classmate with the teacher cc'd in. The teacher responds with constructive feedback; the fellow student writes a short reply. In general, students find it very motivating to know what they write will actually be read.

Teaching tip

As the course progresses, start giving your students feedback on their writing using the official marking criteria. You will have noticed that in the **Answer key** (see TB109 for an example) of *Ready for B2 First* there are examiner comments for each sample answer to the writing tasks, which give feedback on **content**, **communicative achievement**, **organisation**, and **language** . These are the four criteria used by official examiners. The feedback you give your students does not have to be this in-depth, but it would be helpful to let your students know in which of these areas they still need to improve. For more information about the way the writing is assessed on the *B2 First*, go to the **Ready for Writing** section.

7 VALUE FOR MONEY

4 Students do the exercise individually and then compare their answers with a classmate. Check the answers as a whole group.

5 Students could do this exercise in pairs or small groups. Elicit some of their ideas in open class.

Answers

a *Openings and closings:* Dear Mr Simpson *and* Yours sincerely *in A;* Hi Rob *and* All the best *in B.*
*The use of nouns in A (*the date of your arrival*; a wide choice of; because of its location) compared to verbs in B (*when you're coming; plenty of … to choose from; being in the centre*). Formal/neutral words in A (*Thank you; very; very large; a great deal of*). More informal equivalent words in B (e.g.* Thanks; really; enormous; a lot of*).*
Latinate verb tolerate *in A; phrasal verb* put up with *in B (though note that* look forward to *in A is a phrasal verb).*

b *Dashes (*I'd definitely recommend the area – it's really lively*) and exclamation marks (*five supermarkets!*) are features of informal writing, which appear in B, but not in A.*

c *Use of contractions in B (*you're*; *it's*; *it'd*; *Justa's*; *there's*; *can't*): no contractions in A.*
*Ellipsis (omission of words) in B ((*I*) hope this is useful/(*I*) Can't wait to see you): no ellipsis in A.*

6 Give students time to read the task and then focus their attention on the **Useful language** and the **Don't forget!** boxes. Elicit what style would be appropriate for the task. Encourage them to incorporate some of the useful language given here and on page 193 in the **Ready for Writing** section into their letters. The final writing could be done in class (timed, 40 minutes) or set for homework. If students do the writing at home, stress the importance of simulating exam conditions as much as possible by sitting in a quiet place where they can write their letters uninterrupted from start to finish. Make sure they time themselves. No breaks!

Sample answer

Hi Patrick,

Thanks for you email. Sorry for not come shopping with you, but you know I'm always busy. However, it's true that I know very well the town.

If I were you, I'd go to Computer House. It's one of the best shops to buy computer equipment. But if the price doesn't convince you too much, you could try looking in Cath's Computer, there is also good equipment. I've also got a friend who works there, maybe he could help you choose a better thing.

And if you want some casual clothes, make sure you have a good look round in Tiffosy Shop, which is a bit far away, in Belgic Street, but their clothes have reasonable prices. However, if you don't want to go so far away and you want something near the town, it will be good if you get across Funny and Punk Shop. You can find great things in both of them.

I hope that's useful. Good look and let me know how you get on.

Best wishes

Madalina

174 words

Examiner comments

Content: All the content is relevant and very informative. Two alternatives are suggested, both for printers and clothes, with consideration given to price (*if their price doesn't convince you too much; reasonable prices*) and quality (*good equipment; great things*).

Communicative achievement: The conventions of letters are used appropriately, with good opening and closing comments. The register is consistently informal and the tone friendly and helpful, holding the reader's attention to the end.

Organisation: The letter is well organised into logical paragraphs, and a range of linking words and other cohesive devices are used (e.g. *However; But; And;* *which; in both of them; I hope that's useful*). More could have been used to aid cohesion in the second paragraph.

Language: A range of everyday language is used appropriately (e.g. *busy; computer equipment; a bit far away; reasonable prices*) and a range of structures is used to give advice (*If I were you; you could try looking; make sure you have a good look round*). The incorrect use of *get across* does not prevent understanding.

Both simple and complex forms are used with good control and errors do not impede communication (*Thanks for you email; Sorry for not come; I know very well the town; Good look*).

Mark: Pass to good pass

VALUE FOR MONEY

3 Read the following answer to writing task B in Exercise 1, ignoring the numbered gaps. The style is appropriately informal and, apart from three minor factual differences, the content is the same as the content of the answer to writing task A in Exercise 2. Can you find the three factual differences between answer A and answer B?

Mirador to school by train: A less than twenty minutes B under thirty minutes
Supermarkets in Mirador: A four B five
Justa to school: A within easy walking distance B you can cycle

B

Hi Rob
Thanks for letting me **(0)** _know_ when you're coming. There are **(1)** _plenty/lots/loads_ of cheap rented flats to choose from all over the city, and here are just a couple of areas worth **(2)** _thinking_ about.
Mirador is a really pleasant district with loads of trees, and although it's on the edge of the city, you can get a **(3)** _train_ into the centre very easily. It'd take you under thirty minutes to **(4)** _get/travel_ to the school. There are more than **(5)** _enough_ shops there, including an enormous indoor market and five supermarkets!
Another possibility is Justa, where rents are a **(6)** _bit/little_ cheaper than in Mirador, even **(7)** _though/if_ Justa's closer to the centre and there are a lot more shops. **(8)** _But_ of course, being in the centre, there's a lot of noise from the traffic. If you can **(9)** _put_ up with that, though, I'd definitely recommend the area – it's really lively and you can cycle to the school from here.
Anyway, hope this is useful. Can't **(10)** _wait_ to see you in August.
All the best
Susana

4 Use the numbered words in bold in answer A to help you complete the numbered gaps in answer B. Write one word in each gap. There is an example at the beginning (0).

5 Read and compare the two answers (A and B) again. Comment on any further differences you notice between them. Consider:
a differences in the language used to express the same idea
b differences in the use of punctuation
c any other differences you notice.

6 Now write an answer to the following Part 2 question.

This is part of an email you have received from your Irish friend Patrick, who lives in your country.

Cristina and I are going into town next Saturday. I want to buy a printer for my computer and we both need some casual clothes – good quality but not too expensive. I know you can't come shopping with us but you know the town very well – where do you suggest we should go?
Thanks
Patrick

Write your email in 140–190 words.

Useful language

Making suggestions
If I were you, I'd go to …
You could try looking in …
Make sure you have a good look round in …
The best place to buy computer equipment is …
If you want to buy decent casual clothes, you can't go far wrong in …

Talking about price
You can buy decent printers at low/reasonable/competitive/affordable prices.
Their clothes are cheap/reasonably priced/affordable/good value for money.

Don't forget

› Plan your email.
› Include a brief, relevant opening paragraph.
› Use linking expressions.
› Write in a consistently appropriate style.

For more information on writing informal emails see **page 193**.

7 REVIEW

Vocabulary Shopping

Complete each sentence with a word from the box.

bargain   charge   money   penny   price   refund   sales   stock

1 Well-made and reasonably priced, it's excellent **value for** ___money___.
2 What do you think of these trousers? I bought them **in the** ___sales___.
3 Our new online shopping app can be downloaded **free of** ___charge___.
4 Booking a holiday last minute is a good way to **pick up a** ___bargain___.
5 It didn't work properly, so I took it back and **asked for a** ___refund___.
6 Our full range of ceramic cookware is now **on sale at half** ___price___.
7 I tried to get a copy, but none of the bookshops have it **in** ___stock___.
8 We paid a lot of money for the car, but it was **worth every** ___penny___.

Reading and Use of English Part 2 Open cloze

For questions 1–8, read the text below and think of the word which best fits each gap. Use only one word in each gap. There is an example at the beginning (0).

GIGAMANSIONS

If you come into **(0)** ___A___ few hundred million dollars, and can't quite **(1)** ___make___ up your mind what to spend the money **(2)** ___on___, why not consider buying a 'gigamansion' in an exclusive area of California?

'Gigamansion' is the term used to describe the new class of luxurious houses that are springing up **(3)** ___like___ mushrooms all over the hills of Bel Air, Beverly Hills and Holmby Hills. Historic 1920s mansions are being knocked **(4)** ___down___ to make way for homes valued at well over $100 million. These include the most expensive house **(5)** ___in___ the United States, a $500 million residence known **(6)** ___as___ 'The One', which has four infinity pools, a 40-seater cinema, a bowling alley and **(7)** ___its___ own nightclub.

Residents complain that their neighbourhood has been turned **(8)** ___into___ a huge construction site, and the new buildings are ruining its appearance, but developers point out that the transformation is pushing up the value of the area's existing homes.

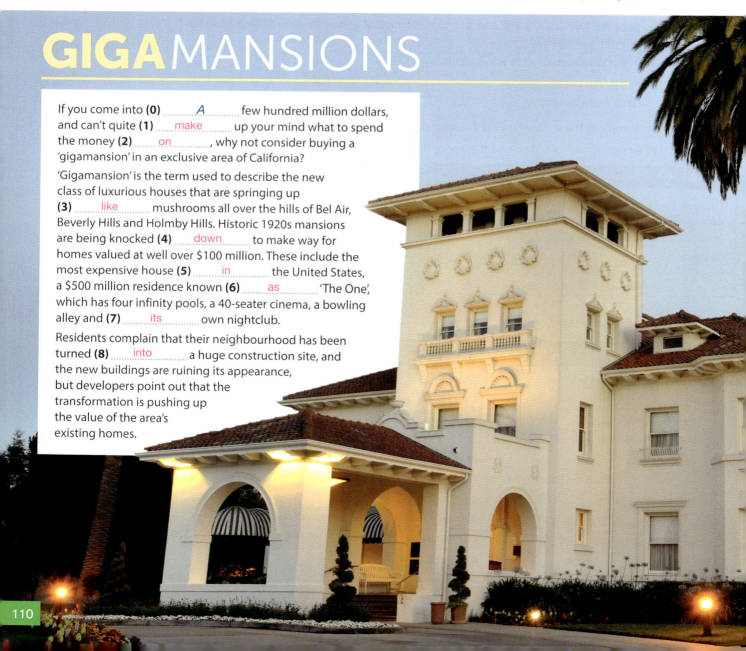

REVIEW 7

Reading and Use of English Part 4 Key word transformation

1 Match each sentence (1–3) with two sentences (a–f) which both express a similar idea.

1 I haven't done this before.
2 I haven't done this for five years.
3 I've been doing this for five years.

a It's five years since I started doing this.
b It's five years since I last did this.
c I've never done this.
d The last time I did this was five years ago.
e It's the first time I've done this.
f I began doing this five years ago.

2 Complete the second sentence so that it has a similar meaning to the first sentence, using the word given. Do not change the word given. You must use between two and five words, including the word given.

1 I haven't spoken to her since she had her baby.
   TIME
   The _last **time** I spoke to_ her was before she had her baby.

2 I haven't eaten Slovak food before.
   FIRST
   This is the _**first** time I have/'ve eaten_ Slovak food.

3 Jasmin only started her blog in May and she's already got thousands of followers.
   WRITING
   Jasmin's only _been **writing** her blog since_ May and she's already got thousands of followers.

4 He hasn't seen his sister for ages.
   LAST
   It's a long _time since he **last** saw_ his sister.

5 The last time I went abroad was five years ago.
   BEEN
   I _haven't/have not **been** abroad for_ five years.

6 I've never seen a supermarket as big as this before.
   EVER
   This is the _biggest supermarket I have/'ve **ever**_ seen.

Writing Part 1 Essay

In your English class you have been talking about shopping. Now, your English teacher has asked you to write an essay.

Write an essay using **all** the notes and giving reasons for your point of view.

> **Some people say that large shopping centres are a bad idea. What do you think?**
>
> **Notes**
>
> **Write about:**
> 1 being able to buy everything in one place
> 2 spending time with family and friends
> 3 .... (your own idea)

Write your essay in 140–190 words.
See the Teacher's Resource Centre for a Sample answer with Examiner comments for this task.
For more information on writing essays, see **pages 189–191**.

7 VALUE FOR MONEY

Pronunciation Contrastive stress

1 ▶ 7.3 Stress can be used to indicate contrast or to correct previous information. Listen to how the underlined words in the sentence below are stressed.

Being successful is not about <u>wealth</u>, it's about <u>happiness</u>.

2 Underline the words with contrastive stress in sentences 1–5.
  1 It's the <u>red</u> jacket I want to buy, not the <u>green</u> one.
  2 It's not <u>what</u> you know but <u>who</u> you know that counts.
  3 <u>I</u> didn't pay for it, <u>Saskia</u> did.
  4 <u>Speaking</u> the language is fairly easy; <u>understanding</u> it is another matter entirely.
  5 He doesn't <u>like</u> shopping. He <u>loves</u> it.

3 ▶ 7.4 Listen to check your answers to Exercise 2.

4 **SPEAK** Work in pairs. Write down three things you believe to be untrue about your partner. Then read your sentences to each other. Correct your partner using contrastive stress.

  A: You play basketball on Saturday afternoons.
  B: No, we play on Saturday mornings.

5 **SPEAK** Work in pairs. Choose two of the items below but don't tell your partner. Try to identify your partner's items by asking questions. The person who guesses their partner's items with the fewest number of questions is the winner.

  A: Have you got a blue bag?
  B: No I haven't.
  A: Have you got a yellow bag?

Pronunciation

1 ▶ 7.3 Word stress is determined by the language; sentence stress, on the other hand, is decided by the speaker. When we stress a particular word in order to contrast it with an alternative, this is called *contrastive stress*. You could raise students' awareness of contrastive stress by boarding the sentence *I never said I loved you* and saying it various times, adding a different meaning each time by stressing a different word.

2–3 ▶ 7.4 Students could do this in pairs or individually.

4 Students do the exercise as suggested. Monitor their use of contrastive stress.

5 Pre-teach (change) purse, ear buds and wok. Monitor and encourage the students to use contrastive stress when asking their questions. Were some of the items chosen more often than others?

8 ON THE MOVE

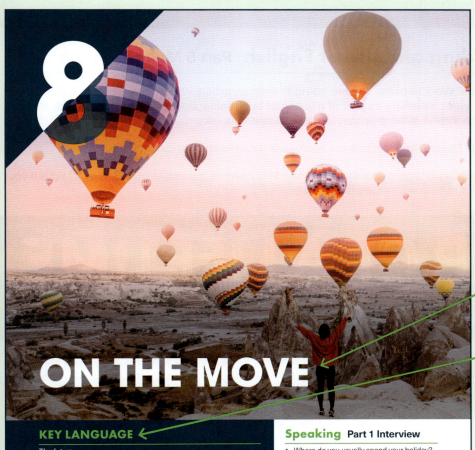

Travel and holidays are the themes of this unit. Reading, writing, listening and speaking tasks explore topics such as gap years, transport, different types of holidays and places people like to go on holiday.

Read the unit objectives to the class.

KEY LANGUAGE
The future
Contrast linkers
Make and *do*
Travel and holidays
Phrasal verbs
Adjectives

PRONUNCIATION
Chunking

EXAM PRACTICE
Reading and Use of English Parts 1, 3, 4 & 5
Writing Parts 1 & 2
Listening Parts 1 & 3
Speaking Parts 1 & 2

Speaking Part 1 Interview
1. Where do you usually spend your holiday?
2. Where are you going to spend your next holiday?
3. What types of things do you like doing on holiday?
4. Would you enjoy going on holiday on your own?
5. What is the best holiday you have ever had? And the worst?
6. Is there anywhere you would particularly like to visit? Why?

SPEAKING Part 1 Interview

Focus students' attention on the picture. Ask the class: *Has anyone ever gone for a ride in a hot-air balloon? Would you like to? What do you think people might enjoy about this activity?*

Put the students into groups of three. Assign one student to be the examiner; the other two are candidates. Only the examiners have their books open, so only they can see the questions. On the board, write or project the following script for the examiners to read:
Good morning/afternoon/evening. My name is ……… . And your names are? Where are you from (Candidate A)? And you, (Candidate B)? First, we'd like to know something about you.

Tell the examiners to go back and forth between the candidates, giving them an equal opportunity to speak.

If a candidate starts giving too much information, the student in the role of an examiner should cut them off politely with a firm *Thank you*, the same way a real examiner would. Remind the students that candidates don't talk to each other during Speaking Part 1 and that this part of the test lasts approximately two minutes.

ONLINE MATERIALS

The Future Board Game (**Teacher's Resource Centre**)
Let's grade each other! (**Teacher's Resource Centre**)
Linkers topic cards (**Teacher's Resource Centre**)
Unit 8 Test (**Test Generator**)
Unit 8 Wordlist (**Teacher's Resource Centre**)
Unit 8 On-the-go-practice (**App**)

8 ON THE MOVE

Reading and Use of English Part 5 Multiple choice

1 **SPEAK** Work in pairs. You are going to read an article written by a woman called Rosie, who went travelling as part of a gap year between school and university. Look at the photographs. Where do you think each one was taken?

2 Read *The trip of a lifetime* to check your ideas from Exercise 1.

3 Read the text again and for questions 1–6, choose the answer (A, B, C or D) which you think fits best according to the text.

THE TRIP OF A LIFETIME

Rosie Casterton describes how she spent her gap year between school and university.

I felt slightly ashamed when my exam results came out, despite the loyal praise from my parents. The grades were more than respectable, but they weren't quite good enough for the university degree course I was hoping to do. I called the admissions office, asked them to reconsider, but the reply was unequivocal – I hadn't met the entry requirements, so I should make alternative plans. I slowly pulled myself together, gathered some perspective, began to feel proud of my achievements and vowed to turn disappointment into opportunity. I would take time out to travel, then reapply the following year for a different course.

It would be stretching the truth to say that I intended to broaden my horizons, develop as a person, discover my true self. Things may have turned out that way in the end, but at the time, I knew only that I had a year on my hands, and an extended trip abroad sounded like a worthwhile way to spend it. Or at least part of it – I'd need to work first to fund myself, so I took a job as a receptionist at a local doctor's surgery. It was a tough six months; the patients were very demanding and I often got shouted at, but it gave me the opportunity to gain some work experience, develop some useful skills, and importantly, save money for the more enjoyable part of the year.

In the meantime, I managed to talk a friend from school into coming with me – Lowri, who also failed to get the grades she needed. After months of planning, we set off for Cuzco in Peru, where we'd volunteered to work for two weeks in an orphanage. I'm not sure what good we thought we could do there. We took gifts of toys and played with the children, but I don't think our presence was of much value. The owners didn't expect a great deal from us and seemed more interested in the money we'd paid to be there, which went towards food, clothes and the upkeep of the building. Everything appeared unstructured and disorganised, but the children were full of life and clearly happy, so the orphanage was obviously doing something right.

The next six weeks we spent travelling around South America as part of a tour group. In Peru we went white water rafting, horse riding and then sandboarding on dunes by the desert oasis of Huacachina. In Bolivia, some courageous, if foolhardy members of the group cycled down the infamous Death Road. This no doubt earned them bragging rights for years to come, though personally, I'm content with being able to tell everyone that I saw the incredible Uyuni Salt Flats, vast plains of white salt which stretch out as far as the eye can see. Then in Brazil we spent time exploring parts of the Amazon, before finishing the tour in Rio de Janeiro.

After Rio we flew to South Africa, where we stayed for two weeks with friends in Johannesburg and Cape Town, and relaxed mostly, before moving on to the third and final stage of our trip in Thailand, Vietnam and Laos; another continent, different cultures, new experiences. Unlike in South America, nothing was pre-planned. We booked all the transport and cultural trips ourselves using local tour companies in each country, which added an element of spontaneity, and gave us more freedom of choice and a greater sense of independence.

And yes, when it all came to an end, I did feel I'd developed as a person. Travelling taught me so much. I learnt how to manage my money; I had to be organised and continually think ahead; I became more flexible and open-minded, readily adapting to a wide range of places, people and their cultures. Perhaps Lowri and I overdid things in this respect; maybe we should have heeded the old adage that 'less is more'. We packed as many countries into the four months as possible, and in doing so, gained only a very general idea of life in each one. Still, I'm sure I'll find time to go back to some of them in the future. Won't I?

114

8 ON THE MOVE

Lead-in

Images are often a great way to introduce a topic and spark discussion. Find four or five pictures of people doing activities associated with gap years: volunteering, backpacking, adventure travel, teaching abroad, being an au pair, etc. Project the photos or put them up on the board. In pairs, students discuss for a minute what they might have in common. Elicit or provide *gap year*. Discuss the topic in open class. *What are the advantages and disadvantages of taking a gap year? Would you like to take/have taken one? Overall – good idea or bad idea?*

Reading and Use of English

1 For this task, you could put a few of the expressions for speculating from the **Useful language** box on page 3 up on the board.

2 Tell the students that for this skimming task you are going to set a countdown timer for three minutes. Be strict. Note that one common complaint on the *B2 First* is not having enough time to answer the questions properly. In class, it's important to get students into the habit of reading very quickly.

Teaching tip

Sometimes it makes sense to simply give the students the answers and let them correct themselves, rather than eliciting the answers one by one to the board, which can be an inefficient use of class time. This is most easily done by displaying the answers using a projector or directing the students to the **Answer key** in the back of the Student's Book (or on the **Student's** and **Teacher's Resource Centres**). Afterwards, discuss and clarify any questions that were particularly tricky in open class. This way of correcting exercises offers the same opportunities for students to resolve doubts and learn from their mistakes—and it can be a great deal faster.

Extra activity

Put the students in groups and have them plan a gap year together. Ask them to come up with a number of ideas first, and then negotiate and agree on a plan. After they have decided what to do, regroup the students and have them share their gap year plans with their classmates. Encourage the students who are listening to ask for more information, e.g. *How are you going to pay for all this?* Round off the activity in open class by asking: *Who do you think had the most exciting plan? The most educational?* This activity is a good way of 'testing' the students' ability to use the future tenses, which are covered on page 116. So take notes on any notable strengths and weaknesses with this grammar to keep in mind during the Language focus section to come.

ON THE MOVE

3 Check the meaning and pronunciation of *orphanage* /ˈɔːfənɪdʒ/ (question 3). Give the students time to pair check before going over the answers as a class.

4 Students discuss the questions in small groups. Feedback in open class.

READY FOR GRAMMAR

8 The future

1 *Will* + infinitive without *to* can be used to talk about:
  a hopes, expectations and predictions. Use verbs such as *believe, expect, hope* and *think*. Adverbs such as *definitely, (almost) certainly* and *probably* may also be used; they usually come after *will* and before *won't*. A present tense can also be used after *hope*.
  *United **will probably win** the league again this year.*
  *I **hope** you **behave**/**'ll behave** yourself today.*
  b decisions/offers made at the moment of speaking.
  *We**'ll babysit** for you if you want to go out.*
  c future facts; events which the speaker knows or believes are certain to happen.
  *Summer **will be** here soon.*

2 *Be going* + infinitive with *to* can be used to talk about:
  a personal intentions and plans made before the moment of speaking. *To go* can be omitted.
  *I**'m going to stay** in tonight and read my book.*
  *I**'m** not **going (to go)** anywhere.*
  b predictions, as an alternative to *will*.
  *I**'m not going to do** very well in the exam.*
  If there is evidence now that something is certain to happen, we usually use *going to*.
  *Stand back! The building**'s going to collapse**!*

3 Modal verbs express degrees of possibility when talking about:
  a intentions.
  *I **may/might go** swimming tomorrow. (possibility)*
  b predictions.
  *It **may/might/could well rain** tomorrow. (probability)*
  *If I leave now, I **should be** home by six. (probability)*

4 The present continuous can be used to talk about future arrangements which have already been made.
  *Sue and Alan **are getting** married in June.*

5 The present simple can be used:
  a to talk about timetabled or scheduled events.
  *The film **starts** at 9.15, just after the news.*
  b to refer to the future after time linkers such as *when, while, after, until, by the time, as soon as*.
  *Give me a call **as soon as you arrive**.*
  Other present tenses can be used in this way.
  When you're having lunch, I'll still be in bed.
  *You can't go out **until you've tidied** your room.*

6 The future continuous, *will* + *be* + *-ing*, is used to talk about actions or events which we predict will be in progress at a certain time in the future.
  *This time tomorrow I**'ll be flying** over France.*

7 The future perfect simple, *will* + *have* + *past participle*, is used to talk about actions and events that will be completed by a certain time in the future.
  *By the end of today we**'ll have driven** over 500 km.*

8 The future perfect continuous is used to talk about actions and events which continue to a certain time in the future.
  *On 21 May I**'ll have been living** here for exactly 10 years.*

9 *Be about to* + infinitive/*be on the point of* + gerund can be used to talk about the immediate future.
  *Can I phone you back? I**'m** just **about to have** lunch.*

10 *Be (un)likely* + infinitive with *to* expresses probability.
  *They've got a map with them so they**'re unlikely (not likely) to get** lost. (= they probably won't get lost)*

11 *Shall I/we* + infinitive without *to* is used to ask for suggestions, advice and instructions.
  *Where **shall we** go tomorrow night?*

12 A number of other verbs can be used to talk about future hopes, plans, intentions and expectations.
  *We **hope/expect to win** tomorrow.*
  *Are you **planning to go/on going** out tonight?*
  *We're **thinking of moving** abroad.*

ON THE MOVE 8

1 How did Rosie react after she received her exam results?
   A She felt that her family could have been more supportive.
   B She realised the goals she'd set herself had been unrealistic.
   C She thought her exams might have been marked incorrectly.
   (D) She gradually changed the way she felt about her grades.
2 What does Rosie say was her reason for travelling?
   A It would be more fun than working.
   (B) It seemed like a good use of her time.
   C It was a chance for self-improvement.
   D It would help her university application.
3 What does Rosie say about her experience in the Peruvian orphanage?
   A She thought the owners were not doing enough for the children.
   (B) She felt that her work was of little benefit to the orphanage.
   C She sensed that the children did not appreciate her gifts.
   D She had suspicions that the owners were corrupt.
4 What does 'earned them bragging rights' mean in line 43?
   A entitled them to receive special treatment
   B made them feel fortunate to have survived
   (C) gave them the opportunity to impress people
   D helped them appreciate the beauty of the country
5 What does 'which' refer to in line 55?
   A each country
   B local tour companies
   C transport and cultural trips
   (D) making our own bookings
6 In the final paragraph, Rosie suggests that she and her friend Lowri
   (A) might have benefited from visiting fewer places.
   B didn't leave themselves enough time to relax.
   C should have spent less time in each place.
   D took too many things with them.

4 SPEAK Work in groups. If you could take a year off school or work, what would you do? Where would you go? How would you fund yourself?

115

8 ON THE MOVE

Vocabulary Make and do

1 Complete the gaps in 1–6 with the correct form of *make* or *do*. Write one or two words in each gap. Here are two examples from the reading.

[My grades] weren't good enough for the university degree course I was hoping __to do__.

I hadn't met the entry requirements, so I should __make__ alternative plans.

1 I don't always __do__ my homework; I know I should __make__ more of an effort.
2 I always __make__ sure I __do__ some form of physical exercise every day.
3 I'm not very good at __making__ decisions; it takes me ages __to make__ up my mind.
4 If I were asked __to make__ a speech in public, I'd __do__ my best, but I'd be so nervous, I'd probably __make__ a mess of it.
5 I've been __doing__ nothing but study lately; it would __do__ me good to go out more in the evenings. It certainly wouldn't __do__ me any harm.
6 I'd love __to do__ a job that has something __to do__ with travel; it would be a great way __to make__ a living.

2 SPEAK Work in pairs. Discuss how true each of the sentences in Exercise 1 is for you.

Language focus The future

1 Rosie uses *will* to make the following prediction at the end of *The trip of a lifetime*.

I'm sure I'll find time to go back to some of them in the future.

Look at the following predictions for the year 2035. Decide whether the words and expressions in bold express:

a certainty   b probability   c possibility

1 We **are likely** to see a lot of self-driving cars on our roads. b
2 All cars **will** be electric, everywhere in the world. a
3 Bicycles **may well** be the most common form of transport in our towns and cities. b
4 Public transport **might** be completely free for all local residents in my area. c
5 School holidays **will probably** be much shorter than they are now. b
6 We **won't** have to put up with electric scooters on our pavements – they**'ll** be banned. a
7 Commercial space travel **probably won't** have caught on. b
8 Flights abroad **may not** be as cheap as they are now. c

2 SPEAK Work in pairs. Discuss the predictions in Exercise 1. Where necessary, make your own predictions, using the words in bold. Give reasons for your opinions.

1 We might see self-driving buses, but self-driving cars probably won't be available to the general public. It would be far too dangerous and I think ...

3 Go to **Ready for Grammar** on **page 222** for rules, explanations and further practice.

4 SPEAK Discuss these questions with your partner.

1 What will you be doing this time tomorrow?
2 What plans have you made for next weekend?
3 Are you planning to buy anything special in the near future?
4 How will your life have changed in ten years' time?

ON THE MOVE 8

Vocabulary

1–2 In many European languages, only one verb is used for both *make* and *do*. This often leads to confusion. One way to introduce the vocabulary in monolingual classes is to put up five phrases in the students' L1 that would be translated as *make* or *do* and ask: *How do you say these in English?* During feedback, encourage students to create pages in their vocabulary notebooks for both *make* and *do*, and include any unfamiliar collocations from this vocabulary section.

Language focus

1 If possible, aim to cover all the material in this and the **Ready for Grammar** section on pages 222–223 (see TB115 and below) in one lesson. Books closed. In pairs, invite the students to make predictions about transport in the year 2035. Monitor and make notes about how well they are using the future tenses. This will inform where to focus your attention during this grammar lesson. Let the students work through Exercise 1 in pairs. One fun way of correcting this type of exercise in class is to assign a gesture to each option. Read each sentence aloud and the students make the assigned gesture, for example, thumbs-up for *certainty*, nodding for *probability*, palms up for *possibility*.

2 Students do the exercise as suggested.

3 Direct the students to the **Ready for Grammar** section on page 222 (see TB115 and below). Note that Exercise 1 is a guided discovery task and should be done before the students read the grammar explanations.

4 While the students discuss the questions in pairs, monitor their use of the target language.

You may wish to use **The Future Board Game** on the **Teacher's Resource Centre** to extend this lesson.

READY FOR GRAMMAR

8 The future

1 Match each of the underlined forms in Rosie's sentences 1–5 with an explanation a–e.

1 <u>I'm going to use</u> the money I earn at the doctor's surgery to help fund my trip.   c

2 My friend Lowri wants to come, so <u>we're meeting</u> in a café tomorrow to talk about it.   b

3 Really?! A cycle ride down Death Road! In that case, <u>I'll stay</u> here and read my book.   a

4 This time tomorrow <u>we'll be getting on</u> the plane to Johannesburg.   e

5 By the end of the four months, <u>we'll have visited</u> seven countries.   d

a decision made at the moment of speaking

b an arrangement made with another person

c a personal intention or planned decision

d an action or actions that will be completed by a certain time

e an action that will be in progress at a certain time

2 Underline the correct alternative in 1–8. Give reasons for your answers. For each sentence, decide which city is being referred to.

I think *I'll meet* / <u>*I'm meeting*</u> Silvia at 11 o'clock at the Colosseum. I'm pretty sure that's what we arranged, anyway.

The present continuous is used for arrangements which have already been made.
The Colosseum is in Rome.

1 You've lost your coat? OK, look, *I run* / <u>*I'll run*</u> back to the Prado to see if you left it there. You wait here **until** <u>*I get*</u> / *I'll get* back.   Madrid

2 **As soon as** <u>we get</u> / *will get* there, we're <u>*planning*</u> / *thinking* to go straight to the Parthenon.   Athens

3 I think we're *doing* / <u>*going to do*</u> well in tomorrow's game. **If** we <u>*win*</u> / *will win*, we're *about to* / <u>*going to*</u> celebrate in the Champs-Élysées.   Paris

4 **After** we <u>*have visited*</u> / *will have visited* the Tower, we're <u>*thinking of*</u> / *on the point of* going up the Shard.   London

5 You're ten hours behind us, so **by the time** you <u>*get*</u> / *will get* up tomorrow morning, we'll already *spend* / <u>*have spent*</u> the day on Bondi Beach.   Sydney

6 **While** <u>*you're sitting*</u> / *you should sit* in a traffic jam during the rush hour tomorrow evening, <u>*I'll be playing*</u> / *I play* beach volley on Copacabana Beach.   Rio de Janeiro

7 Our train <u>*leaves*</u> / *will have been leaving* tomorrow morning at 10.15, and if there are no delays, we *must* / <u>*should*</u> get into Grand Central Station around 4.30 in the afternoon.   New York

8 I'm looking at the Bolshoi's website and I'm just *likely* / <u>*about*</u> to book the tickets. <u>*Shall*</u> / *Might* we go to the early performance? Then we can go out for dinner afterwards.   Moscow

3 Which tenses are used to refer to the future after the linking words and expressions in bold in Exercise 2?
Present tenses (simple, continuous, perfect) are used after these linkers to refer to the future.
Go back to page 116.

TB116

8 ON THE MOVE

Listening

▶ **8.1** Students read the instructions and the **Don't forget!** box. During feedback, you could play the part of the recording once more for any particular question students struggled with. Ask the students: *Why is the correct answer correct? Why are the incorrect answers incorrect? Were there any distractors?* Refer students to the **Audioscript** on pages 241–242 (see below and TB118) to check their answers if necessary.

AUDIOSCRIPT

Listening Part 1 Multiple choice

▶ 8.1

H = Hotel manager W = Woman M = Man

1 You hear a hotel manager talking to his staff.

H: As you know, it's been a difficult season for the hotel. The level of occupancy has been unsatisfactory, and with nearly half our rooms empty each week, we're running at a loss. Unfortunately, we have no control over the weather and it seems likely that the situation will only get worse in the coming weeks. It'll probably Q1 come as no surprise to you to hear, then, that some of you on the temporary staff will, I'm afraid, have your contract terminated. Those affected will be asked to come to my office later this morning and I'll provide anyone who requires it with a reference.

2 You hear a married couple talking about a campsite they stayed at.

W: That campsite just outside Florence was good.

M: Yeah, it was. We never actually went in to the city, though, did we?

W: No, we should have done, it was so close. But I couldn't pull you and the boys away from the pool.

M: Oh come on – you spent just as much time there as Q2 we did. And then there was the sauna, the gym … and that games room was great for the kids.

W: Yeah, there was plenty to do. We'll have to go back there.

M: But on our own, when the boys have grown up, and we can have some peace and quiet.

W: Right. And see Florence, too.

3 You hear two people talking about a place they have just visited.

M: I'm really pleased we did the guided tour. You don't normally get to see *that* side of things.

W: It was amazing sitting in the director's box. I felt just Q3 like royalty.

M: Yeah, it was great. I was really impressed with the trophy room, as well. All those cups on display – I've never seen so much silverware in one place.

W: Shall we come back tomorrow night? It's only an exhibition match, but I'd love to see what the place looks like with people in it. It was weird seeing it empty.

M: OK. It'll be a great way to finish the holiday.

4 You overhear a woman leaving a voicemail message for her friend.

W: Hi, Alison. Really sorry to hear you can't come away with us to Brighton next month. Steve just told me. He was a bit upset, I think – he was looking forward Q4 to seeing you again. Anyway … you and I are seeing each other next week, aren't we? I can't remember if we said Wednesday or Thursday. I've just agreed to go and visit my parents on Wednesday, so if that's the day you and I are meeting up, I'll have to phone them and rearrange things. They won't mind, but can you just remind me what we decided? Thanks. Bye.

5 You hear two people on a plane talking about the airline they are flying with.

W: It says in their magazine they're one of the 'World's Most Improved Airlines'.

M: I saw that. But it doesn't say what's better. I mean, there's definitely still room for improvement in the way they speak to people – like that poor woman just now whose cabin bag was too big.

W: Yeah, I felt really sorry for her.

M: Hmm. Sometimes they're in such a hurry to get you on the plane and up in the air on time they forget to be nice. Still, credit where credit's due – they *are* Q5 efficient and I have to say, it's good to see the days of dried-out meat and sad-looking salads are gone.

W: Definitely.

6 You hear a woman talking about tourists in her town.

W: I shouldn't complain really. I mean, the whole economy of this town is based on tourism and if they stopped coming, then a lot of people would be out of work and struggling to make ends meet. But I wish they'd show a little more respect. Loads Q6 of them have music blaring out of their cars during the day, and then in the evening, you get big groups of them coming into the centre for the nightlife. And they don't seem to care that we can't get a decent night's sleep with them making such a racket.

7 You hear two tourists talking about their tour guide.

W: Come on. Let's get back to the coach. We don't want to upset the guide.

M: Yeah, she really lost her temper with that couple this Q7 morning.

W: Hmm, and they were only a couple of minutes late. But apart from that, she's alright. She seems to know what she's talking about.

M: Well, I checked what she said about the cathedral on my phone and she got one or two things really wrong.

W: Yeah, but you can't believe everything you read on the internet. Anyway, she puts things across well. She'd make a good teacher.

M: As long as everyone pays attention.

W: Right. She wouldn't bother to explain things twice.

TB117

ON THE MOVE

Listening Part 1 Multiple choice

8.1 You will hear people talking in eight different situations. For questions 1–8, choose the best answer (A, B or C).

1 You hear a hotel manager talking to his staff.
   What is he doing?
   A informing them of something
   B inviting them to do something
   C criticising them

2 You hear a married couple talking about a campsite they stayed at.
   What did they both like about it?
   A It was quiet.
   B It was near a city.
   C It had good facilities.

3 You hear two people talking about a place they have just visited.
   What kind of place is it?
   A a stadium
   B a museum
   C a palace

4 You overhear a woman leaving a voicemail message for her friend.
   Why is she calling?
   A to check an arrangement
   B to cancel a planned trip
   C to make an apology

5 You hear two people on a plane talking about the airline they are flying with.
   The man thinks the airline has improved
   A its punctuality.
   B the quality of its meals.
   C its treatment of passengers.

6 You hear a woman talking about tourists in her town.
   What is she complaining about?
   A They have no money to spend.
   B There are too many of them.
   C They make too much noise.

7 You hear two tourists talking about their tour guide.
   What do they agree about her?
   A She isn't very good at explaining things.
   B She isn't very knowledgeable.
   C She isn't very patient.

8 You hear a man talking about a beach he recently visited.
   What did he like about the beach?
   A the quality of the sand
   B the temperature of the sea
   C the closeness of the shops

> **Don't forget!**
> You will hear distractors. Listen carefully both times before deciding on your answer.

8 ON THE MOVE

Vocabulary Travel and holidays

1 Complete each of the gaps 1–6 with a word from the box.

   cruise   flight   journey   tour   travel   trip

   1 When there's a public holiday, I often **go on a day** ___trip___ to the coast or to the mountains with my family.
   2 I've never **been on a long-haul** ___flight___; the furthest I've flown is from London to Berlin.
   3 I'm a huge fan of **rail** ___travel___; I'd love to take the Trans-Siberian railway or go from one coast of the United States to the other by train.
   4 I wouldn't like to **go on a Caribbean** ___cruise___: I'd probably be seasick and I'd rather get to know one island well than visit lots of different ones.
   5 I think the best way to see the sights in a city is to **go on a guided** ___tour___.
   6 I sometimes read when I **go on a long car** ___journey___, and I sleep a lot, too.

2 **SPEAK** Work in pairs. Discuss how true the sentences in Exercise 1 are for you.

3 Read the online advertisements A–C quite quickly and match each one to a holiday type in the box.

   adventure holiday   camping holiday   seaside holiday
   self-catering holiday   sightseeing holiday   working holiday

4 Underline the correct alternatives in A–C.

5 Look again at the holiday types in the box in Exercise 3. Rank them from the one you think you would enjoy most (1) to the one you would least like to go on (6).

6 **SPEAK** Work in pairs. Compare your list from Exercise 5 with your partner, giving reasons for your choices.

camping holiday

A (1) Placed / Fixed / *Set* in an area of outstanding beauty, Langton Farm is an ideal location for getting away from it all. We have over 300 spacious (2) *pitches* / parcels / lands for caravans and tents, as well as a number of bungalows which are (3) disposable / obtainable / *available* to rent. There's always (4) *plenty* / variety / choice to do at Langton Farm. In addition to the heated, covered pool and games room, we provide a (5) long / *wide* / high range of activities for all the family every day of the week.

seaside holiday

B Book a relaxing (6) accommodation / reserve / *stay* in one of the country's top holiday (7) *resorts* / stations / posts and discover the stunning western shoreline. The four-star Blue Bay Hotel (8) poses / *offers* / stands breathtaking views of the ocean, and the spectacular mile-long sandy beach is just a short walk (9) afar / *away* / aside. An excellent selection of shops, restaurants and nightclubs is also within easy (10) *reach* / stretch / touch, making this the perfect place to spend your holiday on the coast.

self-catering holiday

C Whether you're looking for a pet-friendly cottage in the countryside or a city-centre flat with disabled (11) *facilities* / instalments / elements, we have something to (12) agree / *suit* / allow your requirements. Search our extensive database for the perfect accommodation in a variety of popular holiday (13) destinies / *destinations* / designations. And if you're planning a last-minute (14) runaway / breakaway / *getaway* we offer special discounts for late bookings. All properties are (15) *fully* / greatly / entirely equipped with bed linen, towels and kitchen appliances to make your holiday as easy as possible.

ON THE MOVE 8

AUDIOSCRIPT continued

8 You hear a man talking about a beach he recently visited.

M: Now, normally I prefer a beach with fine sand, you know, so it's not painful to walk on. This one, though, had small stones – well, more like pebbles, actually – and I don't remember the brochure saying anything about *that*. But anyway, we bought ourselves a pair of flip-flops each at one of the shops next to the beach, so that didn't matter too much. And then **Q8** we spent most of our time there in the water. It was just like being in a warm bath. I could have stayed there all day.

Vocabulary

1. Students of many language backgrounds have the tendency to use *travel* as a noun when *trip* or *journey* would be more appropriate. Elicit or explain the related but distinct meanings of these words.
   - *journey* (countable noun): the act of going from one place to another, especially in a vehicle
   - *trip* (countable noun): going somewhere and coming back, usually for a short time
   - *travel* (verb): to make a journey
   - *travel* (uncountable noun): a generic term for the activity of travelling

2. Give the students time to discuss the sentences with a classmate and then get feedback from the class. Monitor their use of the target language. Note that there are instances of both intrusive sounds and consonant-vowel linking in these lexical items, e.g. *go on a day trip* /gəʊwɒn ədeɪtrɪp/. This would be a good opportunity to revisit these features of connected speech introduced in Units 5 and 6, respectively.

3-4 Students do the exercises as suggested. To consolidate any of the collocations students are less familiar with, ask them to write sentences containing the lexical items about a place in their own country.

5-6 Encourage the students to use some of the collocations from the lesson while justifying their choices. Round off the lesson by asking which types of holiday were most popular.

You may wish to use **Let's grade each other!** on the **Teacher's Resource Centre** as an extension to this lesson.

Teaching tip

At times, it is worthwhile to set aside class time for the students to transfer new lexis to their vocabulary notebooks. Ideally, this work is better left for outside the lesson, but for those students who have lost the habit of recording new lexical items, or perhaps simply haven't made time, it can help get them back into the habit. It's also a good opportunity to reflect on how and how often students are using their notebooks outside of class. Research shows that students who are more organised in the way they learn and record new language tend to progress much faster, so time spent in class reinforcing good study habits is always well spent.

Extra activity

Collocations lend themselves well to gamification. If you are using technology in class, there are a number of websites like Quizlet and Kahoot that allow you to create competitive games. A low (no) tech option is to write the two parts of the collocations on individual sticky notes and put them around the classroom (under tables or chairs, on the door or window, etc.) before a lesson or during a break. Put the students in pairs and assign them a section of the board. Together with their partners, students must find as many matches as they can and stick them on their part of the board.

8 ON THE MOVE

Speaking

1-2 Focus the students' attention on the **Useful language** box. Point out that speculation is something the examiners will be listening for on the speaking exam.

If your students over-rely on the verb *seem* when describing photos, contrast the difference with *look* using these example sentences:

He seems like a nice person. (we assume you met the person)

He looks like a nice person. (judgment on appearance alone)

However, we don't use *look* to talk about subjective impressions; *seem* is used e.g. *It seems like a bad idea to …*

Students could do this Speaking Part 2 in pairs and time each other, or in groups of three with one student in the role of the examiner, who keeps the time and asks the follow-up questions.

Teaching tip

The **Teaching tip** on TB48 explained the value of focusing on emergent language — that is, student language that comes up unpredictably during a lesson. Here are some further ideas for working with emergent language:

- Make sure to leave enough time for a proper corrective feedback stage after a speaking activity. It's easy to take a lot of good notes while the students are talking and then not have enough time to go over them. Plan for at least five minutes, but better ten.
- Start by boarding some good language, which you can praise, personalise or expand on by eliciting or providing other ways of saying the same thing (or the opposite).
- Include pronunciation — this is a particularly good way to raise awareness.
- Emergent language can become part of the course. Revise it from time to time, especially the type of persistent, fossilised errors students keep making.
- Get students to record relevant errors in a special page in their vocabulary notebooks, perhaps with the error on one side and the correction on the other.

Extra activity

A speaking Part 2 task is relatively easy for students to create themselves. Ask students to look at a number of Speaking Part 2 tasks in *Ready for B2 First* or from past paper books and elicit the following characteristics of the task:

- Two colour photographs showing people doing an activity like working or studying, or people in a situation, e.g. on holiday, at home, etc.
- One direct question above the photos starting with a question word, e.g. *What are the people …? Why have the people chosen to …?*
- Candidates need to be able to compare the photos, discussing similarities and differences, so the photos are related in some way (but not too closely).
- Students create their tasks for homework — or in class, if there is access to technology or magazines they could cut photos out of. Collect and save these tasks to practise Speaking Part 2 in future lessons.

ON THE MOVE

Speaking Part 2 Long turn

Before you do the following Speaking Part 2 tasks, read the Useful language box below.

1 Look at photographs 1 and 2. They show people on holiday.

   Student A: Compare photographs 1 and 2 and say why you think the people have chosen to go on these different holidays.

   Student B: When your partner has finished, say whether you would like to go on either of these types of holidays.

Why have the people chosen to go on these different holidays?

Useful language

Student A Use a range of structures to speculate about the photographs.

look + adjective	They look very <u>relaxed</u>.	**Modal verbs**	They <u>might</u> be going to work.
look like + noun	They look like <u>tourists</u>.		They <u>must</u> be very interested in wildlife.
look as if + verb phrase	They looks as if <u>they are enjoying themselves.</u>	**Other verbs**	I <u>imagine</u>/<u>expect</u> they like the outdoor life.

Student B Use a range of structures to express preferences.

I'd prefer/love/hate to go on a safari.   I'd be nervous about/enjoy riding one of those.

I'd rather do this than that.   I'd be thrilled/scared to travel like that.

2 Now change roles and look at photographs 3 and 4. They show people travelling in different ways.

   Student A: Compare photographs 3 and 4 and say why you think the people are travelling in these different ways.

   Student B: When your partner has finished, say whether you would enjoy travelling in either of these ways.

Why are the people travelling in these different ways?

8 ON THE MOVE

Listening Part 3 Multiple matching

1 **SPEAK** Work in pairs. When, if ever, do you use a bicycle? How common is it for people to cycle in the cities in your country? How safe is it?

2 ▶ 8.2 You will hear five different people speaking on the subject of cycling in the city. For questions 1–5, choose from the list (A–H) what each speaker is talking about. Use the letters only once. There are three extra letters which you do not need to use.

A a move in the right direction
B the consequences of breaking the law
C the need to educate the public
D a lack of open spaces to cycle in
E the problem of pollution
F a feeling of freedom
G the dangers of not being visible to drivers
H the intolerance of other road users

Speaker 1	C	1
Speaker 2	F	2
Speaker 3	A	3
Speaker 4	H	4
Speaker 5	E	5

B, D & G not used

3 **SPEAK** Work in groups. What measures can be taken by the government and/or local authorities in your country to encourage cycling?

Vocabulary Phrasal verbs

1 Use the context to help you work out the meanings of the phrasal verbs in bold in these extracts from the listening.

1 I get shouted at by people who still haven't **caught on** that it's me that has right of way, not them. *(begin to understand)*
2 I get off the train, put on my helmet and **head for** the office. *(go somewhere)*
3 Someone in the town hall **came up with** a nice idea to promote cycling in the city. *(think of)*
4 There's a real festival atmosphere now, with thousands of cyclists of all ages **turning out** every month. *(attend/take part in an event)*
5 Sometimes you **come across** some really nasty drivers in the city. *(meet (by chance))*
6 People don't generally use a bike to **get about** the city. *(travel around)*

2 **SPEAK** Work in pairs. Discuss the following questions.

1 Where are you heading for after this class?
2 Did you come across any friendly people on your last holiday?
3 What is the best way to get about your town or city?

ON THE MOVE

Listening

1 Alternatively, you could dictate the questions and then ask the students to open their books and check before discussing in pairs. Point out that *cycle* is the verb for bicycle; we also say *ride a bicycle*.

2 ▶ 8.2 Check the meaning of *a move in the right direction*. Note that students from some language backgrounds will use *contamination* when *pollution* would be more appropriate (as well as the verb *contaminate* instead of *pollute*). Sometimes the terms are interchangeable, but in general *contamination* is more specific. It refers to when we make something dirty, polluted or poisonous by adding a chemical, waste or infection. *Pollution* is more general, referring to the process of damaging the air, water or land with chemicals or other substances.

One interesting way of correcting this listening Part 3 exercise is to enlarge the Audioscript on page 242 (see below), or use the photocopiable version on the **Teacher's Resource Centre**, and put the five extracts around the room. While the students walk around and check, they discuss their answers with their classmates.

3 Get some feedback from the class after the students have discussed the questions in groups.

Vocabulary

1 Explain that you will now be focusing on some phrasal verbs that came up in the listening. These phrasal verbs appear in red in the Audioscript, so the exercise could be done with the students looking at page 242 (see below) instead. See the **Teaching tip** on TB82 for ideas about teaching phrasal verbs.

2 You could give the students a few minutes to write at least two more questions using the phrasal verbs from Exercise 1 for other pairs to discuss. Round off the activity with some open class feedback.

AUDIOSCRIPT

Listening Part 3 Multiple matching

▶ 8.2

Speaker 1 There's a cycle path that goes right round the city, and various shorter ones within it. Now, these paths are up on the pavement rather than in the road, so it's pedestrians, not motorists, that have to be careful they don't wander onto them. Some people don't seem to understand this, and walk along them as if they had every right to. I really think the authorities could do more **to inform pedestrians, to make them aware of how it works**. [Ex 2 C] Every day I cycle to work and every day I get shouted at by people who still haven't caught on that it's me that has right of way, not them.

Speaker 2 Mine's a folding bike, so I get off the train, put on my helmet and head for the office. I *could* take the bus or the underground, but there's no pleasure in that – they both get so crowded. On the bike I feel the wind in my face and **a sense that the city's mine – I can go where I want, when I want**. [Ex 2 F] I know I shouldn't, but I can even get up on the pavement to avoid traffic lights or go the wrong way down one-way streets. And of course, cycling is just so healthy – I've never felt fitter. Some say it's risky too, but I find motorists tend to go more carefully when cyclists are around.

Speaker 3 A year or two ago, someone in the town hall came up with a nice idea to promote cycling in the city. On the first Sunday in every month, a number of the main streets in the centre are closed to traffic for two hours and given over to bicycles. It's gradually grown in popularity, and there's a real festival atmosphere now, with thousands of cyclists of all ages turning out every month. **It's a start, and it's certainly helped to get people out on their bikes. But there's still a long way to go.** [Ex 2 A] We need a whole series of additional measures to make our roads more cycle-friendly.

Speaker 4 Sometimes you come across some really nasty drivers in the city. I can be cycling along, minding my own business, when some car or van comes right up close to me, almost touching my back wheel. It's really dangerous – sometimes I lose my balance and nearly fall off. It seems to be worse in the evening. I've got my bike lights, my luminous cycling jacket, my reflective cycle clips – so they can see me all right. But **they seem to resent me being there and get impatient if they have to slow down for me. I get beeped and shouted at all the time** [Ex 2 H] – it's very unpleasant.

Speaker 5 It's more a recreational activity here than a means of transport. People don't generally use a bike to get about the city. They might spend a Sunday morning cycling in one of the big parks in the suburbs, or on the cycle path that runs alongside the river. But they won't ride a bike in the centre to get from A to B or to go to and from work. It's just not an attractive option, given **the quality of the air here. We're in the middle of a huge industrial area, and many pedestrians wear face masks.** [Ex 2 E] So people are hardly likely to expose themselves to more danger by cycling in amongst the traffic.

8 ON THE MOVE

Word formation

1 These sentences will have already been heard (and possibly even seen, if you have used the **Audioscript**) in the Listening Part 3 task on page 120. So ideally this exercise, as well as the one on phrasal verbs, should be done in the same lesson as the listening. While going over the answers to Exercise 1, elicit that all the words in the gaps are adjectives formed with suffixes.

2-3 Students complete the table in pairs. Encourage them to copy the table into the Word formation section of their vocabulary notebooks. Note that it is much faster and easier to correct this type of exercise by either projecting the answers on the board or asking the students to check their answers in the **Answer key**, instead of eliciting the words one by one to the board. Fast finishers can mark up the word stress.

Check the pronunciation of *additional* /əˈdɪʃənl/, *impatient* /ɪmˈpeɪʃnt/, *industrial* /ɪnˈdʌstriəl/, *humorous* /ˈhjuːmərəs/, *original* /əˈrɪdʒənl/, *beneficial* /ˌbenɪˈfɪʃl/, *ignorant* /ˈɪgnərənt/ or any other words your students might find troublesome. Point out that the word stress sometimes shifts, e.g. *origin* /ˈɒrɪdʒɪn/ and *original* /əˈrɪdʒənl/. There are also spelling changes, e.g. *humour* and *humorous*. Students from many language backgrounds confuse *hungry* /ˈhʌŋgri/ and *angry* /ˈæŋgri/, so this could be a good time to elicit and discuss the difference in pronunciation.

Reading and Use of English

You could lead into this exercise by asking the students what they know about monorails. This exercise could also simply be used as 'exam practice' and limit yourself to revisiting helpful exam strategies with questions like: *Should you read the text just once or more than once?* When you go through the answers, encourage students to write down any new forms of words in the Word formation section of their vocabulary notebooks. Elicit the shift in word stress with *signify* /ˈsɪgnɪfaɪ/ and *significant* /sɪgˈnɪfɪkənt/, *environment* /ɪnˈvaɪrənmənt/ and *environmental* /ɪnˌvaɪrənˈmentl/.

READY FOR GRAMMAR

8 Contrast linkers

1 *But* contrasts two ideas in the same sentence.

*The weather was bad **but** she enjoyed the trip.*

In informal writing, *but* is often used at the beginning of the sentence.

*John's got the flu. **But** the rest of us are fine.*

2 *Although* and *though* (informal) are also used to contrast ideas in the same sentence. They can go at the beginning of the sentence or in the middle.

***Although** the weather was bad, she enjoyed the trip.*
*I liked the book, **although** I wouldn't recommend it.*

Even used before *though* emphasises the contrast.

*He still wears his ring, **even though** he's divorced.*

3 *However* contrasts ideas in two different sentences. It often goes at the beginning of the second sentence and is followed by a comma.

*The hotel was expensive. **However**, the others were full, so she had to book it.*

It can also go in the middle of a clause or sentence, or at the end.

*Tim hated York. He did not, **however**, want to move.*
*Amy often tells lies. She would never steal, **however**.*

4 *Nevertheless* is a more formal alternative to *however*.

*It was snowing. **Nevertheless**, the game went ahead.*

5 *In spite of* and *despite* are both followed by a gerund or a noun. They can go at the beginning of a sentence or in the middle.

*We enjoyed the meal **in spite of** the poor service.*
***Despite** feeling terrible, she still went to work.*

If the subject of the gerund is different to the subject of the main verb, a noun, an object pronoun or possessive adjective is added.

*She paid for the meal despite **me/my** telling her not to.*

The words *the fact that* are added before a verb clause.

*Chloe invited Steve to her party, **despite the fact that he had treated** her so badly.*

6 *Whereas*, *while* and *whilst* (formal) are used to contrast two things, people or situations in the same sentence.

*Jake likes heavy metal **whereas/while** I prefer rap.*

ON THE MOVE 8

Word formation Adjectives

1 Use the word in capitals at the end of each of these extracts from the listening to form a word that fits in the gap in the same sentence. There is an example at the beginning (0).

0 There's a cycle path that goes right round the city, and __various__ shorter ones within it. VARY
1 It's pedestrians, not motorists, that have to be __careful__ they don't wander onto them. CARE
2 And of course, cycling is just so __healthy__ – I've never felt fitter. HEALTH
3 We need a whole series of __additional__ measures to make our roads more cycle-friendly. ADDITION
4 It's really __dangerous__ – sometimes I lose my balance and nearly fall off. DANGER
5 They get __impatient__ if they have to slow down for me. PATIENCE
6 I get beeped and shouted at all the time – it's very __unpleasant__. PLEASE
7 It's just not an __attractive__ option, given the quality of the air here. ATTRACT
8 We're in the middle of a huge __industrial__ area. INDUSTRY

2 Copy the following table with adjective suffixes into your notebook. Complete the table by writing the adjectives you wrote for Exercise 1 in the appropriate columns.

-ous	-ful	-y	-al	-ent	-ant	-ive
various	careful	healthy	additional	impatient	unpleasant	attractive
dangerous	peaceful	cloudy	industrial	different	ignorant	protective
poisonous	beautiful	hungry	original	apparent	tolerant	decisive
mysterious	successful	foggy	financial	obedient	hesitant	destructive
humorous			beneficial			

3 Use the appropriate suffixes from Exercise 2 to create adjectives from the following words in the box. You may need to make further spelling changes. Add the words to the table in your notebook. There are three words for each column.

> ignore differ origin poison peace protect cloud
> beauty hunger appear decide tolerate mystery finance
> fog humour destroy hesitate benefit succeed obey

Reading and Use of English Part 3 Word formation

For questions 1–10, read the text below. Use the word given in capitals at the end of some of the lines to form a word that fits in the gap in the same line. There is an example at the beginning (0).

MONORAILS

Monorail systems are (0) __FREQUENTLY__ associated with airports, zoos and amusement parks. They can, however, also be integrated into a city's main transport infrastructure and in recent decades a (1) __significant__ number have been built around the world for this purpose. In particular, there are (2) __numerous__ examples in Asia, with Japan leading the way. Elsewhere, Sydney, Moscow and São Paolo all have modern monorails. Perhaps the most (3) __unusual__ system in operation was also one of the first to be built: the 'Schwebebahn' in Wuppertal, Germany, whose trains are suspended from its track, was opened in 1901. Monorails run over short (4) __distances__, providing a quick and efficient method of urban transport. Supporters point to their (5) __impressive__ safety record and the fact that, because they are electrically powered, they have an (6) __environmental__ advantage over other more polluting forms of city transport. They are also (7) __inexpensive__ to operate. However, among the objections to monorail systems are the high costs of construction and the unpleasant (8) __appearance__ of the elevated tracks.

FREQUENT
SIGNIFY
NUMBER
USUAL
DISTANT
IMPRESS
ENVIRONMENT
EXPENSE
APPEAR

8 ON THE MOVE

Language focus Contrast linkers

2

They can, however, also be integrated …

The word *however* can be placed at the beginning of the sentence, or in the middle of a clause, in this case separating the modal verb from the passive infinitive.

3

The weather was bad. However, she enjoyed the trip. / She enjoyed the trip, however.

Although the weather was bad, she enjoyed the trip. / She enjoyed the trip although the weather was bad.

Despite the bad weather, she enjoyed the trip. / She enjoyed the trip despite the bad weather.

Despite the fact (that) the weather was bad, she enjoyed the trip./ She enjoyed the trip, despite the fact (that) the weather was bad.

1 Complete the gap in this extract from *Monorails*. Write one word.

They are also inexpensive to operate. __However__, among the objections to monorail systems are the high costs of construction …

2 Check your answer on page 121, and find another example of the same word in the text. What do you notice about the position of the word in the two examples?

3 Rewrite the following sentence in three different ways using *however, although* and *despite* instead of *but*.

The weather was bad but she enjoyed the trip.

4 Use the words from the box to complete these opinions from two people, Harry and Jodie, comparing trains and cars.

although   despite   however   spite   though   whereas

Harry

1 'Rail travel is more expensive than going by car. __However__, you don't suffer traffic jams in a train.'

2 'I'd always much rather catch a train, in __spite__ of the higher cost. Trains pollute less than cars.'

3 '__Although/Though__ cars are more convenient, driving is more tiring than sitting on a train.'

Jodie

4 '__Despite__ being slower than trains, cars get you to your destination more quickly.'

5 'Cars take you door to door, __whereas__ trains do not.'

6 'Even __though__ trains are usually punctual, passengers can still suffer delays.'

5 **SPEAK** Work in pairs. Which do you prefer, travelling by car or by train? Why?

6 Go to **Ready for Grammar** on **page 220** for rules, explanations and further practice.

Writing Part 1 Essay

1 **SPEAK** Work in pairs. Read the following Writing Part 1 instructions. How would you answer the essay question and what could you say for each of the three 'Things to write about' in the Notes?

In your English class you have been talking about travel and tourism. Your English teacher has asked you to write an essay.

Write an essay using **all** the notes and giving reasons for your point of view.

Is it better to spend a summer holiday in the countryside or on the coast?

Notes

Things to write about:

1 leisure options
2 climate
3 .... (your own idea)

ON THE MOVE

Language focus

1-2 This Language focus section is linked to the Word formation text from page 121. It starts by getting students to 'notice' how the linker *however* is used. Note that students often use the wrong punctuation with *however*. Use a semi-colon before and a comma after *however* when you are using it to combine two simple sentences into a compound one. If *however* is used to begin a sentence, it must be followed by a comma.

3 Elicit sentences from the students to the board. If they are incorrect, that's fine. Write them up on the board anyway and elicit the correction. Explore the rules for these linkers using concept questions, e.g. *Can we also move the clause starting with* although *here?* Use the grammar rules from the **Ready for Grammar** section on page 220 (see TB121) to help you. Point out that *despite* is a preposition and is therefore followed by a noun phrase (including *the fact that*) or a gerund. Students will encounter this word again in the **Ready for Grammar** section in Unit 12: Prepositions and gerunds.

4 The correction stage of this exercise could also be used as a teaching stage, using concept questions to elicit the rules for *despite/in spite of*, *though/although*, *while/whereas*, e.g. *Could we also use* although *here? Can anyone say this same sentence using* despite *instead?* Again, use the rules in the **Ready for Grammar** section on page 220 (see TB121) to help you. Note that both *while* and *whereas* can be used for contrast, but only *while* can be used as a time linker, e.g. *While I was parking the car …*

5 When you feedback this **SPEAK** section as a class, encourage students to refer to the points made by Harry and Jodie.

6 Alternatively, the key word transformation exercise in the **Ready for Grammar** section could be set for homework or saved for revision if students have demonstrated a good understanding of the contrast linkers by this point.

You may wish to use the **Linkers topic cards** on the **Teacher's Resource Centre** to round off this section.

Writing

1 Books closed. Start by discussing the question from the task in open class. The students then open their books, read the task and discuss what they could write about the three options with a classmate. In open class, discuss some of their ideas for the third 'your own idea' part of the task.

READY FOR GRAMMAR

8 Contrast linkers

Complete the second sentence so that it has a similar meaning to the first sentence, using the word given. Do not change the word given. You must use between two and five words, including the word given.

1 Mel and I have a lot in common but we don't really get on.

   EVEN

   I don't really get on _____*with Mel even though*_____ we have a lot in common.

2 I enjoyed Khalid's concert, but I only knew a few of the songs he performed.

   ALTHOUGH

   I enjoyed Khalid's concert, _____*although I didn't/did not know*_____ many of the songs he performed.

3 It'll probably rain on the coast, but we'll still take a picnic.

   FACT

   We'll take a picnic to the coast, despite _____*the fact (that) it's/ it is*_____ likely to rain.

4 New York is noisy and crowded, but I still love going there.

   SPITE

   I love going to New York _____*in spite of the noise (NOT noises)*_____ and the crowds.

5 Although he doesn't do a lot of exercise, Jaden seems very fit.

   MUCH

   Despite _____*not doing (very) much exercise*_____ Jaden seems very fit.

6 I told Chloe to walk, but she continued to run.

   DESPITE

   Chloe carried _____*on running despite me/my telling*_____ her to walk.

Go back to **page 122**.

ON THE MOVE

2 Give the students time to read the questions and the sample essay individually before talking to their partners. Conduct brief open class feedback.

3 Elicit the purpose of each paragraph to the board in open class.

Answers

Paragraph 2: leisure options – one reason why it is better to spend a summer holiday on the coast

Paragraph 3: climate and making friends – two further reasons to support the writer's opinion

Paragraph 4: summarising comment restating the writer's opinion

4 This exercise highlights an important point about the essay section of the *B2 First*: there are two types of essay candidates are expected to know how to write. (See models of both types in the **Ready for Writing** section.) It's important that students get plenty of practice with both types.

Answers

The sample answer in Unit 3 is a balanced essay, considering both sides of the argument before giving an opinion in the final paragraph. The sample answer here in Unit 8 is not balanced; the writer considers just one point of view, providing only reasons which support the opinion already expressed in the first paragraph.

5–6 If possible, project the text on the board and underline the linkers and linking devices there.

7–9 Focus on the **Don't forget!** box. Note that this could be adapted into a checklist, e.g. *Does the essay include a brief introduction and conclusion?* Students then read the instructions and plan their essay individually. Point out that these exercises take the students through the planning process they should ideally be following each time they sit down to write an essay. The final writing could be done in class (timed, 40 minutes) or set for homework (still timed if done at home).

Sample answer

The best way to travel in my area is by car, which generally has more advantages from using public transport.

Firstly, there are not trains and the busses in my area are not often. You can wait thirty minutes to find a bus. They can be very slow and you can waist a lot of time going to a diferent place. In the car, you can travel more fastly to a variety of places.

Second point, although busses are not expensive to by tickets, they are not too clean so it is not nice to sit on them for long time. It is better to go to a place in the car because the car is more plesant.

Finally, the busses do not go to many diferent places and you can have problems to go where you want. In the car you can decide what to visit in my area. It is not surprising that all of the people in my town use the car to go somewhere.

In my opinion, then, the car is the best way to travel in my area because it saves time, costs cheaply and you can go where you want.

196 words

Examiner's comments

Content: All content is relevant and the reader is fully informed. Although the question of cost receives only a brief mention, all three points in the notes are dealt with and the writer's opinion is clearly stated.

Communicative Achievement: The register is consistently neutral, though the answer might have benefited from a more objective approach rather than repeated use of *you*, e.g. *you can wait; you can have problems.* There is a clear essay structure with an opening statement, a series of supporting arguments and a final, summarising sentence. Straightforward ideas are communicated.

Organisation: The answer is generally well organised and coherent, although the third paragraph begins with a comment on the cost of bus tickets, and ends with the statement *'the car is more plesant (pleasant)'* without any real comparison of cost in-between. There is adequate use of simple linking devices e.g. *Firstly, although, because, Finally,* though the introduction to the third paragraph *(Second point)* is rather abrupt. Repetition could be avoided e.g. *It is better to go to a place in the car because the car is more plesant.*

Language: Everyday vocabulary is used appropriately with some use of collocation e.g. *waist (waste) a lot of time; a variety of places; saves time.* Although the frequent errors do not obscure meaning, they do distract the reader. These include incorrect use of adverbs (*more fastly* instead of *faster*; *costs cheaply* instead of e.g. *is cheap*; *not too clean* instead of *not very clean*), comparisons (*more advantages from* instead of *than*), misuse of infinitive (*have problems to go* instead of *going*) and basic spelling mistakes (*waist; diferent; by; plesant*). [The usual plural of the noun *bus* is *buses*.]

Some ideas are expressed awkwardly: *there are not (no) trains and the busses in my area are not often (frequent)* and *busses are not expensive to by tickets (bus fares are not expensive).*

Some more complex grammatical forms are used successfully (e.g. *The best way to travel in my area is by car; you can decide what to visit*).

Mark: Pass

ON THE MOVE 8

2 Read the answer to the question in Exercise 1. Answer the questions.
   1 What is the writer's 'own idea' for number 3 of the Notes section in the question?
   meeting new people – The fact that there are more opportunities to make new friends on a seaside holiday than in the countryside.
   2 How similar is the essay to the one you would have written if you had answered the question?

☀ A summer holiday by the sea

Without doubt, the best place to spend the summer is on the coast, which generally has far more advantages for the holidaymaker than the countryside.

For one thing, in the countryside there is not much to do apart from walking and visiting villages, whereas the coast offers a wider range of possibilities for the tourist. You can stroll around seaside villages, but you can also spend the day on the beach, take part in watersports such as sailing and surfing, eat in a variety of restaurants and go to clubs and bars in the evening.

Secondly, in July and August it is usually cooler on the coast than in the countryside, and therefore much more pleasant. It is not surprising that most people head for the beach during the hot summer months. Another positive point is that, because so many people choose the coast as their holiday destination, there are more opportunities to make new friends than in the countryside.

In my opinion, then, the coast offers the chance of a far more varied and enjoyable summer holiday than the countryside.

3 What is the purpose of each paragraph in the sample answer?
   Paragraph 1: a general opinion in answer to the question

4 Compare the paragraph structure of the sample answer with that of the sample answer on page 42 in Unit 3. In what way are they different?

5 What linking devices does the writer use to introduce each of the three points from the Notes section in the question (e.g. *For one thing* …).
   Secondly; Another positive point is

6 What other linking devices do they use? *Without doubt; which; whereas; but; also; therefore; because; In my opinion*

7 You are going to write an answer to the following Part 1 task. Read the instructions, but before you write your essay, do Exercises 8 and 9 and read the advice in the Don't forget! box.

   In your English class you have been talking about travel and transport. Your English teacher has asked you to write an essay.

   Write an essay using **all** the notes and giving reasons for your point of view.

   > **Is it better to use the car or public transport in your town or area?**
   >
   > **Notes**
   > **Things to write about:**
   > 1 journey times
   > 2 cost
   > 3 .... (your own idea)

   Write your essay in 140–190 words.

8 Decide on your third point. This will depend on the situation in your area and the answer you give, but here are some possible options:
   - comfort
   - frequency
   - noise and pollution
   - parking facilities

9 Make a brief plan before writing your essay. Write down ideas for each of the three points in the Notes section. Select those you wish to include and decide how you will organise them into paragraphs.

   Now you are ready to write your essay.

   For more information on writing essays, see **pages 189–191**.

Don't forget!
- Include a brief introduction and conclusion in your essay.
- Write in a consistently formal or neutral style.
- Include a range of language and avoid repetition.
- Use appropriate linking devices (see page 42–43 of Unit 3, Language focus on page 122 and Exercises 5 & 6 above).
- Check your work when you have finished.

8 REVIEW

Language focus Contrast linkers

Underline the most appropriate option. Sometimes more than one option is possible.

1 We enjoyed our day in the countryside, in spite of *raining* / *it rained* / <u>*the rain*</u>.
2 Although I got to the airport late, *they wouldn't let me check in* / <u>*I still caught my plane*</u> / *I didn't have my passport*.
3 Elena and I got on well during the holiday, despite *of the fact she's older than me* / <u>*her being older than me*</u> / <u>*our age difference.*</u>
4 I'm not keen on package holidays, whereas *I'm not fond of camping* / <u>*my brother loves them*</u> / *my sister doesn't like them either*.
5 My grandparents are going on a cruise next month, even though <u>*they don't particularly like boats*</u> / *they like visiting different places* / <u>*they both get seasick*</u>.
6 We usually spend part of our summer holiday by the sea. This year, *whereas,* / <u>*however,*</u> / *although,* we've rented a cottage in the mountains.

Reading and Use of English Part 1 Multiple-choice cloze

For questions 1–8, read the text below and decide which answer (A, B, C or D) best fits each gap. There is an example at the beginning (0).

Seville

Situated on the banks of the river Guadalquivir, Seville **(0)** _C_ the best of Andalusian culture, with its rich Moorish heritage, fine food and passionate flamenco music. Hidden within the narrow streets of its historic centre are beautiful courtyards **(1)** _D_ of flowers, bringing an air of calm to an otherwise vibrant city.

Begin your **(2)** _B_ to Seville with a guided tour aboard an open-top bus or one of the many horse-drawn carriages which **(3)** _A_ off from the cathedral. Then climb the Giralda tower for a spectacular **(4)** _B_ of the city, before strolling around the gardens of the Alcázar palace. Seville, of course, is **(5)** _C_ for its delicious 'tapas', so if you need a break from sightseeing, **(6)** _B_ Triana or Santa Cruz, where you can sample the delights of southern Spanish cuisine.

If you have time, take a **(7)** _D_ out to the Roman ruins of Italica, birthplace of the emperors Trajan and Hadrian. Just a short bus **(8)** _A_ away from the city centre, Italica boasts an impressive Roman amphitheatre and numerous mosaics.

0	A discovers	B explores	C <u>offers</u>	D involves
1	A plenty	B lots	C crowded	D <u>full</u>
2	A stay	B <u>visit</u>	C sight	D arrival
3	A <u>set</u>	B put	C get	D give
4	A vision	B <u>view</u>	C aspect	D appearance
5	A seen	B looked	C <u>known</u>	D heard
6	A come across	B <u>head for</u>	C move on	D take to
7	A travel	B trail	C track	D <u>trip</u>
8	A <u>ride</u>	B walk	C pass	D run

REVIEW 8

Language focus The future

Complete each gap with one word. There is an example at the beginning (0).

I **(0)** _am_ just about to go on a three-day business trip to St Petersburg. My husband's going with me, but while he's out enjoying himself, looking around the city, I'll be **(1)** _taking_ part in meetings. I'm not planning **(2)** _on_ doing much sightseeing myself, as I don't expect **(3)** _to_ have a great deal of free time. However, if I do get the chance, I **(4)** _may/might/could_ well pay a quick visit to the Hermitage Museum. I'm a huge fan of Leonardo da Vinci, and I know for certain that two of his works **(5)** _will_ be on display there. Being February, it **(6)** _is_ likely to be very cold, but I might **(7)** _not_ notice that too much as I'll be inside most of the time. It's really not going to **(8)** _be_ much fun for me.

298 Retweets   **643** Likes

Reading and Use of English Part 4 Key word transformation

Complete the second sentence so that it has a similar meaning to the first sentence, using the word given. Do not change the word given. You must use between two and five words, including the word given.

1 He was about to decide when his phone rang.
   POINT
   He was _on the **point** of making_ up his mind when his phone rang.

2 The weather probably won't improve for several days.
   LIKELY
   The weather is _not/n't **likely** to get (any/much)_ better for several days.

3 Dan wants to start his own travel business.
   SETTING
   Dan's planning _on **setting** up_ his own travel business.

4 The plants will probably be dead when we eventually get home.
   HAVE
   The plants may well _**have** died by_ the time we get home.

5 Let me know the moment you think of a solution to this problem.
   COME
   Let me know as _soon as you **come** up_ with a solution to this problem.

6 It was hot and humid, but we still enjoyed our holiday.
   SPITE
   We enjoyed our holiday _in **spite** of the heat_ and humidity.

Writing Part 2 Article

You see this announcement in an international magazine for young people.

Write your article in 140–190 words.

HOLIDAY COMPETITION

Write an article about a holiday destination you know well, giving details of what tourists can see and do there. The top ten articles will be included in the next edition of our magazine.

Use the multiple-choice cloze text on Seville on page 124 as a model. Consider the following:

- How many paragraphs are there?
- What type of information does each one contain?
- Are there any expressions which you could use in your own article?

See the Teacher's Resource Centre for a Sample answer with Examiner comments for this task.
For more information on writing articles, see page 192.

8 ON THE MOVE

8 ON THE MOVE

Pronunciation Chunking

1 ▶ 8.3 Listen to this extract from a talk show. Notice how the speaker makes a slight pause in between each group of words or 'chunk' of speech.

> Well, / a few years ago / I was in South Africa with a few of my friends / and we'd nearly finished the first part of an all-day climb. / I was just pulling myself up / when I saw a huge snake / right in front of me. / I'm terrified of snakes, / so I just froze / and watched as it started to hiss at me / and arch backwards. / I waited for another few minutes, / not moving, / and then it just seemed to get bored / and it slithered back into a crack in the rock. / It was the most terrifying moment ever / and it had nothing to do with climbing!

2 Read the box below, then practise reading the extract in Exercise 1 aloud, pausing slightly after each chunk of speech.

> **Chunking**
>
> When speaking, we regularly make pauses between groups of words, or 'chunks' of language, such as phrases or clauses. Chunking helps the listener make sense of what the speaker is saying in the same way that punctuation helps the reader make sense of what is written.

3 Read the following extract from a story. Chunk the extract, marking each pause with a forward slash (/).

> So, anyway, / a few months ago / I was staying at my parents' house / when this strange thing happened. / We were all in the lounge, / enjoying the warmth of the fire, / listening to the storm raging outside. / We could hear the rain pouring down heavily, / and the strong wind / roaring through the trees. / Suddenly, / we heard the sound of glass smashing upstairs / and something heavy banged on the floor. / We rushed upstairs, / and in our bedroom, / we saw an enormous branch / which had come crashing through the window. / We stood, / open-mouthed, / wondering what to do next.

4 ▶ 8.4 Listen and compare with your ideas in Exercise 3.

5 **SPEAK** Work in pairs. Take turns to tell the story in Exercise 3.

126

Pronunciation

1 ▶ 8.3 Play the recording and students listen for the pauses. You can play the recording more than once if students still appear a bit uncertain about the idea of chunking.

2 Alternatively, you could elicit the information from the box using the chunked text in Exercise 1. The importance of chunking could be demonstrated by reading the text aloud and purposely not pausing appropriately between phrases or clauses.

3–5 ▶ 8.4 Note that there is no one correct way to chunk a text. So make sure the students know their version isn't 'wrong' if it's different from the one in the recording, as long their pauses are logically placed between phrases and clauses. Different speakers may pause in different places for different reasons, for example, to emphasise a certain detail or idea.

9 MYSTERY AND IMAGINATION

In this unit, students will explore the themes of mystery and imagination, doing tasks related to ghosts, mystery donors and superstitions, among other topics. They will also get useful practice writing reviews.

Read the unit objectives to the class.

SPEAKING Part 1 Interview

Write *mystery* vertically on the board. In pairs, students have to think of words that either start with a letter from *mystery*, e.g. *superstition* for the letter 's', or contain one of the letters, e.g. *aliens* for the letter 'e'. They create vertical poems to be shared in open class.

When discussing the Part 1 questions, an extra challenge could be added by projecting or writing them on the board with some of the words gapped:

1 Are you a fan _____ scary films, series or books?
2 Do you enjoy _____ puzzles and doing crosswords?
3 Have you ever _____ a friend or a member of your family a big surprise?
4 Describe a time when you lost something, _____ temporarily or permanently.
5 Which magicians are famous _____ your country? Have you seen one perform live or _____ television?

The missing words could be elicited to the board in open class. The students could also simply open their books and check there.

ONLINE MATERIALS

Jump to conclusions (**Teacher's Resource Centre**)
Keep talking (**Teacher's Resource Centre**)
Unit 9 Test (**Test Generator**)
Unit 9 Wordlist (**Teacher's Resource Centre**)
Unit 9 On-the-go-practice (**App**)

9 MYSTERY AND IMAGINATION

Listening Part 4 Multiple choice

1 **SPEAK** You are going to listen to a radio interview with a ghost walk guide. What do you think happens on a ghost walk? What does the guide do?

2 ▶ 9.1 Listen to the interview. For questions 1–7, choose the best answer (A, B or C).

1 Alan says his job as a ghost walk guide has enabled him to
   A become an expert on local history.
   B combine his different talents.
   C improve his acting skills.

2 Alan says that participants in the ghost walks
   A are never disappointed.
   B want to be frightened.
   C laugh at all his jokes.

3 According to Alan, what quality enables a storyteller to frighten audiences?
   A self-confidence
   B a loud voice
   C good timing

4 What type of people do not usually enjoy the ghost walk so much?
   A people who have not been anticipating it
   B people who come as part of a group
   C people who do not like surprises

5 What does Alan say about playing different characters on the ghost walks?
   A Some of the roles help to improve his mood.
   B He dresses up as real people from history.
   C Acting helps maintain the audience's interest.

6 When talking about the possible existence of ghosts, Alan says that
   A he respects other people's belief in ghosts.
   B he believes ghosts are part of people's imagination.
   C he suspects people of inventing stories to impress others.

7 When talking about his favourite ghost story, Alan says that
   A he does not want to give all the details.
   B he does not tell it on many ghost walks.
   C he does not think everyone enjoys it.

3 **SPEAK** Discuss the following questions.
   1 Have you or has anyone you know ever had 'a paranormal experience'?
   2 Do you believe that ghosts and haunted buildings exist?
   3 Would you be interested in going on a ghost walk? Why/Why not?

MYSTERY AND IMAGINATION

Listening

1 Give the students time to discuss the questions in pairs. Then bring the class back together and nominate a few students to share their ideas. Note that *enable* in question 3 contains the *en-* prefix that students encountered in unit five, page 76, which here turns the adjective *able* into a transitive verb.

2 ▶ 9.1 Before the students read the task, elicit some exam strategies, e.g. underline key words in the questions; while doing the task, listen for the answer to the question or sentence beginnings instead of the options, etc. Then set a time limit for how long the students can read the task before the recording starts. Be strict. On the exam, candidates will have only a minute, but you can still give them a bit longer at this point in the course.

3 Students discuss the questions in pairs or small groups. To extend this **SPEAK** activity, ask the students to share any good ghost stories they have heard.

AUDIOSCRIPT

Listening Part 4 Multiple choice

▶ 9.1

I = Interviewer   A = Alan Stanford

I: In the Talkabout studio today we have a ghost walk guide. Local man, Alan Stanford, takes groups of people round the town on guided tours, telling ghost stories about the historic buildings which are said to be haunted. Sounds like an interesting job, Alan.

A: Oh, it is, it's fascinating. I've been a tour guide before but mostly abroad and never here in my own home town. I wouldn't call myself an expert, but I've learnt quite a lot about our local history since I started doing this a couple of years ago. Plus, of course, I get to dress up in period costume and **Ex 2 Q1** tell lots of ghost stories in character. Acting and storytelling have always been in my blood, so I'm really just doing the things that come most naturally to me. I have a great time.

I: And how about those who actually go on the tours? Do they get frightened?

A: Well, obviously these are ghost walks, so it wouldn't be much fun if there wasn't a bit of fear involved. Not too much, of course – we often have children **Ex 2 Q2** in the groups, so we have to be careful. But people expect to be scared, and they'd be disappointed if they weren't, so we aim at least to give them goose bumps, and perhaps even a little fright – after which **they all laugh nervously** and enjoy the release of tension.

I: And how do you achieve that, giving them a fright?

A: Well, the mark of a good storyteller is the ability to hold an audience's attention, and that's not too hard to do when the subject is ghosts. You take the listeners into your confidence, create the right **Ex 2 Q3** mood, make them feel safe with you. Then, just at the right moment, when they're least expecting it, you change the tone, give a shout or let out a scream. And they nearly jump out of their skin!

I: Right, yes. And does it work every time?

A: Well, it does with most audiences, people who've been thinking about the ghost walk all day, maybe all week, wondering what's going to happen. **These**

Ex 2 Q4 people usually respond extremely well. Some of the groups we get, though, come along as part of a surprise event. People like these haven't had time to reflect on what they're coming to, they haven't been given the chance to look forward to it, and the effect isn't the same. They don't normally have such a good time, unfortunately.

I: You mentioned dressing up and acting before. Do you have a variety of characters that you play or just one?

A: Oh no, there are several. There's Lord Warwick, for example, a wealthy noble; the old sea dog Jake Redburn; John Simpkins, who's a servant … none of them actually existed, of course, they're all fictitious. The choice of character I play often depends on the route we take and the stories to be told, or also perhaps how I'm feeling that night and the type of audience I'm expecting. As with all acting, it adds a sense of truth to the whole **Ex 2 Q5** thing, makes it more credible. So the audience becomes engaged in the tour and responds in a more positive, sometimes more frightened way.

I: One question, I have to ask you, Alan. Do you believe in ghosts?

A: Regrettably, I have to say that I haven't seen any on the walks, or had any other paranormal experiences to impress you with. Some people in my audiences have said they have, and so have **Ex 2 Q6** some of my friends, and I wouldn't dare dispute that or suggest they're imagining things. Ghosts are real for those people who say they've seen them, and who am I to say they haven't? The most I can say is that I have no personal evidence they exist.

I: And of the stories that you tell on your ghost walks, do you have a favourite?

A: Well, I particularly like stories which involve smells that some buildings are said to give off when ghosts **Ex 2 Q7** are around. I don't want to give away too much here on the programme, but the one I enjoy telling most of all is about an old woman called Florence Hardcastle, who haunts the town hall. When she appears every now and again, the place absolutely stinks. Now at first, some people thought it was a problem with the rubbish, but if you want to find out the real reason, you'll have to come along on the ghost walk.

I: We're curious now, Alan.

TB128

9 MYSTERY AND IMAGINATION

Word formation

1–2 Individually, students complete the sentences and check their answers with the **Audioscript** on page 242 (see TB128). Then, in pairs, students discuss the rules. In open class, elicit these rules to the board.

Answers

Add -ly to the adjective (e.g. *nervously*). This also applies to adjectives ending in -l (e.g. *usually*) or -e (*extremely*). However, if the adjective ends in a consonant +-le then omit the final -e and add -y (e.g. *regrettably*).

3–4 Students could do these exercises individually and then check in pairs; they could also do it in pairs and then check with another pair. Point out that words that already end with -ly like *lively, friendly, silly* have no adverb form; *in a silly way/manner* is the usual way round it. With this type of exercise, it's much more efficient to simply project the answers on the board or have the students check them in the **Answer key** on page 267 (also available on the **Student's Resource Centre** if they don't have the with-key version).

Reading and Use of English

1 Ask the students what *SOS* is and what situations they associate it with. Students read the instructions. Elicit some of the exam strategies from earlier units, e.g. first read the whole text quickly to get a general idea; think about whether the words could be negative or plural, etc.

2 Conduct brief feedback after the students have talked about their stories in pairs. Board some emergent language that comes up during the discussion.

Teaching tip

Give your students practice writing their answers on an official answer sheet. These can be found on the **Teacher's** and **Student's Resource Centres**. Note that it is strongly recommended that candidates write their answers for Parts 2, 3 and 4 of the Reading and Use of English paper in capital letters. Students should therefore get into the habit of always writing their answers this way, even in their notebooks.

Extra activity

To practise the phonemic script, as well as the pronunciation of the words themselves, put the following phonemic transcriptions for the words from the Part 3 Word formation task on the board and elicit the words:

/ɪˈventʃuəli/   /ˈlʌkɪli/   /əˈpærəntli/   /ˈnjuːli/
/ˈseɪfli/   /ɪkˈsepʃ(ə)nəli/   /drəˈmætɪkli/   /ˈʃɔː(r)tli/

Ask the students if there are any symbols they are still a bit unsure about. Elicit or provide a few other words containing the sound corresponding to that symbol and write them in phonemic script on the board.

MYSTERY AND IMAGINATION

Word formation Adverbs

1 In these sentences from the listening, write the adverb formed from the adjective in brackets.
  1 They all laugh __nervously__ (*nervous*).
  2 These people __usually__ (*usual*) respond __extremely__ (*extreme*) well.
  3 __Regrettably__ (*regrettable*), I have to say that I haven't seen any on the walks.

2 Check your answers in the Audioscript on page 242. What are the rules for the formation of the adverbs in the above examples?

3 Write the adverb formed from these adjectives. The same rule applies to both adjectives in each pair. There is an example at the beginning (0).

  0 Example:
     beautiful → beautifully   *total → totally*
  1 complete __completely__   sole __solely__
  2 simple __simply__   responsible __responsibly__
  3 happy __happily__   extraordinary __extraordinarily__
  4 scientific __scientifically__ energetic __energetically__

4 Now write the adverbs formed from these words. These should be learnt separately.
  1 whole __wholly__   2 shy __shyly__   3 full __fully__
  4 public __publicly__ 5 true __truly__   6 day __daily__

Reading and Use of English Part 3 Word formation

1 For questions 1–8, read the text below. Use the word given in capitals at the end of some of the lines to form a word that fits in the gap in the same line. There is an example at the beginning (0).

In this particular text, all the missing words are adverbs. For numbers 1, 2, 6 and 8, the word in capitals is a verb or a noun. In order to create an adverb from these words, you first need to consider the adjective form.

2 **SPEAK** Tell the class about any other survival stories you know.

A MYSTERY SOS

When a helicopter pilot spotted an SOS sign made from rocks at Swift Bay, Western Australia in May 2017, a search (0) __IMMEDIATELY__ began for a missing person. Someone had (1) __apparently__ made a call for help in this (2) __exceptionally__ remote part of the country, but police were unsure whether the sign was (3) __newly__ constructed or if it had been there for some time. They were unable to find anyone, although evidence of a camp was discovered. The mystery was solved when, (4) __shortly__ after hearing about it, a man told police that the sign had been made in 2013 by his brother, Robert Rudd, after his yacht had become stranded in the bay. Rudd and a travelling companion had made it to shore (5) __safely__ in a small boat, but only after (6) __dramatically__ surviving an attack from a crocodile. They were (7) __eventually__ rescued after living for several days off rations they had taken with them and fresh water they had found. (8) __Luckily__ for them, another yacht came by and found them before they ran out of food.

IMMEDIATE
APPEAR
EXCEPTION
NEW

SHORT

SAFE
DRAMA
EVENTUAL

LUCK

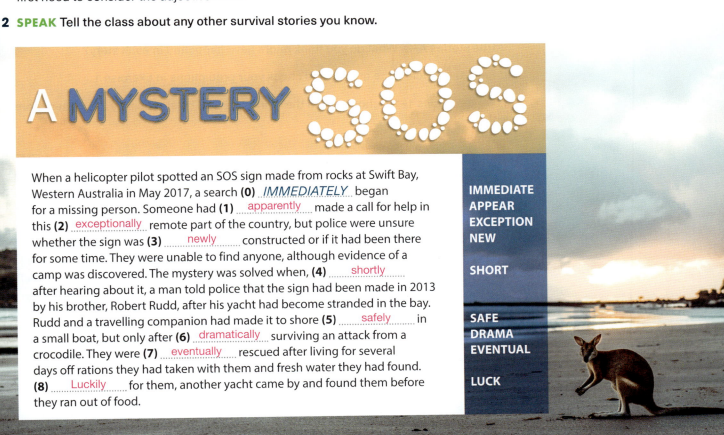

129

MYSTERY AND IMAGINATION

Language focus Modal verbs for speculation and deduction

1 It is possible that the police had the following thoughts when they first saw the SOS sign mentioned in the text on page 129. Read them and answer the question below.

*Someone who was in trouble **must have made** this in the hope that it would be spotted from the air. Their boat **might have become** stranded on the rocks in the bay, or it **may have suffered** damage in a storm. They **can't have come** here overland because the nearest town is over 600 miles away.*

Which of the forms in **bold** express

a possible explanations for what happened?   might have become; may have suffered

b certainty about what didn't happen?   can't have come

c certainty about what happened?   must have made

2 Go to **Ready for Grammar** on **page 222** to check your answers to Exercise 1 and for further rules and practice.

3 Speculate about what might have happened in the following situations. Write at least two sentences for each using modal verbs. There is an example at the beginning (0).

0 Angela's crying.

She could have just received some bad news.

She may have had an argument with a friend.

She might have been peeling onions.

1 Paul's face and hands are very dirty. He may have got his hands dirty and then wiped his face, or he might have been playing football and fallen over several times.
2 The kitchen window is broken. Someone may have thrown or kicked a ball through it, or a burglar might have broken into the house.
3 There's a red mark on Steve's shirt collar. He might have cut himself while he was shaving, or he could have been painting and got some red paint on his shirt.
4 Lucy was late for school. She might have overslept or the bus may have been late.
5 Nobody in the class did their homework last night. It could have been too difficult for them, or they might have all been watching something on television.

4 **SPEAK** Work in pairs. Take turns to read out some of the sentences you wrote in Exercise 3. Your partner should guess which situation each sentence applies to.

Reading and Use of English Part 7 Multiple matching

1 **SPEAK** Read the introduction to the article *Mystery donors*, as well as the titles of the true stories A–D. What do you think might have happened in each story?

2 Read the article quite quickly and check your predictions in Exercise 1.

3 For questions 1–10, choose from the stories (A–D). The stories may be chosen more than once.

Which story

mentions an unsuccessful attempt to identify the donor?	1 C
describes a source of irritation for the recipients of the donations?	2 B
suggests why people might initially question the suitability of the donations?	3 A
says that one gift helped someone encourage other people to make donations?	4 D
mentions a suggestion from the donor as to how the donations could be used?	5 B
says that one person initially mistook the intentions of the donor?	6 C
says that most people did not want it to be known who the donor was?	7 A
mentions the donor's recent piece of luck?	8 C
refers to unpleasant incidents which may have motivated the donations?	9 B
says there was only one exception to the type of recipient of the donations?	10 D

4 **SPEAK** Discuss the following questions.

1 Which story do you like best? Why?

2 Imagine you unexpectedly came into a lot of money, and decided to give half of it away. Who would you give it to, and why? What would you do with the remaining half?

MYSTERY AND IMAGINATION

Language focus

1-2 Students look at the examples in Exercise 1. Students discuss questions a–c in pairs and then check their answers in the **Ready for Grammar** section on page 222 (see below). If students show a good grasp of the grammar, you could set the two exercises in the **Ready for Grammar** section for homework or save them for revision.

3-4 Monitor while the students write their sentences to check how well they are using the grammar. You may wish to use **Jump to conclusions** on the **Teacher's Resource Centre** to extend this lesson.

Reading and Use of English

1-2 Check the meaning of *donor* in the title. Ask: *What's the verb?* (donate.) Elicit some of the students' predictions in open class after they have talked in pairs.

3-4 Get the students to compare their answers in pairs, justifying their choices, before going over them in open class. While students discuss the questions, write down some emergent language.

READY FOR GRAMMAR

9 Modal verbs for speculation and deduction

If we are fairly certain about something, *must*, *can't* and *couldn't* can be used to express this.

1 For present situations the modal verbs *must*, *can't* and *couldn't* are followed by the infinitive without *to*.
   'I haven't slept for two days.' 'You **must be** so tired!'
   I can hear singing, so the stadium **can't be** far now.
   The continuous infinitive can also be used.
   He **couldn't be going** to school – it's Saturday today.

2 For past situations we use the same modal verbs + *have* + past participle (the perfect infinitive without *to*).
   I can't find my book. I **must have left** it at school.
   This essay is poor. You **can't have spent** long on it.
   The continuous form can also be used.
   The road's wet – it **must have been raining**.

If we are not certain about something but think it is possible, we use *may (not)*, *might (not)* or *could* (but not *could not*).

1 For present situations these modal verbs are followed by the infinitive without *to*. The continuous infinitive is also possible.
   'Ed hasn't replied.' 'He **might be** on holiday.'
   He **could be telling** the truth, but it's hard to believe.

2 For past situations we use the same modal verbs + *have* + past participle (the perfect infinitive without *to*. The continuous form is also possible.
   I think we **may have taken** the wrong road.
   'Lee was quiet.' 'He **might not have been feeling** well.'

---

9 Modal verbs for speculation and deduction

1 Match each of the sentences 1–6 with a suitable continuation a–f.

  1 Don't make too much noise.   _b_   a She might not be working there anymore.
  2 What do you mean you don't know what to do?   _d_   b He might still be asleep.
  3 Would you lend me yours?   _e_   c He can't have got very far.
  4 I can't find her name on their website.   _a_   d You can't have been listening to my instructions.
  5 You should ask her.   _f_   e I must have left mine at home.
  6 I want everyone to search the area.   _c_   f You never know; she might be interested.

2 **SPEAK** Use modal verbs to speculate about possible contexts for each of the sentence combinations in Exercise 1.

  1 *This could be a mother speaking to her children. They might be playing in the house and their father may be ill in bed.*
  2 *This could be a teacher talking to a student about an exercise she has asked the class to do.*
  3 *This might be a friend asking a classmate if he/she could borrow a phone to make a call.*
  4 *This might be work colleagues talking about trying to find a contact on a website in order to write/email them information.*
  5 *This could be friends talking about asking another friend to join them on an activity holiday.*
  6 *This may be a detective talking to police officers about searching for a thief.*

Go back to **page 130**.

9 MYSTERY AND IMAGINATION

READY FOR GRAMMAR

9 Reported speech

Reported Statements

When reporting what someone has said or written we can use either direct speech or reported speech.

When we use direct speech, we report the exact words which someone has used.

'I'm staying here tomorrow,' said Heather.

When we use reported speech, changes may have to be made to verb tenses, pronouns and certain words indicating place and time. We can use *that* after the reporting verb, but it is optional.

Heather said (that) she was staying there the next day.

1 The following changes are usually made to verbs. In each case the verb 'moves back' one tense.

Direct Speech		Reported Speech
Present simple	→	Past simple
*'I **work** in an office,' he said.*		*He said he **worked** in an office.*
Present continuous	→	Past continuous
*'We **aren't going** away on holiday,' she said.*		*She said they **weren't going** away on holiday.*
Present perfect	→	Past perfect
*'I**'ve known** her for a long time,' he said.*		*He said he**'d known** her for a long time.*
Present perfect continuous	→	Past perfect continuous
*'He**'s been playing** tennis,' she said.*		*She said he**'d been playing** tennis.*
Past simple	→	Past perfect
*'I **saw** Ben in town,' he said.*		*He said he**'d seen** Ben in town.*
Past continuous	→	Past perfect continuous
*'We **were trying** to help him,' she said.*		*She said they**'d been trying** to help him.*

The modal verbs *will*, *can* and *may*:

*'I**'ll** let Tim know.'*	→	*He said he **would** let Tim know.*
*'I **can** speak German.'*	→	*She said she **could** speak German.*
*'We **may** not go to Lucy's.'*	→	*They said they **might** not go to Lucy's.*

When reporting obligations, *must* usually changes to *had to*. *Mustn't* does not change.

*'You **must** be home by twelve.'*	→	*Dad said we **had to** be home by twelve.*
*'You **mustn't** tell anyone.'*	→	*She said I **mustn't** tell anyone.*

When reporting deductions, *must* does not change.

*'He **must** be joking.'*	→	*Lina said he **must** be joking.*

2 No changes are made in the verb tense:
  1 if the verb in the direct speech is in the past perfect.
    'He had never spoken about it before,' she said.
    She said he had never spoken about it before.
  2 if the direct speech contains one of the following modal verbs: *would, might, could, should, ought to*.
    'You should go to the doctor's,' he said.
    He said I should go to the doctor's.
  3 if the statement being reported is still true. The tense change is optional.
    'I like fish,' she said.
    She said she likes/liked fish.
  4 if the reporting verb is in the present.
    'It's 40 degrees in Athens at the moment.' (Jamie to his mother on the phone)
    'Jamie says it's 40 degrees in Athens at the moment.' (Jamie's mother to her husband)

3 Pronouns in direct speech may have to change when we use reported speech.
  'I'll see you later,' said Nico.
  Nico said he would see me later.

4 The following changes may also need to be made to words indicating place and time.

Direct Speech	Reported Speech
now	then
today	that day
this morning	that morning
tomorrow	the next/following day
next week	the next/following week
yesterday	the day before / the previous day
two days ago	two days before / earlier
last week	the week before / the previous week
here	there
come	go

MYSTERY DONORS

MYSTERY AND IMAGINATION 9

Here are four true stories of people who performed acts of generosity – and kept their identity a secret.

A Book sculptures appear in Edinburgh's cultural centres

Over the course of a nine-month period, a total of ten sculptures, beautifully crafted from books, were left anonymously in various cultural buildings in the city of Edinburgh. Each was accompanied by a note, which included the words, 'In support of libraries, books, words, ideas and festivals'. Cutting up books may at first seem a rather strange way to show one's support for the written word, but there was unanimous approval of the intricate sculptures from all those lucky enough to view them when they were put on display.

Each sculpture was carefully chosen: a dinosaur for the National Museum or a tiny cinema for the city's Filmhouse. Despite a strong suggestion in one of the notes that the person leaving the sculptures was a woman, journalists at a local newspaper said the donor was a man. They claimed they had discovered his identity, but kept it quiet, given that the general view was that he, or she, should remain anonymous.

B Ambulance crews receive anonymous thank-you notes and cash

In the lead-up to the winter holiday period one year, paramedics in London and the adjoining county of Surrey began finding cards attached to their ambulances with words of thanks for their life-saving work, and up to £10 in cash. The thank-you notes and money may have been a response to recent abusive messages received by ambulance crews who had parked their vehicles in front of people's driveways while dealing with emergency calls.

The professionally printed cards, believed to be the work of a local firm that wished to remain anonymous, told the paramedics 'YOU ARE AWESOME' and included the invitation: 'Coffee and doughnuts are on us today'. To their annoyance, however, the healthcare workers were told by their management to hand over any cash donations, as the ambulance service had 'strict rules and guidelines around the acceptance of monetary gifts'.

C Mystery man gives out money in supermarket

When a man entered a supermarket in Tiverton, England, and began handing out envelopes to shoppers, the recipients were delighted. In each of the envelopes was a fifty-pound note, together with a message which read: 'I have recently been fortunate enough to come into quite a lot of money – more than I need for myself and my family. So I thought that I would share some of it with you.' Believing it to be part of a marketing promotion, one beneficiary nearly threw the blank envelope away. Another went to the bank to check that the note was genuine. The donor's identity remains unknown, in spite of the efforts of one national daily, which asked readers to get in contact if they knew who the mystery benefactor was.

D Philanthropist donates millions to US universities

Donations to educational establishments are nothing unusual, but one year, no fewer than twenty universities in the United States received a total of over $100 million from a single anonymous donor. All but one of the universities were public institutions, and all were run by women. The donations, ranging from $1.5 million to $10 million, were made on the condition that most of the money should go towards financial scholarships for women and minorities, and that the recipients make no attempt to identify the donor. Chancellor Pamela Shockley-Zalabak managed to double her university's donation of $5.5 million by persuading private individuals in Colorado Springs to match the amount. The money was used to fund single parents returning to education, as well as promising students who had to work while attending university.

131

MYSTERY AND IMAGINATION

Speaking Part 3 Collaborative task

1 **SPEAK** Imagine that a wealthy donor wants to give away large sums of money to different institutions and other places in your community. Below are some of the possible recipients of the donations. Talk to each other about how these different recipients could spend their donations.

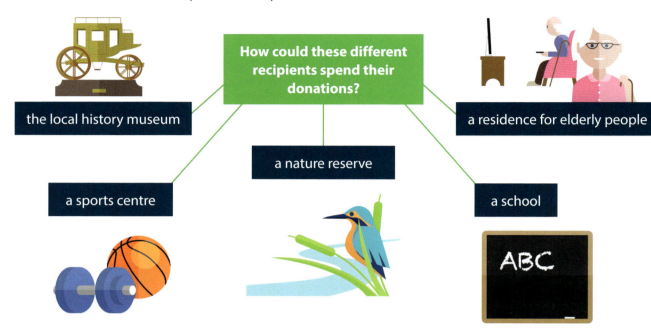

2 Now decide which two donations would benefit the community most.

Useful language

Task 1
Spending the donations
Complete each gap with a word from the box.

| for | in | on | on | out |

1 They could **spend** it ___on___ (computers).
2 They could use the money to **pay** ___for___ (advertising).
3 One idea would be to **invest** ___in___ (new equipment).
4 A sensible thing to do would be to (**take** ___on___ more staff).
5 The money could be used to (**carry** ___out___ repairs).

Task 2
Comparing the different options
(A museum) would not need as much financial help as (a school).
The more help we give to (elderly people), the better for the community.
The community would benefit far more from a donation to (the nature reserve).
The one in most need of a donation would be (the sports centre).

Speaking Part 4 Further discussion

SPEAK Discuss these questions with your partner.

1 What other types of places, institutions or organisations should be considered for a donation? Why?
2 Some people say that money can't buy happiness. What do you think?
3 Is it a good idea for parents to give pocket money to young children?
4 How important is it to save money?
5 Which types of workers in your country do you think deserve to earn more money? Why?
6 Do you think sports stars earn too much money? Why/Why not?

MYSTERY AND IMAGINATION 9

Speaking

1-2 Students read the instructions and then do the gap fill in the **Useful language** box. Before they do the speaking tasks, give students a minute to write two sentences, one for task 1 and one for task 2, using the useful language. Tell them to insert these sentences as naturally as they can into their conversations. At this point in course, it's good to replicate exam conditions as much as possible. Put students into groups of three, with one student in the role of the examiner, who keeps the time, reads the part 3 scenario and asks the questions in part 4. Tell the examiner to tick any expressions from the **Useful language** box used by the students. Put the following script up the board or on a handout for the examiner to read.

Now I'd like you to talk about something together for two minutes. I'd like you to imagine a wealthy donor wants to give away large sums of money to different institutions and other places in your community. Here are some ideas and a question for you to discuss. First you have some time to look at the task. (15 seconds.) Now talk to each other about how the different recipients could spend their donations. (2 minutes.) Thank you. Now you have about a minute to decide which two donations would benefit the community most. (1 minute.) Thank you.

Speaking

Students can work in pairs and take it in turns to ask the questions or put them in groups of three and one person can be the examiner.

You may wish to use **Keep talking** on the Teacher's Resource Centre to extend this speaking section.

READY FOR GRAMMAR

5   *This*, *that*, *these* and *those* may change to *the*.
   '**That** book you lent me is really boring,' he said.
   He said **the** book I had lent him was really boring.

6   The reporting verb *tell* must be followed by a direct object.
   He **told his mother/her** that he was getting married.

The verbs *say* and *explain* are used without a direct object.
She **said/explained** that she wasn't feeling well. ✔
She said/explained me that she wasn't feeling well. ✘

They can, however, be used with an indirect object.
I **said/explained to them** that I'd left my passport at home.

Reported questions
When we report questions, we make the same changes to verb tenses, pronouns and words indicating place and time as we do when we report statements. In addition *do*, *does* and *did* are omitted; the word order is the same as that of a statement; question marks are not used.

'What do you want to do?' he asked me.	He asked me what I wanted to do.
'Where have you been?' she asked him.	She asked him where he had been.
Yes/No questions:	If there is no question word (*what*, *where*, *who*, etc.) in the direct question, we use *if* or *whether*.
'Does she know Joe?'	He asked if/whether she knew Joe.

When we report a request, we can also use the structure *ask* + object pronoun/noun + infinitive with *to*. Compare the following:

Reporting a request: 'Can you help me, please?'	He **asked me to help** him. / He **asked me if could help** him.
Reporting a question: 'Can you ride a horse?'	She **asked me if I could** ride a horse.

TB132

9 MYSTERY AND IMAGINATION

Language focus

1–2 Tell one of the students they are a journalist at a local newspaper and ask them to read aloud the direct speech. Ask what tenses are used in the two sentences (*present simple*; *present perfect simple*). Then read out the reported speech making a 'beep' noise to represent the missing words. Elicit what happens to tenses when we report them (*they move back one tense*), then ask students to fill in the missing words. Students complete the rules in the box.

3 Direct students to the **Ready for Grammar** section on pages 224–225 (see TB131, TB132 and below). Note that reported speech with modal verbs can be challenging as modals don't exist in many other languages. So pay particular attention to these. Students may also be surprised to find that sometimes the verb tense doesn't change, e.g. when the statement is still true.

4–5 Monitor the students closely to see how they are getting on with the grammar.

6–7 Students look at the examples of reported questions and discuss the changes in pairs. They then read the grammar explanation on page 225 (see TB132) in the **Ready for Grammar** section to check their ideas.

8 This exercise is most efficiently corrected by either projecting the answers on the board or allowing students to correct themselves using page 268 in the **Answer key** (also available on the **Student's Resource Centre** if they don't have the with-key version).

Possible answer

Lucy said to Mark that he looked worried and asked him what the matter was. Mark told her he couldn't find his keys and asked Lucy if she had any idea where they might be. Lucy said she didn't, and asked Mark whether he'd looked in the spare bedroom. He replied that he'd looked everywhere in the flat. Lucy asked him when he had last used them and Mark said he'd opened the door with them when he('d) got home that afternoon. Lucy asked him if he'd left them in the door and Mark asked her if she was joking. She said she was deadly serious and said he should have a look. Mark opened the door and asked Lucy how she had known they'd be there.

READY FOR GRAMMAR

9 Reported speech

Reported statements

1 Complete the columns below, to show how verb tenses and other words and expressions can change in reported speech. Write either one or two words in each space. There is an example at the beginning (0).

Direct Speech	Reported Speech
0 'We're meeting her tomorrow.'	They said they _were meeting_ her _the next_ day.
1 'She's been living here for years.'	He told me she _had been_ living _there_ for years.
2 'I spoke to him last week.'	She said she _had spoken_ to him _the previous_ week.
3 'I was working yesterday.'	He told me he _had been_ working _the day_ before.
4 'We'd asked her several times.'	They said they _had asked_ her several times.
5 'I'll phone you later today.'	She told him she _would phone_ him later _that_ day.

2 Name the tense in each sentence in Exercise 1.

0 present continuous → past continuous

1 present perfect continuous → past perfect continuous
2 past simple → past perfect simple
3 past continuous → past perfect continuous
4 past perfect simple → past perfect simple
5 *will* + infinitive → *would* + infinitive

Go back to **page 133**.

Reported questions

3 For questions 1–6, complete the second sentence so that it has a similar meaning to the first sentence, using the word given. Do not change the word given. You must use between two and five words, including the word given.

1 'Did you buy a loaf of bread, Jack?' asked Millie.
HAD
Millie asked Jack _if/whether he **had** bought_ a loaf of bread.

2 'What's your Spanish teacher's name, Oliver?' asked his mother.
WHAT
Oliver's mother asked him _**what** his Spanish teacher was/is_ called.

3 'Do you think you'll pass?' I asked Amy before the exam.
THOUGHT
Before the exam, I asked Amy _if/whether she **thought** she would/she'd_ pass.

4 'Where are you planning on spending your holiday, Liam?' I asked him.
WAS
I asked Liam where _he **was** planning to_ go on holiday.

5 'Can I see your driving licence, sir?' asked the policewoman.
SHOW
The policewoman asked the man _to **show** her his_ driving licence.

6 'What is the width of the bed?' the woman asked.
HOW
The woman wanted to know _**how** wide the bed_ was.

Go back to **page 133**.

MYSTERY AND IMAGINATION 9

Language focus Reported speech

Reported statements

1 Report the direct speech in a by completing the gaps in b with the correct form of the verb in brackets.
   a **Direct speech**   'The donor is a man. We have discovered his identity.'
   b **Reported speech**   Journalists at a local newspaper said that the donor ____was____ (be) a man. They claimed they __had discovered__ (discover) his identity.

2 Check your answers to Exercise 1 in section A of the article on page 131. Complete the rules below with the names of the appropriate tenses.

Reported speech
The present simple in direct speech changes to the ____past simple____ in reported speech; the present perfect simple changes to the ____past perfect simple____.

3 Go to **Ready for Grammar** on **pages 224–225** for rules, explanations and further practice.

4 Write down at least five things that different people have said recently. Think about the following people.

   > family and friends   teachers   classmates   work colleagues   newsreaders
   > politicians   sportsmen and women   other famous people   yourself

   'I think United will win the cup this year.' (my brother)

5 **SPEAK** Report the statements from Exercise 4 to your partner using reported speech.
   My brother said he thought United would win the cup this year.

Reported questions

6 Here are two examples of direct questions, each followed by its reported version. Compare the two versions then answer the question.
   1 'Who do you think made the donation?'
     The interviewer asked the recipient who she thought had made the donation.
   2 'Will you try to identify the donor?'
     He asked her if she would try to identify the donor.

   What changes are made to direct questions when we report them? Consider the following:
   - auxiliary verbs *do, does, did* **disappear**
   - verb tenses **'move back' a tense**
   - word order **the same in reported questions as for statements (subject + verb)**
   - yes/no questions **use *if/whether***
   - punctuation **question marks are not used**

7 Go to **Ready for Grammar** on **pages 224–225** for rules, explanations and further practice.

8 Rewrite the following conversation using reported speech.
   Lucy said to Mark that he looked worried and asked him what ...

The mystery of the missing keys

Lucy: You look worried. What's the matter?
Mark: I can't find my keys. Do you have any idea where they might be?
Lucy: No, I don't. Have you looked in the spare bedroom?
Mark: I've looked everywhere in the flat.
Lucy: When did you last use them?
Mark: I opened the door with them when I got home this afternoon.
Lucy: Did you leave them in the door?
Mark: Are you joking?
Lucy: I'm deadly serious. You should have a look.
(*Mark opens the door*)
Mark: How did you know they'd be there?

9 MYSTERY AND IMAGINATION

Listening Part 2 Sentence completion

1 ▶ 9.2 You will hear a woman called Sally Hurst talking on the radio about the Superstition Mountain Range in the United States. For questions 1–10, complete the sentences with a word or short phrase.

The Superstition Mountains

While she was in the Superstition Mountains, Sally was able to go (1) __hiking__.
Sally does not recommend visiting the area in (2) __summer__.
Sally says the mountains were probably given their name by local (3) __farmers__ in the nineteenth century.
The owner of the lost gold mine was a (4) __German__ immigrant.
The mine owner died in (5) __October__ 1891.
It was estimated at one point that as many as (6) __eight thousand/8,000__ people every year tried to find the lost mine.
According to one clue, when the sun is (7) __setting__, it shines into the entrance of the mine.
The section on the mine in the Superstition Mountain Museum contains a collection of (8) __maps__.
Goldfield is now a (9) __ghost__ town, visited by many tourists.
Dutchman's Gold is the title of a (10) __song__ about the lost mine.

2 **SPEAK** Do you know any places with mysteries or legends attached to them?

Vocabulary Give

Phrasal verbs with *give*

1 Use the context to work out the meaning of the phrasal verbs in bold in these two extracts from the listening.

  1 But he didn't **give away** [the mine's] location to anyone, and it's a mystery which remains unsolved to this day.   *tell someone about, reveal*

  2 Even now, many people still haven't **given up** searching …and they continue to head for the region to look for the gold.   *abandon, stop*

2 Now work out the meaning of the phrasal verbs in bold in the following sentences.

  1 Tired of running, he **gave himself up** at a police station and confessed to the crime.
     allow oneself to be arrested by the police, surrender
  2 I'm going to **give out** the test papers now but you mustn't begin until I tell you.
     give something (physical) to several people
  3 You should never **give out** your personal details or financial information online.
     give information to a lot of people
  4 If you **give in** your homework now, I'll mark it tonight and **give** it **back** tomorrow.
     give something to a teacher; return
  5 My parents said no at first, but eventually they **gave in** and let me go to the party.
     agree to something after initial resistance

MYSTERY AND IMAGINATION 9

Listening

1 ▶ 9.2 Students read the instructions. Check the meaning of *mine*, which appears frequently throughout the task. Elicit a few useful exam strategies for this listening task, e.g. while you read the task, think about what kind of information might fit in the gaps; you will hear distractors – information that could fit in the gap but is not the correct answer, etc. Give the students no more than a minute to read the task before starting the recording. The answers could be elicited to the board or students could check them in the **Audioscript** on page 243 (see below).

2 Students discuss the question in pairs or small groups. Conduct brief feedback.

Vocabulary

1–2 *Give* is similar to verbs like *take*, *get*, *make* and *do* in that it can have a wide variety of meanings depending on which words it's combined with. Encourage students to add a page to their vocabulary notebooks for *give* and note down any new phrasal verbs or collocations in Exercises 2 and 3. After the students have discussed the meaning of the words from the context, they could check their guesses on www.macmillandictionary.com if mobile phones are allowed or use the **Wordlists** available on the **Student's Resource Centre**. See the **Teaching tip** and **Extra activity** on TB82 for more ideas for teaching phrasal verbs.

AUDIOSCRIPT

Listening Part 2 Sentence completion

▶ 9.2

S = Sally Hurst

S: Hi, I'm Sally Hurst and I've just got back from Arizona, where I spent two weeks in the Superstition Mountain Range, near Phoenix. Besides being known for its luxury desert golf courses, the area also attracts enthusiasts of more energetic outdoor activities like rock climbing or mountain biking. **[Ex 1 Q1]** And I was lucky enough to go **hiking** when I was there. There are miles of paths and the scenery is absolutely spectacular.

As you'd expect, it can get quite hot in the desert. It's late spring now, of course, and that's not unbearable. Autumn isn't too bad either, but I'd **[Ex 1 Q2]** certainly advise against going there in **summer**. Temperatures can reach the high forties – and that's more than a little uncomfortable for most.

The reason I went there was to research some of the legends and mysteries of the area for a radio documentary. The very origin of the name, 'Superstition Mountains' is itself a bit of a mystery. One theory says they were given their name by sixteenth-century Spanish settlers, some of whom inexplicably vanished when they went exploring there. But the more likely explanation is that it came about in the nineteenth century, when it was discovered that the local Pima Indians were **[Ex 1 Q3]** frightened of the mountains. **Farmers** in the area attributed this fear to superstition, and they decided to give that name first to one mountain, and then the whole range.

Perhaps the most talked-about mystery in the area is that of the so-called, 'Lost Dutchman's Mine', which is supposedly somewhere in the Superstition Mountains. Far from being Dutch, however, the owner of the gold mine in question, Jacob Waltz, **[Ex 1 Q4]** was in fact **German**, or *Deutsch* in his native language. Waltz arrived in the United States in November 1839, and spent virtually all his life there prospecting for gold, firstly in North Carolina, then Georgia, California and finally Arizona. When he **[Ex 1 Q5]** passed away in **October** 1891 he took the secret of his mine with him to his grave.

You see, apparently Waltz had found what was believed by some to be the richest gold mine in the world. But he didn't give away its location to anyone, and it's a mystery which remains unsolved to this day. According to one estimate in the late **[Ex 1 Q6]** nineteen seventies, up to **eight thousand** people a year attempted to locate the mine. Even now, people still haven't given up searching, despite the ban on mineral prospecting in 1983, and many continue to head for the region to look for the gold.

Waltz left a few clues, but without revealing very much. In one of them, for example, he says, 'The **[Ex 1 Q7]** rays of the **setting** sun shine into the entrance of my mine', but that could be just about anywhere.

I did a lot of my research for the documentary in a museum; The Superstition Mountain Museum. It's full of information on the Lost Dutchman's Mine, **[Ex 1 Q8]** including a whole set of **maps** which are thought to show its location – not that that's been of any use to anyone! So far, anyway.

And I saw another exhibit on the mine in a museum in nearby Goldfield. Now Goldfield was a prosperous mining town at the end of the nineteenth century, but when the gold ran out, everyone left and now it's a **[Ex 1 Q9] ghost** town. It's become a popular tourist attraction as well, of course, with museums, rides and shows, but it's still quite impressive, nevertheless.

Now you may have seen a film that was made in 1949 about the Lost Dutchman's Mine entitled *Lust for Gold*, starring Glenn Ford in the role of Jacob Waltz. But here's another piece of trivia for **[Ex 1 Q10]** you: in 1960, actor Walter Brennan recorded a **song** on the subject called *Dutchman's Gold*. We're going to play it to you right after the news.

TB134

MYSTERY AND IMAGINATION

3 Check the meaning of *thrilled*, *pay rise* and *nasty*. Students do the exercise individually and then pair check. Get students to cover up the sentence endings in the right-hand column and see how many of the nouns they can remember for the corresponding verb + adjective combinations on the left.

4 Before doing the speaking task, if time allows, get students to create flash cards, with the phrasal verb or collocation on one side and the definition or translation (with monolingual classes) on the other.

Reading and Use of English

1 Direct students to the **Additional materials** section on page 200 (see below). They discuss the rituals and think of any other examples. Get feedback from the class. Alternatively, Students A and B each get two cards. They take turns miming the ritual and describing them. Get them to create at least one card of their own about another famous sportsman or woman for another pair.

2 Students read the instructions. Elicit a couple of exam strategies for this task, e.g. read the task once quickly to get a general understanding; consider the meaning of the whole sentence and the words both before and after the gap, etc. If possible, project the text on the board and elicit the answers there.

3 This question could be discussed in pairs or in open class. A fun way to finish the lesson would be to play a little bit of the song mentioned in the listening, *Dutchman's Gold* by Walter Brennan.

Reading and Use of English Part 2 Open cloze

Read the examples of sportsmen and women's superstitious rituals. Do you know any more like this?

> Former world number one tennis star Serena Williams always ties her shoelaces in exactly the same way, and wears the same pair of socks for every match, without washing them.

> In the 1998 football World Cup, French player Laurent Blanc would kiss the bald head of goalkeeper Fabien Barthez before every game. France won the trophy that year.

> Before each race, swimming legend Michael Phelps used to listen to music, then take off his headphones and swing his arms three times before stepping up onto the starting block.

> British former boxer James DeGale always used to put his left glove on before the right one, whether he was training or about to go in the ring for a professional fight.

Go back to **page 135**.

MYSTERY AND IMAGINATION

Collocations with *give*

3 Match each sentence beginning 1–7 on the left with a suitable ending a–g.

1 Pat saw the mouse, **gave a piercing**   a **sigh**, and sent her yet another text.
2 Thrilled at the news, he **gave a broad**   b **surprise** yesterday; a 5% pay rise!
3 Your gifts of soft toys will **give great**   c **smile**, showing all his teeth.
4 He looked at her photo, **gave a deep**   d **look**, as if he didn't recognise her.
5 She waved, but he **gave** her **a blank**   e **shock** when they saw her phone bill.
6 Jasmin's parents were **given a nasty**   f **scream** and ran out of the room.
7 My boss, Megan, **gave** me **a pleasant**   g **pleasure** to the orphaned children.

4 **SPEAK** Describe an occasion when someone or something:
- gave you a nasty shock.
- gave you a pleasant surprise.
- gave you great pleasure.
- gave a broad smile.

Reading and Use of English   Part 2 Open cloze

1 **SPEAK** Go to the Additional materials on page 200.

2 For questions 1–8, read the text below and think of the word which best fits each gap. Use only one word in each space. There is an example at the beginning (0).

SPORTING SUPERSTITIONS

Most of **(0)** _us_ have routines, habits and superstitions. We'll wear our lucky shirt to an interview, arrange our cutlery in a particular way or turn the oven off three times, just to **(1)** _be/make_ sure. In a competitive environment, in **(2)** _which_ athletes are all going for gold, years of training, drastic diets and intense coaching might just **(3)** _not_ be enough … so, sometimes, the Olympians turn **(4)** _to_ luck for extra support.

'Superstition is very common in sport most of all because of the uncertainty of the outcome,' says sports psychologist Dr George Sik. 'Athletes use it so they can rely on something else other **(5)** _than_ their own consciousness. Sport is generally based on repetition and superstition means being in control, adding a safety net. It affects the mind and not the body. If you convince **(6)** _yourself_ that you are in luck, you'll boost your confidence and tend to perform better. And if you fail, you can always blame it **(7)** _on_ the luck.'

So, **(8)** _although/though/while/whilst_ they may know deep down that a 'lucky' pair of socks won't take them over the line any faster, many athletes stick to their rituals for that little bit of confidence, belief and a sense of security.

3 **SPEAK** How much does superstition affect your behaviour?

9 MYSTERY AND IMAGINATION

Language focus Reporting verbs

Earlier in this unit you looked at reporting statements using verbs like *say* and *tell*. A number of other verbs can be used to report what people say.

Reporting verbs followed by a preposition

1 Complete the gap in this sentence from the listening on page 134 with an appropriate preposition.

   I'd certainly **advise** ___against___ going there in summer.

   Check your answer in the Audioscript on page 243.

2 Match each sentence beginning 1–10 on the left with a suitable ending a–j. Complete each of the gaps with an appropriate preposition.

   1c

   1 Go and **apologise** to Amy ___for___
   2 The cyclist **blamed** me ___for___
   3 I forgot to **thank** Charlie ___for___
   4 I'm often **told off** at school ___for___
   5 Politicians were **criticised** ___for___
   6 My friend's mum **insisted** ___on___
   7 We **congratulated** Harry ___on___
   8 Our employees **complain** ___about___
   9 Signs at the lakeside **warn** ___against___
   10 The musician was **accused** ___of___

   a helping me. He probably thinks I'm ungrateful.
   b driving me home. 'It's too cold to walk,' she said.
   c losing her book, and offer to buy her a new one.
   d stealing the melody for his hit from another song.
   e causing the accident, but it was his fault, not mine.
   f working long hours, but we pay them really well.
   g swimming there after periods of heavy rainfall.
   h laughing in class. My teachers are far too serious.
   i passing all his exams. He deserved to do well.
   j being completely out of touch with public opinion.

3 Choose three of the sentence beginnings from Exercise 2 and write your own ending for each one.

4 **SPEAK** Read out your endings to your partner, who will try to guess the beginning of each sentence.

Reporting verbs followed by an infinitive

5 Look at these different ways of reporting what people say:

   a 'I'll buy you a new book,' said Jack to Amy.
      Jack told Amy he would buy her a new book.
      Jack **offered to buy** Amy a new book.

      offer (verb + infinitive with *to*)
      ask, promise, refuse, threaten

   b 'You should go and see a doctor,' said Elisa.
      Elisa said I should go and see a doctor.
      Elisa **advised me to go** and see a doctor.

      advise (verb + object + infinitive with *to*)
      ask, encourage, invite, persuade, recommend, remind, tell, warn

   Which of the following verbs have the same pattern as *offer* (verb + infinitive with *to*) and which are like *advise* (verb + object + infinitive with *to*)? Make two columns in your notebook.

   ask   encourage   invite   persuade   promise   recommend
   refuse   remind   tell   threaten   warn

6 Go to Ready for Grammar on page 226 to check your answers to Exercise 6 and for further rules and practice.

7 **SPEAK** Work with a partner. You each have various problems and you would like your partner's suggestions and advice.

   Student A turn to the Additional materials on page 201.
   Student B turn to the Additional materials on page 203.

MYSTERY AND IMAGINATION

Language focus

1 Note that the sentence is taken from the second paragraph in the Audioscript on page 243 (see TB 134).

2-4 If you think your students will find this exercise challenging, board the possible prepositions (*for, about, on*, etc). You could quiz students by asking which verbs go with *for, on*, etc. While students write their sentences for Exercise 3, monitor their use of the target language. After students have done Exercise 4, nominate a few students to share their sentences with the class. To finish, students discuss the last time they: apologised; were congratulated; thanked someone; were told off; were accused of doing something; complained about something.

5-6 Alternatively, start with books closed and the first sentence from a on the board. Elicit the reported sentence with *told*, then elicit the one with *offered*. Repeat for b. Tell the students the sentences follow two common patterns for reporting verbs. Books open. In pairs, students divide the verbs into verb pattern 1 or 2. They then check their answers in the Ready for Grammar section on pages 226–227 (see below).

7 Direct students to the Additional materials (see TB137). Allow time to think about the best verbs to use to report their classmate's suggestions before switching partners.

READY FOR GRAMMAR

9 Reporting verbs

A Reporting verbs followed by a preposition:

The following reporting verbs can be used with a preposition followed by a noun or a gerund: *accuse someone of, advise (someone) against, apologise (to someone) for, blame someone for, complain (to someone) about, congratulate someone on, criticise someone for, insist on, thank someone for, tell someone off for, warn (someone) against*

I **complained about the noise** from the street and **insisted on changing** rooms

B Reporting verbs followed by an infinitive:

a verb + infinitive with *to*

ask, demand, offer, promise, refuse, threaten

We **refused to pay** for our meal and **asked to see** the manager.

b verb + object noun/pronoun + infinitive with *to*

advise, ask, beg, encourage, invite, order, persuade, recommend, remind, tell, urge, warn

They **invited Liz to play** the piano at the ceremony and even **persuaded her to sing** a few songs.

C Reporting verbs followed by a gerund:

admit, deny, recommend, suggest

My flatmate **admitted taking** my bike but **denied breaking** the front light.

Jodie **recommended/suggested joining** a gym.

The following pattern can also be used after both *recommend* and *suggest*:

I **recommended/suggested (that) he (should) eat** less chocolate.

The infinitive with *to* can only be used after *recommend*.

He **recommended me to go** to the chemist's. ✔
He **suggested me to go** to the chemist's. ✘

9 Reporting verbs

1 Report the following sentences using an appropriate verb from the box. There is an example at the beginning (0).

| encourage | ~~promise~~ | refuse | remind | tell | threaten | warn |

0 'I'll give you the £10 back next week,' he told her.
He _promised to give her the £10 back the following week_.

1 'I'm not going to clean my room!' she said.
She _refused to clean her room._

2 'Don't forget to take your sandwiches, Noah,' said his father.
Noah's father _reminded him to take his sandwiches._

3 'If you don't turn your music down, I'll call the police,' said my neighbour.
My neighbour _threatened to call the police if I didn't turn my music down_.

4 'Don't take the car out. The roads are very icy,' said Millie's friend.
Millie's friend _warned her not to take the car out (as/because/since the roads were very icy)_.

5 'Put your chewing gum in the bin,' said the maths teacher to Alicia.
The maths teacher _told Alicia to put her chewing gum in the bin._

6 'You really ought to report the theft to the police,' my friend told me.
My friend _encouraged me to report the theft to the police._

2 Underline the correct alternative.

1 Lucy *invited* / offered / promised me to spend the weekend with her at her house in the country.

2 Angry protesters stormed the Town Hall and *demanded* / ordered / urged to speak to the Mayor.

3 When Josh showed me the spots on his chest, I insisted / *advised* / suggested him to phone the doctor for an appointment.

4 Penn was arrested for complaining / denying / *refusing* to co-operate with the police.

5 Don't *accuse* / blame / criticise me of something I didn't do!

6 The Finance Minister *admitted* / told off / apologised having lied about the state of the economy.

Go back to **page 136**.

9 MYSTERY AND IMAGINATION

Writing

1 Ask the class what kind of reviews they read and why. Give them an example, e.g. *I read online restaurant reviews because …* Students read the task and, with a classmate, discuss what they might review.

2 Students read the review and write the name of the album and band. You could take this opportunity to play one minute of four songs from *Abbey Road*, one composed by each member of the band: *Come together*, John Lennon; *Oh Darling*, Paul McCartney; *Something*, George Harrison; *Octopus's Garden*, Ringo Starr. Don't tell them who wrote each song. Ask them to rank them from best to worst. Discuss in open class. Then reveal each song's composer.

3 Students reread the review and make notes on questions 1–5. They then compare their ideas with a classmate. If possible, project the review on the board during the feedback stage.

4-5 Monitor and provide assistance as necessary while the students plan and write their reviews. Set a time limit of 40 minutes and be strict. If any students finish quickly, skim their reviews and give them one or two suggestions for improving it. Note that this type of peer correction is valuable because in the process of giving each other feedback students improve their ability to see how their own work could be improved.

Language focus Reporting verbs

Student A

1 Tell each other your problems (see below) and give each other suggestions and advice. Use the following structures:

You should …   *Why don't you …?*   *If I were you, I'd …*
Make sure you …   *Try* + gerund

- I'm finding it difficult to sleep at night.
- I have problems learning English vocabulary.
- I'm addicted to my smartphone. I spend six hours a day on it.
- I think someone in this class is stealing things.
- I get very nervous when I take exams.

2 Change partners and report your conversations using the verbs *suggest, recommend* and *advise*.

I told Ana I was finding it difficult to sleep at night, and she suggested I should stop looking at my phone in the evening.

Go back to page 136.

Language focus Reporting verbs

Student B

1 Tell each other your problems (see below) and give each other suggestions and advice. Use the following structures:

You should …   *Why don't you …?*   *If I were you, I'd …*
Make sure you …   *Try* + gerund

- I've got a bad cold.
- I find it hard to concentrate when I study.
- I eat a lot of junk food because I'm so busy and have no time to cook.
- I have no idea what I want to do when I leave school.
- My parents want me to go on holiday with them, but I'd rather go with my friends.

2 Change partners and report your conversations using the verbs *suggest, recommend* and *advise*.

I told Diego I had a bad cold, and he suggested I should drink lots of water.

Go back to page 136.

MYSTERY AND IMAGINATION

9

Writing Part 2 Review

1 Read the following Writing Part 2 instructions. What item would you choose to review?

You have seen this notice in your school's English-language magazine.

1 Yes. Good points: para 2 and first line of para 3. Bad point: last line of para 3. Recommendation: last para.

2 Yes. See info above and para 1 is the introduction.

3 Yes. *So; Despite; However; and; as well; but; so; Unfortunately*

REVIEWS WANTED ☆☆☆

We would like you to write a review of something you have bought recently. It could be a computer game, a book, a magazine, a smartphone … anything you like!

Describe the good and bad points of your purchase and say who you would recommend it to.

The most interesting reviews will appear in next month's edition.

4 Yes (see underlining in the review).

5 Yes, it is informal, with contractions, a dash, exclamation marks and direct address. It is appropriate as the readers will be other students.

2 Read the following review of a music download. Do you know what album is being reviewed? Write the name of the album and the band on the record.

Abbey Road by *The Beatles*

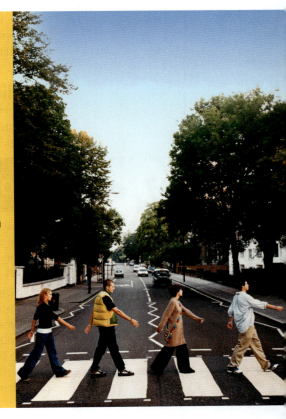

This classic album, named after the band's London recording studio, has been in our family for over forty years. It's my dad's vinyl version, and it's been played so often that it's too scratched to listen to now. So last week I bought the download.

Despite its age, it still sounds as fresh as when it was first released in 1969. Most of the tracks, of course, were composed by Lennon and McCartney, always a guarantee of quality music. However, my favourites are the two written by George Harrison – gentle songs of love and hope.

The Liverpool band's use of vocal harmony on the album is outstanding, and there's a good mix of fast and slow tracks, with one or two humorous ones as well. Ringo's contribution about the octopus is the weakest, but he was always a better drummer than a singer, wasn't he?

The album has songs to suit every generation, from children to grandparents, so I'd recommend it to everyone. Unfortunately, of course, the artwork of the 'Fab Four' on the zebra crossing is tiny on my smartphone, but we still have the cover from the vinyl version!

3 Read the review in Exercise 2 again and answer the following questions about it. Give examples from the review to support your opinions.
1 Has the writer described both good and bad points and said who they would recommend it to?
2 Is the review organised into suitable paragraphs?
3 Are ideas connected with appropriate linking words?
4 Is there a good range of vocabulary and structures?
5 Is the style of the review formal, informal or neutral? Is the style appropriate?

4 Use questions 1–5 in Exercise 3 to help you plan and write your own answer to the question in Exercise 1. To add an element of mystery, do not mention the name or title of the item you are reviewing.

Write your review in 140–190 words.

5 **SPEAK** Work in pairs.
1 Read your partner's review and try to guess the name or title of the item he or she has written about.
2 Read the review again and give your partner feedback on it, using questions 1–5 in Exercise 3. Give examples from the review to support your opinions.
3 If necessary, rewrite your own review, incorporating the points your partner has mentioned.

For more information on writing reviews, see **page 197**.

9 REVIEW

Vocabulary Prepositions

Complete each gap with one word.

1 We ran out __of__ milk yesterday and my flatmate blamed me __for__ not writing it on the shopping list. Then she started complaining __about__ always having to think of everything and criticised me __for__ not doing my fair share of the housework. I'm not sure I can put up __with__ her much longer.

2 Our son insisted __on__ having a motorbike, but we weren't keen __on__ the idea and tried to put him __off__ it by talking about the possible dangers. Eventually, though, we gave in, and even offered to pay __for__ lessons.

3 The neighbours were going to have some repairs carried __out__ on their flat, and they came round to apologise in advance __for__ any disturbance this might cause. We thanked them __for__ being so thoughtful, and told them not to worry. I was studying for exams at the time, so I invested __in__ some decent noise cancelling headphones and I didn't hear a thing.

Reading and Use of English Part 1 Multiple-choice cloze

For questions 1–8, read the text below and decide which answer (A, B, C or D) best fits each gap. There is an example at the beginning (0).

Solving a mystery

A scuba diver has (0) __C__ a British family with the photos from a camera they lost on a canoeing (1) __B__ on the Dordogne river in France. The camera fell into the water when their canoe hit a bridge and (2) __C__. The father, Andrew Sully, dived down to look for it, but soon (3) __D__ up, as the water was too muddy to see clearly.

Soon afterwards, however, French student Kevin Quirin came (4) __C__ the camera while exploring the river. (5) __A__ the camera was broken, the memory card was still intact, so he downloaded the photos and followed the (6) __B__ to trace the owners. He found two humorous photos of Andrew standing next to signs with the word 'Sully' on them and (7) __B__ that might be their surname. There were also photos of Andrew taking (8) __D__ in a charity bike ride in Paris: searching the internet, Kevin found an Andrew Sully on the participants list and forwarded the photos to the family in Wales.

0	A replaced	B encountered	C reunited	D joined
1	A travel	B trip	C voyage	D cruise
2	A dropped	B divided	C overturned	D drowned
3	A held	B put	C turned	D gave
4	A up	B towards	C across	D over
5	A Although	B Apart	C Since	D Despite
6	A suggestions	B clues	C ways	D directions
7	A assured	B guessed	C worked	D judged
8	A place	B prize	C pose	D part

138

REVIEW 9

Word formation Adverbs

Complete each gap with an appropriate adverb formed from the noun or verb in capital letters at the end of the line.

1 Cover the saucepan and cook _gently_ over a medium heat. **GENTLE**
2 The audience applauded _enthusiastically_ at the end of the concert. **ENTHUSIASM**
3 Cycling is becoming _increasingly_ popular in this city. **INCREASE**
4 This museum was _originally_ built as a palace. **ORIGIN**
5 Mike's still in hospital, but his condition is improving _daily_. **DAY**
6 The Government's response to the crisis is _wholly_ inadequate. **WHOLE**
7 Tim was stopped by the police and accused of driving _carelessly_. **CARE**
8 Lynne does a lot of exercise. However, she eats far too _unhealthily_. **HEALTH**

Reading and Use of English Part 4 Key word transformation

For questions 1–6, complete the second sentence so that it has a similar meaning to the first sentence, using the word given. Do not change the word given. You must use between two and five words, including the word given.

1 Janie has been ill recently, so perhaps she isn't running in the marathon today.

   TAKING

   Janie has been ill recently, so she might _not be **taking** part_ in the marathon today.

2 I expect you were very pleased to have your book published.

   GIVEN

   It must _have **given** you great pleasure_ to have your book published.

3 'It was David's idea to put butter on the door handle!' said Alex.

   ACCUSED

   Alex _**accused** David of coming_ up with the idea of putting butter on the door handle.

4 He promised that he would buy a new coat with his money.

   SPEND

   He promised _to **spend** his money on_ a new coat.

5 'Can you swim, Sarah?' asked her teacher.

   HOW

   Sarah's teacher asked her _if/whether she knew **how** to_ swim.

6 'You should employ a secretary, Paul,' advised his accountant.

   TAKE

   Paul's accountant suggested _(that) he (should) **take** on_ a secretary.

Writing Part 2 Report

A multinational company based in your area has made a large donation to your town and wants the money to be used for building either a sports centre or a theatre. Write a report for the town council, describing the benefits to the town of each facility and saying which one you think should be built and why.

Write your report in 140–190 words.
See the Teacher's Resource Centre for a Sample answer with Examiner comments for this task.
For more information on writing reports, see **page 196**.

MYSTERY AND IMAGINATION

  MYSTERY AND IMAGINATION

Pronunciation Using intonation to show interest

1 ▶ 9.3 Listen to this exchange between two friends. Notice how the woman uses intonation to show interest in what the man says. Repeat what she says using the same intonation.

2 ▶ 9.4 Listen to the same exclamations said in two different ways. For each exclamation, choose the speaker (a or b) that shows the most interest.
  1 How embarrassing!   a / (b)
  2 Really?!   (a) / b
  3 That's ridiculous!   a / (b)
  4 That's amazing!   a / (b)
  5 What a nightmare!   (a) / b

3 Write down three interesting facts about yourself and/or experiences you have had.
  1 _____
  2 _____
  3 _____

4 **SPEAK** Work in pairs. Take turns to tell each other your facts from Exercise 3. Use intonation to express interest. Then ask follow-up questions for more information.
  A: I travelled around America last summer.
  B: That's amazing! Where did you visit?

> **Useful language**
> **Showing interest**
> Really? That's amazing!
> Wow! That sounds brilliant/fantastic!
> What a laugh!
> I bet that is/was good fun/a good experience!
> You must have enjoyed that!
> Wow! What a nightmare!
> Oh no! That sounds terrible/awful!
> How embarrassing!
> I bet that is/was frightening/exhausting!
> You must have hated that!

Pronunciation

1 ▶ 9.3 Books closed. Ask a student to say what they did yesterday. Use the simple interjection *mmm …* to respond to a student's comment in two ways: to express 1) interest (*rise fall intonation*), and 2) boredom (*falling*). Students match which intonation you used. Use arrows to help students visualise these intonation patterns. Books open. Play the recording twice and then invite the students to repeat, copying the intonation pattern of the speaker as best they can.

2 ▶ 9.4. Play the recording more than once if the students are finding the exercise challenging.

3–4 Before the students practise their exchanges, focus their attention on the **Useful language** box. Note that these expressions could be used to good effect in Parts 3 and 4 of the speaking paper. During the activity, monitor students' intonation patterns.

MYSTERY AND IMAGINATION

READY FOR SPEAKING

Introduction

The **Speaking** paper consists of four separate parts and lasts 14 minutes. You will probably take the test with another candidate, although it is possible to be part of a group of three; in this case, the test lasts 20 minutes. There are two examiners: the interlocutor, who conducts the test and asks the questions, and the assessor, who listens to the test and assesses your performance. The interlocutor also assesses and contributes to your final mark.

Speaking Part 1 Interview   Total time: 2 minutes

The interlocutor asks you questions which require you to give basic personal information about yourself. You are not actively invited to speak with your partner in this part.

1 Choose three of the following categories and for each one, write three questions you could ask another student.

> family and friends   future plans   hobbies and interests   sport and keeping fit
> travel and holidays   TV and internet   work and study

Begin your questions with the following words:

> Do/Are/Have/Would you …?   How …?   How long/often/much/many …?
> What …?   When …?   Where …?   Who …?   Why …?

If you write a question which only requires a short answer, write another which will encourage the other student to say more.

Where do you live? What do you like about living there?

2 Work with another student. Interview each other using the questions you have prepared. Develop your answers, making sure they are relevant to the question.

3 ▶ 0.5 Listen to two students, Silvia and Luca, doing Part 1 of the Speaking test and answer the following questions.

  1 Does the interlocutor ask any of the same questions you prepared?
  2 Why does the interlocutor interrupt Silvia at the beginning?
  3 What advice would you give to Luca to help him improve his performance?

2 Silvia has obviously come with a prepared speech. The interlocutor asks where she is from and, having answered the question, she begins to talk about her family and school.

3 He should develop his answers more, without pausing too much. He does improve by the end of Part 1, when he answers more confidently.

> **Don't forget!**
> - Do not learn long, pre-prepared answers for this part of the exam. They may not be entirely appropriate to the question you are asked and they will probably not sound very natural.
> - Do, however, make sure you know individual items of vocabulary which are relevant to yourself. For example:
>   **Your hobbies and interests**
>   *'I'm really keen on rock climbing.'*
>   **The course you have decided to study**
>   *'I would like to study for a degree in aeronautical engineering.'*
>   **What your parents do**
>   *'My mother's a systems analyst.'*

READY FOR SPEAKING

Introduction

Put the following numbers on the board: 2, 3, 4, 14, 20. Tell the students to read the introduction quickly and remember the significance of each number. Quiz them afterwards. The **Audioscripts** for the **Ready for Speaking** tracks are available on Student's Book pages 249–251 and on the **Teacher's Resource Centre**.

Speaking

1 Monitor and check the students' questions for accuracy. If any students struggle to think of questions, direct them to the unit openers, which have Speaking Part 1 questions.

2 Remind the students that their answers shouldn't be too short or too long. Two or three sentences is usually about right.

3 ▶ 0.5 After the listening task, finish by looking at the information in the **Don't forget!** box.

MYSTERY AND IMAGINATION

READY FOR SPEAKING

Speaking Part 2 Long turn   Total time: 4 minutes

You have one minute to compare two photographs, and then say something else about them in response to instructions given to you by the interlocutor. You also have about 30 seconds to comment on your partner's pictures. You do not talk to your partner in this part.

1 **Student A:** Look at these photographs. They show children learning new skills. Compare the photographs and say why it might be useful for children to learn skills like these.

   Student B: When your partner has finished, say what new skill you would like to learn.

2 Now change roles. Go to the Additional materials on page 202 and do the Speaking Part 2 task.

3 ▶ 0.6 Listen to Silvia and Luca doing the Part 2 task and answer the following questions
   1 How well does each person carry out their task when they are Student A?
   2 How well do they use the 30 seconds when they are Student B?

Useful language

Comparing the photographs
In both pictures ...
One (obvious) similarity/ difference is that ...
In this picture .... whereas/while in the other one ....

Speculating
*It **might** be useful in the future for (work).*
*He'**ll probably** have to do it himself one day.*
*It **looks as if** they're enjoying (the sun).*
*It **looks** quite (exciting).*

Fillers
Words or phrases which enable you to think while you are speaking.
Well ...   Let's see ...
What else (can I say)?

How to go about it

Student A
- Point out the similarities and differences between the photographs. Avoid language such as *I can see*, as this may lead you simply to describe the photographs rather than compare them.
- Leave sufficient time to deal with the question which is printed above the photographs. This part of the task, in particular, gives you the opportunity to produce a wide range of language.
- Keep speaking until the interlocutor stops you; make the most of your minute to demonstrate your language abilities.

Student B
- Speak for the full 30 seconds.
- Develop your answer by giving reasons for your opinions and, where relevant, examples.

Why might it be useful for children to learn skills like these?

Speaking

1–2 Focus the students' attention on tip boxes.

3 ▶ 0.6 Students listen and discuss the questions.

Answers

1 *Silvia compares the photos well, using language such as* both pictures *and* whereas. *She addresses the second part of the task with a reasonable range of language* (holding the spoon; could be useful for the future; foreign language; live on his own) *and she successfully corrects herself when she says 'a work'.*

Luca doesn't compare the photos except when he says: This one doesn't look so exciting. *His range of language, however, is very good, particularly the vocabulary specific to the situations in the photos* (waterfalls; rough; calm; hired the boat; *and even* rescue jackets, *for* life jackets). *He uses a range of structures to speculate* (she looks as if she is enjoying herself; they may have hired the boat or they could be the owners; I imagine; This one doesn't look so exciting; it's probably quite relaxing; I expect; They might be happy).

2 *Silvia gives a much more complete answer than Luca, who doesn't fill the 30 seconds he is given for this part.*

READY FOR SPEAKING

Speaking Part 3 Collaborative task   Total time: 4 minutes

After explaining the task, the interlocutor listens while you and your partner discuss a question together for two minutes. The interlocutor then gives you a further minute to try to agree on a decision related to your initial discussion.

1 Some people think that teenagers who go to school should also do some part-time work. Below are some things they think about and a question for you to discuss. Talk with your partner for two minutes about whether teenage schoolchildren should do part-time work.

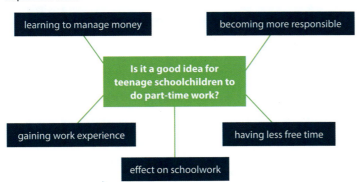

2 Now you have about one minute to decide what you think is the most important reason for teenage schoolchildren to do part-time work.

How to go about it

- In task **1**, you are not expected to discuss all five prompts; aim to speak about three or four of them in the two minutes you are given for this task.
- Express and justify your opinions, ask your partner what they think and respond to what they say by agreeing, disagreeing or adding a further comment.
- Take turns with your partner to speak; do not dominate the discussion.
- In task **2**, summarise your discussion in task **1** and work towards a decision. It does not matter if you do not agree with your partner, and you will not lose marks if you do not reach a decision.
- In both tasks, continue your discussion until the interlocutor asks you to stop. Make the most of the time you are given to demonstrate your English and your conversation skills.

3 ▶ 0.7 Listen to Part 3 and answer the questions.
  1 How does Silvia encourage Luca to talk in the first task in Part 3?
  2 How many of the five discussion areas do they talk about in the first task?
  3 In the second task, what do Silvia and Luca decide is the most important reason for teenage children to do part-time work?

1 Silvia asks Luca questions to encourage him to speak. *Is it the same for you, Luca? What do you think? Do you agree?*
2 They both talk about three areas; having less free time, effect on schoolwork and gaining work experience. At the end, Silvia briefly mentions becoming more responsible.
3 Becoming more responsible.

Useful language

Asking your partner for their opinion
What do you think?   How do you feel about that?   Do you agree (with me on that)?

Agreeing and disagreeing
I agree with you (up to a point).   I think you're right/wrong.   I think so, too.
I don't agree.   I (completely) disagree.   I (really) don't think so.

Changing to another topic
Let's talk about ... first/next.   Shall we move on to ... now?

Summarising your discussion
As we said before ...   We both agreed before that ...   You made a good point before about ...

143

Speaking

1–2 After students read the instructions, focus their attention on the **How to go about it** box. Ask some follow-up questions, e.g. *Why is it important to justify your opinions? Why is it bad to dominate the conversation? Why do you think it's not actually a requirement to reach a decision?* Then focus on the **Useful language** box. Put students into pairs. Either time the students yourself or ask one member of each pair to keep the time. Go around the room and monitor. Then give the class feedback on how well they performed the task. Ask the class: *Were there any aspects of the task you found challenging?*

3 ▶ 0.7 After listening, students discuss the questions in pairs. Conduct open class feedback.

MYSTERY AND IMAGINATION

READY FOR SPEAKING

Speaking Part 4 Further discussion Total time: 4 minutes

The interlocutor asks further questions related to the topic introduced in Part 3. You might each be asked individual questions, or you may be encouraged to interact with your partner and comment on what each other says.

1 SPEAK Discuss the questions below with your partner.

> **Don't forget!**
> - Develop your answers, justifying your opinions and giving examples if necessary.
> - Interact with your partner, listening and responding to each other's comments.

1. How easy is it for young people to get part-time work in your country?
2. Should teenagers who work give some of the money they earn to their parents?
3. Is it better for young people to get a full-time job after they leave school or should they go on to further education?
4. How well do you think schools prepare young people for the world of work?
5. Do you think it is better to work for other people or to be self-employed?
6. What do you think it would be like if you never had to work?

2 0.8 Listen to Part 4 and answer the following questions.
1. How well do Silvia and Luca interact with each other in Part 4?
2. How well do they develop their answers?

1 For the first two questions, Luca has to be prompted to respond to Silvia's initial reply. Then Silvia responds to Luca's comment on the lack of suitable jobs for graduates and from that point, the interaction becomes more fluid and natural.

2 They develop their answers very well, including Luca, who by the end of the test, is much more relaxed than he was at the beginning.

> **Useful language**
>
> **Giving your opinion**
> In my opinion …   Personally, I think that …   To my mind …
>
> **Gathering your thoughts**
> I'm not quite sure, but I think …   I don't really know, but I imagine …
> I haven't thought about it before, but perhaps …
>
> For language of **Agreeing and Disagreeing**, see **page 143**.

144

Speaking

1 Once students have read the instructions, focus on the **Don't forget!** box. Remind them that on the official exam one of the marking criteria is called *interactive communication*. The better they listen and respond to what their partner says, the higher their mark will be for this criterion. Alternatively, put the students into groups of three, with one student acting as the examiner, who keeps the time and asks the questions.

2 0.8 Encourage students to take notes related to questions 1 and 2 while listening. They then discuss the questions in pairs. Bring the class back together and nominate a few students to share their observations with the class.

10 NOTHING BUT THE TRUTH

This unit deals with the topic of crime. There is an article about private investigators and an interview with a crime writer. Students will also practise writing articles.

Read the unit objectives to the class.

SPEAKING Part 1 Interview

Focus students on the image. What does it show? Elicit contexts where fingerprints are important, e.g. at a crime scene, when a baby is born, for national identity cards, to unlock your phone, etc. Ask students how they feel about more and more biometric data being collected and used by governments and private companies.

To add an extra challenge, with books closed, board the questions as written below and ask the students to choose the correct option.

1 Do you always *say/tell* the truth?
2 Do you enjoy *watch/watching* reality programmes which show the police *doing/making* their job?
3 Who is your favourite *fictional/fiction* detective?
4 Is there a lot of graffiti *on/in* your area?
5 If you *found/find* a wallet or purse with a few coins in it, would hand it *on/in* to the police?

The correct options could be elicited to the board in open class or students could open their books and check there. They then ask and answer the questions in pairs.

ONLINE MATERIALS

Pelmanism (**Teacher's Resource Centre**)
Truth or lie? (**Teacher's Resource Centre**)
Unit 10 Test (**Test Generator**)
Unit 10 Wordlist (**Teacher's Resource Centre**)
Unit 10 On-the-go-practice (**App**)

10 NOTHING BUT THE TRUTH

Vocabulary Crime and punishment

1 **SPEAK** Talk about a crime which has been in the news recently. Say what you know about the facts of the crime and, where relevant, the investigation and the trial.

Crimes and criminals

2 Match the crimes in the box with each of the people in sentences 1–8. The first one has been done for you.

> burglary   drink-driving   identity fraud   internet piracy
> ~~mugging~~   shoplifting   drug trafficking   vandalism

1 A young man attacks another and robs him of his wallet. _mugging_
2 A 78-year-old woman steals a scarf from a department store. _shoplifting_
3 A 14-year-old sets fire to litter bins and breaks car windows. _vandalism_
4 A driver stops to sleep in his car; he has had three glasses of wine. _drink-driving_
5 A criminal gang earns millions from buying and selling narcotics. _drug trafficking_
6 A group of teenagers illegally distributes films online. _internet piracy_
7 A man has tricked people into emailing him their bank details; he uses this information to take money from their accounts. _identity fraud_
8 A journalist breaks into the town hall to steal documents that will prove the mayor is guilty of corruption. _burglary_

3 What title would be given to each of the criminals in Exercise 1?

1 mugging – mugger 2 shoplifter 3 vandal 4 drink-driver 5 drug trafficker
6 internet pirate 7 identity fraudster 8 burglar

Punishment

4 Look at the following types of decisions which can be taken by courts. Put them in order 1–5 from the least to the most severe.

_5_ to sentence someone to life imprisonment
_3_ to order someone to do 200 hours of community service
_1_ to acquit someone of all charges
_2_ to order someone to pay a fine of £2,000
_4_ to give someone a two-year prison sentence

5 **SPEAK** Decide what punishment, if any, should be given to the person or people in Exercise 1 above. Discuss your ideas using some of the language of agreement and opinion in the Useful language box below.

Useful language	
Giving opinions	**Agreeing and disagreeing**
In my opinion/view ...	That's right/true. I think so, too.
To my mind ...	I agree (up to a point).
Personally, I think ...	I really don't think so.
I strongly believe ...	I completely disagree.

NOTHING BUT THE TRUTH 10

Lead-in

Books closed. In open class, elicit to the board 15–20 words related to the topic of *crime* — anything that comes to the students' minds. Then put the students in small groups and tell them to create categories for the words, justifying why each word fits into a particular category. In open class, students compare the categories they created.

Vocabulary

1 Check the meaning of *trial*. To encourage students to go into more detail in this task, you could give them a couple of minutes to find and read about a recent crime (if mobile phones are allowed). This research could be done in English or the students' L1. Warn them against choosing a crime that would be upsetting to discuss. While the students talk, go around and monitor, feeding in vocabulary as necessary. Nominate a few students to share what they learnt from their partners. Board any good crime-related vocabulary that comes up during the activity.

2 Students read the instructions and do the exercise on their own. Invite them to compare their answers with a classmate. Check the pronunciation of *burglary* /ˈbɜːgləri/, *fraud* /frɔːd/, *piracy* /ˈpaɪrəsi/, *mugging* /ˈmʌgɪŋ/ and *vandalism* /ˈvændəlɪzəm/. Note that in North America people say *drunk driving*. You may also want to highlight the difference between *rob* and *steal*, as these are often confused. *Rob* focuses on the victim of the crime, while *steal* focuses on the object taken. Fast finishers could quiz themselves by covering the words in the right-hand column and trying to remember them.

3 Students do this exercise in pairs. Correct in open class. Ask students which is the worst type of criminal and why.

4 Check the meaning of *fine* and *sentence*, as well as both the meaning and pronunciation of *acquit* /əˈkwɪt/. In pairs, students rank the punishments. Feedback in open class. At this point in the lesson, encourage students to tick the vocabulary items they would like to record in their vocabulary notebooks after class.

5 Put students into small groups, preferably with people they have not yet worked with during the lesson. Monitor and provide on-the-spot correction of the target language as appropriate. Any other common errors can be written down and discussed later in a corrective feedback stage. You may wish to use **Pelmanism** on the **Teacher's Resource Centre** to consolidate the vocabulary or as a revision warmer at the start of the next lesson.

Teaching tip

Websites like Quizlet enable you to create vocabulary sets which students can use to revise new language from home or on the go using the app. Show the students how the website works in class and assign each student a vocabulary section from *Ready for B2 First*. The students then create their vocabulary sets for homework and share them with the class. These sets can be used for revision or as a filler/warmer.

Extra activity

Spelling in other languages is often much easier than it is English. So students are often puzzled by the phenomenon of spelling bees, which sometimes appear in Hollywood films. This popular contest is easily adapted to the ELT classroom, and it's a worthwhile activity in this context for the same reason it's popular in American schools: spelling can be quite difficult in English, even for native or proficient speakers of the language, and it requires study and practice in order to be good at it. Traditionally, spelling bees are played individually, but in class it's more fun to play in teams. Points are awarded for each word spelt correctly. Start with easier words from page 146 and finish with harder ones. Students are allowed to ask for a definition of the word or an example sentence (it would be a good idea to make use of the **Wordlists** on the **Student's** and **Teacher's Resource Centres** for this activity).

10 NOTHING BUT THE TRUTH

Listening

1 Students discuss the question in pairs. If you have access to technology, play a short clip from one or two of the crime series that came up in the students' conversations. Would they recommend the series to their classmates? Why or why not?

2 ▶ 10.1. Tell the students to read the questions and predict what Justin will talk about during the interview. Elicit their ideas in open class. Check the meaning of *appealing* (question 4). Note that students encountered *to be set in* (question 3) in the vocabulary section on page 48, but they may still be unfamiliar with the related word *setting* (question 2).

3 During the feedback stage, ask students if their own city or town would make a good setting for a crime novel. Why or why not?

AUDIOSCRIPT

Listening Part 4 Multiple choice

▶ 10.1

I = Interviewer   J = Justin Blakelock

I: With us today is local crime writer, Justin Blakelock. Justin, perhaps I should begin by asking you why you decided to write crime fiction rather than any other genre?

J: Whenever I'm asked that question, people think I'm going to say it's because I've always loved reading crime novels. Well, I have, but I'm actually much more of a science-fiction fan than anything else, and that's the kind of thing I was writing when I first started out as an author. But then my editor – an ex-policewoman curiously enough – saw elements of crime writing in my work and she gently pushed me in that direction. *(Ex 2 Q1)*

I: And was it her idea to set your novels here in Brighton?

J: No, that was mine. Firstly, because I love the place so much and despite the crime theme, I do try to show it in a positive light. But also, even though I'm writing fiction, I want my stories to be as real and accurate as possible. And because I grew up in this area, because I know it so well, it makes sense for me to set them here. There are too many novels that lack credibility because they're set in fictional places, or they're set in real places which are not accurately described. *(Ex 2 Q2)*

I: You show two versions of Brighton in your books, don't you?

J: That's right. To the visitor, Brighton seems a very peaceful city. It has this gentle, calm exterior – the very solid seafront buildings and pleasant shopping streets. But like many other cities it has its darker, more criminal places – the rundown buildings and areas that the tourist rarely sees. And that's also true of many of the characters I create. At first, they seem to be very gentle, very pleasant people, but there's something darker, more criminal hiding below the surface. *(Ex 2 Q3)*

I: And how about your protagonist, Detective Inspector George Trent? He's a little more straightforward, isn't he?

J: Yes, yes he is. He does have the occasional moment when he surprises everyone – if not, he'd be too dull. But essentially, what you see is what you get with George. He's very scruffy, slightly overweight, and completely disorganised. He doesn't worry about things like dressing up or combing his hair – he thinks he's good enough as he is; he's very comfortable with the way he looks. And that's really what makes him such a likeable character, I think. *(Ex 2 Q4)*

I: Yes, he's not attractive, but he's very human, isn't he? Now, Justin, you have a very popular website. Can you tell us about that?

J: Yes, sure. Well, the original idea behind the site was to get my name out there more and promote my books. But it gradually evolved into a blog – usually articles aimed at crime writers who were just getting started. And then other established authors began reading and commenting on my posts, and now it's effectively become a forum, a kind of debating club. *(Ex 2 Q5)*

I: Can you give us an example of the kind of advice you give?

J: Well, I've just posted a list of things you should remember to include in a crime novel. So for example, make sure your detectives have enough paperwork to keep them busy. Real detectives have loads to do, so your fictional ones should be doing their fair share too. To be honest, it's the kind of thing writers ought to pick up themselves by watching what goes on in a police station. There's absolutely no substitute for that. But it's good to compare notes and for every ten pieces of advice I give, you can read twenty more in the comments from other writers who've done their own research. It's a support service, a secondary source. *(Ex 2 Q6)*

I: And a very useful one. Now Justin, your last book, *Western Road*, is currently being made into a film. You must be delighted.

J: Yes, I am. More or less. The American producers wanted to move the action to Chicago, but I made it a condition that it had to be filmed in Brighton with British actors. I only wish I'd insisted on having more control over the script. It moves too fast for my liking. But that's the film world for you – what can you do? *(Ex 2 Q7)*

I: Not much, I guess.

NOTHING BUT THE TRUTH 10

Listening Part 4 Multiple choice

1 **SPEAK** Work in pairs. Discuss the questions.
   1 What was the last crime novel you read or crime series you saw?
   2 Why do you think crime novels and films are so popular?

2 ▶ 10.1 You will hear an interview with a crime writer. For questions 1–7, choose the best answer (A, B or C).
   1 Why did Justin become a crime writer?
      A His favourite genre as a reader has always been crime.
      B He had previously worked in the police force.
      C He was encouraged to do so by his editor.
   2 The setting for Justin's novels helps him create
      A a sense of authenticity.
      B a mood of optimism.
      C a degree of tension.
   3 Both the city in which Justin's novels are set and his fictional characters
      A are physically very attractive.
      B have two very different sides.
      C are very unwelcoming.
   4 According to Justin, what is his main character's most appealing feature?
      A He is very unpredictable.
      B He is happy with his appearance.
      C He looks like a typical detective.
   5 Justin initially set up his website in order to
      A publicise his work.
      B help new crime writers.
      C encourage an exchange of ideas.
   6 Justin says writers should carry out their main research by
      A working closely with a detective.
      B consulting criminal documents.
      C observing police professionals.
   7 What is Justin not happy about with the film version of his latest book?
      A the actors
      B the script
      C the location

3 **SPEAK** If you were writing a crime novel, where would you set it? Why?

10 NOTHING BUT THE TRUTH

Reading and Use of English   Part 5 Multiple choice

1 SPEAK Work in pairs. Discuss the questions.
1. Why might somebody hire a private detective?
2. What image do you have of private detectives?
3. What qualities do you think are required to do the job well?

2 Read through *Private investigators investigated* and compare your ideas in Exercise 1.

PRIVATE INVESTIGATORS INVESTIGATED

David Lee investigates the world of the private eye – and uncovers some surprising truths.

When I walk into the offices of Wright & Wrong Ltd, a predominantly female firm of private investigators, I am a little disappointed. My only previous contact with private detective agencies has been through black and white films from the golden age of Hollywood. So I am half expecting to see a small, dark, smoke-filled room, a single desk with an empty in-tray and a long, scruffy raincoat hanging from a hat stand. *Clearly, my romantic image of the profession needs updating.* Wright & Wrong Ltd's offices are light and spacious and there are no ashtrays in sight on any of the dozen or so desks. These are tidy and free of paper, but concentrated faces at large computer screens give the place a busy feel.

Jenny Wright, founder of the agency, is not surprised at my error and with *a note of irritation in her voice*, points to further misconceptions. *'Cinema and television are mostly to blame for our reputation.* Contrary to popular belief, we always work strictly within the law – there's no violence, no break-ins, and certainly no guns. The laws relating to our activities are very tight and if we don't stick to them, there's a very real danger that the evidence we obtain will not be accepted in court.'

The types of cases her agency deals with are varied *but the day-to-day work is often far from stimulating.* Wright & Wrong Ltd handles anything from infidelity in a marriage or tracing a missing person to insurance fraud, employee theft and advising companies on security measures. 'Resolving a case is very rewarding,' says Jenny, *'but the actual investigation can be rather dull.* When we're not dealing with paperwork or internet searches, we're usually involved in surveillance. *And that normally means just sitting around in cars or cafés for hours, waiting for something to happen.'*

Not surprisingly, then, patience is an important asset for anyone doing this kind of work. Is that why nine of the twelve investigators in her team are women? 'Obviously, women don't have a monopoly on patience,' replies Jenny, 'but perhaps it's no coincidence that they tend to stay in the job longer than men.'

Jenny tells me that people's perceptions of women make them popular with clients, and also, consequently, with her as an employer. Women are often considered to be more sensitive than men. They're looked upon as less threatening when it comes to making inquiries. 'People open up to women more readily,' she says, 'and are relieved when a woman picks up the phone to speak to them. We're also good at breaking bad news. What may be a victory for the agency – filming someone doing something they shouldn't be doing, for example – tends not to be such a pleasant discovery for the client, and there's a right and wrong way of handling that information.'

Most of Jenny's clients are wealthy. The hourly rate is anything between sixty and a hundred pounds, so the cost of a single case will often run into thousands of pounds. Even with the latest hi-tech equipment, such as long-range listening devices, a surveillance campaign can last several days. 'The technology is freely available and most of what we do could be done by the clients,' explains Jenny, 'but *they're reluctant to get involved. Finding out the truth is often just too painful to do on your own.'*

I ask Jenny, a former night club owner, how she came to be a private detective. *Her face turns red, she gives a slight grin and drops her voice to a whisper so as not to be overheard by her staff.* 'I used to read a lot of crime novels,' she confides, 'and I started to think "I could do that". I went on a training course and realised I was in the wrong job.' I am about to ask her whether she ever wears a long, scruffy raincoat, when her phone rings and she is called away on business.

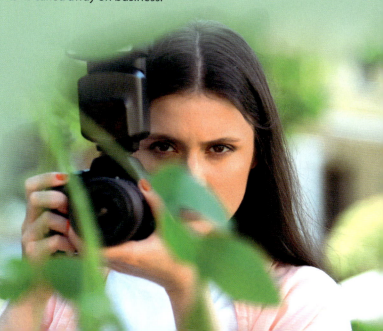

NOTHING BUT THE TRUTH 10

Reading and Use of English

1 In pairs, students discuss the questions. During the feedback stage, board some of the qualities and ask: *Which of these do you think is the most important? Why?*

2 Give the students two minutes to read the text and then stop them. Ask if any of their ideas were mentioned.

Teaching tip

The exam tasks in *Ready for B2 First* are carefully designed to get harder and harder, unit by unit, until they are of equal difficulty to the real exam by the end of the book. In order to pass the *B2 First*, students will need to get above 60% overall in the four papers. Logically, therefore, if a student is getting well above 60% in each individual exam task at the end of the book or on past papers, they should pass comfortably. However, if there is an individual task that a student is consistently getting well below 60% in, then that will slightly drag down their overall score. For this reason, it's important to help students identify the parts of the exam where they are still weak. (If they are using the **Digital Student's Book**, the **gradebook** function will keep a record of their scores in exam tasks.) Make sure they are updating the 'Ready' and 'Almost ready' columns in their notebooks (see teaching tip on TB102). If you find that one task is difficult for a number of students in the class, try to identify why the students are still finding it hard. Then make time to work on the subskills or language they still need to improve on.

Extra activity

Important writing skills for the *B2 First* exam can be developed through reading, for instance, developing an argument through a text and using examples to support main ideas. Board the following questions and ask the students to discuss them in pairs.

1 *What examples does the writer use to support the main idea that the job of private investigators is widely misunderstood?*

2 *How successful is the writer in making this argument?*

You could also get the students to answer the same questions about another main idea: *women make good private investigators.*

TB148

10 NOTHING BUT THE TRUTH

3 Elicit a few exam strategies for this task, e.g. read the question and find the answer in the text before looking at the options; words from the questions repeated in the text are often a sign of a distractor, etc.

4 Students discuss the question with a partner. In open class, try to find students who think they would make good detectives and invite them to explain why.

Word formation

1 Note that students worked on this same grammar point in unit 4 on page 50. Take the opportunity to remind students about how we use the present participle as an adjective to describe the person or thing that produces a feeling. The past participle, on the other hand, is used to describe how we feel about someone or something. You could also remind students about the pronunciation rules for the -ed endings (see TB50).

2 Students correct the exercise as suggested.

Extra activity

Invite students to write sentence stems using the participle adjectives and adverbs from this activity for other students to finish. Model an example on the board: *I found it very surprising that …* or *I felt a bit disappointed when ….* Once the students have written at least five of their own, ask them to get out of their seats (with their notebooks). They then do a 'mingle' activity, in which they move from one classmate to another reading and then finishing each other's sentence stems. Encourage the students to briefly explain why before moving on.

Teaching tip

Make your classroom more learner-centred and democratic by including an element of choice. For example, you could allow students to assign their own homework. Ask them to think about which part of the exam or language area they most want to practise. In class, you could give your students two options from time to time, e.g. doing more controlled practice with a particular grammar point or moving onto a speaking activity or game. You might be surprised how often they choose the grammar exercises!

NOTHING BUT THE TRUTH **10**

3 Read the article again. For questions 1–6, choose the answer (A, B, C or D) which you think fits best according to the text.

1 What does the writer discover on his visit to the offices of Wright & Wrong Ltd?
- A The firm is not as dynamic as he had been told.
- B The offices have recently been modernised.
- C All the private detectives in the firm are women.
- **(D)** He has an old-fashioned idea of private detectives.

2 Jenny Wright is annoyed by
- A the strict laws controlling private detectives.
- B the inflexibility of the law courts.
- **(C)** the way her profession is represented in films.
- D the violence used by other detective agencies.

3 According to Jenny, most of the work of a private detective is
- **(A)** monotonous.
- B challenging.
- C exhausting.
- D enjoyable.

4 Jenny is influenced in her decision to take on women by
- A women's ability to get results.
- B the speed at which women work.
- C women's tendency to speak openly.
- **(D)** the way clients see women.

5 What do we learn about Jenny's clients?
- A They cannot afford to buy the surveillance equipment.
- **(B)** They do not want to do the detective work themselves.
- C They object to paying such high prices for the work.
- D They prefer more than one detective to work on a case.

6 How does Jenny feel about telling her story in the last paragraph?
- **(A)** embarrassed
- B frightened
- C proud
- D angry

4 SPEAK Work in pairs. Do you think you would make a good private detective? Why/Why not?

Word formation Participle adjectives and adverbs

1 Complete each gap in these sentences from *Private investigators investigated* with the correct adjective or adverb formed from the word in capitals at the end of the line. There is an example at the beginning (0).

0 David Lee ... uncovers some __SURPRISING__ truths.	**SURPRISE**
1 When I walk into the offices ... I am a little __disappointed__. (3)	**DISAPPOINT**
2 Jenny Wright ... is not __surprised__ at my error. (14)	**SURPRISE**
3 The types of cases her agency deals with are __varied__ ... (23)	**VARY**
4 ... but the day-to-day work is often far from __stimulating__. (24)	**STIMULATE**
5 'Resolving a case is very __rewarding__,' says Jenny. (28)	**REWARD**
6 Not __surprisingly__, then, patience is an important asset. (33)	**SURPRISE**
7 They're looked upon as less __threatening__ when it comes to making enquiries. (42)	**THREAT**
8 People ... are __relieved__ when a woman picks up the phone to speak to them. (44)	**RELIEF**

2 Check your answers in the article. The relevant line numbers are given in brackets.

10 NOTHING BUT THE TRUTH

Vocabulary Paraphrasing and recording

1 In 1–8 below, complete each gap with one word so that the second sentence has the same meaning as the first. The second sentence is taken from the article on page 148. There is an example at the beginning (0).

0 I cannot see any ashtrays.
   There are no ashtrays in ___sight___. (11)

1 Our reputation is mostly the fault of cinema and television.
   Cinema and television **are** mostly **to** ___blame___ **for** our reputation. (16–17)

2 Despite what many people believe, we always follow the law closely in our work.
   Contrary to ___popular___ **belief**, we always **work strictly** ___within___ **the law**. (17–18)

3 We know how to tell people bad news.
   We're ___good___ **at breaking bad news**. (45)

4 We charge anything between sixty and a hundred pounds per hour.
   The ___hourly___ **rate is** anything between sixty and a hundred pounds. (50–51)

5 A single case will often cost thousands of pounds.
   The cost of a single case will often ___run___ **into thousands of pounds**. (51–52)

6 Everyone can obtain the technology.
   The technology **is freely** ___available___. (54–55)

7 Finding out the truth is often just too painful to do alone.
   Finding out the truth is often just too painful to do **on your** ___own___. (57)

8 Jenny used to be a night club owner.
   Jenny is a ___former___ night club owner. (58)

2 Check your answers in the article. The relevant line numbers are given in brackets.

3 Paraphrase the following sentences from the article. You do not need to change every word in the sentence. There is an example at the beginning (0).

0 The desks are free of paper. (12)
   There is no paper on the desks.

1 Concentrated faces ... give the place a busy feel. (12–13)
   Concentrated faces make the place feel busy.
2 Women don't have a monopoly on patience. (36)
   It is not only women who are patient.
3 People open up to a woman more readily. (43)
   People are more prepared to talk about their feelings to a woman.
4 Clients are reluctant to get involved. (56)
   Clients do not want to take part.
5 She gives a slight grin. (59)
   She smiles a little.

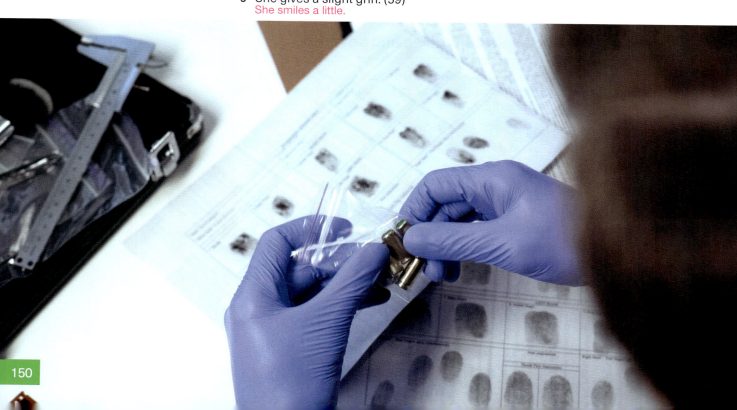

150

NOTHING BUT THE TRUTH 10

Vocabulary

1 Remind students of the importance of paraphrasing by revisiting the information in the **What to expect in the exam** box on page 104. Students do this exercise either individually or in pairs.

2 Once the students have corrected themselves, challenge them to quiz each other in pairs. Student A studies 1–4; Student B, 5–8. They then take turns remembering the paraphrased sentences.

3 Students do the exercise in pairs. Monitor and provide assistance as necessary. Note that the answers provided in the **Answer key** are not the only possibilities. Accept any appropriate alternative.

READY FOR GRAMMAR

10 Passives

We form the passive using the verb *to be* + past participle.

Present simple	Goods worth £750 million **are stolen** from shops each year.
Present continuous	A man **is being held** in connection with the robbery.
Present perfect	Photos of the suspects **have been released** to the media.
Past simple	He **was taken** away in a police van.
Past continuous	The burglar didn't realise he **was being filmed**.
Past perfect	Two people **had been mugged** there on the previous day.
Future simple	All football supporters **will be searched** at the airport.
Future perfect	A thousand new jobs **will have been created** in this town by the end of the year.
Infinitive	He is hoping **to be released** from prison next week.
Gerund	I can't remember **being hit** on the head.
Modal verbs	He **should be sentenced** to life imprisonment.

- The passive is used to focus attention on the person or thing affected by the action, rather than on the agent (the 'doer' of the action). If we are interested in the agent, we use the preposition *by*:
  *Sue and Mark were brought up **by their grandparents**.*

- When we talk about the instrument used by the agent to do the action, we use the preposition *with*:
  *He was hit on the head **with a vase**.*

- The agent is not usually included:
  1 when it is clear from the context who the agent is.
     Colin was arrested for dangerous driving. (by the police)
  2 when we don't know the agent or the agent is unimportant.
     My car was stolen yesterday afternoon.
     This castle was built in the Middle Ages.
  3 in official notices to avoid using *you*.
     Food may not be consumed on the premises.
  4 when the agent is people in general.
     Texas is known as The Lone Star State.

10 NOTHING BUT THE TRUTH

Language focus

1–2 Books closed. Board the following two sentences along with a stick figure or photo of a politician: *I made mistakes. Mistakes were made.* Ask the students which one the politician is more likely to say and why. Books open. Students do the guided discovery exercises in pairs. Elicit the rule to the board. Point out that the passive voice can be used in a variety of tenses but that it always contains the same two elements: the verb *be* and the past participle.

3 Students sometimes ask about the difference between subject and agent, but this can be quite hard to explain, as the first one is a syntactic concept and the latter a semantic one. If asked, just say that during this lesson you'll be using the word *agent* to refer to 'the one doing the action' in passive sentences. Try to avoid any lengthy, abstract explanations.

4 Direct the students to the **Ready for Grammar** section on pages 226–227 (see TB150 and below). Use your judgment on how much time to spend here before returning to the unit. What you don't do in class can be set for homework or saved for revision.

5 Students pair check after doing the exercise individually. When you go over the answers in open class, elicit why it makes sense to use the passive voice in these contexts.

6 Elicit the four methods before the students discuss the questions: *CCTV cameras* (B), *increased police patrols* (C), *fines* (D) and *taking matters into your own hands* (E).

READY FOR GRAMMAR

10 Passives

1 Rewrite the news article using the passive form of the verbs in bold.

> Police **have detained** an animal rights activist for releasing over two thousand pheasants from a game farm in Suffolk. They **arrested** the man at his home in Ipswich after they **had identified** him on CCTV cutting through wire fencing to allow the birds to escape. Local game farms **raise** as many as 50,000 pheasants a year for the shooting industry. The police **are questioning** the suspect about a number of similar incidents in the region. If they **find** him guilty at trial, they **will probably make** him pay a fine, and they **could give** him a short prison sentence.

An animal rights activist (1) _has been detained_ for releasing over two thousand pheasants from a farm in Suffolk. The man (2) _was arrested_ at his home in Ipswich after he (3) _had been identified_ on CCTV cutting through wire fencing to allow the birds to escape. As many as 50,000 pheasants a year (4) _are raised_ by local game farms for the shooting industry. The suspect (5) _is being questioned_ about a number of similar incidents in the region. If he (6) _is found_ guilty at trial, he (7) _will probably be made_ to pay a fine, and he (8) _could be given_ a short prison sentence.

2 Complete the gaps with an appropriate passive form of the verb in brackets.

1. Three million chocolate bars _are produced_ (*produce*) at this factory each week. Over one million of these _are sold_ (*sell*) in the UK, and the rest _are exported_ (*export*) to other European countries.
2. Glenn Lambert _was released_ (*release*) from prison last week, ten years after _being convicted_ (*convict*) of a crime he did not commit.
3. Our car _is being repaired_ (*repair*) at the garage at the moment. I _was told_ (*tell*) yesterday that it should be ready tomorrow.
4. a: I _have been asked_ (*ask*) to give a talk at my company's sales conference.
   b: Have you? Is that the one that _is/'s held_ (*hold*) in Birmingham every year?
5. a: What happened to the two Year Nine boys who _were caught_ (*catch*) spraying paint in the gym last week?
   b: Nothing much. They _were made_ (*make*) to clean it off the next day.
   a: Is that all? They should _be expelled/have been expelled_ (*expel*)!

Go back to **page 151**.

NOTHING BUT THE TRUTH 10

Language focus Passives

1 Look at the following sentences from the article on page 148. In each one underline an example of the passive.

1 *If we don't stick to the laws, there's a very real danger that the evidence we obtain <u>will not be accepted</u> in court.*
2 *Most of what we do <u>could be done</u> by the clients.*
3 *She drops her voice to a whisper so as <u>not to be overheard</u> by her staff.*
4 *Her mobile phone rings and she <u>is called away</u> on business.*

2 Complete the following rules about the passive:

To form the passive, we use an appropriate form of the verb ____to be____ and the ____past____ participle.

3 In sentences with passives, the agents are the people or things who do the action. They appear after the preposition *by*. Look back at the sentences in Exercise 1:

1 Who are the agents in sentences 2 and 3? In sentence 2, the clients and in sentence 3, her staff.
2 Why are there no agents in sentences 1 or 4? In sentence 1, the agent is obvious (the court officials) so does not need to be mentioned. In sentence 4, the agent is not known by the writer, or is not important in this context.

4 Go to **Ready for Grammar** on **page 226** for rules, explanations and further practice.

5 Complete the gaps in the following sentences with an appropriate form of the verb in brackets. Use the words in bold to help you make your choices.

A

Antisocial behaviour ___is defined___ (*define*) as conduct that causes or is likely to cause alarm or distress to other people. Different types of antisocial behaviour **may** ___be categorised___ (*categorise*) as follows:

- nuisance behaviour that affects a community, e.g. noisy neighbours
- acts that target individuals or groups, e.g. threatening behaviour
- environmental antisocial behaviour, e.g. vandalism and graffiti.

B

Closed Circuit Television Cameras ___will be/are going to be installed___ (*install*) on buses in four major cities **next month**. A spokesman for the government, which ___has/have been criticised___ (*criticise*) **in recent weeks** for being 'too soft on crime', said the CCTV cameras would improve passenger safety and help reduce antisocial behaviour such as vandalism.

C

Last month, police patrols ___were increased___ (*increase*) in the town's parks and open spaces. Their aim **is** not necessarily to arrest young people who ___are/have been found___ (*find*) drinking in public places. In most cases **so far**, parents ___have been contacted___ (*contact*) and asked to come and take their child home. 'Parents **need** ___to be made___ (*make*) aware of their responsibilities,' said a police spokesperson. 'We emphasise to them the importance of knowing where their children go and what they do there.'

D

Noisy neighbours who consistently played loud music in their town-centre flat ___were fined___ (*fine*) £300 **yesterday** and ordered to pay £250 court costs. The court ___was told___ (*tell*) that students Joe Cave and Irene Burstall ___were/had been warned___ (*warn*) on several occasions **previously** that legal action ___would be taken___ (*take*) **if** the music ___was not turned___ (*not/turn*) down. Both now have criminal records.

E

'**When I got there**, the little one ___was being pushed___ (*push*) around by the four older boys,' said 70-year-old Mrs Slade. '**They were pushing him quite hard**. I was worried he **might** ___be attacked___ (*attack*) more seriously, so I started hitting them with my umbrella. Then I fell over and they ran off.' **After** ___being treated___ (*treat*) in hospital for minor cuts and bruises, Mrs Slade ___was sent___ (*send*) home **last night**.

6 **SPEAK** How serious a problem is antisocial behaviour where you live? How effective would the above methods, B–E, be in dealing with antisocial behaviour in your area?

10 NOTHING BUT THE TRUTH

Characteristics of a good citizen might include the following:
- willingness to help others
- good manners
- respect for others and their property
- respect for the environment
- selflessness
- compassion
- honesty
- respect for rules and laws
- willingness to volunteer
- willingness to work hard

Writing Part 2 Article

1 **SPEAK** Read the following Writing Part 2 instructions and discuss with your partner how you might answer the question.

You see this announcement in an English-language magazine:

> ### Articles wanted
> #### Good citizenship
> What are the most important characteristics of a good citizen? What are some of the things you do to be a good citizen?
>
> The best articles will be published in our magazine.

2 Now read the following article and compare the writer's ideas with those you discussed in Exercise 1.

How well has the writer answered the question?

Being a good young citizen

How can a simple teenager like me be a good citizen? Obviously, I don't pay taxes and I'm still too young to vote. But there are many small things I do that are beneficial for the community.

For example, whenever I go into a building, I always hold the door open for anyone coming behind me. Unfortunately, not everybody does this, and heavy doors can really hurt if they suddenly close on you. Another thing I always do is use waste paper bins – I never drop litter in the street. And if I'm in the countryside and I see rubbish that someone else has left, I pick it up and take it home with me.

Clearly, I can't drive yet, but I always make sure my parents observe the speed limit, and I tell them to slow down if they're going too fast. Also, recently, they bought a new car and I persuaded them to get an electric one, which is much more environmentally friendly than our old diesel van.

So, you see, no matter how young you are, there is always something you can do to make your world a better place.

NOTHING BUT THE TRUTH 10

Lead-in

Put the following quotations on the board and ask the students to discuss them in pairs, e.g. *Have they heard/read the quotes before? Do they agree with them? Why might the people have said them when they did?* If you have access to technology, put each one on a different slide and bring them up one by one.

"We are citizens of the world." – Woodrow Wilson

"It is not always the same thing to be a good man and a good citizen." – Aristotle

"Ask not what your country can do for you — ask what you can do for your country." – John F. Kennedy

Writing

1 Students read the instructions and discuss the task in pairs. Challenge them to think of at least five characteristics of a good citizen. Board their ideas. Ask the class: *Are some more important than others?*

2 Students read the article, then ask if any of their ideas mentioned. Then focus on the question of how well the writer answered the question. Get the students to look at the task once more and underline the key points. Elicit that the first point about important characteristics is not addressed in the article, which is otherwise very well written. Note that *content* is 25% of the students' writing mark. In order to get top marks here, students have to make sure to address all the points in the task.

Answers

The writer has given a complete answer to the second question (What are some of the things you do to be a good citizen?) *but failed to answer the first. Students must be careful to address all parts of a question.*

Sample answer

Am I a good student?

Perhaps you are wondering how can you be a good student. Well, there are several qualities that you need, some of which are more important than others.

To give an example, you should be participative. Teachers love it when their students put interest in what they are telling them. Clearly, another important quality would be to be well-organised, making clear notes in class, handing in projects before the deadline and leaving enough time to study for exams. And obviously, it's also important to be well-behaved, unless you want to annoy the teacher and get punished.

In my case, I'm a hardworking person, but only for me so that I have a good future, not for anyone else. What's more, I'm respectful with teachers and with my classmates, even if sometimes I'm in a bad mood and suddenly get angry. So, although I don't have a long list of good characteristics, I consider myself a good student. Why don't you make a list of your pros and contras so you can see if you are, too?

Andrea

181 words

Examiner's comments

Content: All content is relevant. The writer answers both questions in the task and the reader would be fully informed.

Communicative achievement: The conventions of article writing are followed. There is a title, with a relevant introduction, and a conclusion which leaves the reader something to think about. The writer maintains interest with an informal register, sometimes addressing the reader directly

Organisation: The article is clearly organised in appropriate paragraphs. There is a good range of cohesive devices, both within paragraphs (*Clearly, another important quality; And obviously, it's also important; What's more*) and from one paragraph to the next (*To give an example; In my case; So, although*).

Language: There is a good range of vocabulary, including relevant adjectives (*participative; well-organised; wellbehaved; hardworking; respectful*) and collocations (*making clear notes; handing in projects before the deadline*). The use of *put interest* instead of *show* or take *interest*, and *pros and contras* for *pros and cons* would not impede communication.

Complex grammatical forms are handled with great control and the only error (in the first sentence *how can you be* instead of *how you can be*) does not impede communication.

Mark: Very good pass

10 NOTHING BUT THE TRUTH

3 This exercise could be done individually or in pairs. If you have access to technology, project the text on the board during the feedback stage and indicate the parts of the texts containing features a–e.

Answers

a Being a good young citizen

b and c How can a simple teenager like me be a good citizen?

d But, And, So (Normally, these are used as conjunctions to link to ideas in the same sentence. Here, they are used informally at the beginning of a sentence to link the ideas which follow with those in the previous sentence.)

e So, you see, no matter how young you are, there is always something you can do to make your world a better place.

4 Students do the exercise individually as suggested.

5 You could either set the final writing assignment for homework or do it in class. In either case, it should be timed (40 minutes), so students get used to producing a finished piece of writing within the prescribed time limit. If mobile phones are allowed, get the students to take a picture of the 8 questions from the **Extra activity** below and encourage them to use them as a checklist. Alternatively, the questions could be emailed or provided on a handout.

Teaching tip

An experienced exam teacher should be able to look at a student's writing and know more or less what mark it would receive on the official *B2 First*. One good way to develop this ability is to look at the sample answers throughout this book and carefully read the examiner comments. These comments are based on the publicly available marking criteria. At this point in the course, you should mark your students' writing according to these official criteria to the best of your ability. It will help your students know how well they would do on the real exam and where they still need to improve.

Extra activity

To help students understand how their writing will be marked on the exam, project or write the following matching activity on the board.

Examiners ask themselves various questions when they read your writing. Match the questions (1–8) to the four marking criteria (A–D).

1 Is the answer organised into paragraphs?

2 Does the answer contain a good range of vocabulary?

3 Is the answer too formal or too informal?

4 Does the answer address all the points in the task?

5 Does the answer contain a variety of linking words and phrases?

6 Does the answer contain errors that make it hard to understand what the writer is saying?

7 Are the writer's ideas easy to understand?

8 Does the answer contain any information that is not relevant to the task?

A Content

B Communicative achievement

C Organisation

D Language

Answers: 1 C, 2 D, 3 B, 4 A, 5 C, 6 D, 7 B, 8 A

Listening Part 3 Multiple matching

Read the article. What reasons are given for children telling lies?

> When children first begin lying, they lie to avoid punishment, and because of that, they lie indiscriminately – whenever punishment seems to be a possibility. A three-year-old will say, 'I didn't hit my sister,' even though a parent witnessed the child hit her sibling. A six-year-old won't make that mistake – she'll lie only about a punch that occurred when the parent was out of the room.
>
> By the time a child reaches school age, the reasons for lying are more complex. Punishment is a primary catalyst for lying, but as kids develop empathy and become more aware of social relations, they start to consider others when they lie. They may lie to spare a friend's feelings. Secret keeping becomes an important part of friendship – and so lying may be a part of that. Lying also becomes a way to increase a child's power and sense of control – by bragging* to assert his status, and by learning that he can fool his parents. *to avoid punishment; to spare a friend's feelings; to keep secrets; to increase a child's power and sense of control*
>
> *talking about achievements or possessions in a proud way that annoys people

Go back to **page 154**.

3 Read the model answer again and find examples of the following common features of articles:

a title
b interesting beginning
c direct questions
d more informal use of linking words
e leaving the reader something to think about at the end

4 These sentences from the model answer contain another common feature of articles.

Obviously, *I don't pay taxes and I'm still too young to vote.*

Unfortunately*, not everybody does this …*

Clearly*, I can't drive yet …*

Each one begins with an adverb which expresses the writer's attitude to or opinion of what follows. In 1–6 below replace the underlined phrase with an adverb from the box.

Amazingly   Interestingly   Luckily   Personally   Understandably   Worryingly

1 <u>As for me</u>, I think any form of physical punishment is unacceptable. Personally
2 <u>I'm astonished that</u> he was sentenced to only two years in prison. Amazingly
3 <u>It's only normal that</u> the victim was upset about her attacker's release. Understandably
4 <u>It was fortunate that</u> she had just taken out insurance against theft. Luckily
5 <u>It is of some concern that</u> many drivers do not wear their seat belt. Worryingly
6 <u>It's worth noting that</u> this law has been in force for two hundred years. Interestingly

5 Either a) write your own answer in 140–190 words to the question in Exercise 1.
Or b) write an answer to the following question:

You see this announcement in an English-language magazine:

Articles wanted

Being a good student

What are the most important qualities of a good student? In what ways are you a good student?

The best articles will be published in our magazine.

Write your article in 140–190 words.

> **Don't forget!**
> - Give your article a title. It may be better to do this after you have written your answer.
> - Include some of the techniques and language features from Exercises 3 and 4.

For more information on writing articles, see **page 192**.

10 NOTHING BUT THE TRUTH

Why do you think the children are being told off?

Speaking Part 2 Long turn

1 Look at the photographs, which show children being told off.

   Student A: Compare photographs 1 and 2 and say why you think the children are being told off.

   Student B: When your partner has finished, say whether your parents often get angry with you.

2 Now change roles. Follow the instructions above using photographs 3 and 4.

> **Useful Language**
>
> Use modal verbs to speculate about what might have happened.
> She **may have done** her homework badly.
> He **might have been doing** X on the computer, when he **should have been doing** Y.
> They **could have had** an argument.

Listening Part 3 Multiple matching

1 Go to the Additional materials on page 203.

2 **SPEAK** Tell your partner about a time when you or someone you know told a lie:
   - as a child.
   - recently.

   What was the reason for telling the lie? What were the consequences?

3 ▶ 10.2 You will hear five different people talking about a time when they told a lie. For questions 1–5, choose from the list (A–H) what each speaker says. There are three extra letters which you do not need to use.

   A I lied to protect a friend.
   B I insisted on my innocence.
   C I apologised for telling a lie.
   D I exaggerated the extent of a problem.
   E I was surprised at someone's reaction.
   F I accused someone of causing damage.
   G I lied to someone who had not treated me well.
   H I intentionally sent someone to the wrong place.

Speaker 1	D	1
Speaker 2	E	2
Speaker 3	A	3
Speaker 4	G	4
Speaker 5	B	5

4 **SPEAK** Have you ever told any similar lies to those of the five speakers?

NOTHING BUT THE TRUTH 10

Speaking

1-2 Direct the students' attention to the **Useful language** box before doing the task. See TB100 for suggestions on how to replicate exam conditions for Speaking Part 2 in class. The more familiar students are with the official exam format, the more comfortable they will feel on the day of the exam. After they finish the task, elicit any problems they encountered, e.g. running out of things to say, spending too long describing the photos, etc. Together, think of strategies for dealing with these problems.

Listening

1 Put the students into pairs. Student A goes to page 203 in the **Additional materials** (see TB153) and reads the text. Student B thinks of reasons and situations in which children might lie. Together they discuss the topic and exchange ideas.

2 In this task, students are given a chance to plan and give a similar monologue to the ones in the Listening Part 3 task to follow. Once the students have done the **Phrasal verbs** section on page 155, which mines the **Audioscript** for useful language related to lying, you could get the students to repeat this speaking task with a new partner, incorporating some of the new language into their monologues.

3 ▶ 10.2. Read the instructions aloud. Then set a time limit of 30 seconds for the students to read through the options and underline key words before starting the recording. Be strict.

4 Students discuss the question in pairs. Tell them they can also talk about lies told by someone they know or people in films or TV series.

AUDIOSCRIPT

Listening Part 3 Multiple matching

▶ 10.2

Speaker 1 The neighbours had some kind of party last Thursday night, and the noise was terrible. I had to **go round** at two in the morning to complain. I told them my wife and I couldn't get to sleep, and their music had woken up our two teenage daughters, who both had an exam in the morning. I **made up** that bit about my girls – they'll sleep through anything. Plus it was the last week of school, so there was no way they had any exams. But it did the trick; they were quiet after that, and the next day they put a card through the door apologising for the disturbance.

Ex 3 D

Speaker 2 In the days before online booking, I once queued up overnight to get a ticket for a David Bowie concert. I was only fifteen, and because I didn't want my parents to worry, I told them I was going to a sleepover at my friend's house. When I got the ticket, though, I was so excited I showed it to my mum, and **owned up** to lying about the sleepover – told her the whole truth. Funnily enough, she said she was sorry I'd felt I'd had to lie to her and told me she'd have let me stay out all night if I'd just asked her. I hadn't expected that – I thought she'd be really angry.

Ex 3 E

Speaker 3 A mate of mine was always getting into trouble at school, and they'd told him that if he put another foot wrong, he'd be expelled. So of course, when someone reported him for smashing a light in the toilets at breaktime, he insisted he was innocent – said he hadn't been anywhere near the toilets. I didn't want him to get **kicked out**, so I **backed up** his story, and said that he'd been with me, in the library. Trouble was, the idiot had left his mobile on one of the sinks, so they knew it was him. He got expelled and I got suspended for a week.

Ex 3 A

Speaker 4 My neighbour **came over** a few weeks ago. She said she'd **run out of** flour and asked if she could borrow some. It was a Sunday afternoon and the shop on the corner was closed and she wanted to bake a sponge cake for her kids. Well, I did have some, and under normal circumstances, I'd have been more than happy to lend it to a neighbour in need. But she'd never done me any favours; in fact, she'd been positively unfriendly to me on occasions. So I said I was sorry, but no, I didn't have any flour, and if she hurried, she might catch the shop down in the town before it closed.

Ex 3 G

Speaker 5 When I was about five or six, I took a pair of scissors out of a kitchen drawer and cut off a big chunk of my hair in front of my friends. I'm not sure why – maybe I was just **showing off**, trying to make myself look big. I kept being asked the same question: 'Have you cut some of your hair off?' My mum, my dad, the hairdresser … And I kept saying 'no'. I said it so many times I almost believed it in the end. I thought I'd **got away with** it, but my mum told me recently she'd always known what had happened.

Ex 3 B

TB154

10 NOTHING BUT THE TRUTH

Vocabulary

1 Direct students to the **Audioscript** on page 244 (see TB154). In pairs, they discuss what the phrasal verbs mean in context. Elicit the meanings of the phrasal verbs to the board in open class.

2 This is a good reminder for students to continue updating their vocabulary notebooks.

3-4 Students could do this activity individually or in pairs. While they write their sentences, circulate and check them for appropriate use of the target language and for general accuracy.

Language focus

1 If possible, aim to cover all the material in this and the **Ready for Grammar** section on pages 228–229 (see below) in one lesson. An alternative way of presenting the grammar, if you have access to technology, would be to do Exercise 1 with books closed in open class, projecting the example sentences up on the board. Elicit the form of the verb after the passive (*infinitive*). Elicit the second sentence starting with *It ....* Ask students if you would be more likely to find these sentences in an essay or in a letter to a friend (*an essay*).

2 Direct the students to the **Ready for Grammar** section on pages 228–229 (see below).

3 Note that in addition to consolidating the grammar, in this lesson students are getting valuable practice with sentence transformations.

4 As students discuss the question, encourage them to say whether they make any of these gestures themselves. Ask them to think of any other tell-tale signs of lying. You may wish to use **Truth or lie?** on the **Teacher's Resource Centre** to round off the topic of lies.

READY FOR GRAMMAR

10 Infinitives after passives

An infinitive can be used after the passive of certain verbs to talk about widely held beliefs or opinions. Verbs used in this way include *believe, consider, expect, feel, know, report, think* and *understand*.

*The vase **is thought to be** over two hundred years old.*   *The President **is expected to arrive** at 9.30 am.*
*The men **are believed to be carrying** weapons.*

Alternatively, a *that* clause can be used after *It* + the passive of these verbs.

*It **is thought that** the vase is over five hundred years old.*   *It **is expected that** the President will arrive at 9.30 am.*
*It **is believed that** the men are carrying weapons.*

The perfect infinitive (*have* + past participle) is used to refer to the past.

*Fifteen people **are known to have died** in the accident.*   *It **is known that** fifteen people **died** in the accident.*

---

10 Infinitives after passives

Rewrite the sentences, beginning with the word(s) given.

1 They do not believe that the escaped prisoner is dangerous.
The escaped prisoner *is not believed to be dangerous*.

2 Police know that the family runs a number of illegal businesses.
The family is known *to run a number of illegal businesses*.

3 They think that Smith broke into several homes.
Smith is *thought to have broken into several homes*.

4 It is expected that they will be given long prison sentences.
They *are expected to be given long prison sentences*.

5 They say that Robinson is enjoying prison life.
Robinson *is said to enjoy/be enjoying prison life*.

6 It is considered that Corelli was the mastermind behind the crime.
Corelli *is considered to have been the mastermind behind the crime*.

7 It is understood that the victims are recovering from their injuries in hospital.
The victims *are understood to be recovering from their injuries in hospital*.

8 People feel the fines are too low to deter offenders.
The fines *are felt to be too low to deter offenders*.

Go back to **page 155**.

NOTHING BUT THE TRUTH 10

Vocabulary Phrasal verbs

1 Look at the **Audioscript** on **page 244** and use the context to help you guess the meanings of the phrasal verbs in bold.

I had to **go round** at two in the morning to complain.

'Go round' means to visit a person or place; in this case, the neighbour in his house.

2 Record the phrasal verbs in your notebook. Include the definition and the sentence from the Audioscript in which the verb appears, as in the example in Exercise 1.

3 Write three sentences, each including one of the phrasal verbs from the Audioscript. Leave gaps where the phrasal verbs should be. Include enough information in your sentences to illustrate the meanings of the phrasal verbs.

I want to _____ to my grandmother's house later – I haven't seen her for a month.

4 Show your sentences from Exercise 3 to another student, who will complete the gaps.

I want to __go round__ to my grandmother's house later – I haven't seen her for a month.

1
make something up = invent an explanation for something

own up to something = admit or confess that you have done something wrong

kick someone out (informal) = force someone to leave a place or organisation; expel

back something up = support an explanation

come over = visit someone in the place where they are, especially their house

run out of something = use all of something so that you do not have any left

show off = behave in a way that is intended to attract people's attention and make them admire you

get away with something = manage to do something bad without being punished or criticised for it

Language focus Infinitives after passives

1 Infinitive forms (*to do, to be doing, to have done*) can be used after the passive of a number of verbs to talk about beliefs and opinions which are shared by many people.

*Young children **are known to lie** to avoid punishment.*

This has the same meaning as:

***It is known that** young children **lie** to avoid punishment.*

Change the following sentence in the same way.

*He **is believed to have made up** the story about being mugged.*

It __is believed he made up the story about being__ mugged.

2 Go to **Ready for Grammar** on **page 228** for rules, explanations and further practice.

3 For questions 1–5, complete the second sentence so that it has a similar meaning to the first sentence. Be sure to use the correct form of the verbs in bold.

1 It is **believed** that continual nose touching **indicates** that someone is lying.

Continual nose touching is _____believed to indicate_____ that someone is lying.

2 It is **said** that people who repeatedly cover their mouth **are trying** to hide the truth.

People who repeatedly cover their mouth _____are said to be trying_____ to hide the truth.

3 It is **considered** that avoiding eye contact **is** a sure sign of deception.

Avoiding eye contact _____is considered to be_____ a sure sign of deception.

4 People **think** that we **use** fewer hand gestures when telling a lie.

We _____are thought to use_____ fewer hand gestures when telling a lie.

5 Everyone **knows** he **lied** because he kept moving about in his chair.

He _____is known to have lied_____ because he kept moving about in his chair.

4 **SPEAK** The statements in Exercise 3 are believed by some people to be myths, widely held beliefs which are simply not true. What do you think?

155

10 REVIEW

Phrasal verbs with *out* and *up*

The following phrasal verbs have appeared either in this unit or in previous units.

1 Complete each gap with the correct form of a verb from the box.

> fall   find   give   run   sort   turn

1. We ____ran____ **out of drink** at the party and had to go and buy some more.
2. The President was reported to have resigned, but it ____turned____ **out to be fake news**.
3. I can't ____sort____ **out your problems** for you; you've got to solve them yourself.
4. Leah hired a detective in an attempt to ____find____ **out the truth** about her husband.
5. Patsy ____fell____ **out with her best friend** last week after a huge argument.
6. I've corrected your homework. Could I have a volunteer to ____give____ **out the books**?

2 Complete each gap with the correct form of an appropriate verb.

1. She never tells the truth; she's always ____making____ **up stories**.
2. Nobody has ____owned____ **up to stealing** the money, but we think we know who did it.
3. Paul's stopped going to karate classes and ____taken____ **up judo** instead.
4. I'm seriously thinking of ____giving____ **up my career** as a lawyer; I can't ____put____ **up with the stress** much longer.
5. Being a parent is so hard; there's nothing more difficult than ____bringing____ **up a child**.
6. ____Cheer____ **up**! Don't look so sad.

Reading and Use of English   Part 4 Key word transformation

For questions 1–6, complete the second sentence so that it has a similar meaning to the first sentence, using the word given. Do not change the word given. You must use between two and five words, including the word given.

1. You should keep dust off the computer screen.

   FREE

   The computer screen should ____be kept **free** of____ dust.

2. The orange walls make the living room feel warm.

   GIVEN

   The living room ____is **given** a warm____ feel by the orange walls.

3. Maia earned five pounds an hour in her last job.

   PAID

   Maia ____was **paid** (at) an hourly____ *or* ____was **paid** at the hourly____ rate of five pounds in her last job.

4. Most cats don't mind it if you leave them at home alone.

   LEFT

   Most cats don't mind ____being **left** on their____ own at home.

5. It was unfair that she was sent to prison.

   DESERVE

   She ____did not/didn't **deserve** to be____ sent to prison.

6. It wasn't Zack's fault that the chair broke.

   BLAME

   Zack was ____not to **blame** for____ the broken chair.

Reading and Use of English Part 1 Multiple-choice cloze

For questions 1–8, read the text below and decide which answer (A, B, C or D) best fits each gap. There is an example at the beginning (0).

Ex-athlete taken in ... again.

The home of **(0)** ..C.. athlete Helen Barnett was burgled this weekend and a large number of sporting medals and trophies were **(1)** ..D.. Ms Barnett, who now **(2)** ..A.. a successful sportswear company, is **(3)** ..B.. to be 'devastated' at the loss.

The burglary took **(4)** ..C.. on Saturday afternoon when Ms Barnett went to investigate smoke coming from a wooded area in her large two-acre garden. The burglar is thought to have **(5)** ..C.. fire to undergrowth in order to attract Ms Barnett out of the house. A young man carrying a large bag was seen climbing over the garden wall, before making his **(6)** ..A.. in a sports car.

The theft comes just ten months after a similar incident in which a man posing as a telephone engineer had **(7)** ..C.. the ex-athlete into leaving the house while another helped himself to her jewels. The thieves were eventually caught and **(8)** ..D.. to four years in jail.

0	A earlierea eare	B sooner	C former	D preceding
1	A robbed	B mugged	C lifted	D stolen
2	A runs	B overtakes	C works	D holds
3	A spoken	B said	C felt	D told
4	A part	B hold	C place	D time
5	A made	B given	C set	D put
6	A getaway	B runaway	C hideaway	D takeaway
7	A succeeded	B managed	C tricked	D obtained
8	A imprisoned	B ordered	C given	D sentenced

Writing Part 1 Essay

In your English class you have been talking about situations in which people might tell lies. Now, your English teacher has asked you to write an essay.

Write an essay using **all** the notes and giving reasons for your point of view.

> It is not always necessary to tell the truth. Do you agree?
> **Notes**
> **Things to write about:**
> 1 when the truth might be painful
> 2 when lying might be harmless
> 3 .... (your own idea)

Write your essay in 140–190 words.
Please go to the Teacher's Resource Centre for a Sample answer with Examiner comments for this task.
For more information on writing essays, see **pages 189–191**.

10 NOTHING BUT THE TRUTH

Pronunciation Stress-shift words

1 ▶ 10.3 Listen to the two sentences. How is 'suspect' pronounced in each case?
   1 Police **suspect** that she had some involvement in the robbery.
   2 She is the chief **suspect** in the investigation.

2 Read the information in the box. Choose the correct options to complete the rules.

> **Stress-shift words**
>
> Some two-syllable words with the same spelling change their stress depending on whether they are verbs or nouns. The nouns are usually stressed on the *first* / *second* syllable. The verbs are usually stressed on the *first* / **second** syllable.

3 In the following sentences, underline the stressed syllables in the words in bold.
   1 There has been a steady **increase** in crime in the area. The problem will continue to **increase** unless the council takes action.
   2 He arrived at court **protesting** his innocence.
   3 There were climate change **protests** in the city centre yesterday.
   4 Andrew has a criminal **record**. He was **convicted** of shoplifting when he was younger.
   5 The former **convict** didn't realise the store's CCTV camera was **recording** him.
   6 The election was a close **contest** between the two main parties.
   7 The losing party has decided to **contest** the result of the election.

4 ▶ 10.4 Listen to the sentences and check your answers in Exercise 3.

5 SPEAK Practise saying the sentences in Exercise 3 with the correct stress.

6 SPEAK Changing the stress on some words can change their meaning. Work in pairs and decide whether the two words in bold in each sentence have a related or different meaning. Then practise saying each sentence.
   1 We **produce** around 400 bottles of juice a week and sell it locally along with our other farm **produce**. related: both the noun and the verb refer to the making or growing of something.
   2 If they **refuse** to pick up their own **refuse**, they will receive a fine.
   3 I want to **present** the facts of the case. All the **presents** had been stolen!
   4 The pupils in his eyes **contracted** as he presented the **contract** to his client.
   5 The school was **conducting** an enquiry into the students' **conduct**.
   6 The **subject** of the enquiry was the humiliating treatment to which prisoners were **subjected**.
   7 Picking up the nearest **object** and raising it above his head, the lawyer shouted 'I **object**!'

2 different: *refuse* (v) means to say you will not do something; *refuse* (n) is a formal word for rubbish.
3 related: *present* (v) means to give, offer or show something to other people; a *present* (n) is something you give to other people
4 different: *contract* (v) means to become smaller; a *contract* (n) is a written legal agreement.
5 different: *conduct* (v) means to carry out (an enquiry); *conduct* (n) means behaviour.
6 different: the *subject* (n) is the main idea, topic or problem being discussed; *subject* (v) *someone to something* means to make someone experience something unpleasant.
7 different: an *object* (n) is a solid thing; *object* (v) *to something* means to express your opposition *to something*.

Pronunciation

1 ▶ 10.3. It's important to point out that this change in meaning due to a shift in word stress only happens in a few specific words in English. By no means does it apply to all English words. In general, these words contain two syllables, though there are a few with three syllables, e.g. *attribute* and *invalid*.

2 Alternatively, the rules in this box could be elicited in open class with books closed and the two sentences from Exercise 1 up on the board.

3–5 ▶ 10.4. Check the meaning of *convict* (noun) and *contest* (verb). Exercises 3 and 4 could be done in pairs or individually. While students practise saying the sentences in pairs, circulate and monitor their pronunciation of the words in bold.

6 Students could use monolingual dictionaries, or www.macmillandictionary.com, if mobile phones are allowed, to help them with this exercise. Check the meaning of *produce* (noun), *refuse* (noun), *subject* (verb) and *object* (verb).

11 WHAT ON EARTH'S GOING ON?

This unit deals with the themes of weather, pollution and other concerns related to the environment. Students will practise writing essays.

Read the unit objectives to the class.

SPEAKING Part 1 Interview

Focus students on the picture. Elicit *polar bear*. For a bit of fun, tell them you have a short quiz to see how much they know about polar bears. If they think the statement is true, they stand up; if false, they stay sitting.

1 Polar bears live in Antarctica. (F – They live in the Arctic.)
2 Polar bears eat meat. (T – Mostly seals.)
3 Polar bears are good swimmers. (T – Some have had to swim 50 kilometres or more without stopping due to melting sea ice.)
4 Female polar bears weigh twice as much as males. (F – It's the opposite.)
5 Polar bears have white fur. (F – It's actually transparent and colourless with a hollow core that reflects light. Bonus fact: their skin is black under their fur.)

For the Speaking Part 1 questions, put students in groups of three, with one student in the role of the examiner who keeps the time and asks the questions.

ONLINE MATERIALS

If or *if not* ... (**Teacher's Resource Centre**)
DIY Speaking Part 3 (**Teacher's Resource Centre**)
Unit 11 Test (**Test Generator**)
Unit 11 Wordlist (**Teacher's Resource Centre**)
Unit 11 On-the-go-practice (**App**)

11 WHAT ON EARTH'S GOING ON?

Vocabulary Weather

1 SPEAK Describe the typical weather conditions in your area for each season.

2 All the words in each of the groups 1–8 below can be used with one of the nouns in the box to form strong collocations. For each group of words write the noun which can be used in the appropriate space. There is an example at the beginning (0).

> breeze   clouds   rain   sea   showers   ~~sky~~   storm   sunshine   winds

0 an overcast / a clear / a stormy — _sky_

1 a lightning / a severe / a tropical — _storm_

2 heavy / torrential / light — _rain/showers_

3 strong / gale-force / light — _winds_

4 warm / bright / glorious — _sunshine_

5 a rough / a calm / a choppy — _sea_

6 thick / storm / fluffy — _clouds_

7 thundery / scattered / snow — _showers_

8 a gentle / a cool / a stiff — _breeze_

3 Study the words in Exercise 2 for two minutes. Then cover up the adjectives and see how many you can remember for each noun.

4 Complete each gap with a two-word collocation from Exercise 2. More than one answer may be possible. The first one has been done for you.

1 There's a lovely ___clear sky___ tonight so we might see a shooting star.
2 Our garden wall was blown down during the night by ___strong/gale-force winds___.
3 Heavy ___snow showers___ will fall on high ground tonight, so skiers can look forward to a good day on the slopes tomorrow.
4 I think it's going to rain – there are some very dark ___thick/storm clouds___ overhead. Look at them.
5 ___Heavy/Torrential rain___ has caused serious flooding throughout the region.
6 We sailed on a beautiful ___calm sea___ with not a wave in sight.

5 SPEAK Describe the photos on these pages using as many of the adjective + noun collocations as possible. What types of weather do you prefer? What weather conditions do you least like?

160

WHAT ON EARTH'S GOING ON? 11

Lead-in

It is worthwhile sometimes to do something completely unexpected to get your students' attention and arouse their curiosity, whether you are working with adults or young learners. For example, you could perform this simple science experiment related to weather. Fill a glass jar with water and then add a big squirt of washing-up liquid. Put the lid on (tightly). When you move the jar quickly in a circle it creates a very convincing tornado. Ask the students to guess what you put in the jar and how the experiment works (*the two liquids move at different speeds*).

Vocabulary

1 After students discuss the question in pairs, nominate a different student to tell you about each of the four seasons. Note that *autumn* is often referred to as *fall* in North America.

2 Remind students about the metaphor of relationships for collocations; words have stronger relationships with some words than with others. This exercise could be done individually or in pairs. Check the meaning of *overcast sky*, *gale-force winds*, *choppy seas*, *fluffy clouds*, *thundery showers* and *stiff breeze*.

3 Students could do one column first and then the other. If the activity is done in pairs, students could quiz each other.

4 Students do the exercise individually and then check with a partner. Go through the answers as a class. Challenge them to make a couple more sentences using other collocations from Exercise 2.

5 In small groups, students describe the pictures and answer the questions. Check their use of the target language. Make note of any interesting emergent language to write up on the board and discuss.

Extra activity

A fun game to play is to put one part of the collocations, such as the nouns in Exercise 2, up on the board. Students stand in two lines. You say the other half of one of the collocations, in this case, one of the adjectives from Exercise 2. The first student to touch the word on the board that completes the collocation gets a point for their team. The two students go to the back of their respective lines and the game continues. Ask students to touch the board with their fingers, not their whole hand, or they will erase the words!

Teaching tip

Students should do a full mock exam at least once before sitting the real *B2 First*. This is important for a couple reasons. First of all, it reduces anxiety about procedural issues, such as finishing both parts of the writing exam within the time limit. It also provides students with an authentic experience of taking the exam which can be reflected on later in class. This often brings to light last-minute questions or concerns.

During the mock, exam-room conditions and timings should be replicated as closely as possible. You can find full practice tests on the **Test Generator**. All answers should be written on official marksheets, which can be found on the **Student's** and **Teacher's Resource Centres**. Finally, the exams themselves should be marked according to criteria of the real *B2 First*.

WHAT ON EARTH'S GOING ON?

Listening

1 Check the meaning of *forecast*. Discuss the question in open class.

2 ▶ 11.1 To replicate the official exam, set a strict time limit of 45 seconds for students to look at the task before starting the recording. Note that the official examination board strongly suggests that candidates write their answers in capital letters, because it reduces the chance of misreading a candidate's answer and marking it wrong. Students should get into the habit of doing this in class.

3 Monitor while students discuss the questions in pairs, providing language support or on-the-spot correction when appropriate.

AUDIOSCRIPT

Listening Part 2 Sentence completion

▶ 11.1

Hi everyone. I'm Craig Stephens. You may know me from *Weather Watch*, a science programme I used to present on children's television aimed at helping younger viewers understand basic aspects of meteorology. But I originally started out in this country as the weather presenter on a TV programme for **farmers**. [Ex 2 Q1] That's actually what I do now, but for a different channel. The programme goes out at 9 o'clock on Sunday mornings, so you may not have seen it. I'm generally known by colleagues and viewers as the weatherman, but officially, someone like me who presents the weather is called a **broadcast** [Ex 2 Q2] meteorologist. It's not quite as catchy, though, is it?

I first got interested in the weather as a teenager, when I was on a family holiday in the Rhône valley in France. We spent three weeks in summer travelling and sleeping in a tent, but in one particular small town, my parents decided it was far too windy to camp so we rented a **holiday apartment** [Ex 2 Q3] next to the campsite we'd intended to stay in. The wind, known as the Mistral, blew for three days non-stop and gave us all a nasty headache. It was really quite irritating. I read up about it later and found out that in winter the wind is much colder and stronger, reaching speeds of 130 kilometres an hour. It can be quite **destructive**, [Ex 2 Q4] causing damage to crops, and even buildings.

I was fascinated by all this and started reading about other winds as well, like the Levante in Spain, the Föhn in the Alps or, in the Adriatic, the Bora, whose name comes from the Greek mythological figure of Boreas, the North Wind. My favourite name for a wind, though, is the Simoom, an Arabic word which sounds nice, but translates as '**poison** [Ex 2 Q5] wind'. This one blows in the Sahara Desert, and often reaches temperatures of 55 degrees, overheating the body and causing heatstroke. So, not so nice.

Anyway, how did I manage to turn this interest into a career? Well, first of all I decided to apply for a degree in meteorology. And to get accepted, I had to do well in my final exams at school. I was worried I wasn't going to get the grade I needed in maths, but as it turned out, it was **physics** [Ex 2 Q6] I struggled with and my result was not quite good enough for me to get on the course. So, I did a gap year and retook the exam the following June – and success! I got into university. But anyway, during that year out, as well as working in a coffee shop, I also volunteered in **hospital radio**. [Ex 2 Q7] That's when I had my first ever taste of presenting. I had to do mundane things, as well, like clean the studio or make the tea, but I was given some really useful training in presentation techniques and even got to read the news and weather. I loved it – I was hooked!

After graduating, I applied for jobs abroad in television. America was my first choice, but nothing came up, and it was a TV network in **Canada** [Ex 2 Q8] that gave me my big break. I worked as part of a team preparing weather reports and forecasts, both for the television presenters and for the website. It was a great experience and I learnt so much from the people I worked with.

For one thing, I really liked the style of the presenters there, and it's one I try to use myself. There was nothing formal or overdramatic about it. It was **conversational** [Ex 2 Q9] and they spoke to their audience as if they were a group of friends. Sometimes, though, it's not so easy to do this. When we give the weather forecast, we're dealing with a lot of information, and what many people don't realise is that most of us don't read from a **script**. [Ex 2 Q10] So, it can be a bit nerve-racking if you trip over your words or forget what you want to say next.

11 WHAT ON EARTH'S GOING ON?

Listening Part 2 Sentence completion

1 **SPEAK** How often do you watch, read or listen to the weather forecast? Why?

2 ▶ 11.1 You will hear a meteorologist called Craig Stephens talking about his work. For questions 1–10 complete the sentences with a word or short phrase.

Craig currently presents the weather on a television programme aimed at (1) ......farmers....... .

His official job title is '(2) ......broadcast...... meteorologist'.

Craig's interest in the weather began when he was staying in a (3) ......holiday apartment...... in a town in the Rhône valley.

Craig says that in winter, the Mistral wind is cold, strong and sometimes quite (4) ......destructive...... .

Craig mentions another wind whose name means '(5) ......poison...... wind' and which can cause heat-related illnesses.

Initially, Craig didn't get the grade he needed in his (6) ......physics...... exam to enable him to study meteorology.

Craig became interested in presenting when he did some voluntary work in (7) ......hospital radio...... .

After university, Craig's first job was with a television company in (8) ......Canada...... .

Craig says he tries to imitate the (9) ......conversational...... style of the presenters he once worked with.

Craig says that most weather presenters work without a (10) ......script...... .

3 **SPEAK** Work in pairs. Discuss the questions.
1 Would you make a good weather presenter? Why/Why not?
2 What effect, if any, does wind have on you?
3 How much do you know about the winds in your country?

11 WHAT ON EARTH'S GOING ON?

Language focus *Too* and *enough*

1 Look at sentences a and b from the listening and answer questions 1–3.

   a ... it was far **too windy** to camp ...

   b ... my result was not quite **good enough** for me to get on the course.

   1 Are the adjectives used before or after the words *too* and *enough*?
   The adjective comes after too *and before* enough.

   2 Which words are used just before the words in **bold** to modify *too* and *enough*?
   Far is used before too *and* not quite *before* enough.

   3 What form of the verb follows the words in **bold**. *The infinitive*

2 In a and b below, complete the second sentence with one word so that it has the same meaning as the first sentence.

   a It was far **too windy** to camp.
   There was far **too** _____much_____ wind to camp.
   too is used before adjectives; too much *(and* too many*) are used before nouns.*

   b I'm not **confident enough** to be a weather presenter.
   I don't have **enough** _____confidence_____ to be a weather presenter.
   enough is used after adjectives but before nouns.

3 Choose the correct options to complete the rules for the use of *too* and *enough* in Exercise 2.

   a We use *too* before **nouns**/**adjectives**. We use *too much* (or *too many*) before **nouns**/**adjectives**.

   b We use *enough* **before**/**after** adjectives but **before**/**after** nouns.

4 Go to **Ready for Grammar** on **page 230** for rules, explanations and further practice.

5 Write eight true sentences using the phrases in the box below.

enough money – My friends are going to the cinema, but I don't have enough money.

   enough money   too difficult   strong enough   too much noise
   old enough   too many people   enough time   too much (home)work

6 **SPEAK** Ask your partner about his or her sentences.

How much does it cost to see a film?

Reading and Use of English Part 7 Multiple matching

1 You are going to read an article about different procedures being used to tackle some of our global issues. Read the article quite quickly and find out:

   a which global issue is mentioned in each section (**A–D**).
   b how the issue is being tackled in each case.

1 Possible answers

A a Population explosion (and need for living space).
b Reclaiming land from the sea for building on.

B a Water scarcity
b Releasing chemicals into clouds, by aircraft or from the ground, to increase the chance of rain or snowfall.

C a Shortage of farmland and need for food.
b Growing vegetables under the sea in large biospheres.

D a Energy crisis and need for fuel.
b Recycling dog waste to create methane and power a streetlamp.

2 Read the article again and for questions 1–10, choose from the procedures (A–D). The procedures may be chosen more than once.

In relation to which procedure does the writer mention

the gradual growth in its use from small beginnings?	1 C
a general lack of awareness of how long it has been in use?	2 B
the place where the idea for it was first thought of?	3 C
the threat it poses to some people's jobs?	4 A
uncertainty about its effectiveness?	5 B
its value as an educational tool?	6 D
the recent dramatic rise in its use?	7 A
the belief that it has potential for wider application?	8 C
the fact that tests were carried out before it became functional?	9 D
growing interest in it from the media?	10 B

3 **SPEAK** Which of the procedures (A–D) would you be most interested to learn more about? Why? Discuss other ways in which global issues are being tackled.

WHAT ON EARTH'S GOING ON? 11

Language focus

1–3 If possible, aim to cover all the material in this and the **Ready for Grammar** section on pages 230–231 (see below) in one lesson. Students work through Exercises 1–3 in pairs. Then get them to read the grammar explanation to check their answers. Alternatively, you could do the grammar presentation in open class with books closed. Board the example sentences and elicit the rules by asking questions, e.g. *Do we use* too *before nouns or adjectives? What about* too many *and* too much?

4 Direct students to the **Ready for Grammar** section on pages 230–231 (see below).

5–6 While students write their sentences, circulate and check them for correct use of the target language and for general accuracy. Students should aim to write true sentences if possible, because it will make it easier to discuss them with a partner later. As always, encourage students to take advantage of this **SPEAK** activity to develop their conversational fluency, engaging with their partner's sentences by asking follow-up questions and giving advice.

READY FOR GRAMMAR

11 Too and enough

Too means 'more than is necessary or desirable'.

1 Too + adjective/adverb

   This jumper's **too big**.   Don't work **too hard**!

2 Too much/Too many (+ adjective) + noun

   I can't eat this. There's **too much salt** in it.

   There are **too many young children** here.

Too much/Too many can also be used as pronouns.

They were lovely cakes, but I ate **too many**.

Too little and *Too few* are also possible. They are quite formal; *not enough* is more common in spoken English (see below).

We had **too little time** to prepare for the exam.

Too few students are opting for science subjects and **too little** is being done to change this.

3 *Too* and *Too much/many/little/few* can be followed by the infinitive with *to*.

   It's **too cold to play** tennis today.

   He spoke **too quickly for me to understand** him.

   There's **too much work for one person to cope with**.

4 *Far*, *much*, *way* (informal), *rather*, *a little*, *slightly* and *a bit* (informal) can be used to vary the strength of *too*.

   This essay is **much too long** and there are **far too many** mistakes. The language is also **a little too informal**.

Enough means 'as much as is necessary'.

1 Adjective/Adverb + enough

   Are you **warm enough** or shall I turn the heating on?

   You haven't done your homework **carefully enough**.

2 Enough (+ adjective) + noun

   We'll have to stand – there aren't **enough chairs**.

   Not **enough new homes** are being built.

   Enough can also be used as a pronoun.

   I'll buy more bread. We haven't got **enough**.

3 *Enough* can be followed by the infinitive with *to*.

   I don't have **enough time to see** you today.

   The floor is **clean enough for you to sit** on.

4 *Nearly*, *almost*, *not quite* and *just* can be used before enough

   Zack's 1.28 m – **not quite tall enough** to go on the roller coaster.

---

11 Too and enough

1 Underline the correct alternative.

   1 You've written too *more* / <u>much</u> / *many* – I asked for a paragraph, not a whole page.

   2 There aren't *much* / *too* / <u>enough</u> young people in this village; most have left to live and work in the city.

   3 This soup is a *way* / <u>little</u> / *rather* too salty for me.

   4 She spoke quietly, but just loud enough <u>for him to</u> / *to him for* / *for him for* hear.

   5 Too *less* / *little* / <u>few</u> politicians understand how serious this issue is.

   6 My son is only seventeen, so he's not *slightly* / <u>quite</u> / *very* old enough to leave home.

2 Complete the second sentence so that it has a similar meaning to the first sentence, using the word given. Do not change the word given. You must use between two and five words, including the word given.

   1 I couldn't hear what they were saying because they were speaking so quietly.
   TOO
   They were speaking ___**too** quietly for me to___ hear what they were saying.

   2 He couldn't see over the wall because he was so small.
   ENOUGH
   He was ___**n't/not** tall **enough** to___ see over the wall.

   3 We'll need more eggs if we want to make an omelette.
   ENOUGH
   There ___**aren't/are not enough** eggs for___ us to make an omelette.

   4 I can't drink this tea because it's too sweet.
   SUGAR
   There ___**is/'s** too much **sugar**___ in this tea for me to drink it.

   5 I didn't go into the bar because it was much too crowded.
   FAR
   I didn't go into the bar because ___there were **far** too many___ people.

   Go back to **page 162**.

WHAT ON EARTH'S GOING ON?

Reading and Use of English

1 Alternatively, you could treat this task as exam practice and get the students to follow the strategy of reading the questions first before reading the text.

2 Elicit the meaning of *threat* (question 4) and *rise* (question 7). Allow the students to check their answers with a partner before going over them in open class.

3 Discuss as a class. If mobile phones are allowed, give students five minutes to read more about one of the topics. They could do this in English or their first language(s). Then ask them to report what they learnt in small groups.

Teaching tip

There are two ways to take the *B2 First*: paper based and computer based. Make time to familiarise your students with both options before they sign up for the test. You could research this yourself, but it would be better to ask the students to do so themselves as a web research task. Give them a few questions to answer, e.g. *How are they different? What are the advantages and disadvantages to each?* Discuss the topic at the beginning of the next lesson.

Extra activity

The following activity encourages students to adopt a critical approach to what they read.

In pairs, discuss the following questions. Support your views by making reference to the text or other sources of information.

1 What do you think was the author's purpose in writing this article?

2 Why do you think the author chose to focus on these particular procedures to tackle global issues and not others?

3 Is the author always objective, presenting both the advantages and disadvantages to these four procedures?

4 Can you think of a reasonable, alternative way of looking at these procedures that would put them in a less favourable light?

5 Did the author convince you that these represent useful procedures to 'tackle some of our global problems'? If so, how did they do this? If not, why not?

CONFRONTING GLOBAL ISSUES

WHAT ON EARTH'S GOING ON?

We look at four procedures being used to tackle some of our global problems.

A LAND RECLAMATION

With a rapidly growing world population, one way for a country to increase the amount of land available for housing is to reclaim it from the sea. Shorelines can be extended, natural islands can be joined to the coastline, and artificial islands can be built from nothing. Some Asian countries have been reclaiming land for the past two centuries – Singapore's land area has expanded by 25 per cent in that time – but the last few years have seen a huge explosion in the number of land reclamation projects. There are numerous examples on China's 14 500 kilometre coastline, including the brand-new city of Nanhui, built on 133 square kilometres of land, almost half of which was reclaimed from the sea. There may be a price to pay, though. Land reclamation can put enormous pressure on the environment, polluting the sea and destroying habitats for marine life. In some areas fish stocks have been drastically reduced, putting the livelihoods of local fishermen at risk.

B CLOUD SEEDING

Some countries, such as the United Arab Emirates, respond to increasing water scarcity with a procedure called cloud seeding, whereby chemicals such as silver iodide or dry ice are released by aircraft or fired from the ground into clouds in order to increase the chance of rain or snowfall. With the UN predicting water shortages for 40 per cent of the world's population by 2030, cloud seeding is receiving an increasing amount of press attention. But what many people don't realise is that it's been around for several decades and has been employed in over fifty countries. Whether it works or not is still open to debate; as yet, there is no definitive scientific evidence that it does, although the six-year Wyoming Weather Modification Pilot Project concluded in 2013 that cloud seeding can increase precipitation by between 5 and 15 per cent. On the downside, it's thought to have been the cause of serious flooding in some of the countries where it's been used.

C UNDERWATER FARMING

Growing vegetables under the sea may seem like something out of a science fiction novel, but Nemo's Garden, situated off the coast of Noli on the Italian Riviera, is very much a reality, producing anything from lettuce and tomatoes to peas, beans, and even flowers. Sergio Gamberini, a scuba diver and amateur gardener, came up with the concept whilst on a diving holiday in the area in 2012. He started off growing basil in a miniature version of the 2 000 litre biospheres currently in use, and over the next few years the underwater habitat just got bigger and bigger as more money was put into the project. The temperature inside the biospheres is stable, no pests can wander in, so there's no need for pesticides, and sea water inside the structures evaporates, condenses on the roof and then drips back down as fresh water to feed the plants. Although still in its early stages, there is optimism that this sustainable form of agriculture could be extended and put to use on a larger scale, offering a possible solution to the shortage of farmland.

D RECYCLING DOG WASTE

A streetlamp powered by dog waste is helping to keep the streets clean, as well as lighting up the area outside the UK home of its inventor, Brian Harper. Dog walkers pick up their pet's mess in a free paper bag, place it into a container and turn a handle to move the mess into a biodigester. Here it is broken down by microorganisms to produce methane, which fuels the light. Harper ran trials on the lamp for over two years before it was put into full working operation at the end of 2017. Ten bags of waste can power the light for two hours, which won't put an end to the world's energy crisis, but it should serve to teach people how waste can be useful. Schemes using dog and other animal waste as a fuel source are being adopted in a number of other countries, from Canada to India.

11 WHAT ON EARTH'S GOING ON?

Vocabulary Put

1 Write one word in each gap to complete the expressions in bold in these extracts from *Confronting global issues*. Then check your answers in the relevant sections of the article.

1 Land reclamation can **put** enormous **pressure** ___on___ the environment … (A)
2 … fish stocks are said to have been drastically reduced, **putting** the livelihoods of local fishermen ___at___ **risk**. (A)
3 … as more **money was put** ___into___ the project. (C)
4 … this sustainable form of agriculture could be extended and **put** ___to___ **use** on a larger scale … (C)
5 … [the lamp] was **put** ___into___ full working **operation** at the end of 2017. (D)
6 Ten bags of waste can power the light for two hours, which won't **put an end** ___to___ the world's energy crisis … (D)

2 Possible answers
1 cause difficulties for
2 threaten 3 invest in
4 make use of 5 start to be used 6 stop

2 **SPEAK** Work in pairs. Discuss the meanings of the expressions in bold that you completed in Exercise 1.

3 Match each sentence beginning 1–9 with an appropriate ending a–i.

1 Paula's joined an amateur dramatics society: they're **putting on**
2 These trousers are far too tight for me now: I must have **put on**
3 I don't really feel like watching anything now: we could **put on**
4 I'm going to have to move out of my flat. My landlord's **put up**
5 Don't shout out the answer, Lara. You know you have to **put up**
6 Robin's coming to London today and I've offered to **put** him **up**
7 The groom had an accident in the morning so they had to **put off**
8 It rained every single day and the tent got flooded. It **put** him **off**
9 She found it hard to study, as several things were **putting** her **off**

a weight.
b for the night.
c camping for life.
d the rent yet again.
e some music instead.
f the wedding to a later date.
d a production of Hamlet in June.
f your hand if you want to say something.
g like the noise of the traffic and the neighbours arguing.

4 The phrasal verbs *put on*, *put up* and *put off*, each have multiple meanings. Use the sentences in Exercise 3 to help you match each phrasal verb to the following groups of meanings.

a increase; raise into the air; accommodate ___put up___
b postpone; discourage from; distract ___put off___
c organise an event; gain; get something ready to listen to ___put on___

164

WHAT ON EARTH'S GOING ON? 11

Vocabulary

1-2 Explain that *put* is a very common word in English and its meaning can vary a great deal depending on which words it's combined with. Students do the exercise in pairs. Once they have checked their answers in the text, give them time to discuss the meaning of the phrasal verbs in context.

3 Students do the exercise as suggested. Challenge them to cover the right-hand column and remember the sentence endings.

4 If mobile phones are allowed, get students to use www.macmillandictionary.com to find a different example sentence for each of the three different meanings of the phrasal verbs in Exercise 4. Students could be split into groups of three, with each group assigned one of the phrasal verbs. Then regroup the students and invite them to share what they found. Together, they write different versions of the sample sentences, perhaps slightly changing the context. These can be shared in open class.

READY FOR GRAMMAR

11 Conditionals

Conditional sentences contain a conditional clause (introduced by words such as *if*, *as long as* and *unless*) and a main clause.

If the conditional clause comes first, a comma usually separates it from the main clause (as in this sentence).

A comma is not needed if the conditional clause comes after the main clause (as in this sentence).

Zero Conditional

if + present simple, present simple

We use the zero conditional to talk about situations which are always true. *If* has the same meaning as *when*, *whenever* or *every time* in such sentences.

My eyes start to hurt if I spend too long on the computer.

If you mix blue and yellow, you get green.

First Conditional

if + present simple, *will* + infinitive without *to*

We use the first conditional to talk about possible situations and their likely results in the future.

She'll be very happy if you phone her.

It can be used for warnings, promises and threats.

I'll send you to bed if you don't behave yourself.

If you pass your driving test, I'll take you out for a meal.

Other future forms and imperatives are possible in the main clause.

We're going to the cinema if my dad gets home in time.

If you see Alan, give him my regards.

Modal verbs can also be used in the main clause. *May*, *might* and *could* express possibility or uncertainty about the outcome. *Should* expresses probability.

If I finish my homework early, I might watch the film.

If you post it today, it should get there by Friday.

Second Conditional

if + past simple, *would* + infinitive without *to*

We use the second conditional to talk about imaginary, unlikely or impossible situations in the present or future.

If I knew the answer to number six, I would tell you.

If I had wings, I'd fly south in winter.

Note the difference between these two sentences:

First Conditional: *If they give me a pay rise, I'll buy a new car.* (I feel there is a real possibility that they will give me a pay rise.)

Second Conditional: *If they gave me a pay rise, I'd buy a new car.* (I feel it is less likely that they will give me a pay rise.)

The second conditional can also be used to give advice.

If I were you, I'd complain to the manager.

Both *was* and *were* are possible in the conditional clause after the subject pronouns *I/he/she/it*. *Was* is more common in spoken English.

If he were a little taller, he'd be an excellent goalkeeper.

Might and *could* can be used in the main clause to express possibility or uncertainty about the outcome.

If you worked a bit harder, you might have more success.

Third Conditional

if + past perfect, *would/might/could have* + past participle

We use the third conditional to talk about imaginary situations in the past and to speculate about their effects on past events or situations.

If we hadn't taken a map, we would have got lost. (But we took a map, so we didn't get lost).

Mixed Conditional

if + past perfect, *would/might/could* + infinitive without *to*

Mixed conditionals are a combination of a second and a third conditional. They can express an imaginary past event and a possible or probable present result.

If you'd listened to my advice, you might/would not be in this situation now.

Alternative words for *if*

As long as, *provided (that)*, *providing (that)* and *on condition (that)* can be used in place of *if* to emphasise the condition.

I'll lend you £10 as long as you give it back tomorrow.

We'll take the boat out provided the sea isn't too rough.

TB164

11 WHAT ON EARTH'S GOING ON?

Language focus

1 Students do the guided discovery in pairs. Check as a class. Point out that *had* and *would* are both often contracted to *'d* before pronouns in spoken English. If students are fairly confident with conditionals use *If or if not …* on the **Teacher's Resource Centre** at this point to check how much they know.

2 This could be done in open class.

Answers
The different modal verbs, will, should *and* might, *express different levels of certainty on the part of the speaker.*

a will *expresses certainty: the speaker feels certain they will be home by midnight.*

b should *expresses probability: he/she thinks they are likely to be home by midnight.*

c might *expresses uncertainty or possibility: he/she is not certain, but thinks it is possible they will be home by midnight.*

3 Direct students to the **Ready for Grammar** section on pages 226–227 (see TB164 and below). Exercise 1 there should be done in class, but Exercises 2 and 3 could be set for homework or saved for revision, depending on how well the students are getting on with the grammar.

4 The meaning of *wet wipes* could be checked with the illustration or realia. Students do the exercise individually and then check their answers in pairs.

5 Ask the students if they can think of any environmental issues with the way we dispose of them (*clogged sewers*). This could be demonstrated by putting 'fat berg' into Youtube.

6 While students do this semi-free practice activity, circulate and provide on-the-spot error correction of the target language. Refer students to the **Additional materials** (see TB166).

READY FOR GRAMMAR

11 Conditionals

1 Complete each gap with one word from the box. You do not need to use all the words.

> condition exclusion far long
> promising providing unless unlike

1 I'll show you my passport photo, as **long** as you promise not to laugh.
2 Her employer will pay for her studies on **condition** that she attends every class.
3 We'll eat in the garden, **unless** of course it rains.
4 I'll let you borrow it **providing** you're careful with it.

2 Each of the following sentences contains one mistake. Find the mistakes and correct them.

1 If I would drink coffee after six o'clock, I can never sleep. *If I drink …*
2 We do not give refunds unless the product isn't damaged. *… unless the product is damaged. / if the product isn't damaged.*
3 If they lose this match, I never go to see them play again. *… I'll/I will never go …*
4 Please email me if you'll find out any more information. *… if you find …*
5 Living here is alright, but I'll prefer it if it wasn't so cold. *… but I'd/I would prefer …*
6 If you'd have asked me, I would have lent you the money. *If you'd/ you had asked me …**

*Note that many native speakers use the incorrect form 'If you'd have asked me'.

3 Rewrite the sentences to form second, third or mixed conditionals.

1 I don't have to pay to get into the museum because I'm unemployed.
   If I wasn't unemployed, I'd have to pay to get into the museum.

2 We don't go abroad on holiday because I'm afraid of flying.
   If I wasn't afraid of flying, we'd/we would go abroad on holiday.

3 We didn't go sailing because there wasn't enough wind.
   We'd/We would have gone sailing if there'd/there had been enough wind.

4 He's broken his leg so he can't drive.
   If he hadn't broken his leg, he could drive.

5 He isn't going to the wedding because he hasn't got a suit.
   If he had a suit, he'd/he would go to the wedding.

6 He's feeling ill because he ate too much last night.
   He wouldn't be feeling ill if he hadn't eaten so much last night.

7 She didn't pass her exams so she couldn't go to university.
   She could have gone to university if she'd/she had passed her exams.

8 They didn't watch the news so they didn't hear about the earthquake.
   If they'd watched the news, they'd/they would have heard about the earthquake.

Go back to **page 165**.

11 WHAT ON EARTH'S GOING ON?

Language focus Conditionals

1 Identify the verb forms in bold in the following conditional sentences. Then underline the correct alternative in each explanation. The first one has been done for you.

Zero conditional
*If you **turn** the handle, the bag of dog mess **goes** into the biodigester.*
turn – present simple   goes – present simple

- a situation in which one event always occurs as the result of another. *If* in this sentence means <u>whenever</u>/although.

First conditional
continue – present simple; **will destroy** – will + infinitive without *to*
*If they **continue** to reclaim land in this area, they **will destroy** the fish stocks.*

- <u>a possible</u>/an impossible situation in the future and its likely result.

Second conditional
had – past simple; **would invest** – would + infinitive without *to*
*If we **had** more money, we **would invest** in more biospheres.*

- an imaginary situation in the past/<u>present</u> or future.

Third conditional
hadn't used – past perfect; **would have lost** – would + perfect infinitive (have + past participle) without *to*
*If we **hadn't used** cloud seeding last year, we **would have lost** all our crops.*

- an imaginary situation in the past, with speculation about its effect on present/<u>past</u> events.

Mixed conditional
hadn't grown – past perfect; **wouldn't be** – would + infinitive without *to*
*If the world's population **hadn't grown** so fast, we **wouldn't be** in this situation now.*

- an imaginary situation in the past, with speculation about its effect on <u>present</u>/past events.

2 Modal verbs can be used instead of *will* and *would* in conditional sentences. Explain the difference in meaning between these three sentences.

  a If we leave now, we'll be home by midnight.
  b If we leave now, we should be home by midnight.
  c If we leave now, we might be home by midnight.

3 Go to **Ready for Grammar** on **page 228** for rules, explanations and further practice.

4 Complete each gap with an appropriate form of the verb in brackets. There is an example at the beginning (0).

  0 If you ___flush___ (*flush*) all those wet wipes down the toilet, they ___will cause___ (*cause*) a blockage. Take them out now!
  1 If a wipe product ___carries___ (*carry*) a 'Do not flush' symbol, that ___means___ (*mean*) you should always throw it in the bin, not the toilet.
  2 Wet wipes ___would not/wouldn't be___ (*not/be*) such a big problem for our sewer systems if they ___were___ (*be*) biodegradable.
  3 Can you do me a favour? My hands are filthy. If you ___open___ (*open*) the packet of wipes, I ___will/'ll take___ (*take*) one out.
  4 Why did you buy these? If you ___had/'d looked___ (*look*) at the packet while you were in the shop, you ___would/'d have seen___ (*see*) that they're non-flushable.
  5 We ___would not/wouldn't have___ (*not/have*) this problem now if wet wipes ___had not/hadn't been invented___ (*not invent*).

5 **SPEAK** When, if ever, do you use wet wipes? How do you dispose of them?

6 **SPEAK** Work in pairs.

  Student A: Turn to the **Additional materials** on **page 201**.
  Student B: Turn to the **Additional materials** on **page 202**.

165

11 WHAT ON EARTH'S GOING ON?

Speaking Part 3 Collaborative task

Before you do the following Speaking Part 3 task, do the exercise in the Useful language box below.

1 **SPEAK** Imagine that you belong to an environmental group and you want to inform people of the environmental issues below. Talk with your partner about what ordinary people can do to help solve these issues.

2 Now decide which two issues ordinary people can do most to help solve.

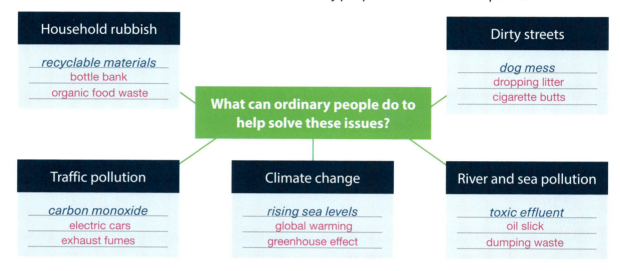

Household rubbish
- recyclable materials
- bottle bank
- organic food waste

Dirty streets
- dog mess
- dropping litter
- cigarette butts

What can ordinary people do to help solve these issues?

Traffic pollution
- carbon monoxide
- electric cars
- exhaust fumes

Climate change
- rising sea levels
- global warming
- greenhouse effect

River and sea pollution
- toxic effluent
- oil slick
- dumping waste

Useful language

One vocabulary item has been given for each of the five issues above. Add two more of the following items to each issue.

oil slick	dumping waste
bottle bank	global warming
electric cars	dropping litter
cigarette butts	organic food waste
exhaust fumes	greenhouse effect

3 Go to the Additional materials on page 203 and do the Speaking Part 4 task.

Reading and Use of English Part 6 Gapped text

1 **SPEAK** Work in pairs. Discuss the following questions.
   1 How many items do you have with you now which are made of or contain plastic?
   2 What other plastic items can you see in the classroom?
   3 In what ways might your daily life be affected if there were no plastic?

2 Read *Oceans of Garbage*. Is there any information in the article which surprises you?

WHAT ON EARTH'S GOING ON? 11

Speaking

1–3 Students do the exercise in the **Useful language** box individually or in pairs. Remind them to 'show what you know' whilst doing the task. Organise students into groups of three for the speaking task with one student in the role of the examiner, who keeps the time and asks the questions. You could also start assigning a fourth student to the role of the assessor (see **Extra activity** below). You may wish to extend this section by using **DIY Speaking Part 3** on the Teacher's Resource Centre.

Students should then turn to the Additional materials on page 203 (TB167) to do Speaking Part 4.

Extra activity

So far it has been suggested that including a student in the role of the examiner (interlocutors) while practising for the speaking exam helps replicate exam conditions. But there is still one person missing from the room: the assessor. On the *B2 First*, the assessor sits apart and does not join the conversation. In class, assign one student the role of the assessor and tell them to take notes on both the performance of the candidates and the interlocutor (the examiner who speaks to the candidates). Provide the assessor with the following questions:

Candidates: *What do they do particularly well? Are they difficult to understand for any reason? Do they give full answers? Do they interact well, listening and responding to what the other candidate says?*

Interlocutors: *Do they keep the time accurately? Do they manage the materials well? Are they friendly and polite? Do they give each candidate an equal opportunity to speak?*

When the speaking test is over, assessors share their notes with the candidates and interlocutor. Remind them to keep their feedback constructive. If time allows, students swap roles and the task is repeated.

Language focus Conditionals

Student A

1 In 1–4 below you are given the second half of four sentences. For each one, write three possible beginnings. There is an example (0) to help you.

   a If I could speak English fluently,
   b If I went to live in the capital,   0 … I'd probably get a good job.
   c If my dad asked the right people,

   1 … I'd probably be extremely popular.
   2 … the world would be a better place.
   3 … I'd never speak to you again.
   4 … I would have passed my exams.

2 Read out the sentence beginnings you have written and your partner will try to guess the sentence endings you were given.

Go back to **page 165**.

Language focus Conditionals

Student B

1 In 1–4 below you are given the first half of four sentences. For each one, write three possible continuations.

There is an example (0) to help you.

                                         a I'd buy a big house in the countryside.
   0 If I were extremely rich,   b I probably wouldn't give up my studies.
                                         c I'd donate some of my money to charity.

   1 If I lived in Britain, …
   2 If I were ten years older, …
   3 If someone stole my phone, …
   4 If plastic hadn't been invented, …

2 Read out the sentence endings you have written and your partner will try to guess the sentence beginnings you were given.

Go back to **page 165**.

11 WHAT ON EARTH'S GOING ON?

Reading and Use of English

1 Once the students have had a chance to talk in pairs, bring the class together and nominate a few students to give examples of everyday items that contain plastic. Ask how their lives would be different without them. Encourage them to use conditional sentences, e.g. *If I didn't have my backpack ….*

2 Set a time limit of no more than two minutes for this skimming task.

3 At this point in the course, start getting your students to do reading tasks more quickly. Set a time limit of around 10–12 minutes and see how they do. Also, remind the students that they can answer the questions in any order they want. In fact, if they leave harder questions to the end, there is a better chance of getting them right, as some of the possible wrong answers will have been eliminated.

4 To add variety, students could be given a couple of minutes to discuss their ideas in small groups and then write them down on a piece of paper. These sheets of papers are then exchanged with another group, who briefly discusses the ideas on the paper. In open class, decide which ideas would be most realistic to put into practice.

Speaking Part 4 Further discussion

SPEAK Discuss the following questions with your partner on the topic of the environment. Give reasons for your opinions.

1 How environmentally aware do you think people are in your country?
2 Some people say that the best way to keep cities clean is to make people who drop litter pay heavy fines. Do you agree?
3 What can local authorities do to reduce traffic pollution in towns and cities?
4 Do you think it's true that some people worry too much about the environment and there are more important problems to solve?
5 Some people think it is too late to repair the damage we have done to the environment. What do you think?
6 Some people say we should set up colonies on other planets, in case we suffer a global environmental disaster here on Earth. Do think this is a good idea?

Go back to **page 166**.

WHAT ON EARTH'S GOING ON?

3 Six sentences have been removed from the text. Choose from the sentences A–G the one which fits each gap (1–6). There is one extra sentence which you do not need to use.

OCEANS OF GARBAGE

The North Pacific Subtropical gyre is an area of twenty million square kilometres in the Pacific Ocean, in which a combination of four currents moves the water slowly round in a clockwise direction. The circular motion of the gyre pulls large quantities of marine debris, including plastics and other rubbish, into the centre, where it becomes trapped and builds up over time. This gyre is sometimes called the Trash Vortex or the Pacific Garbage Patch. Some plastics here will not break down in the lifetimes of the grandchildren of the people who threw them away.

More than 300 million tonnes of plastic are produced each year, and 8 million tonnes of this end up in the sea. If you look around on any beach anywhere in the world, you will invariably find an assortment of disposable plastic items such as shopping bags, food wrappers, bottles and bottle caps, drinking straws, lighters and pieces of fishing net. **1** E

These larger objects are the visible signs of a much larger problem. They do not degrade like natural materials. **2** A A single one-litre bottle could separate into enough tiny pieces to put one on every mile of beach in the entire world.

3 G Unfortunately, however, many items are mistaken for food and swallowed by seabirds and other ocean-going creatures. A turtle found dead on one Pacific island had several hundred pieces of plastic in its stomach and intestines. It has been estimated that plastic kills over a million seabirds and one hundred thousand marine mammals and sea turtles each year.

4 C Absorbed by fish and shellfish, they quickly work their way up to the very top of the food chain. You may not be able to see the tiny fragments hanging in the water, but they are there, nonetheless, and they may one day end up on your plate.

5 F Ocean garbage patches, it seems, are just the tip of the iceberg and the vast majority of discarded plastic is broken down and sinks to the bottom. Here it is swept along by powerful currents and deposited in high concentrations in so-called microplastic hotspots. Researchers recently found as many as 1.9 million pieces of microplastic covering just one square metre of the ocean floor.

The issue of plastic waste is one that needs to be urgently addressed. **6** B Obviously though, there is a need to make those who earn a living from the sea, such as ship owners and fishing boat operators, more aware of the consequences of irresponsible disposal of plastic items.

With so many threats to the world oceans, including pollution, overfishing and climate change, we urgently need to rescue marine biodiversity in the most effective way possible.

A At sea and on shore, under the influence of sunlight and the action of waves, they simply break down slowly into increasingly smaller particles.

B We can all contribute by avoiding plastics in the things we buy and by disposing of our waste responsibly.

C Microscopic particles of plastic, known as microplastics, are consumed by humans, too.

D But this is not the only threat to marine life.

E They have been casually thrown away on land and at sea and carried ashore by wind and tide.

F Of course, not all plastic floats.

G This perhaps wouldn't be too much of a problem if the plastic had no harmful effects.

4 SPEAK Give examples of ways in which we could 'avoid plastics in the things we buy'.

11 WHAT ON EARTH'S GOING ON?

Reading and Use of English Part 3 Word formation

1 **SPEAK** Look at the names of the three World Days highlighted in bold in the text below and the posters. What do you think happens on these days and why?

2 Read through the text quite quickly, ignoring the gaps. Compare what it says with your own ideas in exercise 1.

World Days

Certain days each year are used to draw attention to (0) _GLOBAL_ issues which affect the health of our planet. **World Car Free Day**, for example, on 22 September, aims to raise (1) _awareness_ of the problems caused by our (2) _dependence_ on private cars. Streets are closed to traffic and opened instead to street parties, theatre or bicycle demonstrations, hoping to encourage more (3) _environmentally_ friendly alternatives to the car, such as walking, cycling and public transport.

8 June is **World Oceans Day**, when numerous events and (4) _activities_ are organised, urging people to respect the ocean and (5) _ensure_ that it is healthy for future generations. Similarly, **World Ozone Day** on 16 September emphasises that the (6) _responsibility_ to protect the ozone layer and the climate does not lie solely with governments. We as individuals can do our part to (7) _minimise_ energy consumption and emissions by sensible use, and proper maintenance of air conditioners, refrigerators and other (8) _equipment_ and appliances.

GLOBE

AWARE
DEPEND

ENVIRONMENT

ACTIVE
SURE

RESPONSIBLE

MINIMUM

EQUIP

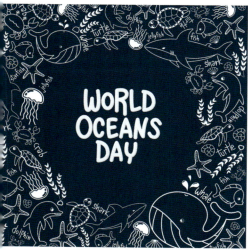

3 **SPEAK** Work in groups. Discuss the following questions.
  1 Do people in your country celebrate any of the days mentioned in the text? If so, how successful are they?
  2 How dependent are you and your family on the car?
  3 What could/do you do to reduce the amount of energy you consume in your home?

Writing Part 1 Essay

In your English class you have been talking about ways in which individuals can help the environment. Now, your English teacher has asked you to write an essay.

Write an essay using **all** the notes and giving reasons for your point of view.

> **There is little that individuals can do to help the environment. Do you agree?**
>
> **Notes**
> **Write about:**
> 1 pollution
> 2 household waste
> 3 .... (your own idea)

Don't forget!
> Plan what you are going to write and how you are going to express your ideas.
>
> *Use the Speaking task and Reading text on pages 166–167, as well as the Word formation text above, to help you with ideas and useful language.*

Write your essay in 140–190 words.

For more information on writing essays, see **pages 189–191**.

WHAT ON EARTH'S GOING ON? 11

Reading and Use of English

1 There are some short, interesting videos on YouTube about each of these three world days, which could make an engaging lead-in to this topic.
2 Ask students to time themselves while they do this task.
3 When discussing question 3, aim to get students using conditional sentences by boarding a few conditional clauses, e.g. *If I didn't …; If my family and I were better about …; If I could find a better way to …*.

Writing

Draw a flow chart on the board and encourage students to follow these steps: *read the task, plan, write, proofread*. Together, agree on how much time would be sensible to spend on each step.

Sample answer

Without doubt, the environment is in danger and all people have a challenge to do something about it. However, even small things that individuals do can make a difference.

First of all, people can try to reduce pollution by taking public transport or by using less energy. Exhaust fumes from cars are a big threat to the atmosphere, so this is one way that an individual can make a contribution to helping the environment.

Secondly, we should try to recycle as much as we can at home in order to cut down on household waste. For example, if everybody brought their old bottles to a bottle bank instead of dumping them, there would be less waste in the natural landscape.

Finally, individuals need to work together as a team. We should encourage each other to recycle more and conserve energy, and educate in our schools about the importance of taking care of our planet.

In conclusion, I disagree with the statement and I believe that individuals can definitely make a difference. If everybody tries a little bit, the result will be effective.

Fehér László
184 words

Examiner's comments

Content: All content is relevant and the target reader is fully informed.
Communicative achievement: The conventions of writing an essay are used successfully to hold the reader's attention. There is a clear essay structure: the opening paragraph challenges the opinion in the question, then each of the next three paragraphs provides suggestions for ways in which individuals can make a difference. The final paragraph restates the writer's opinion.
The register is, in the main, consistent, with *a little bit* in the final sentence as the only example of informal English.
Organisation: The essay is well organised with logical paragraphing and a clear topic sentence in each of the three central paragraphs. There is also good use of linking words and expressions to introduce each main point (*However; First of all; Secondly; Finally; In conclusion*).
Language: There is a range of vocabulary relevant to the topic (*reduce pollution; exhaust fumes; cut down on household waste; bottle bank; dumping; conserve energy*). A wide range of simple and complex grammatical forms is used with control, accuracy and flexibility, including conditionals (*if everybody brought …; there would be …; If everybody tries a little bit, the result will be effective.*) and verb forms (*make a contribution to helping the environment; We should encourage each other to recycle more; the importance of taking care of our planet*).
Mark: Very good pass.

AUDIOSCRIPT

Listening Part 1 Multiple choice

 11.2

W = Woman   M = Man

1 You hear a woman talking about litter.
W: If I was in local government, I'd make sure something was done about the mess on the streets. It's an absolute disgrace. Local people need more help to keep them clean, and that help has to come from the authorities. There aren't enough litter bins, for one thing, so *the pavements outside my premises* are covered with paper, drink cans and cigarette butts. Before I open up in the morning I have to spend about ten minutes sweeping it all up. *I wouldn't sell anything if I didn't.*

(Ex 4 Q1)

2 You hear an environmentalist talking on the radio about a current project.
M: Some species of plants were close to extinction here. People would come out for the day to the countryside, see all these beautiful flowers and pick them, without realising the effect this was having. If we hadn't made this a conservation area and limited the number of people coming in, then we'd have no flowers at all. *The challenge we now face is to ensure the survival of the project – and there's no guarantee of that.* As expected, the new government has shown little interest in the environment and the Minister has even suggested she might *cut the funding for projects like this one.*

(Ex 4 Q2)

TB168

11 WHAT ON EARTH'S GOING ON?

Listening

1–3 Follow the procedure as instructed.

4 ▶ **11.2.** On the official exam, students are given a few seconds to quickly read each question before listening to the individual extract twice. Try to replicate this in class.

AUDIOSCRIPT continued

3 You hear this woman talking to her friend about her holiday.

M: So what was it like?

W: Marvellous. Just what we were looking for.

M: What? Loads of lovely sandy beaches?

W: If we'd wanted that, we'd have gone to one of the other islands – and had to put up with all the crowds of sun worshippers and horrendous traffic.

M: So weren't there many tourists where you went?

W: Well, there were quite a lot more than we expected really. But it didn't matter, because with *the ban on private cars, everywhere was so wonderfully quiet and peaceful.* There were buses and taxis, but because the island's so small, we walked most of the time. *(Ex 4 Q3)*

4 You hear two people talking on the radio about the use of cars in their town.

M: The council wants to introduce a supplementary tax on car owners. Fine, but if we're serious about reducing pollution and easing traffic congestion, *we need to reduce speed limits* on the main roads coming into town and keep all cars out of the centre. *(Ex 4 Q4)*

W: That's all very well, but if you stopped cars from coming into the centre, shop and restaurant owners would be unfairly affected. Likewise, the council's plan would penalise those responsible people who leave their cars at home and use public transport to get about town. *Forcing drivers to slow down seems the only reasonable option.*

M: But it's not enough on its own.

5 You hear a man talking on the radio.

M: Violent storms swept across the south coast last night, causing widespread damage to property. Torrential rain and gale-force winds lashed seaside towns and *several people had to be evacuated from their flooded homes by rescue services.* Train services were severely disrupted by the extreme weather conditions this morning and thousands of *commuters were forced to find alternative transport to the capital or else stay at home.* In Worthing, *a high-sided lorry parked in a lay-by was blown over* by the strong winds, causing serious traffic delays on the A27. *The vehicle was empty at the time and there were no injuries.* *(Ex 4 Q5)*

6 You overhear this conversation between a woman and her neighbour.

W: Hello, Peter. Have you got a minute?

M: What's the problem, Jill?

W: Well, my garden's in a terrible state. I lost quite a few plants last night.

M: It wasn't our cat, was it? I do apologise. I really don't know what to do about him.

W: No, it's alright, it was the wind. Didn't you hear it? It was blowing a real gale. Uprooted all my roses and blew down most of the fence.

M: Oh, I'm sorry to hear that.

W: Not to worry. I'd be very grateful, though, *if you'd give me a hand to clear up the mess.* *(Ex 4 Q6)*

M: Of course. I'll just go and put a jumper on.

7 You hear two people talking about a boy.

M: I think we should all get together and decide what we're going to do. I can't put up with it any more.

W: Neither can we. The noise of that boy's music makes the whole building shake. My husband says it's just like being in an earthquake.

M: Of course, it's the parents' fault, but it's no good talking to them. They're no better than he is.

W: And his teachers can't control him, either. Apparently, he's as rude to them as he is to all of us.

M: So, *let's have a meeting of everyone in the street* and we'll decide how we're going to deal with this. *(Ex 4 Q7)*

8 You hear a woman being interviewed about an environmental issue.

W: Climate change is having a devastating effect on these islands. Cyclones are far more frequent than before and rising sea levels are causing severe coastal erosion. Our aim is to persuade people in wealthy nations to put pressure on their governments to take action and help prevent this situation from arising. *The average person, however, sees the islands as a paradise and not a priority, and fails to understand that what goes on in their own country is affecting people thousands of miles away.* Meanwhile the impoverished islanders can do little except continue to move further and further inland. *(Ex 4 Q8)*

WHAT ON EARTH'S GOING ON? 11

Listening Part 1 Multiple choice

1 Look at the Listening Part 1 question and script below. Choose the best answer (A, B or C).

You hear a man talking about fly-tipping, the illegal dumping of waste. What does he think should happen?

A Stricter fines should be imposed on fly-tippers.
B Businesses should be encouraged to prevent waste.
C Security cameras should be installed in country areas.

> Last year there were nearly a million cases of fly-tipping in this country, with over a third of farmers having rubbish dumped on their land. The Government want to increase penalties Ex 3
> for fly-tipping, but if they did that, they'd have to fill the countryside with CCTV cameras to catch offenders, and let's face it, that's just not practical. The only solution is to attack the Ex 2
> problem at its root: provide incentives for companies to reduce the amount of packaging they use and persuade manufacturers of white goods to make fridges and washing machines that last. And if they don't do that, then make them pay for clearing up the mess.

2 Which part of the script helped you to choose the correct answer?

3 Which grammatical structure is used to distract you and encourage you to consider the incorrect options as possible answers? The second conditional

4 ◉ 11.2 You will hear people talking in eight different situations. For questions 1–8, choose the best answer (A, B or C).

In questions **1–3** below, you will hear conditional sentences. These have been used to create distractors, as in Exercise **1** above.

1 You hear a woman talking about litter.
   Who is the woman?
   A a shopkeeper
   B a town councillor
   C a local resident

2 You hear an environmentalist talking on the radio about a current project.
   How does he feel?
   A concerned about the future of the project
   B disappointed with the results of the project
   C surprised at the lack of public interest in the project

3 You hear this woman talking to her friend about her holiday.
   Why did she enjoy it?
   A There were plenty of beaches.
   B There wasn't much traffic.
   C There weren't many people.

4 You hear two people talking on the radio about the use of cars in their town.
   What do they agree about?
   A Car owners should pay higher local taxes.
   B Cars should be banned from the town centre.
   C Speed restrictions should be imposed on cars.

5 You hear a man talking on the radio.
   What type of information is he giving?
   A a travel warning
   B a news report
   C a weather forecast

6 You overhear this conversation between a woman and her neighbour.
   What is the woman doing?
   A asking for help
   B apologising
   C complaining

7 You hear two people talking about a boy.
   What is the relationship between the two people?
   A They are married.
   B They are teaching colleagues.
   C They are neighbours.

8 You hear a woman being interviewed about an environmental issue.
   What does she find frustrating?
   A It is difficult to convince people of the problem.
   B Governments are not responding to public pressure.
   C The people most directly affected are not doing enough.

169

11 REVIEW

Vocabulary Weather

Match each sentence beginning 1–8 with an appropriate ending a–h.

1 She opened the door and a **gentle**
2 Northern areas suffered **torrential**
3 A tree blown down by **gale-force**
4 There is a possibility of **scattered**
5 The valley was bathed in **bright**
6 The boat struggled through **rough**
7 The appearance of very **thick, dark**
8 It will be a grey day with **overcast**

a **showers** in the region tomorrow.
b **seas** to reach the safety of the port.
c **breeze** blew into the room.
d **sunshine**, like a scene from a painting.
e **clouds** told us a storm was on its way.
f **rain**, which caused heavy flooding.
g **skies** and occasional showers.
h **winds** blocked the road, holding up traffic.

Reading and Use of English Part 4 Key word transformation

Complete the second sentence so that it has a similar meaning to the first sentence, using the word given. Do not change the word given. You must use between two and five words, including the word given.

1 It's a good thing I spoke to you or I would have forgotten her birthday.
   IF
   I would have forgotten her birthday _____*if* I hadn't/had not spoken_____ to you.

2 I only wrote the letter because my mother made me do it.
   HAVE
   If my mother hadn't made me do it, _____I would not/wouldn't **have** written_____ the letter.

3 I will help you only if you tidy your room.
   NOT
   I will _____**not** help you unless you_____ tidy your room.

4 You can borrow it, but you must return it to me next week.
   LONG
   You can borrow it _____as **long** as you give/hand/send_____ it back to me next week.

5 The factory fumes are endangering the health of local residents.
   PUT
   The health of local residents _____is being **put** at_____ risk by the factory fumes.

6 If the sea wasn't so rough, we could go out in the boat today.
   ENOUGH
   The sea _____is not/isn't calm **enough** for_____ us to be able to go out in the boat today.

Vocabulary Put

Complete each of the gaps in sentences 1–6 with one of the words from the box. Use each word twice.

| off on up |

1 Put your hand __*up*__ if you want to ask a question.
2 We're putting __*on*__ a concert to raise money for charity.
3 That job I had in the butcher's put me __*off*__ eating meat for life.
4 Could you put some music __*on*__? It's too quiet in here.
5 When I'm next in London, could you put me __*up*__ for the night?
6 Never put __*off*__ until tomorrow what you can do today.

REVIEW 11

Reading and Use of English Part 2 Open cloze

For questions 1–8, read the text below and think of the word which best fits each gap. Use only one word in each gap. There is an example at the beginning (0).

A ZERO-WASTE LIFESTYLE

I am extremely concerned (0) __ABOUT__ the amount of waste we produce. There is much (1) __too__ much of it. It uses up natural resources, takes up landfill space and, in the case of plastic, makes (2) __its__ way into our oceans. So, I follow the three Rs – reduce, reuse, recycle. I'm trying initially to generate as little rubbish (3) __as__ possible, but my ultimate aim is to lead a zero-waste lifestyle.

Recycling is important, but I do (4) __my__ best to avoid disposable items in favour of reusable ones. So, for example, (5) __instead__ of paper towels, serviettes and tissues, I only ever use cloth ones. I always take several bags with me when I go shopping, and won't buy anything that's wrapped or comes in a container (6) __unless__ the wrapping or container can be reused. (7) __Although/Though/Whilst/While__ I realise what I do won't make a huge difference on its own, it might at least help to influence others. And if we all (8) __did/played__ our part, it would undoubtedly have a positive effect on the environment.

Language focus Conditional sentences

1 If the weather __stays__ (stay) good next weekend, we __will/'ll probably go__ (probably/go) away somewhere.
2 Why didn't you phone us? If I __had/'d known__ (know) you were coming, I __could have prepared__ (could/prepare) something special to eat.
3 I __wouldn't do__ (not/do) a bungee jump even if you __paid__ (pay) me a million pounds, so stop trying to persuade me.
4 I thought this might happen. If you __had/'d taken__ (take) the advice I gave you, you __would not/wouldn't be__ (not/be) in this mess now.
5 Stop being naughty! I __will/'ll send__ (send) you to bed early unless you __start__ (start) behaving yourself right now!
6 It was very kind of you. I don't know what I __would/'d have done__ (do) yesterday if you __had not/hadn't helped__ (not/help) me.
7 My printer's getting old now, but it __usually works__ (usually/work) all right if you __feed__ (feed) the paper in manually.
8 I __would/'d go__ (go) to the cinema more often if I __had__ (have) the time, but unfortunately it's just not possible.

Writing Part 2 Informal email

You have received an email from your Irish friend, Liam.

From: Liam
Subject: January trip

I'm definitely coming in January. Shame you won't be there then, but perhaps you could give me some advice. What's the weather like in your area at that time of year? What sort of clothes should I pack and what can I do there?
Thanks
Liam

Write your email in 140–190 words.
Please go to the Teacher's Resource Centre for a Sample answer with Examiner comments for this task.
For more information on writing informal emails, see page 193.

11 WHAT ON EARTH'S GOING ON?

11 WHAT ON EARTH'S GOING ON?

Pronunciation Consonant clusters

1 ▶ 11.3 Listen and repeat the following words, which all begin with a consonant cluster, a combination of two or more consonant sounds.

> bright   creative   flexible   glorious   previous   scattered
> spoilt   spread   squirrel   strong   switch   throughout

2 **SPEAK** Work in pairs. Complete the words in bold with the consonant clusters in the box.

> -cts   -dth   -fth   -mpt   -nchy   -ngth   -nks   -pth   -sks   -sps   -sts

1 The **cru**__nchy__ **cri**__sps__ were delicious.
2 She **thi**__nks__ this is my first **atte**__mpt__ at the exam, but actually it's my **fi**__fth__.
3 The average **wi**__dth__ of the lake is over ten kilometres; the maximum **de**__pth__ is unknown.
4 Please leave the **te**__sts__ on the **de**__sks__.
5 We take pride in the **stre**__ngth__ of our **produ**__cts__.

3 ▶ 11.4 Listen and repeat the sentences in Exercise 2.

4 **SPEAK** Work in pairs. Read the rules and play the game below.

RULES

You need a coin to play this game.

1 Student A tosses the coin. If it lands on heads, they have to say two words that begin with the consonant cluster in the first block below. If the coin lands on tails, they have to say four words.

2 Student B then chooses any one of the remaining blocks and tosses the coin. Once again, if it's heads, they say two words; if it's tails, they say four words.

3 For each turn there is a time limit of 30 seconds. One point is scored for each correct word. Words from Exercise 1 may not be used.

4 Continue until all the blocks have been chosen. The student with the most points is the winner.

SP — space, Spain, Spanish, speak, special, species, speed, spell, spend, spirit, sponsor, sport, spot

PL — place, plain, plan, plane, planet, plant, plastic, plate, play, pleasant, please, plenty, plot, plus

PR — practice, prepare, present, president, press, pretty, price, prison, private, probably, problem, process, produce, product, production, programme, progress, project, property, propose, protect, provide, proud

SC — scan, scandal, scared, school, score, Scotland, Scottish, scout, screen

SM — small, smart, smile, smell, smoke, smooth

TR — track, trade, traditional, traffic, train, tram, tramp, transport, trap, travel, tread, treat, tree, trick, trophy, trouble, true, truly, trust, try

GR — grade, gradual, graduate, grammar, grand, grant, grass, grateful, great, Greece, Greek, green, grew, grey, group, ground, grow

STR — straight, strange, strawberry, stream, street, strength, stress, stretch, strict, strike, string

CR — crack, craft, crash, crazy, cream, create, credit, crew, crime, crisis, cross, crowd, crown, crucial, cruel, cruise, crystal

GL — glad, glamorous, glance, glass, glimpse, global, globe, glove, glow, glue

THR — threaten, three, threw, thrill, thriving, throat, throne, through, throw

BL — black, blame, blanket, blast, bleed, blind, block, blog, blond, blood, blow, blue, blunt

BR — brand, bread, break, breakfast, breast, breath, bridge, brief, brilliant, bring, Britain, British, broad, broken, brother, brown

FL — flag, flame, flash, flat, flavour, flew, flight, float, flood, floor, flour, flower, fluent, fly

ST — stable, staff, stage, stand, star, start, state, station, stay, steal, step, stick, still, stop, store, story, storm, student, study, style

SW — swan, swallow, sweater, Sweden, Swedish, sweep, sweet, swim, Swiss

172

Pronunciation

1 ▶ 11.3 Books closed. Board the words *spray* and *texts*. Elicit that in English there can be as many as three consonant sounds found together at the beginning of a word, /spreɪ/, and as many as four at the end of the word, /teksts/. Consonant clusters can often be troublesome for students, particularly when the combination in question is not possible in their L1. Books open. Students could listen to the words first and then listen and repeat. Pictures could be used to elicit the meanings of *spoilt* and *squirrel*.

2–3 ▶ 11.4 If you think your students might find this challenging; they could do it in pairs. It can be difficult to get the whole class to repeat a full sentence in unison, so try nominating only two or three students to repeat individual sentences in open class.

4 While students play the game, circulate and check their pronunciation of the consonant clusters. Make note of any sound combinations that are particularly hard for your students.

12 LOOKING AFTER YOURSELF

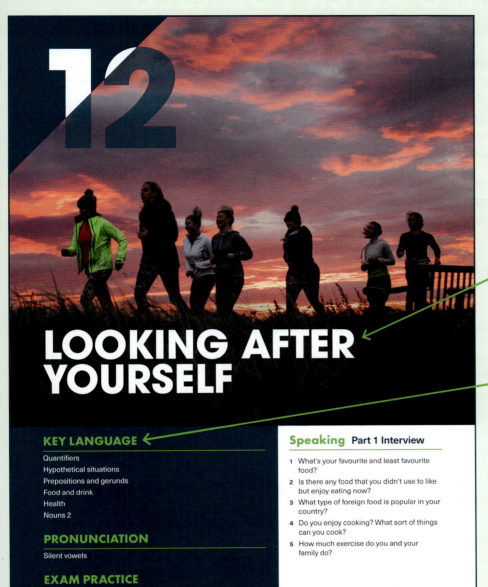

Diet, exercise and health are the themes of this unit. Students will practise Writing Part 2, the report.

Read the unit objectives to the class.

SPEAKING Part 1 Interview

Explain that instead of discussing these questions, they are going to write their own. Give the students a few minutes to go through the book and study the Speaking Part 1 questions at the beginning of Units 1–12. Ask them to answer the following:

- How do the questions usually start? (Most often with question words, e.g. *what*, *how much/many*, or an auxiliary, e.g. *do* or *is/are*. Sometimes with an imperative, e.g. *Describe …*; *Talk about …*. Also sometimes with a conditional clause, e.g. *If you could ….*)
- Can the questions be easily answered with yes or no? (Not usually. If so, there is a follow-up question.)
- What kind of information do they ask for? (Basic personal information about the candidates.)

In groups of four, students write six questions of their own about the themes of the unit: *diet, exercise and health*. They then swap questions with another group and do the task, with one student in the role of the interlocutor and another in the role of the assessor (see the **Extra activity** TB166 for ideas about how to include an assessor).

ONLINE MATERIALS

Sentence endings game (**Teacher's Resource Centre**)
Who can remember the most? (**Teacher's Resource Centre**)
A future interview (**Teacher's Resource Centre**)
B2 First for Schools writing lessons (**Teacher's Resource Centre**)
Unit 12 Test (**Test Generator**)
Unit 12 Wordlist (**Teacher's Resource Centre**)
Unit 12 On-the-go-practice (**App**)

12 LOOKING AFTER YOURSELF

Speaking Part 2 Long turn

1 Look at the photographs, which show people eating in different situations.

   Student A: Compare photographs 1 and 2 and say what might be good or bad for the people about eating in these situations.

   Student B: When your partner has finished, say where you like eating.

2 Now change roles. Follow the instructions in Exercise 1 using photographs 3 and 4.

> **What to expect in the exam**
>
> In Part 2 of the Speaking test, Student A speaks for one minute and Student B has 30 seconds. When you do these Speaking Part 2 tasks, practise keeping to the time limits.

Vocabulary Food and drink

1 Work out the meanings of the words and expressions in bold in the following questions.

   1 Are you a **fussy eater** or do you tend to eat all types of food?
   2 When eating out, do you prefer to **eat a three-course sit-down meal** or just **have a snack**?
   3 Do you **chew** your food several times before you **swallow** it, or do you tend to **bolt it down** quickly?
   4 Which drinks, if any, do you usually **sip** slowly? When, if ever, do you **gulp down** your drink quickly?
   5 When buying or ordering a **soft drink**, do you prefer **still drinks** like orange juice or **fizzy drinks** like lemonade?
   6 Do you often **drink straight from a bottle or a can**, or do you usually **drink from a glass**?

2 **SPEAK** Discuss the questions in Exercise 1 with your partner. Give as much information as possible.

---

1 **fussy eater:** someone who only eats the food they particularly like and refuses to eat anything else.

2 **eat a three-course sit-down meal:** eat a meal with a starter, main course and dessert while sitting at a table. **have a snack:** eat a small quick meal

3 **chew:** bite the food in your mouth into small pieces **swallow:** make food or drink go from your mouth, through your throat and into your stomach **bolt down:** eat food very quickly

4 **sip:** swallow a drink slowly, a little at a time **gulp down:** swallow a drink very quickly

5 **soft drink:** cold, non-alcoholic drink **still drink:** drink without gas bubbles **fizzy drink:** drink with gas bubbles

6 **drink straight from a bottle or a can:** drink something without pouring it out first **drink from a glass:** drink something having first poured it into a glass

---

> What might be good or bad for the people about eating in these situations?

1

2

174

LOOKING AFTER YOURSELF 12

Lead-in

Students could simply carry on the speaking exam practice from TB173 and move directly into this Speaking Part 2 task. The following lead-in could be used before the vocabulary section.

Ask your students to organise the words below into a mind map with the word *food* at the centre. Brainstorm subcategories in open class, e.g. *meat*, *seafood*, *vegetables*, etc. (Note: try to replace some of the words below with ones more typical to the local diet.)

apricot, *beans*, *cabbage*, *cod*, *cured meats*, *pasta*, *pomegranate*, *rice*, *sausage*, *shrimp*, *spinach*, *watermelon*

Then give the students two minutes to add as many extra words to their mind maps as they can. Students share their mind maps in open class.

Speaking

1-2 Focus the students on the **What to expect in the exam** box. In groups of four, students do the Long turn task. Assign one student the role of the interlocutor (examiner who talks to the candidates) and another the role of the assessor. Both, ideally, should keep the time. See TB100 for an examiner script that could be adapted for this speaking task and TB166 for a peer-feedback task for the assessor.

Vocabulary

1 Students work in pairs and discuss the meaning of the words. Make monolingual dictionaries available and encourage them to look up any vocabulary items they are unsure of. If mobile phones are allowed, direct students to www.macmillandictionary.com. Check the pronunciation of *fussy* /ˈfʌsi/, *swallow* /ˈswɒləʊ/ and *gulp* /gʌlp/. Note that the /t/ sound in *bottle* may sound quite different depending on where you were born or where you learnt your English. In these cases, it's best to simply teach your own accent, while at the same time acknowledging and accepting linguistic variation if the issue comes up in class.

2 While students discuss the questions in small groups, monitor their use and pronunciation of the target language, providing on-the-spot error correction when appropriate.

Teaching tip

In many schools, there will be groups of students who have already studied for and passed the *B2 First* exam, for example, students in *C1 Advanced* preparation course. Recruit one or two brave members of another course to come to your class one day and talk about how they prepared for the exam, how much work they had to do, how they achieved the score they did, etc. Your students should prepare questions to ask the invited guests. It seems invariably true that advice from a fellow student is more powerful and leaves a longer lasting impression than if the same advice came from a teacher.

Extra activity

With the exam date looming, it's good to give your students some common-sense advice, such as *get enough sleep the night before the exam*. Rather than lecture your students, however, and risk the advice going in one ear and out the other, get the students to write their own advice. This provides useful language practice with imperatives and conditionals in particular. A more fun variation is to get the students to write bad advice instead of good advice. Model this with a funny example, such as *Stay out late with friends the night before the exam. You've got nothing to lose!* Or: *Go slow and spend as much time as you need on each question. There's always plenty of extra time*. This activity always makes for a good laugh, which exam preparation courses could always use a bit more of!

12 LOOKING AFTER YOURSELF

Listening

1. ▶ 12.1 Books closed. Explain to the students that on the official exam they will only have 30 seconds to read the task for Listening Part 3 before the recording starts. Ask the students how they think this time would be best spent. Discuss their ideas in open class. Books open. Read the task instructions aloud and then start the timer. Start the recording after 30 seconds.

2. Alternatively, students could read the question and then quickly scan the **Audioscript** on page 246 (see below) and find a minimum of five collocations that might be useful for them while describing the best or worst meal they have ever had, e.g. *genuine home-cooked food* (speaker 1), *surprisingly tasty* (speaker 2) or *the food was to die for* (speaker 4). They then try to slip these lexical items as naturally into their conversation as possible.

AUDIOSCRIPT

Listening Part 2 Multiple matching

▶ 12.1

Speaker 1 It was a fairly inexpensive restaurant on the edge of the city, but low prices are no excuse for poor hygiene. We'd decided to get away from all the people and noise in the centre, where tourist restaurants charge tourist prices, and try something more local, more authentic. The reviews we'd read spoke about the genuine home-cooked food and the size of the portions, with only one or two negative comments about having to wait a little too long for the food to arrive. What they didn't mention **[Ex 1 B]** were the sticky tables that hadn't been wiped, the stained cutlery and the filthy floor. We just ordered a main course, and left as soon as we could.

Speaker 2 My partner and I went to a new vegan restaurant that had just opened in town. We weren't expecting very much from the food, but everything we ordered was surprisingly tasty. There wasn't a massive amount of variety on the menu but, to be honest, I'd rather have just a few decent things to choose from than a huge number of dishes, some of which might not be particularly well cooked. What spoilt it, though, was the large group of people on **[Ex 1 E]** the table next to ours, all talking at the tops of their voices. Neither of us could hear what the other was saying, so we had to shout most of the time.

Speaker 3 The only time I've ever made a complaint about anything was when I went for a meal once **[Ex 1 H]** with my parents. I told the waiter the meat in my stew was chewy, and should have been left in the oven longer. My dad said he thought I'd been rude to the waiter, but my mum told me I was right to complain. Her attitude is, if something's not right, then kick up a fuss, make a noise about it, otherwise nothing will get changed. As it was, the waiter said he couldn't change it, but he wouldn't charge for my dessert. So I ordered the most expensive one on the menu!

Speaker 4 Recently, we treated ourselves to dinner in a five-star seafood restaurant. We'd heard several negative things about the place before we went: the food was overpriced, the waiters were too formal, you didn't get much on your plate … But we're not big eaters and we felt like spoiling ourselves, so we ignored the warnings and booked. Well, the food was to die for; the crab, the mussels, the seabass – absolutely delicious. And whoever said **[Ex 1 F]** the portions were small was lying. We just wished they'd been a bit quicker about bringing the food out. They certainly weren't in any hurry, and we'd run out of things to say to each other by the time the main course arrived.

Speaker 5 My wife and I are both quite fussy eaters, so if we eat out, there have to be plenty of dishes to choose from. Unfortunately, the restaurant in the **[Ex 1 C]** hotel we stayed at with our walking group offered hardly any choice at all – just a few starters and a couple of mains – so we only ate there once. We had no complaints about the food we actually ordered, and the service was second to none. In fact, most of the people from our group liked the place so much they had dinner there every evening. We might have come across as antisocial, but we preferred to eat in some of the other restaurants in the area.

LOOKING AFTER YOURSELF 12

Listening Part 3 Multiple matching

1 ▶ 12.1 You will hear five short extracts in which people are talking about a restaurant they went to. For questions 1–5, choose from the options (A–H) what each person says about the restaurant. Use the letters only once. There are three extra letters which you do not need to use.

A The food was too expensive.
B The restaurant was dirty.
C The menu was not varied enough.
D The food portions were too small.
E There was too much noise.
F The service was slow.
G The waiters were rude.
H The food was not well cooked.

Speaker 1 B 1
Speaker 2 E 2
Speaker 3 H 3
Speaker 4 F 4
Speaker 5 C 5

2 **SPEAK** Do any of the sentences A–H above apply to meals you have had in a restaurant? What are the best and the worst meals you have had?

175

12 LOOKING AFTER YOURSELF

Language focus Quantifiers

1 Complete each gap in the script from the listening with a word from the box.

any   couple   every   few   most   no   plenty   some

> My wife and I are both quite fussy eaters, so if we eat out, there have to be (1) __plenty__ of dishes to choose from. Unfortunately, the restaurant in the hotel we stayed at with our walking group offered hardly (2) __any__ choice at all – just a (3) __few__ starters and a (4) __couple__ of mains – so we only ate there once. We had (5) __no__ complaints about the food we actually ordered, and the service was second to none. In fact, (6) __most__ (*some* is also possible) of the people from our group liked the place so much they had dinner there (7) __every__ evening. We might have come across as antisocial, but we preferred to eat in (8) __some__ of the other restaurants in the area.

A large/massive/huge, etc. amount of is used before singular uncountable nouns. (*Variety* can be both countable or uncountable, but here it is used uncountably.)

A large/massive/huge etc. number of is used before plurals (*dishes*).

2 Underline the correct alternatives in the following sentence from the listening. Give reasons for your choices.

There wasn't a massive (1) <u>amount</u>/number of variety on the menu but, to be honest, I'd rather have just a few decent things to choose from than a huge (2) amount/<u>number</u> of dishes.

3 ▶ 12.2 Listen to check your answers to Exercises 1 and 2.

4 Go to **Ready for Grammar** on **page 230** for rules, explanations and further practice.

Reading and Use of English Part 7 Multiple matching

1 **SPEAK** Work in pairs. Discuss the following questions.
   1 What types of food can and can't vegans eat?
   2 Why do you think people become vegan?
   3 What are some of the difficulties that vegans face?

2 You are going to read an article in which people talk about becoming vegan. For questions 1–10, choose from the people (A–E). The people may be chosen more than once.

Which person states the following?

I received a great deal of help and advice from other vegans.	1 D
My attempts to reassure someone had the opposite effect.	2 B
I regret not having become a vegan before.	3 E
I understand someone's resistance to me going vegan.	4 A
Some people are not as supportive as they could be.	5 E
I lacked the necessary determination to be a vegan.	6 C
There were concerns that I was putting my health at risk.	7 B
It's important to make the change to a vegan diet gradually.	8 D
People are always surprised by how tasty vegan food can be.	9 A
Being vegan is a defining feature of my identity.	10 B

3 **SPEAK** If you are a vegan, why did you decide to become one? If you are not a vegan, do you think you might ever become one? Why/Why not?

12 LOOKING AFTER YOURSELF

Language focus

1–3 ▶ **12.2** If time allows, aim to cover all the material in this and the **Ready for Grammar** section on pages 230–231 (see below and TB177) in one lesson. Students work through Exercises 1 and 2 individually and then check their answers with a partner before listening to the recording.

4 Direct students to the **Ready for Grammar** section on page 230, where they can check their answers for Exercises 1–2 by reading the grammar explanation. Alternatively, you could elicit the rules for *amount/number* in open class before turning to the **Ready for Grammar** section. Highlight that we use *a lot of*, not *much*, in affirmative sentences, e.g. *I didn't spend much money/I spent a lot of money*. In their writing, students should be encouraged to use *a large amount of/a great deal of/a large number of* as alternatives to *a lot of*, particularly, though not exclusively, in tasks requiring more formal English, such as essays or reports (as in this unit). Using an example sentence, elicit that *of* is often reduced to one of its weak forms, /əv/ or /ə/, when it follows a quantifier, e.g. *couple of* moves from /ˈkʌpəl ɒv/ to /ˈkʌpələv/.

READY FOR GRAMMAR

12 Quantifiers

We use quantifiers to give information about the quantity of people or things. They tell us *how much* of something, or *how many* people or things there are.

1 Quantifiers can be used:
- before countable nouns: *both, a couple of, each, every, a few, (very) few, fewer, (not) many, several, a (large/small) number of*

  We saw **several** lions but **not many** giraffes.
- before uncountable nouns: *less, a little, (very) little, (not) much, a great deal of, a large/small amount of*

  I did **a great deal of** work, but made **little** progress.
- before both countable and uncountable nouns: *all, (hardly) any, enough, (quite) a lot of, lots of, a load of, loads of*, more, most, no, plenty of, some.*
  *Loads of and a load of are informal.

  I love **all types** of cheese; **all cheese** is delicious.

  Plenty of means *a lot of* or *more than enough*.

  Don't hurry – we've got **plenty of time**.

2 Most of the above quantifiers can be used with *of* + *the, this, that, these, those, my, your,* etc plus a noun, to talk about members of a specific group.

Add **a few of** the olives and **most of** the cheese.

of is optional with *all* and *both* before a noun.

All (of) my friends have seen **both (of)** those films.

The same quantifiers can be used with *of* plus a pronoun. *Of* is not optional with *all* or *both*.

The exam was easy, but **all of us** got **some of it** wrong.

None is used instead of *no* before *of*.

None of us got full marks in the exam.

Neither of is used instead of *none of* when talking about two people or things.

Neither of my parents is very sporty.

3 Most quantifiers can also be used as pronouns on their own. *Plenty of*, *a lot of*, *lots of*, etc are used without *of* in this case.

'How much money have you brought?' '**None**.'

'Have you got enough peas?' 'Yes, thanks, **plenty**.'

4 *each* and *every*

These two quantifiers are used with singular nouns and verbs to mean *all*. *Each* is used to talk about two or more people or things; *every* is only used to talk about more than two.

He held a glass in **each hand**.

Each/Every child who **takes** part **receives** a prize.

Each, but not *every*, can be used with *of*. A plural noun is used followed by a singular verb.

Each of my sisters was wearing a dress.

5 *little* and *few*

These two quantifiers have quite negative meanings. They mean *not much/many* or *not as much/many as desired or expected*.

This recipe requires **little time** and **few ingredients**.

6 *a little* and *a few*

These have more positive meanings. They mean *some* or *more than expected*.

After **a little practice** and **a few failures,** I made a perfect tortilla.

Quite a few means a fairly large number or quite a lot.

I've read **quite a few of her books**; maybe six or seven.

12 LOOKING AFTER YOURSELF

Reading and Use of English

1 If you don't think your students will necessarily know the answers to these questions, allow students to do some web-based research on their mobile phones. This could be done in English or the students' first language(s).

Possible answers

1 Vegans can eat all plant-based food but nothing which has involved the exploitation of animals, including meat, eggs, dairy produce, honey, etc.

2 People might become vegan for a variety of ethical, environmental and/or health reasons.

3 Some difficulties might include getting enough protein and other nutrients, as well as suffering criticism and misunderstanding.

2 Give your students no more than 12–15 minutes to finish this task.

3 Get open class feedback after the students have discussed the question in pairs.

READY FOR GRAMMAR

12 Quantifiers

1 Underline the two correct alternatives in each sentence. There is an example at the beginning (0).

0 I eat <u>plenty of</u> / a large amount of / very much / <u>very few</u> vegetables.

1 Lot / <u>None</u> / Each / <u>Most</u> of the food I eat is very healthy.

2 We eat <u>very little</u> / a small number of / <u>quite a lot of</u> / not many meat in our house.

3 I eat pizza <u>several</u> / every / <u>a couple of</u> / any times a week.

4 I do no / <u>hardly any</u> / <u>some</u> / few of the food shopping for my family.

5 I can cook a great deal of / <u>a large number of</u> / a little / <u>a few</u> different dishes.

6 How many spoonsful of sugar do I put in my coffee? <u>A lot</u> / <u>None</u> / Plenty of / Much.

7 At home, we eat <u>all</u> / some / every of / <u>most of</u> our meals in the kitchen.

2 **SPEAK** Tell your partner which of the two correct answers in each sentence in Exercise 1 is closer to the truth in your case. Develop your answers.

0 *I don't exactly eat plenty of vegetables but I do eat quite a few – perhaps four or five portions a week. I realise they're important, but I'm not very keen on them. The ones I hate the most are …*

Go back to page 176.

LOOKING AFTER YOURSELF **12**

GOING VEGAN

Five people share their experiences of becoming vegan.

A JACK

I first wanted to go vegan a few years ago, when I was about thirteen, and learnt about the effects of the meat industry on the environment. But my mum told me to wait until I was older and better informed about what being vegan meant. It was probably sound advice, though I now know it was partly because she couldn't face cooking special meals for me. I totally get that, though, and don't hold it against her. Now that I am a vegan, I'm very much aware of the extra effort involved for non-vegans who invite me round for a meal. I always offer to take a dessert, and the other dinner guests are invariably amazed at how delicious it is.

B SARAH

I went vegan when I left home and went away to university. My parents were worried I was missing out on essential nutrients and that this could have serious consequences for me. My dad had the biggest problem with it, and he kept sending me articles warning of the pitfalls of a plant-based diet. I tried to put his mind at rest by telling him I was taking supplements, but that just served to reinforce his idea that I wasn't eating properly. Over time, though, they've both gradually come to accept my change to veganism, and that's really important to me, because it's a major part of who I am. My dad even cooks some of the vegan recipes I send him.

C MAYA

My sister went vegan after she was diagnosed with an autoimmune disease which causes pain in the joints and tiredness. Her doctors encouraged her to follow a raw plant-based diet to help manage her symptoms, and I decided to support her by going vegan as well. My sister has kept at it faithfully for over five years and shown amazing willpower. I just wish I could say the same for myself. There were too many types of food I missed, and I threw in the towel after a few months. On the plus side, I learnt a surprising amount about nutrition and the health benefits of certain foods. I still eat loads of fruit, nuts, pulses and vegetables, and feel much healthier than I used to.

D JUSTIN

I started off by swapping one product at a time; soya milk for cow's milk, coconut oil for butter, maple syrup for honey. Many people try to make the switch overnight and it can prove too much, so they give up and go back to their vegetarian or meat-based diet. The key is to do it in stages. It gives you time to work out what works for you and what doesn't. While I was going vegan, I got loads of useful tips from a social media group I joined. If I had any questions or concerns, like which health supplements to take, how to reassure my parents I knew what I was doing, or where to buy vegan products, there was always someone who could give me the benefit of their knowledge and experience.

E RHONA

I've only recently changed to a plant-based diet. I wish I'd done it ages ago. I'd become increasingly aware of the suffering we cause to animals by what we eat, and I felt it was high time I took a stand against the way we treat them. It's not easy, though. My friends only ever want to meet up in burger restaurants, and my parents seem determined not to try vegan food, let alone cook it, which is disappointing – it's not asking much for them to show a little interest. So, anyway, I just cook all my meals for myself now. I'm gradually getting the hang of it, and I like the independence it brings.

177

12 LOOKING AFTER YOURSELF

Language focus Hypothetical situations

1 Complete each of the rules (1–3) with words from the box.

> the past perfect   the past simple   would

1. We use *wish/if only* + <u>the past simple</u> to express unhappiness with present situations, e.g. *I wish I had as much willpower as my sister.*
2. We use *wish/if only* + <u>would</u> to express irritation at other people's actions or behaviour, e.g. *If only people would treat animals with more respect.*
3. We use *wish/if only* + <u>the past perfect</u> to express regrets about things that happened or didn't happen in the past, e.g. *I've only just changed to a plant-based diet. I wish I'd done it ages ago.*

2 Choose the correct alternative in the following sentences.

1. It's time you <u>went</u> / *will go* / *go* to bed now.
2. I'd rather you <u>didn't</u> / *wouldn't* / *mustn't* tell anyone – it's a secret.

3 Go to **Ready for Grammar** on **page 232** to check your answers to Exercises 1 and 2 and for further practice.

4 You have decided to spend the day complaining, telling different people how you would like them to change! The people you are going to speak to are:

- your mother or father
- your brother, sister or cousin
- one of your friends
- a neighbour
- the leader of your country
- another person of your choice.

Write one sentence for each person beginning with one of the following phrases:

I wish you …   It's time you …   I'd rather you …

5 SPEAK Explain to your partner why you would say each of the sentences.

> *I'd say to my dad, 'I wish you would stop telling bad jokes.' When I was younger I used to think his jokes were funny, but not anymore. It's embarrassing when …*

Reading and Use of English Part 2 Open cloze

1 SPEAK Look at the title of the text below. What do you think the text will say?

2 Read the text quite quickly, ignoring the gaps. Are any of the ideas you discussed in Exercise 1 mentioned?

3 Read the text again and for questions 1–8 and think of the word which best fits each gap. Use only one word in each gap. There is an example at the beginning (0).

Sleep myths

Modern living places great demands **(0)** <u>ON</u> our time, and as we try to balance work or school pressures with leisure and social commitments, **(1)** <u>it</u> is often our sleep that suffers. We would **(2)** <u>rather/sooner</u> spend fewer hours sleeping than give up time dedicated to family, friends and free-time activities. Yet this disregard for the importance of sleep is putting our health **(3)** <u>at</u> risk, and can lead to serious issues such as heart disease, obesity and diabetes.

A recent study carried **(4)** <u>out</u> at NYU School of Medicine has identified a number of widely held myths which contribute to the problem. Most damaging of all is some people's belief that they can **(5)** <u>get</u> by on just five hours' sleep and suffer absolutely **(6)** <u>no</u> harmful effects. Also, it seems, taking naps when you routinely have difficulty sleeping at night **(7)** <u>is</u> not the solution. The researchers, led by Rebecca Robbins, PhD, suggest **(8)** <u>we</u> create a regular sleep routine for ourselves, and aim to sleep for at least seven hours a night.

4 SPEAK Do you sleep enough hours each night? Why/Why not? What do you think would be a sensible sleep routine for you?

LOOKING AFTER YOURSELF 12

Language focus

1–3 Aim to get through all the material in this and the *Ready for Grammar* section in one lesson if possible. Books closed. Project or show a picture of an old man feeling sad. Board *I wish* and *If only*. Explain that the man is unhappy with his life and has many regrets. Ask the students to imagine what he is thinking. Model a few sentences about both the present and past, e.g. *I wish I lived in the countryside instead of this noisy city. If only I had travelled more. Now it's too late.* In pairs, students think of other examples. Books open. Once students have completed the rules in Exercises 1 and 2, direct them to the *Ready for Grammar* section on pages 232–233 (see below and TB179). You could make a link to the earlier conditionals lesson on page 165 by eliciting that we use past forms after *I wish/If only/It's time/I'd rather* just as we do for the second, third and mixed conditionals, which also describe unreal or hypothetical situations. Point out that sentences with *if only* start with *if* like other conditional clauses but are frequently used without the second clause, e.g. *If only we could move into a bigger place.*

4–5 While the students write their sentences, monitor their use of the target language. Write down any interesting emergent language from this **SPEAK** activity to put up on board and discuss afterwards.

Reading and Use of English

1–2 A good lead-in to this task would be to enter the words 'Rebecca Robbins NYU Sleep myths' into your search engine and watch the short video. Ask the students to take notes and then discuss them in pairs afterwards. Was anything surprising? They can then skim the text and see if any of the ideas from the video are mentioned.

3 You should aim to get your students moving through these shorter Use of English tasks at a good pace. Time is short on the official exam.

4 Board *If only, I wish, I hope, It's time*. Tell the students to use at least one sentence with the grammar for hypothetical situations during their conversations.

READY FOR GRAMMAR

12 Hypothetical situations

Wish and if only

Wish or *if only* can express how we would like things to be different if we had the power to change them. *If only* is often considered more dramatic than *wish*.

1 We use *wish/if only* + past simple when we are unhappy about a present situation and would like it to be different, even though this may not be possible. Stative verbs such as *be, have, know, live* and *understand* are used.

I wish I was/were taller.

If only I knew how to play the guitar.

2 We use *wish/if only* + *would* when we want something to happen or someone to do something. Active verbs (verbs describing actions) are used.

I wish you would go away.

If only this wind would stop blowing.

Wish/if only + *would* is used if we want to express irritation at other peoples' actions or behaviour.

I wish you wouldn't keep tapping your foot.

Wish/if only + past simple can also be used if the action occurs habitually.

I wish you didn't/wouldn't smoke so much.

If the subject of *wish* is the same as the subject of the verb which follows (*I wish I ..., she wishes she ...* etc), we use *could*, not *would*.

I wish I could remember the name of that actor.

3 *Wish/if only* + *would* or *could* can be used to express wishes for the future. This use of *wish* suggests that the action will probably not happen.

I wish I could go on holiday with you in summer. (I know that I can't go with you.)

If there is more possibility that the action will happen, we use *hope*.

I hope I can go on holiday with you in summer. (I don't know if I can or not.)

4 We use *wish/if only* + past perfect to express wishes and regrets about the past.

I wish I hadn't left school when I was 16.

should have + past participle can also be used to express wishes and regrets about the past.

We **should have got** the train. This traffic's terrible.

Would rather/sooner

We use *would rather/sooner* + past simple when we want someone else to do something in the present or future.

I'd rather/sooner you told Leah the news yourself.

[Compare: **I'd rather/sooner tell** Leah the news myself.]

It's time

We use *it's (high/about) time* + past simple when we want something to happen or be done now. It implies that the action should have been done already.

It's high time we bought a new car – this one's far too unreliable.

12 LOOKING AFTER YOURSELF

Vocabulary

1-2 You could lead into this vocabulary section with a quick review of the parts of the body. Check the pronunciation of *stomach* /ˈstʌmək/, *ache* /eɪk/ and *throat* /θrəʊt/. See the **Extra activity** boxes on TB118 and TB160 for additional ideas for practising collocations.

3 Check the pronunciation of *stitches* /ˈstɪtʃɪz/, *bandage* /ˈbændɪdʒ/, *receipt* /rɪˈsiːt/ and *recipe* /ˈresəpi/. If time allows, ask the students to write new sentences in order to make some of the wrong answers right, e.g. Jason cut his leg quite badly and he still has a couple of scars.

4 Elicit the meaning of the collocations in bold with concept check questions.
- cold (noun) – *an illness that affects the nose and/or throat, making you cough, sneeze, etc. A heavy cold is a particularly bad one.*
- burn (verb) – *to destroy, damage, injure by fire or extreme heat.*
- sting (verb) – *to touch your skin or make a very small hole in it so that you feel a sharp pain*
- faint (adjective) – *feeling weak and tired and likely to become unconscious.*
- nose bleed (noun) – *flow of blood from the nose.*

READY FOR GRAMMAR

12 Hypothetical situations

1 In 1–5 below, underline the correct alternative in each sentence.
1. I wish I <u>could</u> / would / did remember where I put my glasses.
2. I wish I don't / <u>didn't</u> / won't have to do so much homework. I never have any time to myself.
3. The car has broken down again! I'm beginning to wish we wouldn't buy / didn't buy / <u>hadn't bought</u> it.
4. I wish they didn't / <u>would</u> / had turn their music down next door. I can't hear myself think.
5. If only you'll listen / you'd have listened / <u>you'd listened</u> to me! None of this would have happened.

2 In 1–8 below complete each gap with the correct form of the verb in brackets.
1. What glorious sunshine! I bet you wish you **were** (*be*) on the beach right now, don't you?
2. I wish you two **would stop** (*stop*) shouting! You're driving me mad!
3. It has rained every day of this holiday. If only we **had/'d gone** (*go*) to Greece instead!
4. If only I **had** (*have*) more time. There are so many films I want to see.
5. One minute you want to come, the next minute you don't. I wish you **would/'d make** (*make*) up your mind!
6. It's time you **bought** (*buy*) some new trainers. Those ones are falling apart.
7. I'd rather nobody **knew** (*know*) I've applied for the job, so don't tell anyone.
8. Jill wants to go out for a meal, but I'd rather **eat** (*eat*) at home.

Go back to **page 178**.

LOOKING AFTER YOURSELF 12

Vocabulary Health

1 In parts A and B below complete the collocations with one of the words from the box.

A

| blood ear heart ~~nose~~ stomach tooth |

0 If you get a **___nose___ bleed**, pinch it with two fingers until it stops.
1 She'll have a **___heart___ attack** when she sees what you've done!
2 He'll have serious **___tooth___ decay** if he doesn't clean them regularly.
3 Of course he has a **___stomach___ ache**. He ate far too many cream cakes.
4 With such high **___blood___ pressure** you should eat less salt.
5 She's got a bad **___ear___ infection** so she can't come swimming.

B

| ankle eye neck nose throat |

1 That's a nasty **black ___eye___**. Did somebody hit you?
2 She's got a very **sore ___throat___**. She can hardly speak.
3 I've got a **stiff ___neck___**. It hurts when I turn my head.
4 You've got a **runny ___nose___**. Would you like a handkerchief?
5 It's just a badly **sprained ___ankle___**. You haven't broken anything.

2 Study the collocations in the shaded boxes in Exercise 1 for one minute, then cover up the words on the right in each one. How many can you remember?

3 Choose the correct alternative in each sentence.
   1 Jason cut his leg quite badly and needed fifteen *points / scars / stitches*.
   2 You've cut your finger. You should put a *blister / plaster / sticker* on it.
   3 When I broke my arm, I had it in *plaster / bandage / wrapping* for about 5 weeks.
   4 The doctor gave me a *receipt / recipe / prescription* for a course of antibiotics.
   5 The nurse *put / gave / made* him an injection in his arm to help him sleep.

4 **SPEAK** Work in pairs. Discuss the following questions.
   1 Have you recently suffered any of the medical problems in Exercise 1?
   2 What help or advice would you give to somebody who:
      a has **a heavy cold**?
      b has **burnt their hand** with hot water?
      c has been **stung by a wasp**?
      d is **feeling faint**?
      e has **a nose bleed**?

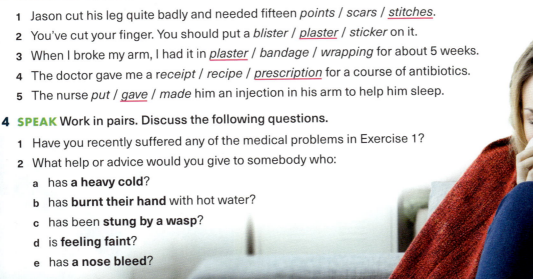

12 LOOKING AFTER YOURSELF

Listening Part 4 Multiple choice

1 **SPEAK** The photograph shows a woman working with a personal trainer. What do you think the job of a personal trainer involves?

2 **◉ 12.3** You will hear an interview with a personal trainer. For questions 1–7, choose the best answer (A, B or C).

1 When Naomi takes on a new client, what is the first thing she does?
  A give the client advice on what food to eat
  B ask the client to do some basic exercises
  (C) find out the client's personal aims

2 Naomi says she has specialist knowledge in helping
  A athletes improve their performance.
  (B) sportspeople recover from injury.
  C older people control their diet.

3 What quality does Naomi believe a personal trainer should have?
  (A) a sense of fun
  B a love of hard work
  C an ability to impose discipline

4 How does Naomi's business differ from that of other personal trainers in the area?
  A She operates from her converted garage.
  (B) She conducts some of her classes outdoors.
  C She has a large number of exercise machines.

5 What did Naomi find frustrating in her job at the gym?
  (A) The clients changed frequently.
  B There were too many clients.
  C The clients were treated badly.

6 Naomi finally decided to leave her job at the gym when she was asked to
  A work at weekends.
  B wear specific clothes.
  (C) sell the gym's products.

7 How does Naomi find new clients?
  (A) Her existing clients recommend her to others.
  B She advertises for clients in the local press.
  C Her previous employer sends her clients.

3 **SPEAK** If you had a personal trainer, what would your aims be? What do you do to keep fit and healthy?

LOOKING AFTER YOURSELF 12

Listening

1 Alternatively, you could lead into this listening with a 'speed dating' activity. Arrange the chairs in two rows so students sit facing one another. Students in row A are clients; in row B, they are personal trainers. They talk for two minutes. At the end of the time, students on one side move one seat to their left. Repeat the activity at least three or four times. The goal is for personal trainers to get as many clients as possible. The clients must decide which person they would prefer to hire as a personal trainer.

2 ▶ 12.3 Hand out copies of the official marksheets for the listening paper (available on the **Student's** and **Teacher's Resource Centres**), to give your students practice transferring their answers. It's important to do this accurately on the day of the test.

3 Students discuss the questions in pairs. After rounding off the activity in open class, write a few common errors on the board and invite the students to self-correct.

AUDIOSCRIPT

Listening   Part 4 Multiple choice

▶ 12.3

I = Interviewer   N = Naomi Price

I: On Health Matters today we have personal trainer Naomi Price. Naomi, what exactly does a personal trainer do?

N: Well, my main aim is to improve people's quality of life and overall health. So besides helping them develop their fitness, strength and posture, I also work on their diet and lifestyle habits. Of course, **each client has their own specific, individual goals, so before we do anything I carry out a needs analysis in order to establish exactly what it is they want to achieve.** This includes asking them about their eating habits, their injury history and any medical complaints or conditions, such as high blood pressure. Then basically, I design exercise routines and give advice on nutrition in response to the information they give me. *(Ex 2 Q1)*

I: And what reasons do clients have for coming to see you?

N: Oh, there's a wide range. I get a lot of clients, especially older ones, who simply want to lose a bit of weight or lower their cholesterol levels. I also have a large number of younger **clients who've been injured while doing sport and want to get back to full fitness – that's my area of expertise.** I also help one or two people train for marathons and triathlons, but mostly it's people who just want to improve their all-round fitness and as a result, their general self-confidence. *(Ex 2 Q2)*

I: And I imagine it's important to build up a good relationship with your clients.

N: Yes, it is. I'm not one of those fitness instructors you sometimes see in films shouting orders at people to do fifty press-ups or run ten times round the park. Certainly, clients have to be dedicated and prepared to work hard when they're with me, but I also want them to enjoy exercising as well. **So it's important, I think, for trainers to keep it light-hearted, introduce an element of playfulness into their sessions.** There's usually a fair amount of laughter in mine. *(Ex 2 Q3)*

I: Now, your workplace is your garage, isn't it, Naomi?

N: Well, yes, what used to be my garage. I don't park my car there any more – it's full of equipment. There's a rowing machine, two treadmills, two exercise bikes and loads of weights and things. I've also got a massage table, but that's in my lounge, where it's warmer. And then with some people **I go to the park or a nearby wood to run** or simply to add a bit of variety to the classes. Clients appreciate that – **they've told me that other local trainers they've been with always hold their sessions inside.** *(Ex 2 Q4)*

I: You haven't always been your own boss have you?

N: No, I used to work in a gym. The good thing about that was I learnt a lot from watching the other gym instructors and their interaction with the clients – both good and bad examples. I also got experience of working with a lot of different clients, but **the trouble was, I rarely had the chance to build up longlasting relationships with them. The client list was different every month** – someone would join the gym in April, say, and by June they'd be gone. *(Ex 2 Q5)*

I: And is that why you left?

N: It wasn't the only reason. I was getting tired of working on Saturdays, for one thing – I'd only had two or three Saturdays free in over a year. But **it was the whole sales thing that I was least happy about. When they told me I had to persuade people to buy things with the gym's logo on it, that's when I made the decision to resign.** I didn't feel comfortable pushing T-shirts and baseball caps, or things like protein supplements, which most people take without needing to. It just wasn't my style. *(Ex 2 Q6)*

I: Are you pleased you became self-employed?

N: Oh, yes, I've got so much more freedom, and so far, touch wood, things are going really well. I thought I might have to put adverts in the local newspaper to get business but **those clients I brought with me from the gym tell all their family and friends about me and those people tell all their friends … and so it goes on. The power of word of mouth.** *(Ex 2 Q7)*

I: Let's hope your success continues, Naomi. Thank you for coming in to the studio.

TB180

12 LOOKING AFTER YOURSELF

Language focus

1-3 Students do Exercises 1–3 individually and then check with a partner. Before turning to the **Ready for Grammar** section (see below and TB182), draw students' attention to numbers 1 and 2 in Exercise 2. Elicit that the verb after the gap is different to the subject of the verb before it. You could also remind students about the following rule with *despite* from page 220 in the **Ready for Grammar** section: 'If the subject of the gerund is different to the subject of the main verb, a noun, an object pronoun or possessive adjective is added, e.g. *She paid for the meal despite me/my telling her not to*.' Elicit what pronoun would be used instead of *Sam* (Exercise 2, 1) or *the cat* (Exercise 2, 2). In the **Ready for Grammar** section, if students find Exercise 2 tricky, you can project the following clues on the board:

- 1 & 5 The word *how* is needed in the answers to both of these.
- 2 The expression required here first appeared on page 8 in Unit 1.
- 4 Look again at sentences 1 & 2 in Exercise 2 on page 181.
- 5 What phrasal verb means 'discover'?

4-5 Students do the exercise as suggested. Monitor their use of the target language.

You may wish to use the **Sentence endings game** on the **Teacher's Resource Centre** to extend this lesson.

READY FOR GRAMMAR

12 Prepositions and gerunds

1 Verbs which come immediately after prepositions must be in the gerund form.
   *Craig was told off **for crossing** the road **without looking**.*

   If the subject of the gerund is different to the subject of the main verb, we add a noun, object pronoun or possessive adjective.
   *We're not happy about **James** riding a motorbike.*
   *They insisted on **me/my** showing them the photos.*

2 These noun + preposition combinations are commonly followed by gerunds:
   (be no/little) point in, (have) difficulty in, (be or have a good/not much/no) chance of, (be in) favour of, (have an/no) objection to
   *There's no **point in inviting** her; she won't come.*
   *Is there any **chance of you playing** tennis later?*

3 Gerunds are used after a number of phrasal verbs containing prepositions, such as *carry on, get over, give up, look forward to, move on to, put off, put up with, take to, turn to.*
   *He **gave up phoning** her and **took to texting** her poems.*
   *I can't **put up with Jason and Lee arguing** all the time.*

4 These linking words and expressions can also be used as prepositions and followed by a gerund: *after, apart from, as a result of, as well as, before, besides, despite, in addition to, in spite of, instead of.*
   ***Apart from tasting** great, it's also very good for you.*
   *She opened the window, **despite me asking** her not to.*

LOOKING AFTER YOURSELF 12

Language focus Prepositions and gerunds

1 In Unit 2 you saw that if a verb follows a preposition, the gerund is used. Complete the gaps in these extracts from the listening with a preposition.

1 And what reasons do clients have ___for___ coming to see you?
2 I learnt a lot ___from___ watching the other gym instructors ...
3 I was getting tired ___of___ working on Saturdays ...
4 ... protein supplements, which most people take ___without___ needing to.

2 Gerunds are also used after phrasal verbs which end in a preposition.

*I've **given up trying** to lose weight; I like food too much.*

In 1–5 complete each gap with a preposition.

1 I'm **looking forward** ___to___ Sam **coming** tomorrow: I haven't seen her for ages.
2 Raul isn't ready for a new pet yet: he still hasn't **got** ___over___ his cat **dying** last year.
3 Breakfast in the hotel wasn't brilliant, but it won't **put** us ___off___ **going** back there next year.
4 When I was in my forties I gave up all team sports and **took** ___up___ **playing** golf instead.
5 Many people choose to **carry** ___on___ **working** after their official retirement age.

3 Go to **Ready for Grammar** on **page 232** for rules, explanations and further practice.

4 Complete three of the sentence beginnings below. Use a gerund immediately after the prepositions in bold. Two of your sentences should be true and one should be a lie.

- I'm looking forward **to** ...
- I've decided to give **up** ...
- Yesterday, I was told off **for** ...
- I have a very good chance **of** ...
- I have great difficulty **in** ...
- I'm very good **at** ...

5 **SPEAK** Work in pairs. Ask questions about your partner's sentences in Exercise 4. Then guess which one is a lie.

12 LOOKING AFTER YOURSELF

Word formation Nouns 2

1 Complete each gap with the correct noun form of the verb in brackets.

I carry out a needs (1) __analysis__ (*analyse*) … This includes asking them about their eating habits, their (2) __injury__ (*injure*) history and any medical (3) __complaints__ (*complain*) or conditions, such as high blood (4) __pressure__ (*press*). Then basically, I design exercise routines and give (5) __advice__ (*advise*) on nutrition in (6) __response__ (*respond*) to the information they give me.

2 Check your answers in the Audioscript on page 246.

3 In 1–8, form nouns by adding the same suffix from the box to all four words in each group. You may need to make further spelling changes. There is an example at the beginning (0).

-age -al -cy -ight -ing -ship -th -ure ~~-y~~

0 honest	difficult	safe	poor
honesty	*difficulty*	*safety*	*poverty*
1 say	meet	build	advertise
saying	*meeting*	*building*	*advertising*
2 fail	depart	please	sign
failure	*departure*	*pleasure*	*signature*
3 arrive	refuse	survive	approve
arrival	*refusal*	*survival*	*approval*
4 warm	deep	true	grow
warmth	*depth*	*truth*	*growth*
5 fly	see	weigh	high
flight	*sight*	*weight*	*height*
6 friend	member	champion	partner
friendship	*membership*	*championship*	*partnership*
7 short	store	pack	marry
shortage	*storage*	*package*	*marriage*
8 accurate	efficient	vacant	frequent
accuracy	*efficiency*	*vacancy*	*frequency*

4 Complete each gap with an appropriate noun formed from the word in brackets. The first one has been done for you.

1 __Laughter__ (*laugh*) is the best medicine.
2 The secret of __success__ (*succeed*) is hard work.
3 Too much __choice__ (*choose*) is a bad thing.
4 A little __knowledge__ (*know*) is a dangerous thing.
5 The worst thing about becoming famous is the __loss__ (*lose*) of __privacy__ (*private*).
6 Protecting freedom of __speech__ (*speak*) is more important than protecting people from being offended.
7 There is no __proof__ (*prove*) that alien life exists.
8 Your __beliefs__ (*believe*) don't make you a better person, your __behaviour__ (*behave*) does.

5 SPEAK Work in small groups. Discuss each of the statements in Exercise 4.

Writing Part 2 Report

1 SPEAK Read the following Part 2 task. Which places would you recommend in your area? Why?

A group of foreign students is going to be staying in your area for a month this summer. They are keen to keep fit during their stay and the group leader has asked you to write a report giving advice on the best places to go running, swimming and cycling. In your report you should explain why these places will be of interest to the group.

LOOKING AFTER YOURSELF 12

Word formation

1-2 You could start this lesson by revisiting the suffixes in the Word formation section on page 35 in Unit 3, which also focuses on nouns. When students check their answers to Exercise 1, remind them that spelling is important in this part of the exam. Highlight the change in pronunciation in *analyse* /ˈænəlaɪz/ and *analysis* /əˈnæləsɪs/.

3 You may want to put students into pairs for this exercise if you think they will find it challenging. Fast finishers can mark up the word stress. Note that this type of exercise is most efficiently corrected by displaying the answers or directing the students to the **Answer key** (at the back of the book or on the **Student's Resource Centre**). Highlight the change in pronunciation in *please* /pliːz/ and *pleasure* /ˈpleʒə(r)/, *sign* /saɪn/ and *signature* /ˈsɪɡnətʃə(r)/, *deep* /diːp/ and *depth* /depθ/, *see* /siː/ and *sight* /saɪt/. Make note of any words students have trouble spelling and revise these at the end of the lesson.

4 Elicit the change in pronunciation in *know* /nəʊ/ and *knowledge* /ˈnɒlɪdʒ/, *lose* /luːz/ and *loss* /lɒs/. Before moving onto the **SPEAK** activity, encourage students to put a tick next to any new words (or ones they had trouble spelling) that they would like to write down later in the Word formation section of their vocabulary notebooks.

5 Monitor students' use and pronunciation of the target language. Any other common mistakes can be written down and discussed in open class during a corrective feedback stage.

READY FOR GRAMMAR

12 Prepositions and gerunds

1 Complete each sentence on the left so that it has a similar meaning to the sentence on the right. In the first gap write one of the words from the box; in the second gap write an appropriate preposition.

> chance   difficulty   favour   objection   point

1 He'll have no ___difficulty___ ___in___ doing it. — He will find it easy to do.
2 There's not much ___chance___ ___of___ him doing it. — He's very unlikely to do it.
3 There's no ___point___ ___in___ him doing it. — It's senseless for him to do it.
4 I have no ___objection___ ___to___ him doing it. — I don't mind him doing it.
5 We were all in ___favour___ ___of___ him doing it. — We all wanted him to do it.

2 For questions 1–6, complete the second sentence so that it has a similar meaning to the first sentence, using the word given. Do not change the word given. You must use between two and five words, including the word given.

1 Paul eats lots of fried food, even though he knows it's very bad for his health.
  UNHEALTHY
  Paul eats lots of fried food despite ___knowing how **unhealthy**___ it is for him.

2 Although I threw away a lot of my old clothes, I still don't have much room in my wardrobe.
  RID
  In spite ___of getting **rid** of___ a lot of my old clothes, I still don't have much room in my wardrobe.

3 Rachel decided not to drive to work, and went there by bus.
  INSTEAD
  Rachel decided to get the bus to work ___**instead** of driving___ there.

4 Sven missed the meeting because his flight was delayed by three hours.
  RESULT
  Sven missed the meeting as a ___**result** of his flight being___ delayed by three hours.

5 She discovered the age of the vase, and also learnt that it had once belonged to royalty.
  OUT
  As well ___as finding **out** how___ old the vase was, she learnt that it had once belonged to royalty.

6 He's a good guitar player, and he also has an excellent singing voice.
  WELL
  In addition ___to playing the guitar **well**___, he has an excellent singing voice.

Go back to **page 181**.

12 LOOKING AFTER YOURSELF

Writing

Note: if your class are taking the *B2 First for Schools* exam, please use the **B2 First for Schools** writing lessons on the Teacher's Resource Centre. Writing a report is not an option on this version of the exam.

1 Students discuss the task in pairs. During open class feedback, make a mind map of the students' ideas on the board, with bubbles for *running*, *swimming* and *cycling*. Ask the students to justify why these are particularly good places to do these activities.

2 Remind students to ignore the gaps for now. After they have read the report, discuss any similarities or differences to the places on the board.

3 Linking words are one thing examiners will be looking for specifically when they read students' writing. If students use them effectively, it will improve their mark in *organisation*, one of the four categories in the official marking criteria. See the **Teaching tips** on TB108 and TB153 for more information about how the writing paper is marked.

4 This exercise helps students identify a more subtle organisational pattern that creates cohesion and helps guide the reader through a text. If used, this kind of pattern will also improve students' marks in *organisation*.

5 Remind students that *content* is 25% of their writing mark. Point out that, in comparison to the other three criteria, it's relatively easy for candidates to get the highest mark in *content* if they carefully read the task and include all the points in their answers.

6 Focus the students' attention on the **Don't forget!** and **Useful Language** boxes after they have read the task. Note that the information in this box could be adapted into a checklist for students to complete along with their report, e.g. *Does each paragraph have a heading?* The final writing assignment could be done in class or at home, but it must be done to a strict time limit of 40 minutes in either case.

As you come to the end of the course you may wish to use **Who can remember most?** and **A future interview** on the Teacher's Resource Centre to help student's reflect on what they have learnt.

Sample answer

Report

The aim of this report is to tell you the best places to eat cheaply in my area and say why. I will also say why, in addition to the reasons of cost, I think the students will enjoy eating in these places.

Where can you eat cheaply

If I were you, I'd go to the shopping centre out of town. Here there are many restaurants from different countries like Italian, Mexico, Chinese, Spanish and also Greece. In addition you eat very well and it is not espensive, you can do shopping or see a film in the cinema which is there. The students will enjoy to see a film after they eat.

Furthermore, I recommend you the area next the sea. Here are many good restaurants for eating fish and the prices are affordable. The best restaurant is 'Ocean Blue' where everything is blue, example chairs, tables, walls etc. The fish is catched local and is delicious. Also, the atmosphere is pleasant, friendly and lively.

Conclusions

To sum up, the students can eat tasty, delicious and cheap food in the shopping centre and next the sea.

Regina

189 words

Examiner's comments

Content: All content is relevant and the group leader would be fully informed. Two distinct places are mentioned for restaurants: the shopping centre and by the sea, and a number of reasons are given as to why students will enjoy eating in each location.

Communicative achievement: The conventions of writing a report are used reasonably well to hold the reader's attention, and the register is neutral and generally consistent, though *If I were you, I'd* and *Also* at the beginning of the penultimate sentence are more informal. Sub-headings are simple but useful, although the main heading does not give the reader a clear idea of the contents of the report that follows.

Organisation: The text is clearly divided into appropriate sections. Some conventional linking devices are used, such as *Furthermore* and *To sum up*, but *In addition* is used inaccurately in the second paragraph (*In addition you eat very well*) and *for* is missing from *for example*.

Language: Everyday vocabulary is adequate and there is some appropriate use of relevant adjectives (*affordable; pleasant; friendly; lively; tasty; delicious*). The word *expensive* is misspelt. More of an effort could have been made to reword the opening paragraph, which is almost identical to the question.

A range of simple and some more complex grammatical forms is used. While some errors occur when these more complex forms are attempted (*In addition you eat very well; I recommend you (go to) the area*), others are more basic (*enjoy to see; next the sea; catched local*). These errors, however, do not impede communication.

Mark: Pass to good pass

LOOKING AFTER YOURSELF 12

2 Read the following answer to the task in Exercise 1, ignoring the gaps. How similar is the area described in the report to the area in which you live?

Introduction
The aim of this report is to describe the best places in this area for your students to go running, cycling and swimming during their stay here.

Running
The town has one of the longest promenades in the country. As (1) ___well___ as being wide and flat, it offers spectacular views out to sea. A run (2) ___here___ just before breakfast is the perfect way for your students to start the day and prepare themselves mentally for their English classes.

Cycling
Cycling is forbidden on the promenade, (3) ___but___ there is a cycle path on the outskirts of town, (4) ___where___ your students can burn a few calories after class. (5) ___This___ takes cyclists through an area of woods and hills, with more superb views of the town and the sea.

Swimming
Swimming in the sea is not recommended, (6) ___as___ the water is not particularly clean. (7) ___However___, there is a lake just outside the town, (8) ___which___ is pleasant to swim in and less crowded than the town's swimming pool.

Conclusion
This area offers plenty of opportunities to keep fit and your students will be able to do sport and enjoy beautiful scenery at the same time.

3 All answers for the Writing paper should contain evidence of linking. Eight words which link ideas in the report above have been removed. Complete each gap (1–8) with a word from the box.

| as | but | here | however | this | well | where | which |

4 How has the writer of the report created links between
1 the paragraphs on running and cycling? In the paragraph on running, the writer refers to the promenade. He/She then begins the paragraph on cycling with *Cycling is forbidden on the promenade, but* …
2 the paragraphs on cycling and swimming? The writer finishes the paragraph on cycling by mentioning the views of the sea. He/She then begins the paragraph on swimming with *Swimming in the sea is not recommended, as* …

5 You must address all the points in the question. Underline those sections of the report above where the writer has addressed the point: *you should explain why these places will be of interest to the group.*

Running – A run here just before breakfast is the perfect way for your students to start the day …

6 Write an answer to the following Writing Part 2 task.

A group of foreign students is going to be staying in your area for a month. You have been asked to write a report for the group leader giving advice on eating out. Describe the best places to eat cheaply in your area and say why, in addition to the reasons of cost, you think the students will enjoy eating in these places.

Write your report in 140–190 words.

Useful language

The food is cheap/inexpensive/reasonably priced/affordable.
The price is/prices are low/reasonable/competitive/affordable.
The atmosphere is pleasant/friendly/relaxed/lively.
The portions are generous/huge/(more than) adequate.
The food is tasty/delicious/healthy/homemade.

Don't forget!
> Plan your answer before you write.
> Give each paragraph a heading.
> Address all the points in the question.
> Use a variety of linking devices.
> Write in a neutral or formal style.

For more information on writing reports, see **pages 56–57** in Unit 4, and **page 196** in Ready for Writing.

183

12 REVIEW

Reading and Use of English Part 4 Key word transformation

For questions 1–6 complete the second sentence so that it has a similar meaning to the first sentence, using the word given. Do not change the word given. You must use between two and five words, including the word given.

1 I don't weigh as much as I did when I last saw you.

   LOST

   I ____**have/'ve lost (some) weight since**____ I last saw you.

2 I'm amazed by how much he knows about wild flowers.

   OF

   His ____**knowledge of wild flowers amazes**____ me.

3 'There'll be very few people at the meeting tomorrow,' she told Roger.

   NOT

   She told Roger there ____**would not be (very) many**____ people at the meeting the next day.

4 It's a pity we don't live nearer the school.

   CLOSER

   I wish we ____**lived/could live closer to**____ the school.

5 I really regret not accepting that part-time job offer.

   WISH

   I really ____**wish I had not/hadn't turned**____ down that part-time job offer.

6 My parents would prefer me not to wear jeans to the wedding.

   RATHER

   My parents would ____**rather I did not/didn't wear**____ jeans to the wedding.

Reading and Use of English Part 3 Word formation

For questions 1–8, read the text below. Use the word given in capitals at the end of some of the lines to form a word that fits in the gap in the same line. There is an example at the beginning (0).

FLEXITARIANISM

Eating, of course, is a **(0)** _NECESSITY_, but a study published by a team of **(1)** _scientists_, led by Dr Marco Springmann of the University of Oxford, warns of the dangers of our diet for the planet. Food production is already responsible for releasing huge amounts of carbon dioxide into the atmosphere. It also brings about deforestation and the **(2)** _loss_ of freshwater sources. With the continued **(3)** _growth_ in population, the problem will get worse, as the **(4)** _pressure_ on resources increases. To reduce our carbon footprint, and at the same time improve our health, the **(5)** _advice_ of the study is that we should adopt a flexitarian diet, which is mostly vegetarian yet still allows for the **(6)** _occasional_ dish containing meat or other animal products. This could cut greenhouse gas emissions from agriculture by more than half. A **(7)** _failure_ to take action, on the other hand, could have serious consequences for the planet and may lead to our **(8)** _inability_ to feed ourselves in the future.	**NECESSARY** **SCIENCE** **LOSE** **GROW** **PRESS** **ADVISE** **OCCASION** **FAIL** **ABLE**

184

REVIEW 12

Reading and Use of English   Part 1 Multiple-choice cloze

For questions 1–8, read the text below and decide which answer (A, B, C or D) best fits each gap. There is an example at the beginning (0).

THE DANGERS OF A SEDENTARY LIFESTYLE

Evidence **(0)** ..C.. that a sedentary lifestyle can have a serious **(1)** ..C.. on your health. According to the World Heart Foundation, physical inactivity **(2)** ..B.. the risk of heart disease by 50%.

You should, therefore, **(3)** ..A.. of spending too long in front of your computer without taking breaks. Sitting for lengthy periods at your desk may cause your shoulders, neck and upper back to become **(4)** ..C.., and you are likely to become increasingly unproductive as your concentration begins to wander. In an attempt to remedy this, you may try to keep yourself going with junk food, sweetened coffee or **(5)** ..D.. drinks, leading to weight gain and perhaps even high blood **(6)** ..D...

If taking time out for vigorous exercise is not a possibility, you should at least get up from your desk at regular **(7)** ..A.. to do stretching exercises or walk around. Drink **(8)** ..C.. of water too – it improves concentration, and the resulting trips to the toilet will keep you active.

0	A advises	B warns	C <u>suggests</u>	D persuades
1	A harm	B damage	C <u>effect</u>	D importance
2	A rises	B <u>increases</u>	C gains	D grows
3	A <u>beware</u>	B avoid	C discourage	D care
4	A tough	B hurtful	C <u>stiff</u>	D intense
5	A floppy	B foggy	C furry	D <u>fizzy</u>
6	A tenseness	B movement	C problem	D <u>pressure</u>
7	A <u>intervals</u>	B interruptions	C stops	D delays
8	A much	B full	C <u>plenty</u>	D lot

Writing   Part 2 Article

You see this announcement in an English-language magazine:

HOW TO BEAT STRESS

Write an article giving us your tips for beating stress at work or in your studies. In particular, we'd like you to tell us:
- how you prevent yourself from getting stressed.
- how you relax and unwind if you're feeling stressed.

The best articles will be published in next month's magazine.

Write your article in 140–190 words.

Please go to the Teacher's Resource Centre for a Sample answer with Examiner comments for this task.
For more information on writing articles, see **page 192**.

12 LOOKING AFTER YOURSELF

Pronunciation Silent vowels

1 In the middle of each of the following words there is a vowel which is not usually pronounced. Cross out the silent vowels and write down the number of syllables in each word. The first one has been done for you.

1 choc~~o~~late 2
2 veget~~a~~ble 3
3 fact~~o~~ry 2
4 fright~~e~~ning 2
5 typ~~i~~cally 3
6 bisc~~u~~it 3

2 ▶ 12.4 Listen to check your answers to Exercise 1.

3 ▶ 12.5 Read out the following sentences. Take care to pronounce the words in bold with the correct number of syllables given in brackets. Then listen and check.
   1 I work as a **secretary** (3) in a **reasonably** (3) large catering **business** (2).
   2 **Everyone** (3) has **different** (2) tastes and **preferences** (3).
   3 The **temperature** (3) in the **restaurant** (2) was very **comfortable** (3).
   4 I found the **documentary** (4) on the **history** (2) of food preparation very **interesting** (3).
   5 There are **several** (2) good **dictionaries** (3) of cooking terms in our food **literature** (3) section.

4 Complete the sentences so that they true for you.
   • My favourite type of chocolate is …
   • The last documentary I saw was …
   • I'm not at all interested in …

5 **SPEAK** Work in pairs. Read aloud your sentences using the correct pronunciation.
   My favourite type of chocolate is milk chocolate with fruit and nuts in it.

Go to **Collocation Revision** Units 1–12 on **page 187**.

Pronunciation

1-2 ▶ **12.4** Explain that the word *vowel* is used with two meanings in English, as it is in most languages: 1) to refer to vowel sounds we hear or produce, e.g. /æ/ or /ɪ/, and 2) to letters A, E, I, O, U and sometimes Y. *Vowel* is used in the second sense in this section. Note that the 'o' in *factory* may not be silent in your accent, as the word is also commonly pronounced /ˈfæktəri/.

3 ▶ **12.5** You may want to suggest that the students go through and underline the syllables before they practise reading them together with a partner. After they have listened to the recording, do some choral drilling with any of the words that students are still having trouble producing accurately.

4-5 Challenge fast finishers to create a few more sentence beginnings for their partners to finish using words from the lesson. Monitor their pronunciation of the target language, providing on-the-spot correction as appropriate. At the end of the lesson, encourage students to write down any words they would like to continue practising in the Pronunciation section of their notebooks.

COLLOCATION REVISION UNITS 1–12

In each of the spaces below, write one word which collocates with *all* three of the other words. You will need to write nouns in the left-hand column and verbs in the right-hand column. The numbers in brackets refer to the relevant units of the book where the words you require first appeared.

Adjective + noun

1. baggy / scruffy / trendy — clothes/trousers (1)
2. a percussion / a wind / a stringed — instrument (2)
3. a horror / an action / a science-fiction — film (4)
4. a challenging / a monotonous / a well-paid — job (5)
5. flowing / shoulder-length / curly — hair (6)
6. a prosperous / a thriving / a run-down — town/city/neighbourhood/area (7)
7. a business / a day / a weekend — trip (8)
8. a life / a two-year / a prison — sentence (10)
9. strong / gale-force / light — winds (11)
10. a soft / a still / a fizzy — drink (12)

Verb + noun

1. lead/live/have — an active social life / a traditional way of life / a sedentary lifestyle (1)
2. play — a track / a tune / a chord (2)
3. change — your lifestyle / careers / for the better (3)
4. take — someone's advice / pity on someone / interest in something (4)
5. work — full time / overtime / long hours (5)
6. make — up your mind / sure / more of an effort (8)
7. do — your best / harm to someone / physical exercise (8)
8. give — a piercing scream / a deep sigh / a broad smile (9)
9. put — pressure on someone/something / someone/something at risk / an end to something (11)
10. have — a sore throat / high blood pressure / a runny nose (12)

READY FOR WRITING TASKS AND KEY

Ready for Writing

Introduction

Extracts

A 5b   B 1   C 4   D 5a   E 2   F 3

Register

1

1 d informal   2 e formal   3 a informal   4 c formal
5 b formal

2

B Formal/neutral

The linker, *however*, is fairly formal, and there are no contractions or phrasal verbs.

C Neutral

There are no informal linkers, contractions or phrasal verbs, but neither is there evidence of any formal language.

D Formal

The linker, *consequently*, is formal, as is the use of language such as *gained considerable amount of … experience in this field*; *well suited to the position*.

E Informal

The writer addresses the reader directly with a question, and there are contractions in the second sentence.

F Formal

The language used for making recommendations is formal: *is an option worth considering* and *it is advisable to*. The linker *However*, is fairly formal and there are no features of informal language.

Marking

2 Content   3 Organisation and cohesion   4 Register
5 Accuracy

Planning and checking

2 e   3 c   4 d   5 a   6 f

Task

In your English class you have been talking about education in schools in your country. Now, your English teacher has asked you to write an essay.
Write an essay using **all** the notes and giving reasons for your point of view.

> Some people think that school does not prepare students adequately for real life. Do you agree?
> **Notes**
> Things to write about:
> 1 the content of lessons
> 2 social relationships
> 3 .... (your own idea)

Write your **essay** in 140–190 words.

Sample answer

Part 1 Essay Type 1

The modern life is very different to when our parents and teachers went to school, and a title is not a gaurantee you will get a job now. We need practical skills to prepare us for the life, however the school does not teach that.

The lessons are boring, we just listen to the teachers talking, do exercises in the book and then take exams. Nothing is practical – not much time in the science laboratry, with the computers or speaking English. Basically, no interaction. In addition, I go to a school with only boys, so we don't learn how to relation with girls, and that is a big handicap. The social skills are important in the real world.

However, one positive thing about school is we learn to have autodiscipline and know that if we work hard, we can get good results. Work hard will be important for getting jobs, people who don't work hard will not have the success.

In conclusion, I think that schools do not prepare us adequately for real life. If we work hard and pass exams but we have problems to get a job, the problem are not us, the problem is the school.

199 words

Examiner comments

Content: All content is relevant and the two points in the notes, plus the student's own (*being self-disciplined*) are given sufficient coverage to inform the reader.

Communicative achievement: The conventions of writing an essay are followed, with arguments for and against framed by an introduction and a conclusion. The register is a little too conversational at times, for example in the second paragraph.

Organisation: The ideas are organised into logical paragraphs. There is some good use of cohesive devices (e.g. **In addition,** *I go to a school with only boys,* **so** *we don't learn how to relation with girls, and* **that** *is a big handicap.*) but often these are lacking or poorly used (e.g. *… prepare us for the life, however the school does not ..; Work hard will be important for getting jobs, people who don't work hard will not have the success.*)

READY FOR WRITING TASKS AND KEY

Language: There is an adequate range of topic-related vocabulary, including *do exercises; get good results* and *pass exams,* as well as *practical* and *social skills.* Some words are misused (*title* for *qualification; relation with* for *interact with; autodiscipline* for *self-discipline*) and two are misspelt (*gaurantee, laboratory*) though this does not impede communication.

Complex grammatical structures are sometimes used accurately (e.g. *We need practical skills to prepare us; However, one positive thing about school is we learn to have …*) but sometimes there is a lack of control, such as in the use of articles (e.g. *The modern life is very different; The social skills are important*) or verb forms (e.g. *Work hard will be important; we have problems to get a job; the problem are not us*).

Mark: Pass

Task

In your English class you have been talking about the effects of fame. Now, your English teacher has asked you to write an essay. Write an essay using **all** the notes and giving reasons for your point of view.

Write your **essay** in **140–190** words.

> **Is it better to be famous or unknown?**
> **Notes**
> **Write about:**
> 1. money
> 2. friends
> 3. _____ (your own idea)

Sample answer

Part 1 Essay Type 2

Is it better to be famous or unknown?

Due to all the disadvantages that famous people have to deal with I personally feel that being unknown is way better than being famous.

To begin with, it is believed that all the famous people are rich, but there are many famous people with normal wages, only a few famous people achieve being really rich. Also, there are many unknown people who work very hard and have high wages.

Secondly, if you are rich you won't have a lot of friends but a lot of fake friends that just want to use you as means for some external purpose. Nevertheless, being unknown you have true friends. Maybe there won't be tons of people around you but in my opinion true friendships are worth more.

Finally, and what I think that is the most important advantage of being unknown is having privacy. As famous people are all the time in the public eye they can't have a calm lifestyle and they have to deal with a lot of stress.

In conclusion, while being famous can be more interesting, being unknown has way more advantages.

Elisa Barba Ortiz
194 words

Examiner comments

Content: All the content is relevant, all three points are given equal attention and the target reader is fully informed.

Communicative achievement: There is a clear essay structure and the writer's opinion is evident throughout the answer. The essay is written mostly in a neutral register, though the writer does occasionally use informal English (*way better; way more advantages; there won't be tons of people around you*).

Organisation: The answer is organised into clear paragraphs, each one introduced with an appropriate linking word or phrase. Conjunctions such as *if, but, as* and *while* are used effectively to construct extended sentences. *On the other hand* or *However* would be more appropriate than *Nevertheless* in the third paragraph.

Language: There is some evidence of a range of appropriate language (*high wages; true friendships are worth more; privacy; in the public eye; deal with … stress*), though repetition of *famous people, rich* and *wages* could be avoided in the second paragraph (*e.g. only a few celebrities achieve great wealth* instead of *only a few famous people achieve being really rich*). In the third paragraph, the use of *external purpose* for *ulterior motive* is easily understood.

Simple and complex grammatical forms are used with good control, as shown for example in both sentences of the penultimate paragraph.

Mark: Pass to good pass

Writing Part 2 Article

You see this announcement in an international magazine.

MY IDEAL JOB
We're interested to know what jobs people would most like to do. Write us an article telling us what your ideal job would be and why. The best articles will be published in next month's magazine.

Write your **article** in **140–190** words.

Sample answer

Part 2 Article

<u>Who wouldn't want to be a fashion designer?</u>

It's a fantastic job because you can develop your creativity by designing different clothes all the time and presenting them to the public on catwalks.

It must be wonderful to be able to travel each month to show your collection to other people. You would get to know other designers and places all over the world. For some people this could be exhausting rather than enjoyable but for me it would be a way to try different food and discover new cultures.

With a job like this you can express what you feel through your clothes, although you have to keep thinking about new ideas because fashion is always

READY FOR WRITING TASKS AND KEY

changing. But that is what makes the job so challenging and therefore rewarding when you create something that is different from everything else.

There might be people that want to copy your designs, but that means your clothes are pretty so you can be proud of yourself and happy that you have gained recognition. And that must be one of the best feelings in the world.

Alicia

184 words

Examiner comments

Content: All content is relevant and the target reader is fully informed.

Communicative Achievement: The writer immediately creates interest with a question in the title and uses an enthusiastic tone throughout the article to hold the reader's attention. The piece ends with a short reflection, leaving the reader something to think about.

Organisation: The text is well organised with logical paragraphs, each addressing a different point. There is a range of conjunctions (*because, but, although, so*) and appropriate use is made of pronouns (e.g. *It's a fantastic job;* **this** *could be exhausting; With a job like* **this**; **that** *is what makes the job so challenging; you create something* **that** *is different from everything else*).

Language: A good range of relevant vocabulary is used accurately (e.g. *develop your creativity; presenting them to the public on catwalks; get to know other designers; challenging; rewarding; copy your designs; gained recognition*). Complex grammatical forms appear in every sentence and are used with very good control.

Mark: Very good pass

Task
This is part of an email you receive from your English friend, Simon.

Write your **email** in 140–190 words.

I won't be here next week, as I've rented a holiday cottage with some friends near the coast. Unfortunately, it looks as if it's going to rain a lot, so we want to take some games with us to play in the house. Can you suggest any? How do you play them?
Thanks
Simon

Sample answer

Part 2 Email and letter (Informal)

Hi Simon

Thanks for writing. I'm sorry that it is going to be bad weather. I think I know some games you might enjoy.

The ones I most like and can recomend you are Call of Duty's Black Ops III for Play Station 4, Cluedo and UNO. The aim of Call of Duty is to kill the enemies and avoid them to kill you until the points are achieved or the time runs out.

Cluedo is a board game in which you have to try to find out who commited the murder, where and with which weapon. You do this by asking each other questions and gradually eliminating the suspects, until you discover who is the guilty.

And finally, UNO is a card game in which you have to get rid of all your cards by putting a card with the same colour or number. You have to say UNO when you only have one card, or you will have to take more cards.

I hope that's helpful. Let me know if you need more suggestions about games.

Best wishes

Daniela

181 words

Examiner comments

Content: All content is relevant and the target reader is reasonably well informed about how to play the three games recommended.

Communicative Achievement: The conventions of writing an email are used appropriately to hold the reader's attention. The register is consistently informal throughout.

Organisation: The text is well organised into logical paragraphs, including suitable opening and closing paragraphs. The three central paragraphs explain the objective of each game and, in the case of Cluedo and UNO, how that objective is achieved (*by asking each other questions; by putting a card with the same colour or number*). Repetition is avoided using pronouns (*The ones I most like; You do this; I hope that's helpful*), though in the description for UNO, *have to* is used three times.

Language: There is a good range of vocabulary relevant to explaining games (e.g. *The aim of .... is to ...; board/card game; you have to try to find out; get rid of all your cards*). The misuse of *putting a card* for *putting down* or *laying a card*, and *the guilty* for *the culprit/murderer* do not impede communication. Spelling errors (*recomend* and *commited*) are minimal.

The incorrect use of *avoid them to kill you* (*prevent them killing you* or *avoid being killed by them*) is a rare error in an otherwise grammatically accurate piece of writing.

Mark: Good pass

READY FOR WRITING TASKS AND KEY

Task
You have seen this advertisement in an international magazine.

COASTAL CAMPSITES REQUIRE

- Reception Assistants
- Swimming Pool Attendants
- Bar and Restaurant Staff
- Entertainers

to work in the UK on our busy, five-star campsites this summer. Applicants must have a reasonable command of English and be willing to work long hours.

Write to the director, Mr Peabody, and explain why you would be suitable for the job.

Write your **letter of application** in 140–190 words.

Sample answer

Part 2 Email and letter (Formal)

Dear Mr Peabody,

I saw your advertisement in 'International Camping' magazine and I would like to apply for the job of reception assistant in your campsite this summer.

I am thinking to study Tourism at university next year when I finish the school, so this will be a perfect opportunity for me to gain some relevant experience. In addition, working in the UK will help me to improve my English, which is so important for my future.

I have been camping many times in France and Germany with my family, and I can say that I understand the needs of people who stay on a campsite. I think this is very useful if somebody comes to reception to complain or because they require help. I speak Spanish and English, also I know some French as I picked it up when we were on holiday in France.

I have a friendly, cheerful nature and I am confident I would be suited to the job. I am not afraid to work long hours, because the more time I work, the more possibilities I have to speak to people and practice my languages.

I look forward to hearing from you.

Yours sincerely

Manuel Sanchez

201 words

Examiner comments

Content: The reader would be fully informed. The writer makes a good case for why he would be suitable for the job, and refers to his English level and his willingness to work long hours, both of which are mentioned in the advertisement.

Communicative achievement: The conventions of formal letters of application are used effectively. The register is appropriate for this application, and the letter would have a positive effect on the reader.

Organisation: The letter is well organised into suitable paragraphs. Relative and demonstrative pronouns are used to good effect (e.g. *which is so important for my future; this will be a perfect opportunity*), and there is a range of conjunctions. The only weak point is the use of *also* in the final sentence of the third paragraph.

Language: There is accurate and appropriate use of formulaic expressions for application letters and evidence of a wide range of vocabulary (e.g. *a perfect opportunity; gain some relevant experience; understand the needs of people; require help; picked it up*). With the exception of *thinking to study* and *finish the school*, the language is grammatically very accurate (e.g. *the more time I work, the more possibilities I have …*).

Mark: Very good pass.

Task
A group of foreign teenage students on an exchange programme in your region is planning to visit your town for an afternoon and evening. You have been asked to write a report for the leader of the group, suggesting ways in which the students might spend their time in your town. You should give advice on places to go for shopping and entertainment, explaining why you recommend these places.

Write your **report** in 140–190 words.

Sample answer

Part 2 Report

Introduction

The aim of this report is to give suggestions to your students about where can they go shopping and for entertainment when they come here to visit for the exchange.

Shopping

The best place for shopping is the Plaza shopping centre, which is not far from our school. It is nearly sure that they will go there some time with their host family or a group of exchange students. There it is a variety of shops, and in general, clothes are very cheap. Alternatively, they can go to the downtown to buy. It will be enjoyable to go to the centre but everything is more expensive.

Entertainment

I suggest them to go to the Betcha! night club in the city centre. On Wednesday and Thursday evening it is for under-18s, so this will be perfect for your students. However, if they do not want to go clubbing, there is a multi-screen cinema in Plaza, so they can see a film and then take a drink in one of the cafés, or go bowling.

Conclusion

There is a wide range of activities for your students when they come here next month and I am sure they will enjoy very much.

200 words

READY FOR WRITING TASKS AND KEY

Examiner comments

Content: The content is relevant, though it is not clear if the writer has understood that the students will only be visiting the town for an afternoon and an evening. *It is sure they will go there some time with their host family* suggests not.

Communicative achievement: The conventions of writing a report are used well to guide the reader through the text and the register is consistently neutral.

Organisation: Paragraphs are logical with suitable headings, and there is an adequate range of basic cohesive devices with conjunctions (e.g. *but, so*), adverbs (e.g *Alternatively, However*) and pronouns (*which is not far from our school; this will be perfect*).

Language: The range of vocabulary is sufficient to express the writer's ideas and there is some typical language for reports, particularly in the first and last paragraphs. Grammatical structures are inaccurate or awkward at times: *about where ~~can they~~ they can go shopping; It is nearly sure that they will go there = They are likely to go there; There ~~it~~ is a variety of shops (there); go ~~to the~~ downtown; I suggest ~~them to~~ they go; they will enjoy (themselves) very much*.

Mark: Pass

Task

Either: **a** write your own answer to the task above in 140–190 words; or **b** answer the following question. You have seen this notice in your school's English-language magazine.

TELEVISION REVIEWS NEEDED
We'd like to hear about a television series you watch regularly. Write us a review, telling us what you enjoy about the series and whether there is anything you don't like about it. Don't forget to say who you would recommend it to.

Write your **review** in **140–190** words.

Examiner comments

Content: All content is relevant and the reader would be informed as to what the series is about, why the writer enjoyed watching it, what they didn't like and who it might appeal to.

Communicative achievement: The review successfully holds the reader's attention throughout. The writer expresses opinions clearly and ends with a recommendation (and a touch of humour). The register and tone are both appropriate for this kind of review.

Organisation: The ideas and opinions are organised into logical paragraphs and there is a range of cohesive devices, including good use of elision (*we couldn't wait for the second (season); My favourite (character) is Rasmus; whereas the first (season) had eight (episodes)*). A weakness is the use of the comma in *Rasmus, he's very handsome* and *Danish, it sounds so gentle*.

Language: Good use is made of adjectives to express opinions and feelings (*gripping; disappointed; convincing; frustrated; realistic*) as well as appropriate language for series (*season; episodes; characters; acting; it is set in*). Grammar is accurate throughout (e.g. *After watching the first series, we couldn't wait for the second; Whether you enjoy science fiction or not, you should watch this series*).

Mark: Very good pass

Sample answer

Part 2 Review

My family and I have just finished watching the second season of the gripping Danish series 'The Rain'. After watching the first season, we couldn't wait for the second – and we weren't disappointed.

It is set in Scandinavia after a virus, which falls with the rain, kills most of the people. The story is about a group of young survivors who travel through Denmark and Sweden looking for a safe place and also a cure for the virus. The acting is very convincing and my family love all the characters – we talk about which one we would most like to meet. My favourite is Rasmus, he's very handsome! We also enjoy listening to people speaking Danish, it sounds so gentle and we have even learnt a few words.

The only thing I don't like about it is that the second season only has six episodes, whereas the first had eight. I felt very frustrated when I realised this, and I hope the third and last season is longer. Whether you enjoy science fiction or not, you should watch this series, especially if you appreciate realistic acting and like listening to different languages.

Farvel! (Goodbye in Danish).